Beyond Red and Blue

Beyond Red and Blue

How Twelve Political Philosophies Shape American Debates

Peter S. Wenz

The MIT Press
Cambridge, Massachusetts
London, England

For information about special quantity discounts, please email special_sales@ mitpress.mit.edu.

This book was set in Sabon by Graphic Composition, Inc., Bogart, Georgia, using InDesign CS2.

Printed on recycled paper and bound in the United States of America.

Library of Congress Cataloging-in-Publication Data

Wenz, Peter S.
   Beyond red and blue : how twelve political philosophies shape American debates / Peter S. Wenz.
     p. cm.
   Includes bibliographical references and index.
   ISBN 978-0-262-01295-9 (hardcover : alk. paper) 1. United States—Social policy—1993–. 2. Social problems—United States. 3. Ideology—United States. 4. Political science—United States—Philosophy. I. Title.
   HN59.2.W46 2009
   320.60973—dc22

                                     2008034798

10 9 8 7 6 5 4 3 2 1

320. 6 0973
W

This book is dedicated to our four children
Ami, Felicia, Jason, and Karen

Contents

Acknowledgments

I want to thank the journalists, economists, philosophers, politicians, and other thinkers whose work I was able to draw upon when writing this book. Clay Morgan and others at the MIT Press have been most helpful, as were the anonymous reviewers. My wife Grace Wenz thought through with me the main ideas in this book before any work began and offered good advice whenever I turned to her. Finally, I want especially to thank my friend Deb Berman, who read everything at least once and made many valuable suggestions, thereby, among other things, protecting readers from some really tasteless humor.

Beyond Red and Blue

Introduction

Political Conflicts

Political conflicts exist when people disagree about what the state should do or permit. This book is about those conflicts and the twelve, not merely two, political orientations that guide our deliberations on such matters as these:

Darlene Miller was making decent money dancing in pasties and a G-string at the Kitty Kat Lounge in South Bend, Indiana, but she thought she could do better. Chief Justice William Rehnquist, not a known patron, explained: "Dancers are not paid an hourly wage, but work on commission. They receive a 100 percent commission on the first $60 in drink sales during their performances. . . . Miller wishes to dance nude because she believes she would make more money doing so."[1] But Indiana's public indecency statute required dancers to wear pasties and a G-string when they danced.

The court of appeals ruled against the state, arguing "that nonobscene nude dancing performed for entertainment is expression protected by the First Amendment, and that the public indecency statute was an improper infringement of that expressive activity because its purpose was to prevent the message of eroticism and sexuality conveyed by the dancers."[2]

The Supreme Court reversed the appeals court and held that Indiana was within its rights to outlaw nude dancing. The statute was not aimed specifically at nude dancing, an expressive activity, but at public nudity of all kinds, which has long been considered something bad in itself. Rehnquist concluded: "The statutory prohibition is not a means to some greater end, but an end in itself."[3] Justice Souter, agreeing to uphold the statute, noted Indiana's contention that nude dancing leads to other evils. It "encourag[es] prostitution, increas[es] sexual assaults, and attract[s] other criminal activity."[4] Justice Souter didn't think the state should have to prove any of these claims.

Justice White, writing for the minority of four in a 5–4 decision, thought Indiana's statute unconstitutional.

The purpose of forbidding people to appear nude in parks, beaches, hot dog stands, and like public places is to protect others from offense. But that could not possibly be the purpose of preventing nude dancing in theaters and barrooms since the viewers are exclusively consenting adults who pay money to see these dances.[5]

Then why does the state require pasties and a G-string? White concludes:

It is only because nude dancing performances may generate emotions and feelings of eroticism and sensuality among the spectators that the State seeks to regulate such expressive activity, apparently on the assumption that creating or emphasizing such thoughts and ideas in the minds of the spectators may lead to increased prostitution and the degradation of women. But generating thoughts, ideas, and emotions is the essence of communication.[6]

Preventing such communication violates the First Amendment, according to White and the other dissenters. The Court majority, by contrast, believed that the First Amendment does not cover Ms. Miller's dancing, so pasties and a G-string must.

Should animal sacrifice in religious rituals be outlawed as cruelty to animals or protected as freedom of religion? United States Supreme Court Justice Kennedy explained, "Animals sacrificed in Santeria rituals include chickens, pigeons, doves, ducks, guinea pigs, goats, sheep, and turtles. The animals are killed by the cutting of the carotid arteries in the neck. The sacrificed animal is cooked and eaten, except after healing and death rituals."[7] The religion couldn't continue without animal sacrifice, because the initiation of new priests requires it.

Santeria expert Migene Gonzalez-Wippler emphasizes the difference between animal sacrifice and ordinary slaughter:

The first time I saw an animal sacrifice . . . , my knees and my teeth knocked together all through the ceremony. In an animal sacrifice there is something primeval, something deeply connected with the collective unconscious of the race. It is all so simple. A quick twist of the hand and the chicken's head is gone, and a thick stream of dark-red, hot blood is streaming from the severed neck. But it is not the beheading of the animals that is so earth-shaking. It is the giving of the blood, the acceptance that blood is the life, the spirit; and that it is being returned to the divine source from where it came.[8]

The phrase "washed in the blood of the chicken" may lack religious resonance for most Americans, but the Santeria seem to find it meaningful.

Opponents of animal sacrifice claim that the killings are more painful to animals than ordinary slaughter,[9] and that animals sacrificed for healing and death rituals die for no good reason because they're not eaten.[10] This is cruelty to animals, they say.

Kerrigan and Mock had been living together for twelve years and believed it was about time they got married. The thirteen-year-old babysitter of their adopted Guatemalan twin boys, Fernando and Carlos, assumed they were married, but Connecticut law forbids Beth Kerrigan to marry Jody Mock because both are women. Connecticut's civil union law for gay couples defines marriage as solely between a man and a woman.[11] Kerrigan and Mock sued Connecticut for the right to marry. Most of Connecticut's registered voters, however, thought that civil union is enough. Just over 50 percent opposed gay marriage in polls taken in 2005 and 2006.

Many conservative Christians oppose both civil union and gay marriage because they believe homosexuality conflicts with the laws of God and nature. Brian Racer, pastor of the Open Door Bible Church at the Arundel Mills Mall in Maryland, explained to Russell Shorto of the *New York Times Magazine*:

It's unfortunate that homosexuals have taken the moniker "gay," because their lifestyle and its consequences are anything but. Look what has happened in the decades since the sexual revolution and acceptance of the gay lifestyle as normal. Viruses have mutated, S.T.D.'s have spread. It shows that when we try to change the natural course of things, what comes out of that is not joy or gayness.[12]

Bryan Simonaire, another anti-gay-marriage activist added: "Once you start this, you could have a 45-year-old man wanting to marry a 9-year-old boy. That could be O.K. in 20 years. That's what you get with relative moral truth. Whereas with absolute moral truth, what was O.K. 50 years ago will still be O.K. 20 years from now."[13] From this perspective, we can't be certain that slavery was wrong two hundred years ago without absolute values.

But the inability to marry can jeopardize family life, as Jeffrey Busch and Stephen Davis, partners for sixteen years, found while returning home from Canada. They were traveling with their three-year-old son Elijah when Canadian officials noticed that Elijah's birth certificate listed his mother as "unknown." The official said, "Here you are, two men with a child, how do we know it's not a kidnapping." It shook the couple up. Busch said, "If we were a married couple, I could say, 'I'm Eli's dad and this is my spouse.' But I couldn't, so six weeks after that happened, we decided to enter into the lawsuit to secure our rights."[14] The lawsuit, which claimed that Connecticut's constitution implies a right to same-sex marriage, included Kerrigan and Mock among its plaintiffs.

James Canter is a cancer survivor who used marijuana for medical reasons, a practice later approved by California voters in 1996. Canter writes:

Doctors and patients should decide what medicines are best. Ten years ago, I nearly died from testicular cancer that spread into my lungs. Chemotherapy made me sick and nauseous. The standard drugs, like Marinol, didn't help. Marijuana blocked the nausea. As a result, I was able to continue the chemotherapy treatments. Today I've beaten the cancer, and no longer smoke marijuana. I credit marijuana as part of the treatment that saved my life.[15]

But federal law, which pre-empts state law, lists marijuana as too dangerous for medical use. Accordingly, "the federal government stopped supplying marijuana to patients in 1991. Now it tells patients to take Marinol, a synthetic substitute . . . that can cost $30,000 a year and is often less reliable and less effective."[16] Ed Rosenthal, who grew marijuana in Oakland for medical purposes under state license, was convicted in January 2003 of a federal drug violation. Jurors at his trial were not told that he was licensed by the state.

The federal government worries that if marijuana can be grown legally for medical purposes, much will be diverted for recreation, which can lead to increased drug abuse. Others favor legalizing marijuana for recreation.

State responses to sexual harassment (or is it free speech?) can be controversial. Freelance writer Sarah Glazer describes one such case:

Peggy Kimzey, a Wal-Mart shipping clerk in Warsaw, Mo., was bending over a package when she heard the store manager and another employee snickering behind her. Kimzey stood up and asked what they were doing. "Well," the manager smirked, "I just found someplace to put my screwdriver." When Kimzey asked him to stop crude remarks, he replied, "You don't know, you might like it."[17]

In another case, Lois Robinson sued her bosses at a shipyard because they displayed a picture calendar featuring female models who were fully or partly nude. In nine of the pictures the models' breasts were bare and in two the pubic areas were visible. Robinson was told by a fellow employee, "You rate about an 8 or 9 on a scale of 10."[18] Should the state stop such behavior and require compensation to women who were subjected to it? Most female employees at the shipyard said they didn't mind, but they may have been trying to keep their jobs or avoid worse harassment. Most men didn't find the pictures or comments offensive; just free speech of the jocular variety.

In a third case, a graduate student at the University of Nebraska kept on his office desk a small photo of his wife at the beach in a bikini. Two psychology graduate students who shared the office claimed the photo display constituted sexual harassment by creating a hostile work environment for them. The department head agreed.[19]

Political Pluralism and Ideological Coalitions

How do Americans address such issues as these? One way is through political campaigns and elections, which determine who will legislate on such matters and, often indirectly, who will judge cases brought to court. The United States has what is basically a two-party political system, because most people think that casting a ballot for a third-party candidate, who seldom has a real chance of winning, wastes their vote.

The predominance of two parties leads many people to believe that Americans are divided ideologically into just two camps—Republican and Democratic, right and left, conservative and liberal, red and blue. There's a culture war between the two camps. Republicans are from Mars; Democrats are from Canada. When Republicans and Democrats or conservatives and liberals join together, it is said that politics makes strange bedfellows. Political interests have overcome ideological opposition. These are misperceptions that this book aims to correct.

In the United States today, I claim, arguments about hot-button political issues appeal to at least twelve different political philosophies, not just two. (There may be more than twelve, but I have distilled only twelve from analyses of current debates.) By "political philosophies," I mean organized views about why states are needed and what their goals and functions should be. Regarding hot-button political issues, the most important differences among political philosophies concern divergent views about the state's proper goals and functions. These are matters of values.

Most individuals use at least a half-dozen philosophies in their own political thinking, because they believe the state should promote several goals and perform various functions, whereas each philosophy emphasizes only one or a few major values.

The use of twelve different philosophies in our political discourse clears the way for principled coalitions that reflect convergences of ideologies, not of interests. People with different philosophical commitments come together on an issue when all have reasons within their own, but often different, schemes of values to support the same law or public policy. Political success often follows developing and marketing a position that takes advantage of such ideological convergence.

Ideological diversity is apparent in the major political parties, making each an ideological coalition. Consider the Republicans in 2008. They were divided on several issues, reflecting a diversity of political philosophies in their ranks. Concerning amnesty (or its equivalent) for illegal immigrants, for example, free-market conservatives favored expanding the workforce (and so the economy) with industrious immigrants, while some social conservatives balked at rewarding people for illegal behavior. Regarding evolution, some theocrats among Republicans wanted to require teaching Intelligent Design along with evolutionary theory in biology classes, whereas other Republicans—such as free-market conservatives who want the most educated workforce possible—favored science without religion. On civil liberties, some libertarian Republicans, who champion low taxes and a small government, were concerned that the Patriot Act deprived Americans of too much freedom, while other Republicans supported a get-tough attitude toward potential, suspected, and potentially suspected terrorists and were willing to sacrifice some traditional civil liberties in that cause.

Democrats were internally divided as well. On immigration, for example, cosmopolitan and multicultural Democrats favored policies that fostered increased immigration, with cosmopolitans questioning the ultimate importance of national borders and multiculturalists savoring the cultural diversity that immigrants bring. But contractarians (whose views are explained in chapter 1 and later) worried that immigrants depress the wages of poor Americans. They were wary of policies that encouraged immigration. They were joined by some environmentalists who noted that the American lifestyle is more environmentally damaging than lifestyles in the immigrants' countries of origin. The Earth would be healthier with fewer people achieving the American dream. There was disagreement in the Sierra Club over this issue in the 1990s.

Such ideological diversity within each party allows for ideology-based coalitions both within and between the parties. Suppose, for example, that you favor school vouchers—government vouchers given to parents who can use them either to support public schools or to send their children to private (including religion-based parochial) schools. Such vouchers make private education more affordable to a larger range of families. To build a political movement or candidacy on this issue, it's helpful to know that current support for school vouchers comes primarily from three different political philosophies. Theocrats, who want laws and public policies to reflect the views of their particular religion, favor vouchers because vouchers help families within their religious communities send their children to schools that teach their religion. Free-market conservatives, by contrast, favor vouchers because they believe that efficiency requires competition and vouchers will enable private education to be more competitive with public education. Public schools, private schools, and taxpayers will all benefit from such competition, they think. Social conservatives favor vouchers because they allow religion to be taught in government-funded schools, and they think religion is the firmest foundation for the moral development that students need to become productive, law-abiding citizens. Social conservatives differ from theocrats, however, because theocrats want schools that promote their particular religion (or ones they consider very similar), whereas social conservatives are happy with any world religion that teaches sound morals. Some theocrats in the United States would oppose vouchers being used for Hindu or Islamic schools, whereas social conservatives would not, so long as standard morality is being taught in that religious context.

Voucher supporters are largely Republican. Many Democrats are wary of vouchers, because contractarians among them—who think that the government should help the poorest citizens—worry that current voucher proposals will harm the poor. Such systems give parents a voucher worth less than half the cost of education and therefore benefit most the children in families that can afford to supplement the voucher with additional money. As children from these middle- and lower-middle-class families leave public schools for private ones, the quality of public schools is likely to decline because a smaller percentage of the politically active population will have a personal stake in public education, leading to underfunding. Children of the poorest families will be stuck in these inferior schools.

With this background, a candidate or citizen group that favors vouchers will know that it can garner support across party lines by neutralizing contractarian objections. One way to do this is to support vouchers worth the full cost of education and limiting (e.g., to 10 percent over that amount) what parents or other organizations can add from nongovernment funds. Schools accepting vouchers would also be required to enroll students on the same basis as public schools, including students with a history of disruptive behavior. All students would be subject to the same rules of expulsion as in public school. Such vouchers might promote efficiency, owing to competition, while actually helping the poorest of the poor because they, too, would benefit from that efficiency.

On another matter, consider the sale of meat and dairy products from cloned animals. Free-market conservatives (mostly Republicans) may see in such products a business opportunity, claiming that so long as the products are as healthful as their more natural counterparts, the government should not restrict their production and sale. Some theocrats, by contrast, although they are also mostly Republicans, oppose cloning of all kinds as unwarranted tampering with what they perceive to be God's plan for nature. Cloning strikes them as people trying to play God.

Such theocrats would do well to recognize that many environmentalists (mostly Democrats) embrace a natural law philosophy, which holds that nature is sacred, or nearly sacred. They think of nature as a beautiful system, too complex for people fully to understand, that should be respected as a mother because it produced human beings through evolution. Many theocrats disagree with important aspects of this environmentalist view. They oppose anything that smacks of nature worship; they think it's essential to acknowledge that God created nature; and they disbelieve that evolution explains the emergence of human beings. In the light of these differences, it might be hard for them to see that environmentalists are their potential allies on agricultural cloning and many other issues. Theocrats have in common with environmentalists the view that people should be wary of using their technological prowess to alter nature in radical ways. Banding together, theocrats and environmentalists should try to change the conversation from one about health and safety (assuming that cloned products are safe) to one about human limitations, the inexhaustible wonders of the natural world, and due respect for religious and quasi-religious qualms about manipulating nature.

These are just two examples of how awareness of the twelve political philosophies currently used by Americans and explained in this book can help politicians and political activists refine proposals, find allies, and market their views. In addition, this book can help journalists, concerned citizens, students, scholars, and policymakers better understand politics and elections. The twelve-part division of political thought explained in this book can illuminate the bases of coalitions and the underlying strategies of candidates and parties.

Your Own Political Identity

Finally, these twelve political philosophies can help most people identify and critically assess their own political leanings and priorities. You can get an inkling of your own political identity by looking at the main values featured in each philosophy:

• *Theocracy*—the state should promote the values of a particular religion.

• *Natural law*—state laws should reflect what is natural for human beings and consistent with the proper role of humanity on Earth.

• *Libertarianism*—the state should limit itself to fostering maximum individual liberty while protecting human life and property rights.

• *Utilitarianism*—the state should promote the greatest happiness or preference satisfaction in society.

• *Free-market conservatism*—the state should foster maximum economic growth.

• *Contractarianism*—the state should protect individual liberty and promote economic growth while maximizing benefits to the poorest and most vulnerable members of society.

• *Social conservatism*—the state should preserve and protect social, political, and religious traditions that have served well in the past.

• *Feminism*—the state should ensure that no person is disadvantaged for being female.

• *Multiculturalism*—the state should recognize that no one culture holds all the keys to human flourishing and should therefore tolerate or promote cultural diversity.

• *Environmentalism*—the state should protect people and other species from unnecessary environmental degradation.

• *Communitarianism*—the state should foster bonds of community over tendencies to excessive individualism.

• *Cosmopolitanism*—the state should support certain universal values and norms.

Few people, if any, are moved by the values central to all twelve philosophies. Some people don't care at all if our country contains the cultural diversity that multiculturalists favor. Many individualists have no sympathy with communitarian critiques of individualism and individual rights. Some thinkers, convinced that we can improve on conditions of ages gone by, have no interest in the traditions that social conservatives want to preserve. Those who believe that the international world is so dangerous that good nations must combat evil terrorists "no holds barred" reject cosmopolitanism's universal norms of humane treatment (for terrorists). One way of locating yourself on the political landscape is to identify the values you reject.

Another way is to identify the trade-offs that you find reasonable. Almost all of us experience political ambivalence from time to time, because we respect and want to promote a plurality of values in circumstances where trade-offs are required. For example, just about everyone wants the country to be secure from attack. But most people also respect the principles, championed most forcefully by libertarians, of individual privacy and freedom from government control. Security and liberty are in tension in this context, because the greater the scope for privacy and freedom, the greater the chance for a terrorist to evade detection and attack our country. Where security and liberty are concerned, we must often trade some of one to get more of the other. People differ on how much liberty to sacrifice for more security. Our political identities are revealed to ourselves and others largely by the trade-offs that we find acceptable.

Finding out which values you reject completely and which trade-offs you find reasonable requires delving into specific areas of political controversy. This book features debates on fourteen important contemporary issues: (1) land condemnation for economic growth; (2) letting (or causing) people such as Terri Schiavo to die by removing nutrition and hydration; (3) physician-assisted suicide; (4) the War on Drugs; (5) the War on Terrorism; (6) affirmative action; (7) pornography, child pornography, and the Internet; (8) abortion; (9) homosexuality, same-sex marriage, and polygamy; (10) genetic engineering and designer children; (11) wages and taxes; (12) health care in America; (13) immigration; and (14) globalization.

Some of these matters are related to one another, posing the challenge of creating a unified political philosophy for oneself that includes responses to each issue consistent with responses to related issues. For example, one problem with health care in America is insufficient access to health care among at least forty million Americans. This problem is related to wages and taxes, because other industrial countries achieve universal health care coverage by having higher taxes than we do and using tax money to fund health care. Alternatively, greater health care coverage might be achieved with higher wages, enabling more people to afford private health insurance. So, health care issues are related to both taxes and wages. Wage issues, in turn, are related to immigration and globalization, because both immigration and globalization may reduce the pay of low-wage workers.

Several issues concern limits on individual freedom or self-determination. The government's forced purchase of one's property for economic development pits individual freedom against public welfare. People who favor individual freedom in this context may or may not think that people should be free to have nutrition and hydration removed when they are severely disabled or to have a (willing) physician assist them when they want to commit suicide. Developing a political philosophy involves decisions about when and why individual freedom is overriding in some contexts but not in others. Such decisions affect views about what kinds of drugs, literature, and film should be legally available for purchase, and what limitations should be placed on legal marriage.

Each of the book's fourteen chapters centers on one area of debate, leaving to readers the task of integrating their responses across related areas. Although these fourteen debates are representative of current political disagreements, they are certainly not exhaustive. The same is true of the arguments given on various sides of each debate. But the debates and arguments do reveal enough about the twelve underlying political philosophies and the choices that we make as individuals and communities to enable people interested or active in politics to gain additional insights into their own political values. It can also help improve understanding of the American political drama and point the way toward increased political effectiveness.

1

No Strange Bedfellows

There Are Twelve Beds

What would you think and how would you feel if people told you that they were buying your house, even though you had no intention of selling? Suppose their justification was that their economic use of the property would be better than yours? This is the situation faced by Susette Kelo and her neighbors in New London, Connecticut, leading to a conflict that illustrates the complexity of American political thought. No division between right and left or red and blue, can explain the coalitions that formed around the issue of land condemnation for economic development. It was not that politics made strange bedfellows. All members of both coalitions had reasons grounded in their own political philosophies for the positions they took.

In 2001, Ms. Kelo, a straight-talking woman of medium height and build with red hair and blue eyes, the mother of five sons, explained her distress:

I grew up in southeastern Connecticut and bought my house at 8 East St. in New London in 1997 because it was just what I was looking for; great view of the water, affordable price, nice neighbors. I enjoyed fixing it up and making it a home for my family. I invested a lot of time and energy in this house and in my neighborhood. I worked to clean up the neighborhood.
Neighbors have told me that the place never looked so good.
In 1998, a real estate agent came by and made me an offer on the house. I explained to her that I was not interested in selling, but she said that my home would be taken by eminent domain if I refused to sell. She told me stories of her relatives who had lost their homes to eminent domain. Her advice? Give up. The government always wins.[1]

In 2005, forty-seven-year-old Susette Kelo was still resisting the sale of her home, a pink nineteenth-century cottage in the Fort Trumbull section of New London. By then, she had been made an offer she couldn't refuse: not by gangsters, but by the New London Development Corporation (NLDP), a nonprofit authorized by the city of New London to develop the Fort Trumbull area. The home was not run down, a health hazard, or an eyesore (if you like pink). Avi Salzman wrote in the *New York Times*: "'Blighted' is not a word anyone would use for her house, with its happy family photographs hung on the walls, its stained-glass chandelier in the dining room and cozy moccasins in a basket at the foot of the staircase. Ms. Kelo is a nurse, the kind of professional that many cities hope to attract."[2] She shared the house with her husband Tim.

Kelo fought the city all the way to the Supreme Court, supported by the right-wing Cato Institute and the libertarian Institute for Justice as well as the left-leaning National Association for the Advancement of Colored People (NAACP), the American Civil Liberties Union (ACLU), and the American Association of Retired People (AARP). On the other side were the City of New London and thirty-one state municipal leagues, which were joined by many (usually) right-leaning real estate developers and left-leaning environmentalists.

Is this a case of politics making strange bedfellows? It all depends on how many beds you think there are. People often assume—incorrectly, in my opinion—that there are just two beds, two basic political philosophies, two views about the proper role of government: one for Republicans and the other for Democrats. Republicans are red, conservative, and right-wing. Democrats are blue, liberal, and left-wing.

According to these stereotypes, right-wing conservative Republicans favor strong property rights, low taxes, free enterprise, small government, self-reliance, and traditional religious and family values. This philosophy appeals most to non-minority, business-oriented, religious people in traditional families. Left-wing liberal Democrats, by contrast, are supposed to favor government regulation of business, high taxes, and state-supported programs for the poor, while they question or reject traditional religious and family values. This view attracts mostly poor people, minority members, secularists, environmentalists, elitist professionals, and feminists, many in non-traditional relationships. Between these two poles are moderate Republicans and Democrats who favor compromise with the other side, but who are still guided primarily by the belief system of hard-liners.

These stereotypes are wrong. Although we have only two major political parties, twelve political philosophies shape American debates on such topics as pornography, religious freedom, same-sex marriage, drug control, sexual harassment, property rights and more. Coalitions on these matters include strange bedfellows only if there are just two beds, rather than twelve. Susette Kelo's fight to keep her home illustrates the multiple-bed approach that this book investigates in depth.

Offers They Couldn't Refuse

The story began, Supreme Court Justice John Paul Stevens wrote in his majority opinion in *Kelo v. New London* (2005), with New London falling on hard economic times and the city government trying to stage a comeback. In 1990, the state designated the city a "distressed municipality." "In 1996," Justice Stevens explained, "the Federal Government closed the Naval Undersea Warfare Center, which had been located in the Fort Trumbull area of the City and had employed over 1,500 people. In 1998, the City's unemployment rate was nearly double that of the State, and its population of just under 24,000 residents was at its lowest since 1920."[3]

That is when redevelopment plans took shape. The state authorized bond issues for planning activities in the Fort Trumbull area and for establishment of Fort Trumbull State Park. In February 1998, "the pharmaceutical company Pfizer Inc. announced that it would build a $300 million research facility on a site immediately adjacent to Fort Trumbull; local planners hoped that Pfizer would draw new business to the area, thereby serving as a catalyst to the area's rejuvenation."[4]

Because the area is a peninsula jutting out into the Thames River, it affords beautiful views of the water and of ferry boats passing by. So the New London Development Corporation (NLDC) planned for "a waterfront conference hotel at the center of a 'small urban village' that will include restaurants and shopping," a marina, a river walk, and about "80 new residences organized into an urban neighborhood and linked by public walkway to the remainder of the development, including the state park." It all sounds very up-market: designer shops, expensive coffee, and beautiful views for beautiful people. The rest of the land was to be used for "office and retail space, parking, and water-dependent commercial uses."[5]

If you are a free-market conservative, this makes perfect sense. In addition to personal and national security, which all mainstream philosophies expect of the state, *free-market conservativism* emphasizes the importance of fostering economic growth. That is why we have the Council of Economic Advisors, the Federal Reserve, the Securities and Exchange Commission, the Anti-trust Division of the Justice Department, laws that limit liabilities in corporate investments, education policies and expenditures to train our workforce to be internationally competitive, and much more. All of these institutions and measures are designed to boost the economy. We value material prosperity and expect the government to help secure it. Without a growing economy, people lose their jobs. As Justice Stevens put it in his *Kelo* opinion, "Promoting economic development is a traditional and long accepted function of government." Free-market conservatives place this function (after security) at the center of what they expect of government. The bottom line of their political philosophy is state promotion of economic growth. So, they applauded efforts in New London to improve the local economy.

But there is another side to the story. What about the property rights of people forced to sell their homes to make way for this economic development? Wilhelmina Dery, for example, one of Susette Kelo's neighbors and another plaintiff in the case, lived in a Fort Trumbull–area house that her relatives bought in 1901. She was born in that house and lived there all her eighty-seven years. Her husband, Charles, moved in when they began their marriage of more than sixty years. Their son Matt and his family lived next door. Iver Peterson reported in the *New York Times*, "On a good day, Matt Dery can see Fisher Island, off the tip of Long Island, from his kitchen window here at the mouth of the Thames River. The view is one of the things he loves about his home, and one reason he wants to stay."[6] His parents wanted to stay because it was their home. Matt Dery said, "We get this all the time. 'How much did they offer? What will it take?' My parents don't want to wake up rich tomorrow, they just want to wake up in their own house."[7]

Others wanted to stay because they felt entitled to reap the rewards of time, work, and money invested in their property. News Radio WINS reported the situation of Bill Von Winkle, "a former deli owner who lives in the neighborhood and owns two other rental homes." Von Winkle is quick to point out: "They were not inherited. They were not a gift. I sold sandwiches to buy these properties. It took 21 years." Eventually he owned them mortgage-free. But the city, having allocated only $1.6 million to pay for all fifteen properties of holdout landowners, planned to pay Von Winkle $638,000 for three properties that served as home and additionally yielded $120,000 per year in rent. It wasn't close to fair, Von Winkle claimed.[8]

Libertarianism is a political philosophy that supports these hold-out homeowners. The bottom line for libertarians (besides security) is individual liberty. People should be able to do whatever they want in their personal lives and with their property, so long as they don't harm others. The government exists primarily to protect such freedom for everyone. It should therefore be small. That government is best which governs least. So, if someone wants to sell her property, fine. If she doesn't, that's fine too. The government should seldom force people to sell their property.

Here we have two different political philosophies—free-market conservatism and libertarianism. One promotes economic development for general prosperity and the creation of jobs; the other promotes a small government that protects individual liberty. Different as they are, they often support similar policies, such as low taxes and little government regulation of business. Free-market conservatives believe these policies generally further economic growth, and libertarians think an appropriately small government needs little tax money and should mind its own business.

But the two views clash when the individual rights prized by libertarians stand in the way of the economic progress favored by free-market conservatives. Most of us are pulled in both directions. Who among us can't sympathize with the plight of Susette Kelo and the other plaintiffs? Yet we want the state to foster economic growth to help the unemployed and underemployed earn a living.

The Takings Clause

One path of compromise in this conflict is to allow the government to buy property at market prices from unwilling sellers, but only for certain purposes. For example, national defense may require waterfront property for shipyards to build naval vessels. National defense and modern life require roads so that the military and the public can get where they need to go in a timely fashion. Large cities need parks for public recreation and to combat overcrowding that can endanger public health. Some libertarians may object to forced sales for some of these purposes, but most accept a provision in the Fifth Amendment to the Constitution that no "private property shall be taken for public use without just compensation." This is known as the Takings Clause. It has two elements: public use and just compensation. Both elements were at issue in *Kelo v. New London*, but the public use requirement received most attention.

National defense, public roads, and public parks are public goods. Everyone has access to them. They are owned by the public and exist for the public, so they clearly meet the "public use" requirement of the Takings Clause. But New London had no intention of allowing the public to enjoy the land that it was taking from those unwilling to sell their Fort Trumbull homes. That land was destined for private apartments and condos, according to NLDC lawyer Ed O'Connell. Pfizer was moving in with new jobs.

We need to get housing at the upper end, for people like the Pfizer employees. They are the professionals, they are the ones with the expertise and the leadership qualities to remake the city—the young urban professionals who will invest in New London, put their kids in school, and think of this as a place to stay for 20 or 30 years.[9]

In other words, the government was forcing some people to sell their property so that other private individuals could eventually buy it, after developers had worked their profit-making magic. What happened to the public use requirement of the Takings Clause?

It was hit by trains in the nineteenth century. When railroads superseded horse and buggy as the main method of intercity transport, national defense and modern life required railroads as much as they previously required roads, but railroads are owned by private corporations. Yet they required land taken in eminent domain as much as earlier roads to get around the problem of property owners along a projected route refusing to sell. The Supreme Court obligingly altered the meaning of "public use" to allow land taken in eminent domain to become private property. However, there was still a public use requirement. The privately owned railroads provided a service to the public; they were common carriers. They could not refuse passengers willing to pay for tickets. So, in theory, the public still had use of the land taken in eminent domain.

This is still a far cry from the situation in New London. The fancy restaurants and shops the city wanted would be open to the overpaying public, but the condos of the "young urban professionals" the city hoped would have "the expertise and the leadership qualities to remake the city" would not use their homes to serve the public for a fee. They might be prosecuted if they tried. In the court's more dignified phrasing: "This is not a case in which the City is planning to open the condemned land—at least not in its entirety—to use by the general public. Nor will the private lessees of the land in any sense be required to operate like common carriers, making their services available to all comers."[10] So how is the public use requirement of the Takings Clause being met?

The notion of public use was broadened in a 1954 Supreme Court decision upholding a slum clearance plan in Washington, D.C. Congress had determined in 1945 that "owing to technological and sociological changes, obsolete lay-out, and other factors, conditions existing in the District of Columbia with respect to substandard housing and blighted areas, including the use of buildings in alleys as dwellings for human habitations, are injurious to the public health, safety, morals, and welfare."[11] Most people want and expect the government to promote health and safety, so the law seemed uncontroversial at first. However, the resulting comprehensive plan for redevelopment required tearing down a department store owned by the plaintiff, Mr. Berman, who complained that his store wasn't housing, so it couldn't be substandard housing, wasn't blighted, and was in no way "injurious to the public health, safety, morals, and welfare" of the District. He objected also to the lack of public use of his property in the comprehensive plan. After requiring him to sell his store to the District, private developers would tear it down and replace it with privately owned houses and shops.

Supreme Court Justice William O. Douglas was not persuaded by Berman's arguments. He wrote for the court:

Miserable and disreputable housing conditions may do more than spread disease and crime and immorality. They may also suffocate the spirit by reducing people who live there to the status of cattle. They may indeed make living an almost insufferable burden. . . . The misery of housing may despoil a community as an open sewer may ruin a river.

The concept of public welfare is broad and inclusive. . . . It is within the power of the legislature to determine that the community should be beautiful as well as healthy, spacious as well as clean, well-balanced as well as carefully patrolled.[12]

Mr. Berman's property was in good shape, but had to be sold anyway, according to Justice Douglas, because "The entire area needed redesigning so that a balanced, integrated plan could be developed for the region, including not only new homes but also schools, churches, parks, streets, and shopping centers."[13]

In sum, the Supreme Court expanded the meaning of "public use" over the years. At the start it meant (1) the public owns it, as with a park or road. Then it expanded to include (2) the public has use of it, as with a railroad. Then it expanded again to include (3) the public benefits through removal of something harmful and its replacement with something beneficial. Notice in this three-step process the gradual erosion of property rights and the increase of government power. If you like this, it's progress; if you don't, it's a slide down a dangerous slippery slope. Political conflicts often include fear of slippery slopes, sometimes on both sides of the issue.

Decision and Dissent in *Kelo v. New London*

For better or worse, on June 23, 2005, the 5–4 majority in *Kelo v. New London* advanced the progress or slide of earlier courts. Justice Stevens wrote for the majority:

Two polar propositions are perfectly clear. On the one hand, it has long been accepted that the sovereign may not take the property of *A* for the sole purpose of transferring it to another private party *B*, even though *A* is paid just compensation. On the other hand, it is equally clear that a State may transfer property from one private party to another if future "use by the public" is the purpose of the taking; the condemnation of land for a railroad with common carrier duties is a familiar example.[14]

The issue is whether economic development constitutes "use by the public." As noted earlier, Stevens responds with political philosophy: "Promoting economic development is a traditional and long accepted function of government."[15] Economic development was a major reason for the government to take land for roads, railroads, and urban renewal, so it justifies New London taking land from unwilling sellers. Susette Kelo and the other plaintiffs must sell because, "As with other exercises in urban planning and development, the City is endeavoring to coordinate a variety of commercial, residential, and recreational uses of the land, with the hope that they will form a whole that is greater than the sum of its parts."[16] Plaintiffs' continued residence would mess up the overall plan.

Justice O'Connor wrote for the minority of four who objected to this further erosion of property rights. She pointed out that when Mr. Berman's store was taken in eminent domain in Washington, D.C., in the 1950s, "the neighborhood had so deteriorated that, for example, 64.3% of its dwellings were beyond repair. . . . Congress had determined that the neighborhood had become 'injurious to the public health, safety, morals, and welfare.'"[17] Berman's store was not blighted, but the neighborhood could not be cleaned up without its removal. In sum, "the relevant legislative body had found that eliminating the existing property use was necessary to remedy the harm."[18]

New London is not blighted, O'Connor noted. The plaintiffs' land is being taken in eminent domain not to eliminate harm, but to secure some benefits to the public, "such as increased tax revenue, more jobs, maybe even aesthetic pleasure."[19] O'Connor would allow takings needed to combat harm, but not those needed to confer benefits.

However, the distinction between combating harm and promoting good is sometimes elusive. Although there are clear cases—theft harms people and free education benefits them—many cases are harder to classify. Forcing Susette Kelo and her neighbors to sell their property to spur economic development and create jobs may seem calculated to confer a benefit on the community through increased tax revenue and improved job prospects. But people out of work could look at the situation differently. They could see plaintiffs' unwillingness to sell, resulting in stunted economic growth and their own continued unemployment, as harming them. In such cases, judging whether the state is averting harm or conferring benefits is like deciding whether the glass is half empty or half full. No answer seems uniquely correct.

Justice Kennedy suggested at oral argument in February 2005 that the distinction between averting harm in Washington, D.C., and conferring benefits in New London will be erased by time. He noted that as things were going, New London would be blighted instead of just depressed in five years. He seemed reluctant to delay action until the city was in worse shape.[20] Having thus expanded the doctrine of pre-emption from foreign policy to slum clearance, he ultimately joined Stevens in the majority.

But O'Connor had another argument in principle against taking land for economic development. Such a policy makes everyone's property rights insecure, she claimed. There is no end of economic development. In our society, we favor continued, rapid economic growth. The alternative is usually unemployment for many people. So, she reasoned, if we allow takings for economic development, "any single-family home . . . might be razed to make way for an apartment building, or any church . . . might be replaced with a retail store, or any small business . . . might be more lucrative if it were instead part of a national franchise."[21] In all of these cases, general economic prosperity and local property taxes would increase. No one's property is safe when others could put it to more lucrative use.

In addition, O'Connor noted:

The fallout from this decision will not be random. The beneficiaries are likely to be those citizens with disproportionate influence and power in the political process, including large corporations and development firms. As for the victims, the government now has license to transfer property from those with fewer resources to those with more. The Founders cannot have intended this perverse result.[22]

Justice Thomas backed O'Connor up with facts and figures, which he quoted from scholarly studies of urban renewal.

"Of all the families displaced by urban renewal from 1949 through 1963, 63 percent of those whose race was known were nonwhite, and of these families, 56 percent of nonwhites and 38 percent of whites had incomes low enough to qualify for public housing, which, however, was seldom available to them." In 1981, urban planners in Detroit, Michigan, uprooted the largely "lower-income and elderly" Poletown neighborhood for the benefit of the General Motors Corporation. . . . Urban renewal projects have long been associated with the displacement of blacks; "in cities across the country, urban renewal came to be known as 'Negro removal.'"[23]

In short, allowing land to be taken in eminent domain for economic development harms minority members, the poor, and the elderly, while it favors real estate developers and rich corporations.

Economic discrimination is clear in New London. Susette Kelo asks, "How come someone else can live here, and we can't?"[24] The issue is simply money. Ms. Kelo and the other plaintiffs don't object to having rich neighbors and fancy shops nearby. But Ed O'Connell, the NLDC's lawyer, said that "developers want open space, not a checkerboard of old and new work around, and particularly not the few old houses that remain in Fort Trumbull. . . . You're not going to get a developer to put a $10 million development next to some of these houses."[25] Kelo understood only too well. She told a reporter, "I think they don't want to have to look at us."[26]

Such economic prejudice, however, is a fact of life. That's why the real estate motto is "location, location, location." People want attractive surroundings; they seldom want to live near people much poorer than themselves. So, if the housing of the relatively poor cannot be taken in eminent domain, City Attorney for New London Thomas Londregan pointed out, the city will never be able to compete with the suburbs.[27]

Ideological Coalitions

The negative impacts on minority groups, the elderly, and the poor explain the support that plaintiffs received from the NAACP, AARP, and some left-leaning organizations and individuals, such as the ACLU and Ralph Nader.[28] Their concern for the poor is justified by a political philosophy called *contractarianism*, taken from the word "contract." In ordinary contracts, people agree to rules governing their behavior. One person agrees to vacate her house by a certain date and another agrees to pay her a certain amount of money for it. One person agrees to work for a company and the company agrees to pay a certain wage for that work. It is crucial that *all* parties to the contract *agree* to it. A coerced contract, one signed with a gun to your head, is invalid.

Contractarians believe that laws and public policies should similarly be what all affected parties would agree to without coercion; rules that everyone considers fair. So, the bottom line for contractarians is fairness and their basic reason for objecting to some laws and public policies is this: no one would agree to that if she put herself in the other person's shoes. This isn't a novel idea. It's very similar to the Golden Rule, which most people consider a sound moral guide.

Contractarians are often at odds with libertarians, whose main concern is individual freedom and whose bottom line is: people should be free to do what they want if they are not harming others. Because property is very unevenly divided in the United States (and elsewhere), contractarians often object when the state allows rich people to do as they please with their property while others in society suffer from poverty. Would rich people agree to laws that allow increasing concentrations of wealth if they were in the other person's Payless shoes? Contractarians don't think so. They therefore generally favor government programs that redistribute wealth from rich to poor, including progressive income taxes that fund programs for the poor, such as Medicaid and food stamps. Libertarians object that this amounts to stealing their money to help others. Rich people should be free to help the poor if they want to, but they shouldn't be forced. Libertarians want a very small government, contractarians a much larger one.

Still, they agreed that taking property in eminent domain for economic development is wrong, so they both supported the plaintiffs in *Kelo v. New London*. But their reasons were entirely different. Libertarians wanted to protect the individual property rights of hold-out homeowners, whereas contractarians wanted to end a practice that tends to harm the poor. A rule that states can take property for economic growth, they believe, would not be freely accepted and considered fair by all parties to the social contract. The NAACP and AARP emphasized the tendency of urban renewal projects to harm poor African Americans and older Americans.

The city's supporters contained another unusual coalition of the willing. As we have already seen, free-market conservatives supported the city, because the bottom line of their political philosophy is: government laws and public policies should maximize economic growth and opportunity. That was the city's objective. They were joined by some environmentalists. The bottom-line political philosophy of *environmentalism* is: laws and public policies need to protect nature. For some environmentalists, this promotes long-term human welfare. If we mess up nature, people will suffer in the long run, because we all depend on nature. Other environmentalists—some for religious reasons—believe that we should protect nature also because it is good in itself. They think, for example, that we should protect endangered species—even those of no conceivable benefit to human beings.

Environmentalists often clash with developers who, following the free-market philosophy, want to alter nature to make a profit, which helps the economy grow. Developers want ski slopes on mountains where environmentalists want wilderness. They want logging in old growth forests where environmentalists want habitat for spotted owls. Environmentalists, for their part, want increased government regulation of business, such as tough emission standards for factories to keep the air and water clean. Free-market conservatives worry that such standards will harm U.S. global competitiveness by making our products more expensive than those produced elsewhere. This could impair economic growth.

These ideological foes jointly supported the government in *Kelo v. New London*, but for different reasons. While free-market conservatives hoped for economic growth, environmentalists sought "smart growth." According to *New York Times* reporter Terry Pristin, "Environmental groups say that eminent domain powers must sometimes be used to promote 'smart growth'—that is, denser development in older neighborhoods—as a means of reducing suburban sprawl."[29] Suburban sprawl generally harms the environment because suburbanites take over land that could be used by wildlife. Suburban development often requires filling in wetlands that cleanse fresh water and serve as habitat for migrating birds. Suburban living requires automobile transportation that uses limited natural resources, such as petroleum, and adds to the build-up of carbon dioxide, which contributes to global climate change. In general, therefore, it's better from the environmental perspective for people to live in compact communities where they take up less land and can walk or use public transportation to get around. So, environmentalists supported New London's efforts to create a compact "urban village."

The lesson from this is not that politics makes strange bedfellows but that to understand politics, we need to go beyond the simple divisions between right and left, red and blue, conservative and liberal, Republican and Democrat. In this case, there were two big slumber parties, but everyone brought and slept in her own bed.

All four philosophies—libertarian, free-market conservative, contractarian, and environmental—attract most of us. We want to enjoy our property free of government interference; we want the government to spur economic growth; we believe in the golden rule; and we want to preserve the environment for our own good and for future generations. The Supreme Court's 5–4 decision in *Kelo* reflects not just a close division of opinion in society, but ambivalence within most of us about the issue. We see good arguments on both sides. But those arguments are not based on conservative versus liberal views. Our thinking is much more complex. Political philosophy examines that complexity, making our thinking clearer to ourselves and others.

Twelve Political Philosophies: A Quick Preview

This book examines twelve political philosophies: the four already introduced, plus an additional eight. The eight are feminism, social conservatism, theocracy, communitarianism, utilitarianism, multiculturalism, cosmopolitanism, and natural law. I discuss them to illuminate hot-button political issues. Each philosophy is attractive to many of us, if not to everyone. In some situations, the bottom line of that philosophy is the one we think should decide the case. But other cases give us pause. The bottom line of that first philosophy, although relevant, does not seem as important as the bottom line of a competing political philosophy.

Switching in this way among political philosophies is not necessarily illogical. Relevant differences among issues may justify altering priorities. My brother Robert, for example, is mostly a free-market conservative who wants the government to keep its nose out of the free market so market activity can make the country wealthier. However, he has asked me to join petitions for laws that would require all insurance policies to cover a hospital stay of more than twenty-four hours after a woman gives birth. On free market principles, people should be able to buy whatever coverage they want and can afford. Depending on consumer demand, some policies would guarantee a post-delivery stay of twenty-four hours or more, and others—perhaps the less expensive policies—would not. Why does my brother want to limit the market by outlawing what may be cheaper health insurance policies?

In this case, my brother finds some other basic principle more important than prosperity through the free market. I really don't know what it is, because people who love their families usually avoid talking politics at Thanksgiving. When reminiscence runs out, they watch football. But I can find support for my brother's position in some other political philosophies.

Robert's competing view may be *feminism*. Because early exit from the hospital mostly jeopardizes women, my brother may be influenced by the feminist bottom line: no person should be disadvantaged simply for being female.

Feminists note the disproportionate impact on women of many seemingly neutral policies. Because women do most parental childcare (owing to biological inclination, social expectation, or both), flexible working hours and work-site daycare are feminist issues. They enable women to pursue careers while fulfilling parental responsibilities. Family leave policies that allow people to take time off work without losing position or seniority so that they can care for newborns or sick relatives are also feminist issues, because women do most of this unpaid family work.

Feminists are quick to point out possible prejudice against women and their interests. For example, some people who oppose abortion on grounds that the unborn is a person with a right to life support government funding of stem-cell research that involves killing human embryos. When only women's interests are at issue (abortion), embryos can't be sacrificed, but when men seek cures for diseases that can affect them (stem-cell research), embryos are expendable.[30] Another example: the IRS can collect taxes from citizens, but the male-dominated Congress does not mandate IRS collection of payments from dead-beat dads who owe child support.

Social conservatives oppose feminists on many of these issues. *Social conservatism* places great value on traditions, including religious traditions, because they believe that traditions embody wisdom accumulated over generations. They fear innovations that jeopardize long-term human interests. Innovations they oppose on these grounds include some feminist favorites: women with children working outside the home; men participating equally with women in parenting; and government supplying childcare for working mothers. According to social conservatives, women putting career above maternal duty jeopardizes the traditional family— the bedrock of social life. Most social conservatives also oppose same-sex marriage and abortion. However, they may support special protections for women who have just given birth, as this supports family life.

Theocrats agree with social conservatives that the nuclear family is the foundation of civilization; that same-sex marriage is bad; and that abortion is (almost) always wrong. But *theocracy* rests on different grounds than social conservatism. Social conservatives support religion in general because they think religious training and tradition help curb wayward human inclinations. They are happy to have nativity scenes and the Ten Commandments displayed on public property, but don't object to inclusion of symbols from other great religious traditions. Theocrats, by contrast, want state policy to reflect the tenets of a particular religion—theirs. Many theocrats see the United States as a Christian nation and therefore oppose equal public support of other religions. They oppose abortion and same-sex marriage because they believe God opposes abortion and same-sex marriage. As former Arkansas Governor Mike Huckabee said during his bid for the Republican presidential nomination in 2008, it's easier to amend the U.S. Constitution on such matters than to alter the eternal word of God. Theocrats who think God has mandated a subordinate place for women may oppose equal employment opportunity for women.

A theocrat's position on hospital stays for new mothers depends on her interpretation of her religion. Theocrats may differ among themselves.

Communitarians are like social conservatives and theocrats in their opposition to what all three consider the excessive individualism of libertarianism, free-market conservatism, and feminism. According to *communitarianism*, people are naturally part of a larger social whole and should not demand so many individual rights. However, communitarians are less attached to tradition than social conservatives and theocrats. Communitarians think, for example, that gender roles can change without jeopardizing the family. They don't object to same-sex marriage because they think family can take many different forms and still perform its core functions.

Like feminists and at least some social conservatives, communitarians may want society to protect new mothers from medical complications by requiring insurance companies to cover extended hospital stays. The community should protect its mothers.

Utilitarians could go either way. *Utilitarianism* is the view that the state should do whatever promotes the greatest good of the greatest number. The consequences of public policies are all that matter. So, if a free market in hospital insurance results in more good for more people more of the time, utilitarians favor the free-market approach. But if grave harm to poor women results from the free-market approach and if state mandates of insurance coverage can reduce this harm without creating greater harm in the process (which is a big "if"), utilitarians support government mandates.

Utilitarians resemble communitarians in their flexibility regarding traditions. But utilitarians are more individualist and less discriminating. For utilitarians, the good of society equals the mathematical total of its individual members' well-being as judged by those individuals themselves. For communitarians, the good of the whole is greater than the good of the parts and the standard of goodness transcends current perceptions. Like social conservatives and theocrats, communitarians believe that individuals and society at any given time may be mistaken about what is good for humanity. So, communitarians often support social conservative positions on issues regarding the good life (such as the War on Drugs) against utilitarian objections that individual happiness would be greater with less government control.

A major reason we all use more than one political philosophy is that none gives answers we find acceptable to all the issues we face. Thus, although our three remaining political philosophies don't address the issue of government mandates to insurance companies, they are useful in exploring other matters.

Multiculturalism is the view that no one nation or culture has a monopoly on the path to human flourishing. We should not assume, for example, that Americans are better than people in Hispanic cultures because they enjoy bullfighting and we don't. We should be tolerant of varying cultural traditions in our midst, allowing as much freedom to different religions and ethnic practices as possible.

Feminists clash with multiculturalists when cultural traditions harm women. In some cultures, for example, a man gets a bride by kidnapping a girl as young as twelve and forcing sex upon her. Feminists object to what our culture considers to be rape of a minor. Another example is female circumcision, which can be quite gruesome. Communitarians object that multiculturalism within our society threatens to divide society along ethnic lines, because people from one culture act one way and people from other cultural traditions act differently. Communitarians think society flourishes most when it bonds as a single community.

Theocrats object to traditions in other cultures that violate their understanding of God's law. Social conservatives, by contrast, tend to favor tolerance of other cultural traditions (they tend to favor maintaining traditions) so long as the tradition is maintained in the nation of its origin and not imported to our country, where they might threaten or replace our traditions.

Cosmopolitanism is the view that certain values are universally important, regardless of race, religion, nationality, or ethnicity. Cosmopolitans often join feminists in objecting to ethnic practices that harm women, wherever they occur. Many cosmopolitans object also to aspects of our own culture that seem to degrade humanity, such as the death penalty or the torture of prisoners to extract vital defense information. Although the content of their dos and don'ts differ from those of theocrats, cosmopolitans are like theocrats in believing that on many matters, there's a universal right and wrong that all humanity should respect and follow.

Nature favors certain ways of living over others and people should adapt themselves to nature rather than attempt vainly to get nature to adapt to them. *Natural law* theorists are grossed out by the thought of chickens genetically engineered to have no feathers and children born of only one parent because they are the product of cloning. This view has historical connection with theocracy because many theocrats see nature as a reflection of its creator, God, and therefore oppose meddling too much with nature. For example, theocrats often join natural law thinkers and environmentalists in opposing genetic engineering, because genetic engineering disturbs God's plan (theocratic), interferes too strongly with nature (natural law), and upsets ecological balances (environmental). Some natural law thinkers join theocrats in condemnation of homosexuality, but others think homosexuality, although not the statistical norm, is natural to our species, like being left-handed.

My brother may not know himself why he forsakes free-market conservatism, or even that he forsakes it, by supporting laws limiting health insurance options for women giving birth. If that's the situation, he needs this book to clarify his thought for himself and make sure that he still favors limiting health insurance options after seeing how this idea conflicts with the free market. Self-clarification can also help him argue more persuasively for his view on the matter, whatever it turns out to be, which could improve his political effectiveness. Luckily for him, he'll get a copy of this book free.

The major difficulty in political philosophy, as I see it, is not people applying one philosophy in one situation and another in a different situation, but just the opposite—people thinking they have a political philosophy that solves all problems. I hope to show that all the philosophies we use are good and helpful in some situations, but that none is helpful in all situations to which it might be applied. In some situations where it might be applied, it gives what most people consider poor guidance. The defect is not in the political philosophy so much as in its application beyond the range of cases where it yields results that we consider reasonable. Of course, people will differ from one another about which results are reasonable, but I think you'll find that we agree enough about what's reasonable to reject applying any one political philosophy across the board.

The Aftermath

In spite of the ambivalence many people feel about the competing claims of economic growth (free-market conservatism) and property rights (libertarianism), most seem to side with Susette Kelo in her fight to keep her home. John Broder wrote in the *New York Times* in February 2006, the year after the *Kelo* decision: "In a rare display of unanimity that cuts across partisan and geographic lines, lawmakers in virtually every statehouse across the country are advancing bills and constitutional amendments to limit the use of the government's power of eminent domain to seize private property for economic development purposes."[31] This legislative activity reflects condemnation of the *Kelo* ruling that came from "black lawmakers representing distressed urban districts, from suburbanites and from Western property-rights absolutists who rarely see eye to eye on anything." Even Justice Stevens, who wrote the Supreme Court's opinion, didn't like it. He told a bar association meeting two months after the decision that "he would have opposed it had he been a legislator and not a federal judge bound by precedent."

Some ambivalence remains, however. After the *Kelo* decision, the state of Texas was one of the first to ban taking property in eminent domain for private development. But they made some exceptions. "Among those exceptions is the condemnation of homes to make way for a new stadium for the Dallas Cowboys." Some things may be more sacred in Texas than private property.

The nature and strengths of competing claims may be different for Scott Bullock of the libertarian Institute for Justice who argued for the plaintiffs in *Kelo*. But even Bullock is not an absolutist. He told the *Times*: "Our opposition to eminent domain is not across the board. It has an important but limited role in government planning and the building of roads, parks and public buildings. What we oppose is eminent domain abuse for private development."[32]

The general sentiment against taking the houses in New London helped Susette Kelo and her neighbors. By July 2006, the city had settled with holdout homeowners for much more than the original offer. Bill Von Winkle, who sold sandwiches for years to afford the three properties he owned in the neighborhood, said, "They finally saw it my way." Susette Kelo was allowed to stay in her house for one more year and then the city moved her house for her.[33]

Commercial development of the area remains uncertain. I hope Justice Kennedy, who predicted the city would be a depressed slum in five years without the takings, and therefore favored preemption in slum removal, will look back in five years to check for development or, in its absence, for predicted depression, slums, and WMD (workers massively displaced).

Free-market conservatism and environmentalism do not always support the same side, as they did in *Kelo v. New London*; neither are libertarians and contractarians always united on the other side. Each of twelve political philosophies has distinctive opinions about the role of government in people's lives. Viewing political conflicts through the prism of these twelve philosophies helps illuminate political debates on vital issues, such as whether Terri Schiavo should have been denied artificial nutrition and hydration, which led to her death.

2

Pulling the Plug: Theocrats and Libertarians

Not Dead Yet

I had been visiting my parents' Florida home more frequently because of their increasing disabilities, but this visit was special—they would meet Grace. Grace and I, both divorced after our children were grown, had been dating for several months, and my mother was certain before meeting her that she was perfect. "We love you," Mother told me on the phone before our visit, "and we're looking forward to loving Grace." Mother wanted to die and hoped Grace would see me through the loss.

My parents lived on the Atlantic coast of Florida, only a quarter mile from the ocean. My father was attracted to the area while working as an engineer on the lunar excursion module, the vehicle that took astronauts from the Moon orbiter to the surface of the Moon in 1969. Having had to wear a jacket and tie during much of his working life, my father wanted to retire to where shirts were optional. So, in 1972, Alberta and Irv moved from Long Island, New York, to a three-bedroom ranch house in a neat subdivision in Indian Harbour Beach. My father took up tennis when he was sixty-six-years old and my mother made friends. It became their longest stay in any home during their marriage of more than sixty years, but in 1997 my mother wanted to die.

She had two reasons. My father had dementia. He still knew who everyone was, retained his Democratic political views, and answered *Jeopardy* questions correctly. But he couldn't keep track of things, like home finances, so my mother had to do all the banking. He couldn't find his way home from around the block, so my mother had to do all the driving. He was increasingly quiet, so friends who had enjoyed his lively sense of humor seldom visited or invited them to dinner.

Arthritis was my mother's second reason. Her legs were in constant pain, even though she took medications and walked each day with a walker or shopping cart (mostly the latter). She was otherwise very healthy except for being significantly overweight (even when she's dead, a son doesn't call his mother "obese") and having high blood pressure.

My parents had completed what they considered their major joint project—raising three children. They also traveled and enjoyed friends, but could no longer travel and were losing their friends. They were realistic about death and amazed that others were not. They told us about their old friends Leo and Lillian, who had fallen on hard medical times. Lillian's dementia made her fear Leo after fifty-eight years of marriage and Leo was dying of cancer. Leo said, "I never thought anything like this would ever happen to me." My parents wondered, "What did they expect to happen in old age?"

One time, in her early eighties, my mother commented with humor on the stages of aging. She said, "Getting out of your sixties is easy, getting into your seventies not too bad, getting out of your seventies is tough, and into your eighties a real pain." I said, "I guess getting out of your eighties will be even harder." She said, "Oh no, that's easy. They carry you out."

My mother believed in spirits and expected when she died to live as a spirit, possibly in contact with her deceased mother, brother, sister, and aunt. For her, death was an opportunity, not an end.

Still, she wanted to leave her youngest child in good hands, so Grace and I went to visit over Memorial Day weekend. The second afternoon of our visit, conversation lagged, so we turned on the TV. One of the inane audience-participation shows featured the reunion of young men and women who had met in Florida on spring break about six weeks earlier. Before the guy was brought on, the woman was asked what had attracted her to him. "Cute butt" and "the way he sipped his beer" are the two that I remember. Such attributes seemed to be enough to spark an intense, but short, "relationship." Apparently, the hook-up was good enough for the woman to retain contact information about the man (a good beer-sipper is hard to find), so a television producer could locate him and arrange a televised reunion. The couples greeted one another with awkward friendliness. After three such reunions, my mother said, "You see what's so good about dying. You get to leave stuff like this."

The next day she took an unusually long time in the bathroom, putting us in real jeopardy of missing the early-bird special at their favorite restaurant. When she failed to respond to knocks and calls, I went in and found her seated, slumped over sideways on the sink. She was unconscious and breathing heavily. They told us later her massive hemorrhagic stroke left no possibility of recovery, or even consciousness. Her high blood pressure had finally come in handy.

But she was not dead. Although she had a living will stating that she didn't want to be resuscitated or kept alive on machines, the hospital put her on a respirator to ensure her survival until my brother, sister, and sister-in-law could join us for our goodbyes. Two days later, we stood around her bed, said goodbye, and kissed her before hospital staff turned off the respirator. My mother continued to breathe. What should we do? At any given time in the United States, between ten thousand and thirty thousand people in a persistent vegetative state are being kept alive with artificial nutrition and hydration (ANH).[1] Should my comatose mother join them?

I didn't know of a dispute brewing at the time elsewhere in Florida about the treatment of Terri Schiavo who, like my mother, could breathe on her own but couldn't eat or communicate. Terri Schindler grew up in suburban Philadelphia where she attended an all-girls Roman Catholic high school. In her senior year, she weighed as much as 250 pounds, but then, writes *Newsweek*'s Arian Campo-Flores,

she went on a NutriSystem diet and quickly lost about 100 pounds. Soon thereafter, she met Michael Schiavo at a community college, and he asked her out. . . . After dating for five months, the couple got engaged. They married in 1984 and eventually moved to Florida, where Michael worked as a restaurant manager and Terri as an insurance-claims clerk.[2]

Terri continued to lose weight until she got as light as 110 pounds on her five feet four inch frame. She "had a figure she proudly flaunted by wearing bikinis for the first time."[3] Because she was having trouble getting pregnant, she saw an obstetrician for fertility treatments.

No one suspected at the time that Terri had an eating disorder. Her weight-loss routine may have included bulimic purges that deprived her body of needed potassium. In any case, owing to insufficient potassium, Terri suffered a cardiac arrest in 1990 that deprived her brain of oxygen for about eleven minutes. According to her court-appointed guardian,

Jay Wolfson, this is "some five to seven minutes longer than most medical experts believe is possible without suffering profound, irreversible brain damage."[4]

Terri's husband Michael insisted on medical intervention that kept her alive, "in a coma for the first two months and then in what was repeatedly diagnosed as a persistent vegetative state (PVS)."[5] Patients in this condition have sleeping and waking cycles, open and shut their eyes, blink, grimace, and breathe on their own. But they are completely unaware of their surroundings, owing to loss of brain tissue needed for consciousness. The condition is irreversible, because brain tissue doesn't grow back.

Michael became Terri's legal guardian and took all normal and some unusual steps to help Terri recover. When conventional therapies didn't work,

Michael flew her out to California, where a doctor implanted platinum electrodes into her brain as part of an experimental procedure that ultimately failed. Back in Florida, Michael enlisted family members to record audiotapes of their voices, which he played for Terri on a Walkman. He was fastidious about Terri's appearance, spraying her with Picasso perfume and outfitting her in stirrup pants and matching tops from The Limited. . . . To better care for Terri, Michael even enrolled in nursing school.[6]

He was so demanding about her care that many caregivers despised him. Still, one nurse said, "He may be a bastard, but if I was sick like that, I wish he was my husband."[7]

Initially, Michael and the Schindler family got along well. Michael lived with the Schindlers for awhile as they worked together for Terri's cure. By 1993, the Schindlers encouraged Michael to date other women and get on with his life. But bitterness between them arose later that year. Michael had sued the obstetrician who was treating Terri for infertility, claiming that blood tests should have revealed Terri's potassium imbalance. He won $700,000, kept in a trust for Terri's continuing nursing care, and $300,000 for loss of companionship. The Schindlers and Michael disagreed about the use of the $300,000. Michael told CNN's Larry King that the Schindlers wanted part of the money for themselves; the Schindlers told Larry King they wanted it for more therapy for Terri.

By this time, more than three years after the cardiac arrest, Michael had given up on curative therapies. Although he remained Terri's most regular visitor, he petitioned in 1998 to have Terri's ANH removed, which would result in her certain death. The Schindlers were adamantly opposed.[8] What should be done? As the dispute developed, the most prominent political philosophies appealed to were theocracy and libertarianism. But neither was fully adequate.

Religious Objections

The Schindlers were joined in their opposition to Michael's petition by many theocrats, who opposed removal of ANH as against God's wishes. The bottom-line political principle for theocrats is that state laws and policies should conform to God's plan for humanity. Cal Thomas wrote the following from a religious perspective before Terri died:

> Terri Schiavo's life matters as symbol and substance. Her case is only the latest in a long series that forces us to choose between two philosophies of life.
>
> One philosophy says we are mere material and energy shaped by pure chance in a random universe, evolving from slime with no Author of life, no purpose for living beyond what gives us pleasure and no destination after we die but the grave.
>
> The other philosophy of life says we are created by an infinite, personal God who has a plan for every life in every situation and circumstance and that no one should take a life except under the most extreme circumstances and only through due process or in self-defense.[9]

Terri's death was not mandated by extreme circumstances or self-defense. Friar Frank Pavone, National Director of Priests for Life, pointed out:

> She is not dying. She has no terminal illness. She is not in a coma. She is not on life-support equipment. She is not alone, but rather has loving parents and siblings ready to care for her for the rest of her life. . . .
>
> Yet a battle rages regarding whether Terri Schindler-Schiavo should be starved. She has sustained brain injuries and cannot speak or eat normally. Nevertheless, the only tube attached to her is a small, simple, painless feeding tube that provides her nourishment directly to her digestive system. . . .
>
> News articles have recently characterized Terri's situation by saying that some want to "keep her alive against her husband's wishes." But Terri is not dying. What does "keeping her alive" mean, if not the same thing as keeping you and me alive—that is, by giving us adequate food, shelter, and care?
>
> Some say that Terri's family should "let her go." But this is not a matter of "letting her go," because she isn't "going" anywhere. If, however, she is deprived of nourishment, then she would slowly die in the same way that any of us would slowly die if we were deprived of nourishment. It is called starvation.[10]

The Florida Catholic Conference wrote:

Mrs. Schiavo is a defenseless human being with inherent dignity, deserving of our respect, care and concern. Her plight dramatizes one of the most critical questions we face: To be a truly human society, how should we care for those we may not be able to cure . . . ? There should be a presumption in favor of providing nutrition and hydration even by artificial means as long as it is of sufficient benefit to outweigh the burdens involved to the patient.[11]

To these pro-life activists, Terri was a vulnerable person needing the compassion and protection that Christianity at its best affords the defenseless. Justice requires protecting the vulnerable.

Theocracy in America

Many supporters of Michael Schiavo's decision to remove ANH from Terri objected to religion intruding into politics. They opposed the theocratic political principle that states should do as God commands.

But theocratic reasoning has a long and distinguished history in the United States. In the Declaration of Independence, Thomas Jefferson invoked "the Laws of Nature and of Nature's God" to justify the colonies' independence from Great Britain. Jefferson also wrote in the Declaration, "We hold these truths to be self-evident, that all men are created equal, that they are endowed by their Creator with certain unalienable Rights, that among these are Life, Liberty, and the pursuit of Happiness."[12] In other words, we have "unalienable Rights" because God says so and our laws should reflect God's commands.

The abolitionist movement against slavery also invoked God's commands. David Walker's *Appeal* in 1829 typifies theocratic abolitionism:

How can the preachers and people of America believe the Bible? Does it teach them any distinction on account of a man's colour? Harken, Americans! To the injunctions of our Lord and Master, to his humble followers.

"Go ye, therefore, and teach all nations, baptizing them in the name of the Father, and of the Son, and of the Holy Ghost."

I declare, that the very face of these injunctions appear to . . . not show the slightest degree of distinction [according to race].[13]

In his second inaugural address, President Abraham Lincoln suggested that the bloody Civil War may be God's punishment of the United States for having profited from slavery. He also said: "With malice toward none; with charity for all; with firmness in the right, as God gives us to see the right, let us strive on to finish the work we are in."[14] Lincoln, it seems, came to rely for political policy on what he believed to be God's will—the right as God gives us to see it. This is central to theocratic thinking.

A call to religiously motivated compassion leading to just actions was at the heart of the civil rights movement. Dr. Martin Luther King Jr. wrote in his famous "Letter from Birmingham City Jail":

There are two types of laws: there are *just* and there are *unjust* laws. I would agree with Saint Augustine that "an unjust law is no law at all."

Now what is the difference between the two? How does one determine when a law is just or unjust? A just law is a man made code that squares with the moral law or the law of God. An unjust law is a code that is out of harmony with the moral law. To put it in the terms of Saint Thomas Aquinas, an unjust law is a human law that is not rooted in eternal and natural law. Any law that uplifts human personality is just. Any law that degrades human personality is unjust.[15]

Those objecting on religious grounds to "letting Terri die" included the Reverend Jesse Jackson, a close associate of Dr. King. He saw depriving a vulnerable person of needed food and water as degrading human personality, treating a person's life as unimportant.

President George W. Bush repeatedly invoked God's will to justify policies aimed at increasing human freedom. Shortly after September 11, 2001, he said, "Freedom and fear, justice and cruelty, have always been at war, and we know that God is not neutral between them."[16] In his third debate with John Kerry during the 2004 election campaign, he reiterated, "I believe that God wants everybody to be free. That's what I believe. And that's one part of my foreign policy."[17]

Evangelical Christian and editor of *Soujourners* magazine Jim Wallis sees religious motivation in most major political movements in the United States:

History teaches us that the most effective social movements are also spiritual ones, which change people's thinking and attitudes by appealing to moral and religious values. Those movements change the cultural and political climate, which then makes policy changes more possible, palatable, and, yes, democratic. The best example of doing it right . . . is the American civil rights movement, which was lead by ministers who appealed directly to biblical faith.[18]

In sum, theocracy has at times been a respectable and influential political philosophy in the United States. Defenders of Terri Schiavo's life invoked the equal value of all human beings in the sight of God much as abolitionist David Walker did in his *Appeal*. In 1995, Pope John Paul II

condemned laws authorizing euthanasia in similar terms to Dr. King's
condemnation of laws promoting racial segregation. Under the title "The
Gospel of Life," the pope wrote: "Laws which authorize and promote . . .
euthanasia are . . . completely lacking in authentic juridical validity. . . .
A civil law authorizing . . . euthanasia ceases by that very fact to be a
true, morally binding law."[19] Ten years later, as Good Friday approached
and Terri Schiavo lay dying of dehydration, Friar Pavone quoted the pope
and then added:

The courts have told Terri's loving parents and siblings, who want to care for her
for the rest of her life, that they cannot even give her a cup of water as she starves
to death. In fact, my friend Eva Edl, a concentration camp survivor, tried the
other day to bring Terri a cup of water and was arrested for doing so. The Passion of Christ is being lived out in Terri, and our faithfulness to Christ demands
that we protect her and all who are vulnerable, as she is.[20]

The defense of Terri Schiavo's life reflects a long tradition of theocracy
in America.

Theocracy: Intolerance, Uncertainty, and Disharmony

Intolerance

Theocracy has a checkered past in America, owing to its alliance with injustice and intolerance. The Bible was invoked in support of slavery as
well as abolition. Slaveholders used the story of Noah, explains historian
Winthrop Gordon:

The original story . . . was that after the Flood, Ham had looked upon his father's
nakedness as Noah lay drunk in his tent, but the other two sons, Shem and Ja-
pheth, had covered their father without looking upon him; when Noah awoke
he cursed Canaan, son of Ham, saying that he would be a "servant of servants"
unto his brothers.[21]

The story suggested subjugating black people because the name "Ham . . .
originally connoted both 'dark and hot.'"[22]

Laws against interracial marriage also claimed divine warrant. Chief
Justice Earl Warren explained in 1967:

In June 1958, two residents of Virginia, Mildred Jeter, a Negro woman, and Richard Loving, a white man, were married in the District of Columbia . . . [and then]
returned to Virginia . . . [where] a grand jury issued an indictment charging the
Lovings with violating Virginia's ban on interracial marriages.[23]

Upon their guilty plea in 1959, the trial judge suspended their sentence, but used theocratic terms to justify the law banning interracial marriage:

Almighty God created the races white, black, yellow, malay and red, and he placed them on separate continents. And but for the interference with his arrangement there would be no cause for such marriages. The fact that he separated the races shows that he did not intend for the races to mix.[24]

More recently, the Reverend Pat Robertson invoked God's opinion about homosexuality to dissuade the city of Orlando from supporting "gay pride" by allowing "gay days" flags to be hung from city streetlamp poles:

The Apostle Paul made it abundantly clear in the Book of Romans that the acceptance of homosexuality is the last step in the decline of Gentile civilization. . . . I would warn Orlando that you're right in the way of some serious hurricanes, and I don't think I'd be waving those flags in God's face if I were you. . . . It'll bring about terrorist bombs; it'll bring earthquakes, tornadoes, and possibly a meteor.[25]

Uncertainty

Some people favor theocracy because they want the stability and reliability of God's commands. Human preferences vary among persons and across time. Theocrats worry that such variation introduces dangerous moral relativism.

However, theocratic reasoning is no less relative to persons and times. Following God's commands has led people to contradictory conclusions, making theocracy an unstable basis for public policy. David Walker saw God on the abolitionist side, whereas slaveholders invoked the Bible to support slavery. Dr. Martin Luther King Jr. was inspired by God to promote racial integration, whereas a Virginia trial judge thought God mandated racial separation. President George Bush claimed that America's 2003 invasion of Iraq was justified, in part, by God's preference for freedom, whereas Pope John Paul II's prayerful reflection led him to oppose that invasion.

Subsequent events seldom end disputes about God's preferences. In 2004, Florida was hit by an unprecedented series of hurricanes, but Orlando was mostly spared. Was God showing displeasure at demonstrations of gay pride or at Florida Governor Jeb Bush's intervention in 2003 in the Terri Schiavo case? God only knows.

Disharmony

Theocracy runs counter to America's tradition of religious freedom. On this matter Thomas Jefferson parts company with more recent theocrats. Jefferson's appeals to God were ecumenical. He opposed sectarian religious claims that a particular revelation from God or a particular interpretation of that revelation should guide public policy. He endorsed the claims of the eighteenth-century enlightenment that the most important ethical precepts mandated by God were accessible to everyone as self-evident truths. Accordingly, all churches and religions should be tolerated so long as they respect such basic moral principles. The state should leave religion alone and remain neutral among the various sects to avoid divisive sectarian disputes over the finer points of religious doctrine, as such disputes precipitated wars of religion in Europe.

Jefferson's general tolerance prevails today. On specifically religious matters, Americans expect the freedom to believe and act as they wish. Specifically religious matters are those on which people can disagree without impairing social peace and harmony. Some people believe that God exists; others disbelieve. Some people think God is three persons in one; others think God is merely one. Some people think Mohammed received revelations from God; others disagree. Some people think human beings have immortal souls that God rewards or punishes after we die; others think there is no life after death. These matters are intensely important to many people on both sides; less important to others. But whatever their views and priorities, people who disagree on these matters can live together in peace and harmony.

This is the essential postulate behind religious freedom. The state must supply security; all political philosophies agree. If religious disagreement were incompatible with peace and harmony, it would threaten security and the state should forbid it, imposing religious uniformity on the population. History teaches us, however, that people can differ on religious matters and live in productive peace and harmony. What threatens peace and harmony is theocracy of the sort championed by some recent American religious leaders, which involves the imposition of one group's religious beliefs on everyone. Europe suffered terribly in sixteenth- and seventeenth-century wars of religion, leading most Europeans to prefer tolerance to theocracy. We are heirs to that tradition of tolerance that

Jefferson promoted. In 2006, religious differences were among the factors provoking violence in Iraq.

Some views that many people embrace on religious grounds, such as the equal importance of every human being, are not exclusively religious. A religious person may have this view because she believes we are all God's children and God loves his children equally. But the view is also secular, because it relates directly to the primary business of government, fostering peace and harmony in the population. If the state treats some people as less important than others, the results are likely to be civil dissention and disharmony, which could ultimately endanger everyone's security. Witness the "troubles" in Northern Ireland that lasted a generation in the late twentieth century.

So, regardless of the divine mandate claimed by its proponents, the ideas that "all men are created equal," that none should be slave to another, and that blacks and whites should be equal before the law, can also be seen as secular. Slavery and subjugation provoke dissention and violence. That's why, in spite of the religious inspiration behind, for example, abolitionism and the civil rights movement, the changes they advocated could be enforced by the state without violating religious freedom. Although the *inspiration* for many people was religious, the *justification* was secular as well as religious. Everyone can appreciate the justification—peace and harmony in the long run—regardless of their religious beliefs.

Theocracy's Slippery Slope

Where does this leave decisions regarding Terri Schiavo? Cal Thomas gave as his reason for continuing Terri's ANH that "we are created by an infinite, personal God who has a plan for every life in every situation and circumstance."[26] This is clearly the kind of religious belief on which people can agree to disagree. Basing public policy on such beliefs endangers social harmony. The Florida Catholic Conference, on the other hand, said, "Mrs. Schiavo is a defenseless human being with inherent dignity, deserving of our respect, care and concern. . . . There should be a presumption in favor of providing nutrition and hydration even by artificial means as long as it is of sufficient benefit to outweigh the burdens involved to the patient."[27] This seems closer to a religiously inspired secular view about caring for all people equally, like the civil rights movement.

But they're not the same. The civil rights movement made it possible for people to sit at lunch counters, vote, and find employment, regardless of race. It didn't require anyone, black or white, to sit at a particular lunch counter, vote, or take a certain job. It reduced the freedom of those who wanted to practice racial discrimination, but this was necessary to expand personal freedom generally and promote social harmony in the long run. Wanting Terri Schiavo's ANH continued fits this secular mold only if that is what she would have wanted. A theocratic decision to feed her regardless of her wishes violates her freedom. Yet that is what many theocrats advocated.

Consider Pope John Paul II's allocution regarding ANH. The Catholic Church had long considered ANH to be a medical procedure that people could decline, even when that results in death, if burdens outweigh benefits. However, in March 2004, the pope urged everyone to see patients in a "vegetative" state as fellow human beings with diminished abilities. Then he added:

I should like particularly to underline how the administration of water and food, even when provided by artificial means, always represents a *natural means* of preserving life, not a *medical act*. Its use, furthermore, should be considered, *in principle, ordinary* and *proportionate,* and as such morally obligatory, insofar as and *until it is seen to have attained its proper finality,* which in the present case consists in providing nourishment to the patient and alleviation of his suffering.[28]

On this understanding, failure to provide people in a vegetative state with nutrition and hydration would be murder by starvation, which obviously should be illegal. Even if the individual wanted to be murdered in this situation, it would be wrong for the state to allow it. So, what starts out as a religious claim ends up constraining the options of believers and unbelievers alike, requiring my siblings and me to supply our mother with ANH after her stroke even though she was eighty-three years old, comatose, and adamantly opposed to living a moment longer than necessary. Because she was otherwise healthy, she could have lived another ten or twelve years, against her wishes.

Where would the imposition of specifically religious views on the unwilling public stop? Many Christians, including Reverend Pat Robertson, believe that God abhors homosexuality. Should theocrats be allowed to reimpose bans on homosexual behavior, even consensual sex in private? Should the state allow or require discrimination against homosexuals in housing and employment?

What about women? St. Paul wrote to the church in Corinth: "As in all the churches of the saints, the women should keep silence in the churches. For they are not permitted to speak, but should be subordinate, as even the law says. If there is anything they desire to know, let them ask their husbands at home. For it is shameful for a woman to speak in church."[29] Many Christians interpret this to mean that women should generally be deferential to their husbands and confined to subordinate roles in public life. Many churches, including the Roman Catholic Church, do not allow women to occupy the highest ecclesiastical offices. Would a theocratically led America restrict economic opportunities for women to discourage public roles and encourage subordination?

Some churches interpret the command "Be fruitful and multiply, and fill the earth and subdue it"[30] as implying that God forbids artificial birth control, such as condoms, birth control pills, and spermicidal creams. Would a theocratic government outlaw the use of birth control, as was the case in Connecticut before the Supreme Court declared the law to violate people's right to privacy?[31] Would the "culture of life" that some theocrats promote strangle American freedoms?

Religious people differ greatly on all these matters. Many Christians believe the Bible does not condemn homosexuality, prescribe subordination of women, or forbid artificial birth control. If theocracy were to prevail in the United States, theocrats on all sides of these issues would seek electoral advantage to ensure that their version of God's plan prevailed in the public square. The stakes would be very high, because nothing is more important for religious people than obeying God's commands or for theocrats than ensuring that everyone else does as well. The potential for sectarian strife and violence is obvious, especially because many religious people, like Pope John Paul II and Martin Luther King Jr., believe that following God's commands is more important than obeying contradictory laws. So, taken seriously, theocracy promotes anarchy and threatens our freedoms, peace, and security.

But don't go overboard against religion. A wall of separation between church and state is neither desirable nor possible. First, much of what

religious people want for society has secular as well as religious justification. As abolitionism and the civil rights movement illustrate, religious inspiration can add important perspectives and insights to public
policy debates. Second, religious people can try to convince others to
share their beliefs. For example, if they had convinced Terri and Michael
Schiavo that life, being a gift of God, should be continued indefinitely on
ANH, regardless of disability, Terri would likely be alive today. Religious
conversions change social outcomes even when they disallow the con-
verted to impose their views on everyone else.

Living Wills

Libertarians offer an alternative to theocracy. They want the state to
promote individual freedom, self-determination, and autonomy. People
should be free to do whatever they want so long as they don't harm anyone else. This is the libertarian Harm Principle that would limit the role
of government in private decisions. Nineteenth-century British philosopher John Stuart Mill gave the classic statement of this principle.

> The only purpose for which power can be rightfully exercised over any member
> of a civilized community, against his will, is to prevent harm to others. His own
> good, either physical or moral, is not sufficient warrant. He cannot rightfully be
> compelled to do or forbear because it will be better for him to do so, because it
> will make him happier, because, in the opinion of others, to do so would be wise,
> or even right.[32]

This principle requires government respect for people's exercise of autonomy in decision making. In medical contexts, it means "informed consent."
People should receive information about any proposed medical intervention so they can consent or decline as they see fit. Jehovah's Witnesses, for
example, often forego procedures that include blood transfusions, because
they believe such transfusions violate the Bible's command to avoid drinking blood. Some Jehovah's Witnesses die as a result of declining surgery
or refusing medically necessary transfusions during surgery, but there's no
legal fault. Similarly, competent people who need kidney dialysis may refuse for any reason to continue treatments, thereby bringing on their own
death. The libertarian ideas of autonomy, self-determination, and body
self-ownership justify competent patients making such decisions, and our
laws conform in this respect to libertarianism.

Of course, as Terri Schiavo's case illustrates, it's hard to be a practicing libertarian when your brain is shot. Libertarians therefore favor legally enforceable advance directives that enable people to specify beforehand what they would want done if certain situations arise when they are no longer competent.

The two general categories of advance directives are "the living will," which specifies what the person would want done in certain circumstances of incompetence, and "durable power of attorney for healthcare," which designates someone to serve as surrogate decision maker when the person is incompetent. The surrogate is supposed to make decisions that reflect the patient's values and preferences, when those can be determined, or that serve the patient's "best interest"—an objective judgment of value used when the patient's preferences are unknown or unclear. Because the best interest standard does not reflect patients' wishes, libertarians view it with suspicion.

Living wills are the favorite approach of libertarians, because the living wills express patients' wishes and therefore allow patients to control their own medical destinies, even when they are no longer competent. In the light of my mother's living will, for example, there was never any question of hooking her up to ANH to keep her alive indefinitely.

However, studies of living wills highlight their limitations. Angela Fagerlin and Carl Schneider wrote in *The Hastings Center Report* that whereas most people who need them have regular wills, only eighteen percent of people have living wills. Even among dialysis patients, whose need is greater than most, "only 35 percent had a living will, even though all of them thought living wills a 'good idea.'" The federal government's libertarian-sounding Patient Self-Determination Act, "which essentially requires medical institutions to inform patients about advance directives," has had little impact.[33] Living wills can't solve problems when, as in Terri Schiavo's case, no will exists.

The difficulty of prediction (especially about the future) is one reason many people don't have living wills. "Even patients making contemporary decisions about contemporary illnesses are regularly daunted by the decisions' difficulty," write Fagerlin and Schneider. "How much harder, then, is it to conjure up preferences for an unspecifiable future confronted with unidentifiable maladies with unpredictable treatments?"[34] In most cases, unlike my mother's, people don't know enough about future conditions and alternatives to know what they would want in a living will.

Another problem with living wills is that people change their minds. Conditions that seem intolerable to healthy people become more tolerable during illness. Fagerlin and Schneider quote Wilfred Sheed's memoir of cancer recovery. Sheed "quickly learned [that] cancer . . . has a disarming way of bargaining downward, beginning with your whole estate and then letting you keep the game warden's cottage or badminton court; and by the time it has tried to frighten you to death and threatened to take away your very existence, you'd be amazed at how little you're willing to settle for."[35]

Studies show, Fagerlin and Schneider report, that "over periods as short as two years, almost one-third of preferences for life-sustaining medical treatment changed. More particularly, illness and hospitalization change people's preferences for life-sustaining treatments." Worse yet, not only do preferences change, "but people have trouble recognizing that their views have changed. This makes it less likely they will amend their living wills, as their opinions develop, and more likely that their living wills will treasonously misrepresent their wishes."[36]

Finally, most people prefer surrogate decision making to living wills. They "are content or even anxious to delegate decisions to their families, often because they care less what decisions are made than that they are made by people they trust." Two large studies looked at patients' desires to have their own directives followed as compared to decisions made for them that deviated from their own directives. Researchers in both studies were amazed to find that between seventy and eighty percent of those surveyed "preferred to leave final resuscitation decisions to their family and physicians instead of having their own preferences expressly followed."[37]

In the light of these findings, libertarian proponents of self-determination for incompetent patients may champion surrogate decision making over living wills as better representing what most incompetent people really want. Surrogate decision making has the added advantage over living wills that changes can be made in response to new needs, unanticipated circumstances, and innovative therapies. Surrogate decision making does not require innumerable predictions about the unknowable future.

Surrogate Decision Making and the Law

In 1990, the Supreme Court decided, as libertarians would want, that incompetent people have a constitutional right to use surrogate decision making to refuse unwanted medical treatments. The case concerned Nancy Cruzan, who was in a persistent vegetative state due to lack of oxygen reaching her brain for several minutes after a car accident. Like Terri Schiavo, Nancy was a young woman without a living will specifying whether she would want ANH continued indefinitely. By the time the case reached the U.S. Supreme Court, she had been in PVS for seven years. Because she lacked a living will, the only way that she could influence decisions regarding her treatment was through a surrogate decision maker—her father. After years of trying to "wake Nancy up," he came to believe that she would never recover and that she would prefer to die than to remain in a vegetative state. So he ordered removal of ANH. The state opposed this order, resulting in the case that reached the Supreme Court.

Because surrogate decision makers are supposed to order what the patient would want, and because removal of ANH inevitably results in death, the court allowed states to protect human life by requiring "clear and convincing" evidence that removal is what the patient would want. When such evidence exists, however, the state cannot prohibit removal of ANH. Removal is a matter of individual right.

However, controversy surrounds many claims of clear and convincing evidence. Consider the evidence of Terri Schiavo's prior views. Michael Schiavo's 1998 request to remove Terri's ANH resulted in a trial in 2000, where Michael testified that when he and Terri were watching television coverage of people on ventilators or feeding tubes, she said she didn't want to be kept alive "on anything artificial" and did "not want to live like that." Some years earlier, reacting to the burden on Terri's grandmother of caring for Terri's severely brain-damaged uncle, Terri said, "If I ever have to be a burden to anyone, I don't want to live like that." Michael's brother Scott recalled Terri's views about Scott's grandmother being kept alive on a respirator after she was "pretty much gone." Terri said, "If I ever go like that, just let me go. Don't leave me there. I don't want to be kept alive on a machine." Scott's wife Joan had a similar recollection of Terri's views.[38]

Is this clear and convincing evidence of Terri's views? In the first place, it all comes from Michael and people close to him. It could be selective memory or wishful thinking on their part, because Michael had moved on with his life by starting a family with another woman. Anti-euthanasia activist Wesley Smith wrote in the *Weekly Standard* shortly after Terri's death, "Why Judge Greer did not think it a matter of grave import that Michael had two children with another woman, even as he petitioned the court to hasten the day when death would part him from his wedded wife, will always be a source of bitter wonder to Terri's supporters."[39]

Second, even if Terri did say these things, did she really mean them? Some courts have not considered casual statements made years earlier to constitute clear and convincing evidence of a patient's wishes. Consider the case of Michael Martin, who sustained severe head injuries in a car accident when he was twenty-six years old. Eleven years later, Michael was being kept alive on ANH while in a "minimally conscious state." He "had some ability to communicate and follow simple instructions. He could move his right arm and leg on command, and he sometimes responded to simple yes or no questions with appropriate motions of his head. Other times, however, he was completely unresponsive."[40]

Michael's wife wanted the feeding tube removed, but Michael's mother and sister objected. The Michigan Supreme Court had to decide if there was clear and convincing evidence that Michael would not want to live in his current condition. He had told co-workers that he would not want to "live like a vegetable," but he was not in a persistent vegetative state; he was minimally conscious. The court decided his prior statements were not enough to show he preferred death to minimal consciousness. "Only when the patient's prior statements clearly illustrate a serious, well thought out, consistent decision to refuse treatment under these exact circumstances, or circumstances highly similar to the current situation, should treatment be refused or withdrawn."[41]

Would Terri's prior statements, as reported by Michael and his relatives, pass this test? Do we know, can we know how well thought out, serious, and consistent Terri's views were? Anti-euthanasia advocate Wesley Smith does not think so.

States need to review their laws of informed consent and refusal of medical treatment to ensure that casual conversations—the basis for Terri's death order—are never again deemed to be the legal equivalent of a well-thought-out, written advance medical directive. We don't permit the property of the deceased to be distributed based on their oral statements; surely human lives deserve as much protection.[42]

But if there's no living will and we discount substituted judgment, we've run out of resources for decisions based on libertarian principles. What's left?

Objective Standards, Family Values, and Another Slippery Slope

Some people suggest doing what's in the patient's best interest. But objective measures of human welfare are controversial. At issue here is society's judgment about the value of life in a vegetative state. If society values such life, then the default setting in the absence of reliable evidence about the patient's wishes would be the indefinite use of ANH. In cases of legal conflict, this is our society's current position. The opposite default setting would reflect a negative evaluation of life in a vegetative state. In the absence of reliable evidence about the patient's wishes, ANH would be removed when the diagnosis of vegetative existence is confirmed.

Friar Pavone offers the following justification for favoring continued life in a vegetative state: "Any honest medical expert will admit that there is so much about the human brain we still don't know. What Terri experienced on the inside is a mystery that only she and God know."[43] But "what Terri experienced on the inside" might be horrific, as Pavone would have to agree, because he says it "is a mystery that only she and God know." God may be getting back at her for all the times she missed Mass. Leaving God out of it, if Terri was able to experience life while unable to communicate, due to brain injury, she might be depressed. We are social beings. Inability to communicate could make vegetative living get old fast. But, again, no one can know for sure.

Another consideration is the quality of death. Opponents of removing ANH maintain that dying of dehydration is painful. But experts agree that even among conscious people, death by dehydration need not be uncomfortable.[44] In sum, consideration of possible experiences by people in PVS does not favor either the current default setting or its opposite.

If we assume with the scientific community that no consciousness exists in PVS, living does not directly benefit the patient, although it may benefit family members who don't want to let go, such as the Schindlers, and harm others who want to move on, such as Michael Schiavo. If our standard is the *patient's* best interest, there is no reason to continue ANH unless the patient's prior wishes are known to favor continued life.

But patients are not merely individuals, as Terri Schiavo's case illustrates. They are members of families. So, when relatives are present and there's no clear advance directive from the patient, perhaps the relatives' wishes should prevail rather than either default setting. Tying people's life prospects to decisions of close relatives reflects the basic human pattern. Children's life prospects depend on myriad parental decisions. Married couples are tied together financially in our society, leading to the romantic truth that as long as you're married, you'll never go bankrupt alone. Old people depend mostly on children and other relatives for help in their declining years. So, if the state allows relatives a large role in decisions about removal of ANH from patients in a vegetative state, it reflects and reinforces the importance of family membership, a fact that libertarian thinking tends to ignore.

In our society, spouses count most. Private communication with no other relative is generally immune from judicial inquiry. State laws favor spouses as surrogates for medical decision making. Parents usually come next; then children; then siblings. Leaving Terri's fate to Michael would be an additional way of honoring marriage. Even under current law, had Michael shared Friar Pavone's religious views, Terri would likely be alive today. Whom you marry sometimes turns out to be important.

Conclusion

Our current laws regarding people in PVS combine some family values with libertarian and possibly theocratic elements. Patients can decide for themselves with clear advance directives whether they want to live on ANH. This is the libertarian element. Michael Schiavo continued to insist that he was vindicating Terri's right to have her choice respected.[45] In the absence of clear advance directives, ANH is administered indefinitely if anyone (usually family) objects to its removal. Theocracy may be at work here.

Alternatively, the bias in favor of life may reflect communitarian concerns that were not prominent in news coverage of Terri Schiavo's case. Theocrat Cal Thomas added a communitarian slippery slope argument to his reasons for keeping Terri alive.

The Schiavo case should not be viewed in isolation. It is part of a flow that began in modern times with abortion-on-demand and will continue, if not stopped, with euthanasia. Once a single category of life is devalued, all other categories quickly become vulnerable. . . .

Having been conditioned to accept killing by the state according to an arbitrary standard of who is "fit" to live and who is not, it will be a short step to killing Grandma and Grandpa in their "assisted living" centers, which quickly will be transformed into centers for assisted dying.

Someone will produce a document or hearsay testimony that the elderly person would have "wanted to die" in such circumstances and never intended to be a "burden" to their children.[46]

In short, deliberately depriving any human being of life puts us on a slippery slope toward the inhumane treatment of the weak and helpless. Such communitarian concerns are featured in debates around our next topic—physician-assisted suicide.

The morning after my mother's diagnosis, my father entered the kitchen and announced that my mother had died the night before. Although technically incorrect, he was basically right. He then went looking for pills to kill himself. This is why physician-assisted suicide is our next topic. It pits libertarians against communitarians.

3

Physician-Assisted Suicide: Libertarians and Communitarians

Alive under Protest

My father didn't seem any more lost than usual when he announced on the Sunday before Memorial Day that my mother was dead. As he sat in the kitchen drinking coffee and orange juice and eating his usual bananas and sour cream, Grace starting sorting out the pills to figure out which were his, which my mother's, and whether any were lethal. Our first instinct was to obstruct any attempt Dad might make to kill himself.

Dad suffered from heart failure and colon cancer as well as dementia. Still, he had his normal routine. He couldn't do the checkbook or drive the car, but he could empty the dishwasher and do other chores around the house that had saved my mother painful activity on arthritic legs. During the family cruise to celebrate their sixtieth wedding anniversary nearly two years earlier, Dad had pushed Mom all around "The Big Red Boat" in a wheelchair. Now that she was gone, he had lost purpose in life and the will to live. What was he to do?

When my sister, brother, and sister-in-law arrived later that day, we asked Dad if he wanted to stay living at home or move to an assisted living facility. He chose to stay at home. So, after Grace flew back to meet work commitments and my sister Allene left to drive Mom's car back to California, Judy and I started clearing out the house so that caregivers could come in to help Dad. My brother Robert sorted out the finances and began arranging for caregivers.

Mother was a packrat. Her notion of cleaning out accumulations of family possessions that dated back to her grandmother's generation was to read old letters and, if the author was still alive, mail the letter back so the author could recall old times. Her emptying the pool with tweezers left plenty for Judy and me to do. Dad had always hated Mother's clutter. Still, after two days it occurred to Judy that we were disrupting Dad's living space and he might find this disturbing. But he was true to form. Sitting on the couch in the living room, he said, "Oh, no. I've been waiting sixty years to get this clutter out of here. Could you also get rid of that line of red books on the top shelf over there?" He still knew who he was and what he wanted.

A year earlier, one of his doctors wanted him to have magnetic resonance imagery (an MRI) of his brain for more information about the cause of his dementia. Dad's claustrophobia had made a previous MRI uncomfortable, so he refused the doctor's request, reasoning that no matter what they found it wouldn't improve his condition or its treatment. The demented patient reasoned better than the doctor treating him.

Although Dad reiterated his desire to die as quickly as possible, there was never any serious thought of helping him. Several people had just died trying to climb Mount Everest, but we figured he wouldn't qualify for such an expedition. Our only practical thought, which we didn't share with him, was that he might kill himself by eating anything from the back of the refrigerator.

After we had cleaned out the house and all gone home, leaving Dad's daily care to others, a housekeeper informed the social worker that Dad was depressed. The social worker came over, sat on the sofa with Dad and said, "Irv, they tell me you're depressed." Dad replied, "Of course I'm depressed—my wife just died."

After only a couple of months, Dad's stay at home ended when he tried to kill himself with an overdose of Advil. He was an engineer, not a pharmacist. He was whisked off to the hospital to save his life and placed in the psych ward. The attending psychiatrist called me to complain that my brother, who had durable power of attorney for health care, wouldn't authorize aggressive treatment for depression. My brother was following my father's claim that he was not medically depressed. The doctor said a demented person shouldn't take part in medical decisions and put Dad on Prozac without any authorization. I let the doctor know that my father was correct. Prozac is completely inappropriate for the kind of depression that Dad had correctly self-diagnosed. Dad was demented, but he wasn't stupid, and Robert and I respected his views.

Two weeks later, released by the hyperactive psychiatrist, Dad moved to an assisted living facility near his Florida home. It was a beautiful place and Dad liked it there. In some ways, dementia was among the happiest times of his life, because he imagined he was wealthy and owned the entire facility. He loved the fact that "they take care of everything." He was comfortable.

When we visited we wanted to improve his quality of life. I thought we might set up a system with the staff to help Dad listen to his favorite music. Maybe he would like to sit where he could see people playing tennis or golf. But when asked about his favorite thing Dad said, "Solving problems." His engineering specialty was troubleshooting. He knew that his dementia interfered with that kind of thinking. His life was pleasant, but it lacked meaning. That's why he wanted to die. He had finished his life's work, lost his life partner, and found no meaning in anything that could happen now.

He fell down, broke his hip, and refused corrective surgery. He claimed he felt no pain and that living in a wheelchair was fine. I called friends to see if this was rational. A surgeon said that lack of pain was not unusual and that the danger of surgery was success, permitting my weakening father to walk and fall again. He was safer in a wheelchair. Again, my father was right about his own care.

He was no longer eligible for assisted living, so he moved to a nursing home near my brother in Denver. The last rational telephone conversation I had with him was at Thanksgiving when he again talked about wanting to die. Grace and I visited him in January in Denver and he died in early February, eight months after my mother.

The only wish we had refused him, because we couldn't have granted it legally, was help in dying. He was right about his own care in every other respect. Was he right about this also? Should the law have allowed a doctor to prescribe lethal pills for him to take or ignore as he wished? Is reasonable comfort sufficient reward for an unwanted continuation of life without meaning? Does the law deny medical help in suicide for his sake, or for the sake of others? Who would those others be and how did my father's continued life benefit them?

A Good Death

Some calls for help in dying are more urgent, prompting families and physicians to conspire in suicide. In the *New Yorker*, Andrew Solomon recounts his mother's death. Carolyn Solomon was diagnosed with ovarian cancer in August 1989. Although anger at her condition provoked initial threats of suicide, she soon vowed to fight the cancer in every way possible. She suffered through "an excruciating, humiliating bout of chemotherapy."[1] Solomon reports, "She . . . found the physical damage of chemotherapy intensely painful—her hair was gone, her skin was allergic to any makeup, her body was emaciated and her eyes were ringed with perpetual exhaustion." Exploratory surgery ten months later revealed disappointing results.

At this point Mrs. Solomon demanded pills to end her life, but agreed to a second round of chemotherapy that seemed to be working. Still, Solomon wrote:

I should emphasize that the vomiting, the malaise, the hair loss, and the adhesions were all relentless; that my mother's mouth was one great sore that seemed never to heal; that she had to save up strength for days to have one afternoon out; that she could eat almost nothing, was a mess of allergies, and shook so badly that she was often unable to use a fork and knife.[2]

What made all of these difficulties bearable, according to Solomon, was the certainty that she could end it all whenever she decided. By October 1990, she had secured the needed pills from a sympathetic doctor who had prescribed Seconal for insomnia. Seconal is no longer preferred for insomnia because an overdose is often fatal. Doctors acceding to requests for Seconal knowingly abet suicide unless several other sleeping formulas have been tried first and failed. But intentions can't always be proved. A second doctor, who added to Mrs. Solomon's cache of Seconal, explained why he did it: "She was in the late stages of an illness that was clearly terminal. She had voiced from the start her intention not to suffer. She had made it clear that she wanted to die with dignity, and that wish seemed to accord with the rest of her character."[3]

The cache of Seconal was a boon to the patient and her family.

Everything that had been intolerable to my mother was made tolerable when she got those pills, by the sure knowledge that when life became unlivable it would stop. I would have to say that the eight months that followed, though they led inexorably to her death, were the happiest months of her illness; and that in some obscure way—despite, or perhaps because of, the suffering in them—they were the happiest months of our lives. Once we had all settled the future, we could live fully in the present, something that we had never really done before.[4]

My mother talked in that period about how much she loved us all, and unearthed the shape and structure of that love; she contrived in the course of a few months to resolve old family differences. She set aside a day with each of her friends—and she had many friends—to say goodbye.[5]

When all her affairs were in order and it was clear that no chemotherapy could cure her lethal cancer, Carolyn set a date for her death. Only the family, her husband and two sons, were involved. They had a book of instructions. She took antiemetics and had a light snack to prevent possible vomiting of the pills. Then she took the pills and said her final goodbyes. Solomon recalled her last words to her sons:

"I wanted my love to make the world a happy and joyful and safe place for you." She held my hand for a second, then my brother's. "I want you to feel that that love is always there, that it will go on wrapping you up even after I am gone. My greatest hope is that the love I've given you will stay with you for your whole life."[6]

She turned to my father. . . . "I can't imagine what I would have done if you had died before me, Howard. You are my life. For thirty years, you have been my life."

Then her voice became dreamily torpid. . . . "I've looked for so many things in life," she said, her voice as slow as a record player at the wrong speed. "So many things. And all the time Paradise was in this room with the three of you."[7]

Carolyn soon lost consciousness, but it was another five hours before she stopped breathing and they could call a doctor to pronounce death. To avoid inquiry and autopsy, cancer was put as the cause of death. The last thing Carolyn wanted was to get her family in trouble.

Many people would call this a good death. Carolyn Solomon was lucky to have a supportive family and helpful physicians. People who can't get appropriate barbiturates sometimes resort to guns. Imagine the horror of finding your loved one with his head blown off. Imagine the extra burden of death when you know you have no choice but to expose your family to that horror.

Carolyn was lucky also that she didn't vomit. This is a common problem that has required some patients who lacked backup pills to eat their own vomit in order to kill themselves. This takes some of the dignity out of "death with dignity."

Finally, Carolyn was lucky that the pills worked. They stopped her breathing. In many other cases people continue living and the attempted suicide results in brain damage. To avoid this eventuality, the Hemlock Society suggests that after several hours people attending the dying use a plastic bag to stop the sedated individual's breathing. Sedation supposedly prevents the patient suffering during asphyxiation, but patients' movements (supposedly unconscious and involuntary) to remove the bag can make the death seem like garden-variety murder against the patient's will. Imagine your last memory of Mom being your holding her hands down and the bag tightly over her head as she struggles. Even assuming this was the agreed backup plan if the pills didn't work, it's hardly the last image people want to have of a parent.

The Libertarian Case for Physician-Assisted Suicide

Carolyn Solomon and her family were spared the worst horrors of suicide, but the only way to ensure that others are so fortunate is for the practice to be guided by trained physicians. Physician-assisted suicide (PAS) does not allow physicians to kill patients; it only allows them to help patients kill themselves. These distinctions are important.

Euthanasia, which means "good death," covers several different ways of bringing about someone else's death. In "passive euthanasia," death is caused by the patient's underlying medical problem after others deliberately withhold or withdraw medical intervention. Terri Schiavo and my mom died this way. The underlying cause of their deaths was failure of their brains to function properly, making it impossible for them to eat. Others brought about their deaths by withholding (my mother) or withdrawing (Terri Schiavo) artificial nutrition and hydration (ANH) that could have kept them alive. This withholding and withdrawing was legal, because it was the wish of the patients (somewhat controversial in Terri's case) to avoid long-term ANH. Patient-requested passive euthanasia is called "voluntary" and is justified by the libertarian values of autonomy and self-determination.

"Involuntary passive euthanasia" occurs when withdrawal of medical interventions needed to keep patients alive was not previously requested by the patients. Some patients can't make such requests; they are small children or people with severe, permanent mental disability whose physical problems require treatments to keep them alive. These treatments can be withheld or withdrawn in cases of medical futility or when the burdens of treatment outweigh benefits. Doctors might have considered it futile to treat my mother and removed ANH on that basis. Improvement and recovery were impossible. In other cases, burdens outweigh benefits, as when treatments terrify incompetent patients who can't understand their rationale, making the patients' lives miserable. In these cases, appeal is made to objective standards of medical effectiveness and patient best interest. Because the standards are objective and do not reflect the patients' particular preferences, involuntary passive euthanasia, unlike voluntary passive euthanasia, enjoys no support from libertarianism.

"Active euthanasia" occurs when medical intervention causes the death of a patient who has no medical condition that would kill him at that time. An example is a lethal injection administered to a cancer patient to avoid prolonging her suffering. The 2004 Academy Award–winning movie *Million Dollar Baby* (don't read the rest of this paragraph if you haven't seen the movie yet) depicts the active euthanasia of a boxer whose quadriplegia made life no longer worth living. Active euthanasia, voluntary and involuntary, is illegal in the United States, even when performed by physicians.

PAS is mostly illegal in the United States outside of Oregon, where it is highly controlled. Unlike euthanasia, patients themselves perform the actions that bring about death. Suicide is do-it-yourself euthanasia. Doctors supply medications and advice to patients who decide when and whether to kill themselves. It's always voluntary and therefore in accord with libertarian self-determination. The rationale is that people should be able to kill themselves when living becomes intolerable. Doctors are involved to avoid botched jobs, messy methods, and people suffocating loved ones.

PAS proponents claim that about three percent of patients suffer unavoidable, unspeakable pain when they die of debilitating diseases such as cancer and AIDS. Opponents of PAS agree that people often suffer horrible pain, but say it's because doctors are not adept at pain management. Properly trained doctors can relieve all pain.

But this is an exaggeration. PAS advocate Dr. Timothy Quill writes of an eighty-year-old widower whose cancer treatments proved unsuccessful:

During the fourth month of hospice care Mr. Kline's pain in his neck and chest increased dramatically. He got little relief from daily increases in his round-the-clock doses of morphine, and adjustments in adjuvant pain relievers, including antidepressants, antiseizure medications, and steroids were not helpful. [He was] unable to sleep, eat, or move without severe pain.[8]

Rapidly increasing doses of morphine eventually controlled the pain.

Unfortunately, in addition to becoming somnolent, Mr. Kline became paranoid and began to hallucinate. He believed the nurses and his children were his jailers and attackers. He was unable to feel safe despite constant reassurance that he was among friends and loved ones. . . . To add insult to injury, he was also too confused to help with subsequent decision making.[9]

Mr. Kline's physical and emotional pain were finally controlled by total sedation, a medically induced coma, which essentially removed the patient along with the pain.

Physical pain is seldom the primary concern of patients wanting to die. Many patients are more concerned about avoiding indignity. PAS advocate Lonny Shavelson tells the story of author Mary Bowen Hall, in her late fifties, who was dying of cancer. Near death, she was in the hospital talking to Shavelson, her son Paul waiting in the hall, when suddenly she cried out in pain from twisting her back. Mary had refused pain relief that would put her in a stupor, so her pain was not fully controlled. Upon hearing his mother's cry, Paul came running in.

"I need to go," yelled Mary, shaking from the effort of balancing herself against the bed rail. "I need the bathroom, now!" Paul grabbed a portable commode and put it near the bed. . . . Her pain was excruciating.

"Let me go . . . !" Paul held Mary against his chest, her feet dragging along the floor. "I don't know what to do," he said to the nurses. . . .

Mary looked up at his face, then said firmly, "For God's sake let me go. . . . I will not be dragged to the bathroom to shit in front of my son."

Mary slumped in Paul's arms, and the foul smell of feces filled the room as she lost control and the loose stool ran out from under her diaper. She wept softly. . . .

Paul carried Mary to the bathroom. . . . She relaxed in his arms as he placed her on the toilet.[10]

Psychologist Barry Rosenfeld reports that patients requesting lethal medications in accordance with provisions of Oregon's Death with Dignity Act (ODDA) indicate year after year that the two most common reasons for seeking early death were loss of autonomy and "decreasing ability to participate in activities that make life enjoyable."

Much of the OHD [Oregon Health Department] data reported from 2001 support the trends that have now become apparent, as "losing autonomy" and "decreasing ability to participate in activities that make life enjoyable" remained the most common reasons for patient requests for PAS (reported in 94% and 76%, respectively), whereas inadequate pain control was reported by only 1 patient (5%). Only 24% cited feeling a burden to their friends or family.[11]

My Dad's primary reason for requesting suicide was neither pain nor autonomy, but loss of the ability to do what he found most enjoyable—solve problems. He also felt that after Mom died, he had nothing to live for, and on this matter he seemed competent to me.

From a libertarian perspective, however, reasons are unimportant. Recall John Stuart Mill's Harm Principle. Competent adults should be free to act as they please so long as they harm no one else. Their "own good, either physical or moral, is not sufficient warrant" to interfere with their individual liberty.[12] We often honor this freedom in our society. If we didn't, the tattoo and body piercing industries might suffer. People are free to buy losers on Wall Street and marry losers wherever they find them. Many decisions alter lives and lead to regret, but if liberty didn't include freedom to mess up, we'd be free to do only what others think best, which isn't freedom at all. The true libertarian defense of PAS doesn't claim that people would use PAS well and benefit from it, but that its legality would respect people's freedom and self-determination. In a play on the title of Lesley Gore's 1963 hit song, libertarians would say, "It's My Body and I'll Die If I Want To." (Ask a baby boomer.)

Communitarian Worries about a Slippery Slope

Most religious people who oppose removal of artificial nutrition and hydration (ANH) from patients like Terri Schiavo who are in a persistent vegetative state also oppose legalizing PAS. Life is a gift of God and all people are precious in God's eyes. God will take human life when He decides the time is right. People shouldn't play God.

Although such religious reasoning inspires many people to good work and is properly used in private contexts to encourage and persuade, it's not an appropriate basis for legislation. In our society, people have a right to behave in ways contrary to strictly religious beliefs. Legislation restricting liberty requires a secular justification, one that people can appreciate regardless of their specifically religious views.

Accordingly, many people opposed to PAS on religious grounds join others in arguing that legalizing PAS will promote cultural degeneration that endangers society. We saw that theocrat Cal Thomas bolstered religious arguments with secular, communitarian reasons for opposing the removal of ANH from Terri Schiavo. Wesley Smith expands on communitarian concerns regarding PAS and euthanasia:

Support for euthanasia is not a cause but rather a symptom of the broad breakdown of community and the ongoing unraveling of our mutual interconnectedness [resulting]: in the disintegration of family cohesiveness; in . . . a rise in suicides, drug use, and other destructive behaviors; in the growing belief that the lives of sick, disabled, and dying people are so meaningless, unimportant, and without value that killing them—or helping them kill themselves—can be countenanced and even encouraged.[13]

Smith does not object to individualism and self-determination, but only to its elevation "above all other cultural values." He contends that

unbridled, near-absolute individualism leads to social anarchy that asphyxiates true freedom. That is why self-determination, while very important, is but one of several equally important and sometimes conflicting values . . . . One such competing value, communitarianism, promotes mutual interpersonal care, concern, and support. Communitarianism mandates that the state prevent harm to the weak and vulnerable—for example, by stopping suicides . . . as our human obligation to protect and care for one another.[14]

According to the communitarian political philosophy, the social whole is greater than the sum of its parts, the individuals who make up society, just as a good basketball team is greater than the sum of its players' individual talents. Teamwork elevates some teams above others with equally talented players. Similarly, a society improves when its members work together and care about one another. Developing these social goods is worth constraining individual freedom beyond what libertarians would allow.

Consider an extreme case: legalized lethal dueling with pistols. If the practice were controlled to ensure that only competent adults participated, duels were fair, and others protected from stray bullets, libertarians could hardly object. Competent adults would be doing what they want and harming no one else. But legalized dueling would promote cultural degeneration, because people's desires alter when laws change. If dueling were legal, children might be socialized to believe that dueling is the proper response to certain insults. Social pressure could reduce interest in peaceful conflict resolution and increase interest in dueling. No one's autonomy would be infringed; dueling would never be required. But many people would duel to avoid the shame of being labeled a coward. People in a dueling society would make worse use of their self-determination than in a nondueling society. So dueling remains illegal not because legalization would impair anyone's autonomy, but because, other things being equal, a society with dueling is worse than one without it. Laws against dueling help to preserve a good society.

Many communitarians argue similarly that laws against PAS and all forms of euthanasia are needed to maintain a good society. Unbridled individualism of the sort advocated by libertarians leads down a slippery slope, ultimately endangering social cohesion and cooperation by denigrating the worth of increasing numbers of human lives.

Reason to fear the slide comes in part from arguments already given in support of PAS: it is argued that competent adults already have the libertarian right to refuse medical treatments needed to save their lives. For example, competent adults who need renal dialysis to clean their blood may refuse dialysis and die of blood impurities. PAS proponents claim that it's arbitrary to allow some people to die when they want to, but not others, when the only difference is that some people need to use a certain machine to stay alive, whereas others don't. A renal dialysis patient may want to die because of the same arthritis pain that afflicts others with better kidney function, so they should all have the same right to die. This reasoning was used by Federal Circuit Judge Roger J. Miner in a case that challenged New York State's law against assisted suicide. Judge Miner wrote:

The New York statutes prohibiting assisted suicide . . . do not serve any . . . state interests . . . , in view of the statutory and common law schemes allowing suicide through the withdrawal of life-sustaining treatment. Physicians do not fulfill the role of "killer" by prescribing drugs to hasten death any more than they do by disconnecting life-support systems. Likewise, "psychological pressure" can be applied just as much upon the elderly and infirm to consent to withdrawal of life-sustaining equipment as to take drugs to hasten death.[15]

In Judge Miner's view, the Constitution of the United States requires the legalization of PAS. Although Miner's majority opinion was overturned on appeal, it illustrates the worry that once one thing is allowed, others will be allowed as a logical corollary. This is the logic of the slippery slope.

The slide continues. Proponents currently want PAS to help competent people who are terminally ill end their lives peacefully and painlessly. This was Mrs. Solomon's situation. Terminally ill people are those expected to die within the next six months. However, the restriction to terminally ill patients may also seem arbitrary. Law professor and PAS opponent Yale Kamisar notes:

It would be arbitrary to exclude from coverage persons with incurable, but not terminally ill, progressive illnesses, such as ALS (Lou Gehrig's Disease) or multiple sclerosis. But why stop there? Is it any less arbitrary to exclude the quadriplegic? The victim of a paralytic stroke? One afflicted with severe arthritis? The disfigured survivor of a fire?

If personal autonomy and the termination of suffering are supposed to be the touchstones for physician-assisted suicide, why exclude those with nonterminal illnesses or disabilities who might have to endure greater pain and suffering *for much longer periods of time* than those who are expected to die within the next few weeks or months?[16]

Having by this logic extended PAS to non-terminal patients, it seems equally logical to extend it further to people who are so disabled that they cannot administer the last lethal drug to themselves. What if Mrs. Solomon had wanted to die because of the unremitting pain of non-terminal arthritis but was too arthritic to put pills into her mouth? She needs someone else to administer the lethal drugs. If it seems arbitrary to deny her the right to end her suffering, we go from PAS to active euthanasia.

But it is still voluntary; no one is being forced; the principle of self-determination is strictly observed in these proposals. Nevertheless, de-valuing the preservation of human life may influence people to prefer death when they would otherwise choose to live. Consider the reasoning of Ezekiel Emanuel, writing in the *Atlantic Monthly*:

Broad legalization of physician-assisted suicide and euthanasia would have the paradoxical effect of making patients seem to be responsible for their own suffering. Rather than being seen primarily as victims of pain and suffering caused by disease, patients would be seen has having the power to end their suffering by agreeing to an injection or taking some pills; refusing would mean that living through the pain was the patient's decision, the patient's responsibility. Placing the blame on the patient would reduce the motivation of caregivers to provide . . . extra care . . . , and would ease guilt if the care fell short.[17]

In sum, just as legalizing lethal dueling with pistols would leave people technically free to participate or not but could create social pressure to take part, so legalizing PAS and voluntary euthanasia would build social pressure for people to request death. In both cases, communitarians think such use of individual freedom harms society.

Your Money or Your Life

Monetary pressures can further the slide. In the past, doctors were paid, mostly by insurance companies, for providing services to patients. This is known as "fee-for-service" health care. In the United States, however, increasingly health insurance takes the form of managed care where a health maintenance organization (HMO) allocates a certain amount of money per patient to a primary care provider (PCP) to meet an individual's medical needs. Whereas in the fee-for-service system doctors make money by providing service, in the managed care setting they make money by reducing service while collecting per capita payments for their patients. Dr. Daniel Salmasy of the Center for Clinical Bioethics at the Georgetown University Medical Center thinks that such managed care can easily promote managed death, even by

physicians [who] sincerely . . . respect . . . patient autonomy. A perilous line of argument might . . . emerge: . . . 1) Too much money is spent on health care; 2) certain patients are expensive to take care of (i.e., those with physical disabilities and the elderly); 3) these patients appear to suffer a great deal, lead lives of diminished dignity, and are a burden to others; . . . 4) recognizing the diminished dignity, suffering and burdens borne by these persons and those around them, their right to euthanasia or assisted suicide should be legally recognized; and 5) the happy side effect will be health care cost savings.[18]

The influence of money on medical decisions complicates legalizing PAS, because most people object to wealth determining who lives and who dies. That's why we have Medicaid for poor people and Medicare for the elderly; why hospital emergency rooms cannot turn away indigent patients who need emergency care; why rescue workers in disasters are not supposed to help the wealthy more than the poor; and why buying and selling organs for transplant is illegal. Free-market conservative views that promote market allocations of most goods and services—houses, cars, recreation, and "stuff"—seem out of place to most people where life and death are concerned. Our laws reflect this value, even if implementation is imperfect. One problem with legalizing PAS, opponents claim, is the potential for economic discrimination in health care.

Many patients, especially poor ones, might be influenced by poor pain control to choose death. Smith quotes a report on pain control in the *New England Journal of Medicine*: "Undertreatment of cancer pain is common because of clinicians' inadequate knowledge of effective assessment and management practices, negative attitudes of patients and clinicians toward the use of drugs for the relief of pain, and a variety of problems related to reimbursement for effective pain management."[19] A California Summit on Effective Pain Management, which included more than 120 health care providers, educators, and consumers, emphasized class bias in pain management. Pain is "more likely to be undertreated if the patient is minority, female, elderly, or a child."[20]

Assisted-suicide advocate Timothy Quill acknowledges that policy makers

might be all too willing to embrace physician-assisted death as a money-saving alternative to universal access to good medical care. Vulnerable patients might be subtly or explicitly coerced to choose death over expensive medical treatment or custodial care. Patients might feel a "duty to die" without spending the family inheritance or expanding the national debt.[21]

Wesley Smith goes further and notes that when money is at issue, vulnerable people may be stripped of the right to decide for themselves. He tells the story of Catherine Gilgunn, a woman in her early seventies who had a history of breast cancer, diabetes, heart disease, and chronic urinary tract infections. Nevertheless, when she fell and broke her hip for the third time, Smith writes, she still had

a burning desire to live. Indeed, she was unequivocal: In the event of a health-care emergency, she instructed her doctors and her family, everything that could be done to save her was to be done. She named her daughter, Joan, as her health-care proxy in the event of incapacity. There was no doubt in anybody's mind what Mrs. Gilgunn wanted: medical treatment to prolong her life.[22]

However, seizures during her hospital stay left her in a coma. The hospital's Optimum Care Committee "urged that a DNR [do not resuscitate] order be placed on her chart because *its members believed* that CPR [cardiopulmonary resuscitation] would be 'inhumane and unethical.'" The attending physician complied with this suggestion and also took Mrs. Gilgunn abruptly off the respirator that assisted her breathing so that, in his words, she "would go out with some dignity." She died three days later. When the family sued, the jury sided with the doctors and the hospital. Smith notes: "In the end, it was not Mrs. Gilgunn's or her daughter's opinions, values, or autonomy that counted. Only the opinions of the doctors and hospital administrators mattered."[23]

This case differs from Terri Schiavo's, discussed in chapter 2, because Terri presumably preferred death to life in a persistent vegetative state. Removal of artificial feeding could be justified on the libertarian ground of individual choice. The grounds for removing Mrs. Gilgunn's respirator and not resuscitating her, by contrast, were "objective" views about futility. The assumption was that, given her grim prognosis, no reasonable person would want to live in a coma and endure (if she was capable of experience) CPR (which is often quite brutal). In general, such appeals to futility, Smith writes, "would allow health-care professionals, health insurance company executives, or even community 'consensus' to take precedence over patients' wishes for their care."[24] If libertarians started "the right to die" movement with claims of self-determination, removal of decision making from patients undermines the original rationale. The right to die may come back to bite libertarians in the feeding tube.

In addition, as Rosenfeld points out, medical futility is all about money. It "refers to situations in which meaningful recovery is unlikely and frames the decision to withhold treatment in economic terms, as a justification for rationing health care services that have become increasingly expensive and often insufficient."[25]

On the other hand, what good does it do someone to persist in a coma? I must admit, it does strike me, as apparently it struck the jury in Mrs. Gilgunn's case, as irrational to want to live this way. Perhaps in the extreme situation of a coma, an objective standard is appropriate, especially in view of limited health care resources. But then, Wesley Smith worries, there will be a slippery slope from people in a coma to people in a persistent vegetative state. It will cease to matter if Terri Schiavo did or didn't want continued life. And after that, perhaps people with minimal consciousness or those too demented or mentally retarded to make decisions for themselves would be allowed to die of pneumonia or anything else that might kill them because reasonable people would not want to live in those conditions, and so forth.

Communitarian Arguments for Limited PAS

What these considerations ignore is the good that legalizing PAS can do for patients and their families. Besides honoring people's wishes—a libertarian concern—legal PAS can prolong patients' lives, encourage moral development, and knit families closer together. These are communitarian values.

Andrew Solomon's account of his mother's death testifies to the improved quality of life for the patient and her family once a quick and painless death is assured. Legalizing PAS would give such assurance to all patients and families who wanted it.

PAS advocate Lonny Shavelson tells the story of a San Francisco trapeze artist with AIDS whose life was prolonged and improved by the availability of assisted suicide. His daughter, friends, and caregivers benefited as well.

Pierre Nadeau was proud of his beautiful body until AIDS resulted in skin lesions and wasting away. He initially preferred death to being seen in his new condition. Clarissa, a hospice nurse, recalled Pierre's attitude during a hospital stay for a kidney infection in February 1992:

He'd be lying in bed with the curtains closed, and he'd answer all my questions with just one word. . . . God, I knew he was upset about the disease, the loss of his body image. You know what a beautiful man he was, what a beautiful body he'd had. When Pierre lost this, it seemed there was nothing left. . . . But he had so much else to live for.[26]

Pierre had a daughter Alexa to live for. She would turn seven in five weeks. Living with her mother in another city, she had been told of her father's illness and impending death, but her mother thought it important that she hear about it also from Pierre. It would reduce her sense of abandonment. Pierre's friend Gordon told him, "You are the magic in Alexa's life. . . . Only you can tell her why the magic is going to stop." So Pierre, who was not yet seriously debilitated or in physical pain and who wanted to die out of anger, frustration, and depression, agreed to stay alive until he spoke with Alexa when she came to visit for her birthday in five weeks.

Pierre did this only on the understanding that his friends in San Francisco's gay community would help him die when life with AIDS became intolerable. Shavelson writes, "In gay neighborhoods around the country, euthanasia and assisted suicide for people with AIDS became an acceptable norm and an act that was not legally prosecuted."[27] In fact, just before his February hospitalization, Pierre had asked his friend Stephan for help in dying. Stephan said it was too soon: "I'll do this for you when the time comes. . . . I'll commit to it, but I'm not comfortable with you just choosing to do it now."[28] So Pierre stayed alive for his hospitalization and then for Alexa's birthday.

Amazingly, as the time for Alexa's visit approached, Pierre's anger and depression melted away. He had a wonderful visit with his daughter and her mother Lynn and never again raised the topic of suicide. In the five months between February, when he wanted to die, and his actual death, Pierre experienced excruciating pain and humiliating debilitation. In

April, "he became gaunt from weight loss. Swollen lymph glands in his groin had grown so large they obstructed the flow of fluid from his legs. His feet and ankles swelled to nearly twice their normal size. It was painful to walk. He also developed a respiratory infection and became short of breath when he tried to move about."[29]

Yet he lived on in good spirits. Pierre's hospice nurse Clarissa told Shavelson, "I think Pierre has changed so much emotionally and spiritually. . . . That's been the great thing about taking care of him—to see this amazing spiritual change. And I knew he'd been suicidal. What if he had acted on it?"[30] Eventually, AIDS killed Pierre, not suicide.

Shavelson sees in this case a powerful argument for legalizing PAS: in May, Shavelson asked Pierre about his former depression. "Why do you think the depression is gone now, and you no longer even mention suicide?"

"I was very sick then . . . . Now I'm not. So I feel better emotionally."

Shavelson was shocked because Pierre had never been physically sicker. "He was bedridden, short of breath, weak, and wasted." Shavelson then asked Pierre if he would have committed suicide months earlier during his depression if PAS had been legal. Pierre said "No. . . . Actually, if it was that easy I would wait, because I'd know that I could do it whenever I wanted to. . . . But since it was hard to do—if the chance had come along, I might have taken it. The chance didn't come along and now I'm here."[31] Shavelson concludes:

The irony is that, for Pierre Nadeau, a major factor that allowed for his desire to live, to suffer on, was his awareness that assisted suicide would be available if and when he might truly need it. Had he thought that help in dying would not be within reach whenever he might ask, he likely would have killed himself in fear at the beginning of his illness. Yet Pierre was guaranteed assistance in death only because the gay community chose to disobey the laws of his state, as well as the Judeo-Christian tenets upon which they were founded.[32]

Statistics from Oregon support Shavelson's position. Strictly controlled physician-assisted suicide has been legally practiced there since 1997. Rosenfeld notes that between the first and second year of the program

the median time elapsed between the provision of a lethal prescription and the utilization of this medication increased fourfold, from 22 days . . . to 83 days. . . . This increased length of time . . . supports the "secondary" benefit that many clinicians have cited, providing patients with a sense of relief by knowing that they have the ability to end their life when (or if) they so choose.[33]

Oregon's Death with Dignity Act (ODDA) formalizes safeguards of the kind that Stephan provided for Pierre to ensure that the right to die isn't abused; that people don't kill themselves inappropriately, as Pierre might have done without Stephan's guidance. In Oregon, patients must be diagnosed with an illness that leaves them less than six months to live; a consulting physician must confirm the diagnosis; doctors must discuss with patients the lethal properties of medications prescribed under the act; and patients must be free of any mental disorder that could impair judgment.

The ODDA requires also that patients be encouraged to notify their next of kin (to reduce painful surprises in the family and increase chances for emotional closure) and that physicians report their use of the ODDA to the Oregon Health Division (so the effects of the act can be monitored for unintended, indirect harms).

Strict libertarians would reject all the safety provisions of the ODDA except the requirement that patients are adults of sound mind. Thus, the ODDA represents a compromise between libertarian calls for individual self-determination in dying and communitarian calls for social and family cohesion. So far, it seems successfully to allow some terminally ill people to kill themselves, while protecting—and sometimes advancing—communitarian values. For example, the worry that PAS would harm the poor has not materialized in Oregon. Rosenfeld reports that studies show "patients who requested assisted suicide were not disproportionately poor, uneducated, members of an ethnic minority, or receiving inadequate health care."[34] The worry that health care services would degenerate for those requesting suicide has not yet proved justified either. Instead, "requests for assisted suicide often resulted in a 'marked improvement' in the quality of palliative care provided by the physician, either in the form of hospice services or more aggressive symptom management."[35]

Shavelson notes that some proposals for legal PAS include provisions that would encourage this positive development. Such proposed legislation would create

an Aid-in-Dying Review Committee created specifically to evaluate every request for death. . . . Every patient asking to die must immediately answer one question, "Is the care you are now receiving adequate?" If the patient's answer is "No," or if the consulting physician or committee finds that control of pain, treatment of depression, or assistance in living is unacceptable—then they must first recommend better care for the patient, denying the right to suicide until all of these have been made available.[36]

Currently, communitarians such as Wesley Smith find inadequate pain management a major problem in our society, especially for poor people. Legal PAS could help address, rather than exacerbate, this problem.

Conclusion

Extremism tarnishes both sides of this debate. The right to die can't be absolute or we'd have legalized dueling and lethal prescriptions for jilted lovers in their twenties. The right to life can't be absolute or my mother might still be alive in a coma against her wishes at great emotional and financial expense to her family—an absurd result.

Because both the libertarian and communitarian political philosophies express widely shared values, our laws reflect compromise. People can bring early death to themselves by refusing unwanted medical care. Some care is withdrawn because it's considered futile. In Oregon, terminally ill people can receive lethal medications under strictly controlled conditions. Yet we have not degenerated to murdering Grandma in her sleep because she suffers from an incurable limp.

How far should we go toward promoting early death? Should we grant people who suffer from severe disabilities, but are not terminally ill, the same right as Oregon grants the terminally ill? Should we allow people of marginal competence like my father to avail themselves of any legal provisions for early death? Apart from theocratic concerns, differences of opinion rest mainly on different predictions. Some people worry that current and expanding PAS will erode communal ties and leave the poor even worse off than at present. Others note that this has not yet occurred in the United States.

Worries about a slippery slope have not yet materialized in the Netherlands, either, where both PAS and active euthanasia are legal and have been practiced without legal consequence for over twenty years. Many people consider voluntary active euthanasia—physicians actually killing people who want to die—worse than PAS. But the Dutch did not slip down a slope from PAS to euthanasia. They practiced both, considering them morally equal, all along. Similarly, although in contrast with Oregon terminal illness is not required of those who seek death in the Netherlands, no slippery slope was involved, as this was the original Dutch practice. Finally, communitarian worries about the loss of social cohesion have not proved justified in the Netherlands. General social cohesion remains robust; their social safety net is much stronger than ours; they have universal health coverage; patients continue to receive good medical care and pain management. Of course, things might work out differently in our country. We might become increasingly callous in our treatment of the poor, elderly, and disabled.

Theocrats who believe that God forbids all taking of innocent human life will, of course, oppose legalizing PAS. Communitarians, by contrast, oppose legalizing PAS only when they predict that it puts us on a slippery slope toward social callousness, but support PAS (with significant restrictions) when they believe it can help people end their lives with dignity while actually strengthening, or at least not weakening, communal ties. Finally, libertarians favor adult access to materials and information useful in suicide. This is part of their general stance against paternalistic interference with adults having and using whatever drugs they want. Libertarians consider the War on Drugs, our next topic, an unjustified crusade against individual liberty. Some utilitarians agree.

4

The War on Drugs: Utilitarianism and Social Conservatism

Drugs Impair Lives

Matthew Yeater's life has been devastated by his use of drugs. Matthew's parents divorced when he was a baby and his mother was an alcoholic. He was in foster care at age fourteen when he first tested positive for marijuana. He told Dave Bakke, reporter for the *State Journal-Register*, "I was drinking and drugging. I was 16 and caught 96 counts of burglary, theft and [possession of drug] paraphernalia."[1] Matthew received his GED at a Department of Corrections juvenile center—no prom. Shortly after release, he went to Arkansas with an older woman, where he began using meth. Holly Eitenmiller of *Illinois Magazine* explains the nature and dangers of meth:

Also dubbed ice, crystal or crank, methamphetamine is a volatile cocktail of chemicals that offers its users a fast track to an intense, lengthy high. A sister to crack cocaine in the stimulant class of drugs, meth is concocted of man-made chemicals, unlike crack, which is derived from organic materials. Both drugs typically cost abusers around $500 per week.[2]

Meth's impact is extraordinary. Terry Silvers, a thirty-four-year-old husband and father, had worked for nineteen years at the Shaw carpet mill in Dalton, Georgia, when some drinking buddies convinced him to use meth to wake up for his drive home. He later told *Newsweek* reporter David Jefferson, "I snorted a line and within five seconds it was like I'd had 12 hours sleep and wasn't drunk anymore." After snorting twice a week, he began to smoke it and finally to inject it. "Golly," he said, "It's the best feeling you ever had. It's like your mind is running 100 miles an hour, but your feet aren't moving."[3] When his wife found out and insisted he use his company's drug-counseling service, he quit his job, hit his wife, and ended up in jail. But Matthew Yeater's fate was worse.

In Arkansas, Matthew stayed awake all weekend and lost his job when he failed to show up for work on Mondays. He started making meth for himself and others, selling a gram for $120. He moved to Missouri, where he met the woman he would later marry, ingratiating himself with her parents by getting high with them and teaching his future father-in-law how to make meth. The family that snorts together cavorts together.

They were all risking their long-term health. Besides staying awake for long periods of time, addicts often

go without food and neglect personal hygiene. Long-term abusers end up with heart, liver and kidney problems, infectious diseases, severely decayed teeth, pneumonia and hepatitis. In the throes of drug-induced delirium, speeders will often see "crank bugs" creeping over their flesh, a hallucination caused by constricted blood vessels that itch. They'll pick at those areas until they bleed.[4]

Matthew's situation became worse on December 12, 2000, when he and his new partner went outside in rural Missouri to make some meth. One of the ingredients, anhydrous ammonia, is a cold gas that expands enormously as it warms. Lids on containers must be left loose to allow the gas to escape. Otherwise, pressure builds up and containers explode. That's what happened when the can of corrosive ammonia was only eighteen inches from Matthew's face, as Dave Bakke reports:

It burned into his skin and eyes. His drug-making partner ran for his car and sped away. Through his quickly disintegrating eyes, Yeater saw him run.

Fluids from Yeater's nose, mouth, and lungs leaked onto his face, shirt and pants. He walked into a house where, a few minutes before, his girlfriend and her parents had been getting high with him. He got a glimpse of himself in a mirror. His face looked as if it were melting.

About 20 minutes later, his girlfriend's mother loaded him into her car and took him to a hospital. He was able to walk into the emergency room under his own power.[5]

In the hospital, doctors told Yeater the anhydrous ammonia had fried his eyes. In the days after the accident, doctors routinely lifted his eyelids with a glass rod and scraped his eyeballs to keep them from healing to his lids.[6]

Now blind, Matthew was so determined to get high that he learned to make meth on his own without sight. Unaware of his continuing addiction, doctors considered him a good candidate for a corneal transplant, which he received on April 12, 2001. Matthew recalls, "After that I could see a little bit, a little color, and I'm, like, 'Let's go!'"[7]

Released from the hospital on April 13, he cooked meth right away, and then two days later, staying up for seven days straight. He was soon infected by a dirty needle, the infection reached his eyes, and he lost the minimal sight he had regained from the transplant. Matthew recalled, "That was hard to deal with. I kept getting high. I couldn't stop. I'd stay up at night and cry. I'd do a shot and bawl. I wanted to stop so bad, but I couldn't."[8] His mother eventually turned him in and he served about two years of a six-year sentence in a state prison. Although he was angry and then depressed in prison, he eventually completed a twelve-step recovery program that culminated in his writing a twenty-five-page letter about his mistakes in life. By July 2003, he was out in the community speaking to groups of youngsters about the evils and dangers of drugs.

Educating young people about the dangers of drugs is the first part of the federal government's three-part strategy in the War on Drugs, as explained in the White House National Drug Control Strategy for 2006. An integral part of the education effort is the new "Above the Influence" initiative. The idea is to stop drug abuse before it starts. "Education programs and outreach activities, backed up by scientific studies, have worked to spread the word that illicit substance use can be harmful to a person's health and wellbeing, as well as a detriment to society as a whole."[9]

The second focus is helping drug abusers overcome addiction. "The Administration is focused on expanding intervention programs and increasing the options for treatment. Intervention programs focus on users who are on the verge of developing serious problems.[10]

Finally, the Feds are working to disrupt drug markets. "Drug control programs focused on market disruption attempt to reduce the profits and raise the risks involved in drug trafficking. The desired result is a reduced incentive for traffickers or would-be traffickers to enter or remain in the illicit trade."[11]

Libertarians versus Social Conservatives

Libertarians consider all these efforts misguided. As we have seen, libertarians think the only proper role of government is protecting people from one another, which rules out protecting people from themselves. Psychiatrist Thomas Szasz champions the libertarian cause regarding drugs. People should be able to buy whatever drugs they can pay for through free-market transactions, Szasz argues. Prescriptions shouldn't be required because this requirement forces people to consult doctors, whereas many individuals, like Matthew Yeater, know what they want. Of course, reasonable consumers consult doctors about drugs they know little about, just as reasonable investors consult stock analysts, but the state shouldn't require consultation in either case.

If people had such access to all drugs, Szasz notes, the issue of physician-assisted suicide would never arise, because people would be able to kill themselves whenever they wanted. They would not need medical permission or intervention. Szasz writes, "I believe that one of the main reasons we reject a free market in drugs is because we fear having an unfettered opportunity to kill ourselves (which a free market in drugs necessarily entails)."[12] Szasz does not expect many ill-considered suicides if the state allows unrestricted access to lethal drugs. At present, people can kill themselves in many ways—guns, knives, cars, and jumping off tall buildings—but few people do. We assume adults can safely handle these potential instruments of self destruction and expect them to accept the consequences of their actions. The same should apply to drugs, Szasz thinks. The War on Drugs is an illegitimate state intrusion on personal autonomy.

Social conservatives are among those who reject Szasz's libertarian premises and conclusions regarding drugs. Social conservative James Q. Wilson, for example, rejects the extreme individualism of libertarians who claim that drug use should be legal, because it's a victimless crime; users harm only themselves, and the state shouldn't protect people from themselves. Wilson writes:

The notion that abusing drugs such as cocaine is a "victimless crime" is not only absurd but dangerous. Even ignoring the fetal drug syndrome, crack-dependent people are, like heroin addicts, individuals who regularly victimize their children by neglect, their spouses by improvidence, their employers by lethargy, and their coworkers by carelessness. Society is not and could never be a collection of autonomous individuals. We all have a stake in ensuring that each of us displays a minimal level of dignity, responsibility and empathy. We cannot, of course, coerce people into goodness, but we can and should insist that some standards must be met if society itself—on which the very existence of the human personality depends—is to persist.[13]

Wilson's political philosophy—his beliefs about the proper role of the state in people's lives—reflects his view of human nature. People require nurture to be fully human. Fully human beings have language, for example, but acquire that language through close contact with other human beings who are language users. An infant raised by wolves (if that's really possible) wouldn't have language and would therefore lack a distinctive and admirable human attribute. Although biologically human and perhaps otherwise healthy, she would be profoundly impaired according to normal standards of human excellence. Parents who locked a child in a closet and deprived her of the human contact necessary to learn a language would therefore be subject to criminal prosecution (although not to a subsequent pesky memoir of child abuse).

Meth abusers often ignore their parental responsibilities as they manufacture the drug in their homes, as Holly Eitenmiller reports:

The underbelly of the drug world live almost invariably in filth . . . , the sort of squalor that encourages bug infestation. Not so in homes that foster meth labs. The toxic stench of ingredients is so strong, even cockroaches won't get near it.

Sadly, cockroaches have a choice that children don't have. . . . Myriad . . . children, sometimes newborns, [are] forced to live in homes with meth labs. The pungent fumes are dense. . . . That fact, coupled with the risk of explosions, places children in these homes in great peril.[14]

Parents must do more than communicate language and keep their children physically safe. Children must also learn, in Wilson's words, "a minimal level of dignity, responsibility, and empathy" for society to survive. We are social beings who depend on one another's responsible behavior as dual parents, co-workers in large organizations, and law-abiding citizens. Empathy is needed so that when conflicts arise, each can appreciate the other person's perspective, resulting in mutual accommodation.

Human excellence is another reason for social conservatives to want the state to promote human moral development. Besides the integrity, responsibility, and empathy that make social life possible, human excellence includes the self-determination that libertarians prize. Libertarians take it for granted, but social conservatives believe that, like language and morality, truly human self-determination must be nurtured and protected. Drugs like heroin, cocaine, and meth, because they are mind-altering, destroy human autonomy and should be banned for that reason. Matthew Yeater, for example, was drug-dependent before he ever had a chance at genuine, adult autonomy. Meth is so powerful that Terry Silvers, who was autonomous, lost his autonomy after a single dose. According to Wilson, the moral imperative to protect human autonomy justifies the distinction we now make between nicotine and cocaine. Both are highly addictive; both have harmful physical effects. But we treat the two drugs differently, not simply because nicotine is so widely used as to be beyond the reach of effective prohibition, but because its use does not destroy the user's essential humanity. Tobacco shortens one's life, cocaine debases it. Nicotine alters one's habits, cocaine alters one's soul. The heavy use of crack, unlike the heavy use of tobacco, corrodes those natural sentiments of sympathy and duty that constitute our human nature and make possible our social life.[15]

Because social conservatives believe that some values and priorities are better than others and that the state should promote proper values, their political philosophy is called "perfectionist." They don't want the state to try to make people perfect, but they object to state neutrality on matters of values. Where there's a clear distinction between good and bad values, the state should promote what's good, even in private conduct.

Finally, besides emphasizing the importance of society and of people's ability to maintain society through adoption of proper values, social conservatives are conservative. They believe that we should be cautious about social experiments in defiance of traditional morality because traditional morality has passed the test of time. This is where social conservatives differ from communitarians, who also stress the importance of social ties and oppose libertarianism's radical individualism. Communitarians are more receptive than social conservatives to innovative social arrangements, such as those concerning marriage and family. This makes a big difference on issues affecting women, but may be less important regarding the War on Drugs. In any case, communitarians have not been as prominent in the drug debate as have social conservatives.

Social conservatives, being conservative, believe that innovators who claim to be wiser than the preceding generations that slowly built our moral code are likely seeking personal advantage by denying established moral truths. Thus, people who want drugs call for their legalization. We should be cautious because if we legalize drugs and it turns out, as social conservatives suspect, that human nature is too weak to resist addiction,

we will have consigned millions of people, hundreds of thousands of infants, and hundreds of neighborhoods to a life of oblivion and disease. To the lives and families destroyed by alcohol we will have added countless more destroyed by cocaine, heroin, PCP, and whatever else a basement scientist can invent. . . . Good character is less likely in a bad society. Will we, in the name of an abstract doctrine of radical individualism . . . decide to take the chance that somehow individual decency can survive amid a more general level of degradation?[16]

Wilson and other social conservatives favor tradition over innovative abstract doctrines such as libertarianism's radical individualism.

Utilitarian Critique of the War on Drugs

Nevertheless, others long associated with conservative views—most notably, William F. Buckley Jr.—disagree with Wilson not in the name of libertarianism, but in the name of utilitarianism. After believing for years that the War on Drugs was justified, Buckley became convinced by 1996 that it was not working and could not work. He writes, "That consideration encouraged me to weigh utilitarian principles: the Benthamite calculus of pain and pleasure introduced by the illegalization of drugs."[17]

Buckley refers here to the moral and political philosophy of Jeremy Bentham (1748–1832), the grandfather of modern utilitarianism. Bentham believed that all good and bad relate to pleasure and pain. Other things being equal, pain is bad and whatever produces pain, which includes all manner of suffering both psychological and physical, is therefore bad. Pleasure is good, and other things being equal, whatever produces pleasure, which includes all manner of delight both psychological and physical, is good.

This view, known as "hedonism," opposes the use of hard drugs. Although many drugs are used for pleasure, which utilitarians consider good, much pain accompanies that pleasure. Addicts become so obsessed that they ignore their families, their jobs, and their own health. Life can become a living hell, as in Matthew Yeater's case. Drug addiction isn't good because pains outweigh pleasures.

But utilitarian opposition to drug abuse, a personal behavior, does not mean utilitarian support for the War on Drugs, a political program. Bentham's political philosophy calls for the state to pass laws designed to produce the maximum pleasure and minimum pain in society, which he referred to as the greatest good for the greatest number. Drug laws, like other laws, should be judged by this standard. Many proponents of drug prohibitions believe that the War on Drugs passes this utilitarian test because it protects people from addictions that cause so much pain. Buckley and others argue, to the contrary, that the War on Drugs does more harm than good.

Increased Crime

Buckley claims, for example:

> More people die every year as a result of the war against drugs than die from what we call, generically, overdosing. These fatalities include, perhaps most prominently, drug merchants who compete for commercial territory, but include also people who are robbed and killed by those desperate for money to buy the drug to which they have become addicted.[18]

The financial incentives motivating drug lords to kill competitors and drug addicts to rob and sometimes kill for drug money result from the War on Drugs, not from the drugs themselves. When drugs are illegal, they are relatively expensive, because suppliers run the risk of incarceration. Their business deals are risky, because they are informal agreements, not legally enforceable contracts. Suppliers' lives are at risk from competitors. The commodity is at risk of seizure by government agents. In the drug trade, as in any business, profit must increase to compensate for risk. Additional costs are incurred evading or bribing police. Buckley writes:

> The pharmaceutical cost of cocaine and heroin is approximately 2 percent of the street price of those drugs. Since a cocaine addict can spend as much as $1,000 per week to sustain his habit, he would need to come up with that $1,000. The approximate fencing cost of stolen goods is 80 percent, so that to come up with $1,000 can require stealing $5,000 worth of jewels, cars, whatever. We can see that at free-market rates, $20 per week would provide the addict with the cocaine which, in this wartime drug situation requires of him $1,000.[19]

Steven Duke of Yale Law School argues that "the drug war is responsible for at least half of our serious crime. A panel of experts consulted [in the mid-1990s] by *U.S. News & World Report* put the annual dollar cost of America's crime at $674 billion. Half of that [is] $337 billion. . . . The crime costs of drug prohibition alone may equal 150 percent of the entire federal welfare budget for 1995."[20]

The story that Danny Stern told of his heroin addiction fifty years ago illustrates Buckley's point. Danny, raised in a middle-class home in New York's Upper East Side, became hooked on heroin at age sixteen when a boy at a party "staked everybody to a free shot, and administered it and made a big adventure out of it."[21] By age twenty-three, Danny had spent four years in jail as a result of his habit, but claimed that drug addicts are not inherently dangerous to others: "After speaking to numerous addicts in the jail at Elmira . . . , and in the streets, I find this: that when the dope addict needs money, he doesn't want to hurt anybody; he just wants the money. He will take your money and run. He's meek. . . . Everybody says he's a killer, but he won't kill you. He's afraid."[22] If drugs were legal and inexpensive, such thefts could be avoided.

Crime unrelated to drugs would also be reduced by decriminalizing drugs. Buckley points out that the approximately 400,000 police now devoted to fighting the War on Drugs "would be free to pursue criminals engaged in activity other than the sale and distribution of drugs if such sale and distribution, at a price at which there was no profit, were to be done by, say, a federal drugstore."[23]

International crime also stems from the War on Drugs. Joseph McNamara, former chief of police in Kansas City, Missouri, and San Jose, California, writes:

About $500 worth of heroin or cocaine in a source country will bring in as much as $100,000 on the streets of an American city. All the cops, armies, prisons, and executions in the world cannot impede a market with that kind of tax-free profit margin. It is the illegality that permits the obscene markup, enriching drug traffickers, distributors, dealers, crooked cops, lawyers, judges, politicians, bankers, businessmen.[24]

Futility

In 2001, columnist George Will suggested that the international War on Drugs may be futile.

The number of source countries is not fixed; suppressing production in one (e.g., Bolivia) can displace production to, and destabilize, another (e.g., Colombia). . . .

Interdiction sometimes seems like bailing an ocean with a thimble—no, a sieve. In May the capture off California's coast of 13 metric tons of cocaine, the largest seizure ever, closely followed one of eight tons. The 21 tons could have supplied 21 million street sales. But there was *no* noticeable effect on the street price of the commodity. James Kitfield of National Journal reports that maritime seizures as a percentage of drugs in the supply pipeline are declining.

In 1997 about a million trucks and railroad cars entering the country from Mexico were searched. Drugs were found in six. A few hundred dealers handle most of the 500 tons of cocaine entering the country, but arrest all of them today, and tomorrow there will be a few hundred others.[25]

The federal government's 2006 report on the international War on Drugs admitted that efforts to reduce production of drugs overseas and interdict their transport to our shores have had little effect on drug availability or purity in the United States.[26]

Another sign of futility is the report of Robert Sweet, District Judge in New York City. In 1996, he wrote:

The total federal expenditure on the drug war this year under the proposed budget will exceed $17 billion. Ten years ago the annual expenditure on the drug war was $5 billion for all governments, federal, state, and local.

While our expenditures have increased tenfold, the number of Americans using drugs has remained relatively constant at 40 million. Steady users are estimated to be 6 million, with 1 to 2 million of those seriously disordered. Our present prohibition policy has failed, flatly and without serious question.[27]

Racism

The War on Drugs exacerbates racial tensions, because its casualties are disproportionately black. According to syndicated columnist Carl Rowan, a study conducted by *USA Today* revealed that in 1988, 12.7 percent of the U.S. population was black, as were 12 percent of those who "regularly use illegal drugs." But 38 percent of those arrested on drug charges were black.[28] Figures from the federal government's National Institute on Drug Abuse are worse: "Although only about 12% of those using illegal drugs are black, 44% of those who are arrested for simple possession and 57% of those arrested for sales are black."[29]

These numbers reflect racial profiling in stops and searches for drugs. Libertarian Thomas Szasz writes, "On a stretch of the New Jersey Turnpike where less than 5 percent of the traffic involved cars with out of state license plates driven by black males, 80 percent of the arrests fitted that description."[30] Such racial profiling becomes a self-fulfilling prophecy. Assuming, contrary to objective data, that blacks are disproportionately involved in drug abuse, racial profiling concentrates law enforcement efforts on blacks. The result is that more blacks than whites are caught with drugs and go to jail, which reinforces the original error that "justified" racial profiling in the first place.

Racism appears in the discrepancy between penalties for possessing powdered cocaine and those for possessing crack cocaine. The powder is snorted, whereas crack is smoked, but the drug delivered to the body is the same. Powder is more popular among whites; crack among blacks. Many laws require jail for first-time offenders found with small amounts of crack, but only probation for those with similar amounts of powdered cocaine.[31] The result is more blacks than whites go to jail for drug abuse, which feeds the prejudice that blacks abuse drugs more than whites, which is used to justify racial profiling that feeds the same prejudice by putting still more blacks behind bars.

Family Values

The War on Drugs may be counterproductive by eroding family values as well as by exacerbating racial tensions. Joseph McNamara reports that Baltimore Mayor Kurt Schmoke "visited a high school and asked the students if the high dropout rate was due to kids being hooked on drugs. He was told that the kids were dropping out because they were hooked on drug money, not drugs."[32] Parental authority is undermined when parents working legally at low wages earn less than their children pursuing the American dream as entrepreneurs.

Families are strongest when two parents are in the home. Steven Duke notes that many conservatives "are rightly concerned about the absence of fathers in the homes of so many of America's youngsters." Social conservative William Bennett, for example, links fatherlessness "to infant mortality, crime, joblessness, homelessness, educational failure, and the disintegration of whole neighborhoods."[33] Duke asks, "Where are those fathers? At least half a million are in prison, often for nothing worse than possessing drugs."[34] The War on Drugs is bad for families and neighborhoods.

Police Corruption

When I was growing up, our family friends included the Nallys. Jim was a police officer in our lower-middle-class New York suburb. He and Dorothy had Patsy, Kathy, Maureen, and two or three more children whose names I could never remember. When they moved away to a much pricier suburb, I wondered where they got the money to do so. My mother explained that Jim's father had been a police officer in New York City during Prohibition, resulting in his ownership of a lot of real estate, which Jim had just inherited. I was old enough, and young enough, to be shocked.

Former police chief Joseph McNamara writes:

Police scandals are an untallied cost of the drug war. . . . In New Orleans, a uniformed cop in league with a drug dealer has been convicted of murdering her partner and shop owners during a robbery committed while she was on patrol. In Washington, D.C., and in Atlanta, cops in drug stings were arrested for stealing and taking bribes. New York State troopers falsified drug evidence that sent people to prison.

And it is not just the rank and file. The former police chief of Detroit went to prison for stealing police drug-buy money. In a small New England town, the chief stole drugs from the evidence locker for his own use. And the DEA [Drug Enforcement Administration] agent who arrested Panama's General Noriega [for drug trafficking] is in jail for stealing laundered drug money.[35]

Utilitarianism and Uncertainty

Uncertainty bedevils utilitarian policy recommendations. Utilitarians favor policies that produce the best results, the most pleasure and least pain in society as a whole in the long run. But it's difficult to predict the consequences of public policies. Although the utilitarian case for ending the War on Drugs is impressive, others claim that fighting the war will produce the best results.

James Q. Wilson, for example, who justifies the war on social conservative grounds, claims utilitarian support as well. He doesn't believe that the war creates more crime and misery than it prevents. He points out that in 1972, when he became chairman of President Nixon's National Advisory Council for Drug Abuse Prevention, the drug epidemic of the day was heroin. In 1990, when Wilson wrote on the subject, the number of heroin addicts was the same half million as in 1972 when the War on Drugs started. This is not failure, Wilson claims. The epidemic was stopped. Addicts in 1990 were older on average than those in 1972, a clear sign that fewer people were turning to heroin. Wilson believes heroin use would have become much worse if tough laws against drug abuse had been abandoned and heroin made legal. He writes:

Its price would have been reduced by 95 percent (minus whatever we chose to recover in taxes). Now that it could be sold by the same people who make aspirin, its quality would have been assured—no poisons, no adulterants. Sterile hypodermic needles would have been readily available at the neighborhood drugstore, probably at the same counter where heroin was sold.

Under these circumstances, can we doubt for a moment that heroin use would have grown exponentially? Or that a vastly larger supply of new users would have been recruited?[36]

By 1990 the focus was on cocaine, especially crack. Wilson believes that just as with heroin, legalization would increase use, resulting in great harm. He writes:

Crack is worse than heroin by almost any measure. Heroin produces a pleasant drowsiness. . . . Regular use incapacitates many users . . . for any productive work or social responsibility. . . . By contrast . . . , cocaine produces instant, intense, and short-lived euphoria. . . . Binge users become uninhibited, impulsive, irritable, and hyperactive. Their moods vacillate dramatically, leading at times to violence and homicide.

Women are much more likely to use crack than heroin, and if they are pregnant, the effects on their babies are tragic.[37]

Keeping the drug illegal is essential to reducing its baleful influence.

George Will, writing eleven years later in 2001, agrees. Even though the War on Drugs seems futile at times, when drugs are more costly and less readily available, as they are when illegal, fewer people take them. Some say Prohibition failed because alcohol consumption continued, as reflected in humorist Will Rogers's quip at the time: "Prohibition is better than no liquor at all." George Will counters:

Legalizers who say the 13 years of alcohol Prohibition "didn't work" must concede that consumption declined up to 50 percent and did not reach pre-Prohibition per capita levels until the 1970s. The number of heroin addicts has plateaued at 900,000, and the number of chronic cocaine users (3.3 million) is below the 1988 peak (3.8 million).[38]

In sum, Wilson and Will argue that even if the War on Drugs has not been won, it has made drug addiction less prevalent than it would otherwise be. They note that legalizing drugs for adults will surely entice teens for whom the drugs remain illegal because, as Wilson puts it, "young people have a way of penetrating markets theoretically reserved for adults."[39] Assuming that life as a drug addict is generally more painful than life without such addiction, the War on Drugs has promoted more pleasure than pain in society, according to Wilson and Will. But who can really know? The utilitarian arguments for the War on Drugs seem as uncertain as those against it.

Consider these counter-suggestions by utilitarian opponents of the War on Drugs. Perhaps cocaine abuse results from suppression of heroin abuse. There is precedent for this in Prohibition, Steven Duke points out. "Before alcohol prohibition, we were a nation of beer drinkers. Prohibition pushed us toward hard liquor, a habit from which we are still recovering. Before the Harrison Act [which made cocaine illegal], many Americans took their cocaine in highly diluted forms, such as Coca-Cola."[40] As chronic cocaine use dropped half a million after 1988, many youths turned to chemistry for fun and profit, resulting in Ecstasy at Rave events and meth labs in basements. And just as cocaine is worse than heroin, meth is worse than cocaine. Critics claim that the War on Drugs produces more pain than pleasure by moving people from bad drugs to worse drugs.

Critics note also that where drugs are legal, often with non-criminal government regulations, drug abuse is less than in the United States. Steven Duke writes:

In many countries, heroin and cocaine are cheap and at least de facto legal. Mexico is awash in cheap drugs, yet our own State Department says that Mexico does "not have a serious drug problem." Neither cocaine nor heroin is habitually consumed by more than a small fraction of the residents of any country in the world. There is no reason to suppose that Americans would be the single exception.[41]

The claim that legality for adults will promote illegal use by minors is not supported by a study done in 1994 that compared the use of cannabis, cocaine, and heroin among secondary school students (ages thirteen to eighteen) in the Netherlands and in the United States. In the Netherlands, these drugs are available either legally or with little penalty to adults, whereas in the United States they are generally illegal and possession and use carry stiff penalties. Among fifteen- to sixteen-year-olds, to give typical findings, 35 percent of American kids had tried cannabis, but less than 11 percent of the Dutch. About 7.7 percent of Americans had tried cocaine, but only 2.2 percent of the Dutch. Around 1.3 percent of Americans had tried heroin, but only 0.5 percent of the Dutch.[42]

Danny Stern's experiences with heroin in the 1950s may help to explain these figures. When drugs are illegal, getting them provides the adventure that young people crave. So,

if narcotics was easy to come by, there wouldn't be half as many addicts. To take narcotics right now, it is cloak-and-dagger, it's spy work, it's something out of television, believe me. You have to walk the street, you have to secure a pusher, you have to locate the money to buy this narcotics, you have to check in dark hallways, on roofs, go through cellars, all this running about, all the time keeping one eye out for the police.

All this. This is an adventure or a young man. And when you finally get your narcotics . . . you say to yourself: man, I did it, I beat the fuzz.[43]

Contrasting experiences in the United States and the Netherlands raise the issue of "American exceptionalism," the belief that America is morally superior to other countries and destined to help others achieve righteousness. Utilitarian arguments for the War on Drugs seem to reflect the opposite view, that Americans are exceptionally vulnerable to drugs.

People in other countries can withstand the allure of cheap drugs, but Americans are morally weaker. Danny Stern's account, by contrast, attributes greater drug use among Americans to the criminalization of drugs in the United States rather than to any inherent weakness in Americans' moral character. I don't know.

Harm Reduction: For and Against

Most utilitarians, unlike libertarians, don't advocate a simple free market in drugs, because they believe that drug use causes pain that the state should try to reduce. Believing that the War on Drugs is counterproductive and futile, however, they would replace the war with what they call "harm reduction." William Buckley, for example, considers treatment more effective than criminal sanctions.

Pursuing utilitarian analysis we ask: What are the relative costs, on the one hand, of medical and psychological treatment for addicts and, on the other, incarceration for drug offenses? It transpires that treatment is seven times more cost-effective. By this is meant that one dollar spent on the treatment of an addict reduces the probability of continued addiction seven times more than one dollar spent on incarceration.[44]

Proponents of the war are not so sure. Won't people be more likely to take drugs if the worst that can happen is being subjected to treatment? Wouldn't the threat of prison deter more people from taking drugs in the first place? Also, what will induce people to undergo treatment if incarceration is not the threatened alternative? While he was head of the Drug Enforcement Administration, Asa Hutchinson (a former congressman from Arkansas) said: "Why did [actor] Robert Downey Jr. go to treatment [for drug abuse]? Because he was arrested."[45] Again, the consequences of legalization are uncertain.

Rather than rely on the threat of prison, utilitarian critics of the War on Drugs who advocate harm reduction stress education. Judge Robert Sweet writes:

Alcohol and tobacco have a social cost when abused and society has properly concluded that abuse of these drugs is a health problem, not a criminal issue. Indeed, our experience with the reduction of 50 per cent in the use of tobacco—the most addicting of drugs, which results in 400,000 deaths a year—confirms the wisdom of that policy. To distinguish between these substances and heroin or cocaine is mere tautology.[46]

Educational campaigns are therefore another aspect of harm reduction advocated by utilitarian critics of the War on Drugs. Supporters of the war also want education, but with criminal sanctions to back them up.

Harm reduction advocates support needle exchange programs. One of the worst consequences of intravenous drug use is infection by dirty needles. If drug users have access to clean, inexpensive needles, they will be less likely to spread diseases, including AIDS, among themselves and to the rest of the population. Mayor Kurt Schmoke of Baltimore writes of their needle-exchange program in the mid-1990s: "The program costs $160,000 a year. The cost to the state of Maryland of taking care of just one adult AIDS patient infected through the sharing of a syringe is $102,000 to $120,000. In other words, if just two addicts are protected from HIV through the city's needle exchange, the program will have paid for itself."[47]

Drug addict Danny Stern advocates the state supplying drugs as well as the needles to administer them.

If a dope addict can be maintained so that he will not get sick, he will not commit a crime. He will be content not to be sick.

So I feel they should have some sort of a clinic, where you can come in and get fingerprinted if you want to be a known addict. Let it be known! If you want to be an addict, don't be ashamed of it. Take your card, go in, get your thing to keep you happy. It would kill the crime and they'd live a happy life.

There would be a few that would want more than whatever the clinic would be administering. . . . They'd want a little extra so they could get up to cloud nine. . . . But taking the adventure away would kill a lot of the drugs.[48]

However, this drug maintenance idea seems terribly convenient. It gives drug addicts exactly what they want: free or cheap drugs with no legal consequence.

Opposition to harm reduction strategies comes from two sources besides utilitarian uncertainties about effectiveness. One is the social conservative view that drug use is simply wrong and should be stopped. Even if the War on Drugs results in overall less pleasure and more pain than harm reduction, it's still worthwhile, according to social conservatives, because the war promotes moral improvement over human degradation. Danny Stern writes that when you're on drugs:

The world goes by. You don't care about anything, you have no worries. You're not thinking about Mom paying the telephone bill or your wife being sick. Everything is so great. I want to do everything for everybody. I may act a little spooky and groggy, and appear to be not in my senses, but really I'm in my senses, more so than a lot of people believe. . . . The only thing that's numb is your thinking mind. You can't think abstractly, you can't think of the future."[49]

Social conservatives find happiness on drugs morally despicable. They oppose harm reduction, including needle exchange programs, because it contains no moral condemnation. According to the ACLU, in fact, harm reduction "assumes that drug users' civil rights and individual autonomy should be respected, treats drug users as important participants in the process of gaining or maintaining control over their drug use, and makes no moral judgment based solely upon an individual's use of drugs."[50]

Asa Hutchinson asks: "If child abuse is not declining, should we stop trying to prevent or prosecute it?"[51] Of course not. Because child abuse is morally wrong we should fight it with criminal sanctions whether those sanctions are working or not. Similarly, we should pursue zero tolerance rather than harm reduction to signal society's condemnation of drug abuse.

The Reverend Jesse Jackson adds a theocratic element to the social conservative view. He claims: "Drugs are poison. Taking drugs is a sin. Drug use is morally debased and sick."[52] Reference to sin suggests common ground between social conservatives and theocrats. Social conservatives consider drug use to be morally wrong on secular grounds; people on drugs commit crimes that harm others, ignore their duties to family and employers, and fail to develop their talents for the good of humanity. Theocrats, by contrast, believe that God condemns the use of drugs and this alone would justify zero tolerance.

The temperance movement was theocratic. Historian Herbert Asbury discusses the National Women's Christian Temperance Union (WCTU), which began in 1874 and was instrumental in the eventual imposition of Prohibition on the nation. "The platform adopted at the first meeting emphasized the religious character of the union, and urged the reformation of the drunkard through faith in God." The next year they announced their goal as the "legal prohibition of all intoxicating drink."[53]

In sum, theocrats who believe that God disapproves of drugs and social conservatives who oppose drugs on secular moral grounds object equally to harm reduction because it lacks moral condemnation of drug use.

Libertarian Thomas Szasz is equally unimpressed with harm reduction, but for the opposite reason. Harm reduction assumes that people can't be trusted to use drugs responsibly, so the state must, for example, supply drugs or drug substitutes to addicts in measured doses of government regulated purity to protect against overdosing. State-supplied needles protect against disease. Libertarians object that drug use is none of the government's business; it's a private choice about consumption. Just as some people eat too much pasta or ice cream, become overweight, and die sooner than they otherwise might, some people take heroin. So long as they are adults, people have the right to make choices that may shorten their lives. Libertarians find government programs to reduce drug use no more justified than government subsidy of Weight Watchers to treat people who overeat. If people think they have a problem with overeating or drugs, they can seek help and pay for it themselves. If they don't think they have a problem, government social workers shouldn't push unwanted treatment.

Harm reduction calls for restrictions on advertising and warning labels on packages to educate the public about the dangers of drugs. Libertarians insist only that labels correctly identify substances being purchased. With such identification, purchasers can find out all they need to know. If they're adults who don't care to know what they're snorting, smoking, swallowing, or injecting, that's their funeral. Libertarians object to all government attempts to protect adults from themselves, and that is central to harm reduction, whose inspiration is utilitarian, not libertarian.

Libertarians and utilitarians agree with one another, however, and disagree with both theocrats and social conservatives, on one matter. They agree that the test of goodness lies in people's perceptions and desires. They both reject the perfectionism of theocrats and social conservatives who think that standards of right and wrong, good and bad, transcend current individual and social views. Theocrats believe that transcendent standards come from God and religion; social conservatives rely on tradition (including religious tradition) and their understanding of human nature. Drug use is wrong because it conflicts with God's plan for humanity (theocrats) or with the highest ideals of human development (social conservatives).

Libertarians and Benthamite utilitarians reject all value judgments that don't reflect what people actually value. Libertarians favor free markets where people express their values commercially. Utilitarians, by contrast, think governments should regulate behavior to help people get as much as possible of what they want. Utilitarians don't trust people to act for their own long-term self-interest, so they often advocate government activism. Harm reduction is a case in point.

Conclusion

Pure libertarians don't favor using drugs, but oppose the War on Drugs as well as government programs to reduce drug-related harm. One implication may surprise you. Libertarian psychiatrist Thomas Szasz believes that professional athletes should be free to take whatever drugs they want. He thinks an athlete's "taking drugs before a game is not any more of our business than is his praying before a game,"[54] which is good news for Barry Bonds and other players in many sports accused of using currently illegal drugs.

But if performance enhancing drugs are allowed, professional athletes will not be free to "just say no," because success will soon require drugs. Libertarians counter that people who don't want to take drugs should find other work—it's a free market out there.

Social conservatives and theocrats generally support the War on Drugs to improve human moral attainment and righteous living. Even if the war can't be won, fighting drug use puts the state on the right side of a moral issue.

Utilitarians are divided. Many believe that although using drugs is bad, the War on Drugs is lost and continued fighting does more harm than good. Harm reduction should be pursued, including strategies to reduce demand for drugs similar to programs to reduce demand for cigarettes. Other utilitarians, however, claim that drug use would be worse without the war, pointing to economic postulates regarding price and demand, as well as to the relative success of Prohibition in reducing alcohol consumption.

But the Prohibition precedent can cut the other way. Even though less alcohol was consumed during Prohibition, the program failed due to the corruption and violence it engendered. No national, mainstream politician today favors a return to Prohibition, because its overall effects were bad. Similarly, utilitarian opponents of the War on Drugs contend, the overall effects of the war are bad even if it reduces drug use somewhat.

Whichever utilitarian argument seems most persuasive, this disagreement suggests that using the utilitarian political philosophy is difficult because conclusions often depend on predictions that remain controversial.

Finally, it's interesting that in a country where economic growth is so highly valued, free-market conservatives don't promote drug legalization to stimulate economic activity and create jobs, a position satirically introduced in the movie *Robocop*. It seems that no one really favors economic growth as much as they oppose drug abuse. Perhaps calling any effort a "war" suggests that it's more important than commerce. This is certainly true of the War on Terrorism, our next topic, which pits security needs against the value of liberty and claims about universal standards of humane treatment.

5

The War on Terrorism: Utilitarianism, Contractarianism, and Cosmopolitanism

The Attacks on 9/11

On September 11, 2001, at 8:46 a.m., American Airlines Flight 11 crashed into the North Tower of the World Trade Center (WTC). According to the "Emergency Preparedness and Response Statement Number 13" submitted to the 9/11 Commission:

The plane cut through floors 93/94 to 98/99 of the building. All three of the building's stairwells became impassable from the 92nd floor up. Hundreds of civilians were killed instantly by the impact. Hundreds more remained alive but trapped.

A jet fuel fireball erupted upon impact, and shot down at least one bank of elevators. The fireball exploded onto numerous lower floors, including the 77th, 50th, 22nd, West Street lobby level, and the B4 level, four stories below ground. The burning jet fuel immediately created thick, black smoke which enveloped the upper floors and roof of the North Tower.[1]

Brian Clark, president of Euro Brokers Relief Fund, heard the crash from his office in the South Tower. He told the 9/11 Commission: "I heard a loud boom. The lights in my office buzzed and I glanced up at them and then my peripheral vision, behind me, caught something and I spun in my chair, and just two yards from me outside the glass, 84 floors in the air, was swirling flames. I assumed that there had been an explosion upstairs."[2]

Statement 13 continues: "Within ten minutes of impact, smoke was beginning to rise to the upper floors in debilitating volumes and isolated fires were reported, although there were some pockets of refuge. Faced with insufferable heat, smoke, and fire, and no prospect for relief, some jumped or fell from the building."[3]

Others, below the impact zone, were able to escape by starting to leave almost immediately, among them Claire McIntyre, manager in Administrative Services of the American Bureau of Shipping. She told the Commission:

After going out into the hallway and yelling down that everyone get out, I went into my office to get my pocketbook and also I grabbed the flashlight and my whistle. The flashlight was useful for the first couple of flights going down because it was completely dark, and there was water flowing down so it was dangerous too, and there was some debris, even on the landings. The air quality wasn't too bad, there was some smoke, light, it was never heavy smoke, where you couldn't breathe. And the lights in the stairwells worked all the way down except for the first two or three flights.[4]

David Lim, working for the Port Authority Police Department was among the first responders.

I went up the B Staircase now, and so I proceeded up on that one. While people were coming down on that staircase, there were some people that were burnt and injured—required assistance. So, I could have taken one person and brought that person down I guess, but I thought the greater good would be to get to the 44th floor and assist more people. So I assigned the people that were uninjured to help carry this person down. There is a triage area downstairs, and that seemed to work out. People were more than happy to help each other out.[5]

At 9:03 a.m., United Airlines Flight 175 crashed into the South Tower. Stanley Praimnath, assistant vice president for administration of the Mizvho Corp. Bank, saw it coming.

I am looking to the direction of the Statue of Liberty, and I am looking at an airplane coming, eye level, eye contact, towards me—giant gray airplane. I am still seeing the letter "U" on its tail, and the plane is bearing down on me. I dropped the phone and I screamed and I dove under my desk. It was the most ear-shattering sound ever. The plane just crashed into the building. The bottom wing sliced right through the office and it stuck in my office door twenty feet from where I am huddled under my desk.[6]

Brian Clark responded immediately.

We went down the hallway on the 84th floor, and I happened to turn left to Stairway A. We descended only three floors, to the 81st floor—the group of seven of us—when we met a very heavy-set woman and she just emphatically told our group, "Stop, stop! We have just come off a floor in flames and we've got to get above the flames and smoke." That's about all I heard of her conversation because I heard somebody inside the 81st floor banging on the wall and screaming, "Help, help! I am buried. Is anyone there? Help, I can't breathe!" And, I noticed that my workmates, the heavy-set woman and her traveling companion were starting to go up the stairs. And that day they all perished unfortunately. But they were dealing with the information they had. None of us really had known what had happened or what was about to happen.[7]

What was about to happen was the collapse of the South Tower at 9:59 a.m. and then the collapse of the North Tower twenty-seven minutes later. Joseph Pfeifer, Deputy Assistant Chief, FDNY, recalled:

We heard a loud roar again and someone yelled that the building was collapsing. And, we started to run. With bunker gear, you can't run too far, especially when a building is a quarter mile high. And what happened inside the building now happened outside. This beautiful sunny day now turned completely black. We were unable to see the hand in front of our face. And there was an eerie sound of silence. That day we lost 2,752 people at the World Trade Center; 343 were firefighters. But we also saved 25,000 people. And that's what people should remember because firefighters and rescuers went in and they knew it was dangerous, but they went in to save people. And they saved many.[8]

Two additional planes were hijacked that morning. One flew into the Pentagon and the other crashed in a Pennsylvania field, at the cost of additional lives. These were the 9/11 attacks that sparked the War on Terrorism as we know it today.

The perpetrators were Al Qaeda operatives under the overall inspiration and direction of Usama Bin Laden, an Islamist who hates the United States and its worldwide influence. According to the 9/11 Commission, Bin Laden, drawing

on symbols of Islam's past greatness . . . , promises to restore pride to people who consider themselves the victims of successive foreign masters. . . . He appeals to people disoriented by cyclonic change as they confront modernity. . . . He also stresses grievances against the United States widely shared in the Muslim world. . . . He spoke of the suffering of the Iraqi people as a result of sanctions imposed after the Gulf War [1991], and he protested U.S. support for Israel.[9]

Bin Laden envisions no possible accommodation with America. In his words: "It is saddening to tell you that you are the worst civilization witnessed by the history of mankind."[10] Without accommodation he envisions violence as the only recourse, writing: "the walls of oppression and humiliation cannot be demolished except in a rain of bullets."[11] He and thousands of followers want to destroy the United States through terrorism aimed at civilians, as on 9/11. If similar or possibly worse attacks are to be averted—attacks using chemical, biological, radiological, or nuclear means—the United States and its allies must win the War on Terrorism.

Given the 9/11 attacks and the enemy's stated aims, waging a War on Terrorism is not controversial, but the means employed are. Here we consider three issues. One concerns denying detained suspects all judicial means of contesting their detention. A second is the use of torture to gain intelligence needed to thwart and apprehend terrorists. The third is the use of racial profiling to help identify terrorists.

Detention of Enemy Combatants

The government compares detention of enemy combatants in the War on Terrorism to detention of enemies captured on the field of battle in other wars. Captured soldiers aren't provided lawyers and legal proceedings to contest their detention. Instead, without any charge of criminal behavior, they are detained indefinitely until hostilities cease. Released prior to the end of the war, they might start fighting us again. Catch-and-release is good in fishing, not in war.

Such treatment of enemy combatants is controversial, especially when the captured enemy is an American citizen. At issue in the Supreme Court case *Hamdi v. Rumsfeld* (2004) was the indefinite detention of Yaser Esam Hamdi, who was captured while allegedly fighting alongside the Taliban—an enemy of the United States—in Afghanistan. The War in Afghanistan was part of the War on Terrorism, because the Taliban, who ruled Afghanistan, aided the terror activities of Al Qaeda by providing shelter and materials. Shortly after the 9/11 attacks, the United States attacked Afghanistan and overthrew the Taliban regime to capture and neutralize forces employing terror against us.

One American ally in the Afghan War was the Northern Alliance, Afghans based in northern Afghanistan. They captured Hamdi in 2001 and turned him over to American authorities, who sent him to the internment camp at Guantanamo Bay (in the American sector of Cuba) where the U.S. detained enemy combatants. When it was discovered that Hamdi is an American citizen—he was born in Louisiana in 1980, but his family moved to Saudi Arabia when he was a child—he was transferred to a Navy brig in Norfolk, Virginia, and then to one in Charleston, South

Carolina. The government's intent was to hold Hamdi indefinitely without charging him with any crime or allowing him to see an attorney, just like prisoners in previous wars. Why not?

In June 2002 Hamdi's father, Esam Fouad Hamdi, contested his son's incarceration. He filed documents stating, in Justice Sandra Day O'Connor's summary,

that his son went to Afghanistan to do "relief work," and that he had been in that country less than two months before September 11, 2001, and could not have received military training. . . . The 20-year-old was traveling on his own for the first time, his father says, and "because of his lack of experience, he was trapped in Afghanistan once that military campaign began."[12]

Well, that's his story, and he's sticking to it. And for all anyone knows from physical evidence, authoritative documents, and sworn testimony that stands up to cross-examination, it may be true. The government claimed it had no obligation to provide evidence to justify Hamdi's detention, so initially it supplied none.

Hamdi's father brought his son's case to a Federal District Court, which appointed a public defender for Hamdi, but the Court of Appeals reversed this ruling, denying Hamdi any right to a public defender. The Appeals Court ordered the District Court to conduct "a deferential inquiry into Hamdi's status" before providing Hamdi any legal help. The Bush administration's major contribution to this "deferential inquiry" was a declaration by Michael Mobbs, Special Advisor to the Under Secretary of Defense for Policy. Mobbs wrote, according to O'Connor's summary,

that Hamdi . . . "affiliated with a Taliban military unit and received weapons training" and "remained with his Taliban unit following the attacks of September 11. . . ." During the time when Northern Alliance forces were "engaged in battle with the Taliban," "Hamdi's Taliban unit surrendered" to those forces, after which he "surrendered his Kalishnikov assault rifle" to them.[13]

This would seem to make Hamdi an enemy combatant. But just as I'm skeptical about e-mails promising me riches if I help a Nigerian widow transfer funds (I flatter myself that such widows find my bank account very attractive), the District Court wondered if Michael Mobbs's claims were actually true. All they had was Mobbs's word. He supplied no names of Northern Alliance fighters who captured Hamdi, no date or place of capture, and no names of those who interviewed Hamdi later to confirm the story. It was all hearsay testimony without corroboration. So, an American citizen on U.S. soil is incarcerated indefinitely on the basis of unsubstantiated hearsay with no charges against him and no access to legal counsel. How can this be justified? How can it be constitutional? The Sixth Amendment to the Constitution reads:

In all criminal prosecutions, the accused shall enjoy the right to a speedy and public trial by an impartial jury. . . ; to be informed of the nature and cause of the accusation; to be confronted with the witnesses against him; to have compulsory process for obtaining witnesses in his favor, and to have the assistance of counsel for his defense.

Justice Clarence Thomas supported Hamdi's indefinite incarceration without any "due process" (the process specified in the Sixth Amendment) by claiming that the original understanding of the Constitution allows for this in cases of military need. Thomas gleaned the original understanding from the Federalist Papers, a collection of essays by some of the Founding Fathers. Thomas quotes Alexander Hamilton's Federalist No. 23: "The principle purposes to be answered by Union are these— The common defense of the members—the preservation of the public peace as well against internal convulsions as external attacks." Hamilton wrote that the power to protect the country "ought to exist without limitation. . . . The circumstances that endanger the safety of nations are infinite; and for this reason no constitutional shackles can wisely be imposed on the power to which the care of it is committed."

Thomas continues: "The Founders intended that the President have primary responsibility—along with the necessary power—to protect the national security and to conduct the nation's foreign relations. They did so principally because the structural advantages of a unitary Executive are essential in these domains."[14]

Thomas finds further support for his view in Supreme Court precedents. He quotes Justice Oliver Wendell Holmes Jr., writing for a unanimous court: "When it comes to a decision by the head of the State upon a matter involving its life, the ordinary rights of individuals must yield to what he deems the necessities of the moment. Public danger warrants the substitution of executive process for judicial process."[15] A case in 1987 mentions detentions specifically: "We have repeatedly held that the Government's regulatory interest in community safety can . . . outweigh an individual's liberty interest. For example, in times of war or insurrection, when society's interest is at its peak, the Government may detain individuals whom the Government believes to be dangerous."[16]

Thomas gives two additional reasons for rejecting ordinary due process for wartime detainees. First, such detentions aren't punishments for crimes, just procedures for public safety. People detained in quarantine during epidemics don't have a right to trial by jury. Wartime detainees are in a similar situation. Second, judges and juries cannot be informed of the basis for an executive determination that someone is a wartime danger to society without compromising vital defense information. "A meaningful ability to challenge the Government's factual allegations will probably require the Government to divulge highly classified information to the purported enemy combatant, who might then upon release return to the fight armed with our most closely held secrets."[17]

Thomas concludes that "the Executive's decision that a detention is necessary to protect the public need not and should not be subjected to judicial second-guessing."[18]

Utilitarianism and Justice for the Individual

Thomas' reasoning is utilitarian. In times of peril, public safety is the greatest good. Utilitarians think all public policies should be aimed at producing the greatest good for the greatest number. Each individual's good is included equally with everyone else's in the calculation of the greatest good. No one's good is given more or less weight based on age, race, religion, national origin, sexual preference, or anything else.

However, utilitarians are dedicated to maximizing the total good, and that can mean slighting some people in favor of others. In the words Thomas quotes from a 1987 Supreme Court decision: "Community safety can . . . outweigh an individual's liberty interest." The individual's liberty interest retains its importance; it's included equally in the calculus of the greatest good for the greatest number. But it is outweighed by the greater interest that a larger number of people have in public safety. Thus, utilitarianism can endorse the sacrifice of some individuals to promote the greater good of others.

That was the issue in Hamdi. For all we know, Hamdi was an innocent person doing charity work, a possibility Thomas doesn't deny. Thomas' point is that the due process measures needed to ensure that Hamdi was guilty—access to counsel, disclosure of documents, and cross examination of witnesses—would jeopardize national security. Ensuring justice for Hamdi isn't worth it. In times of war, national security, which is the greatest good for the greatest number, requires allowing the president to detain anyone he thinks dangerous to the war effort, citizens included. He shouldn't have to justify these detentions in any court.

This utilitarian reasoning is less appealing in the light of Brandon Mayfield's ordeal. Mayfield became a subject of investigation in the wake of the terrorist bombing in Madrid on March 11, 2004, that killed 191 people and injured thousands. It was an Al Qaeda–related terrorist attack, just as in New York.

In a van near the explosion, "Spanish National Police discovered a blue plastic bag containing detonation materials similar to the devices used in the bombings. On this bag, a number of latent fingerprints were observed."[19] One of these was matched by the FBI (international cooperation in the War on Terrorism) to former U.S. Army lieutenant Brandon Mayfield. They considered it a 100 percent match. They had no doubt that Mayfield's finger had been on the bag found in Madrid.

Mayfield may have fit the suspect profile because he's a Muslim married to a woman of Egyptian origin; he advertised his legal services (he's an attorney) on a Muslim Web site; and he once represented a man in a custody battle who was later convicted on federal terrorism charges. On May 6, Mayfield was arrested on a material witness warrant and held without bail. Given the government's reasons for arresting him, he was clearly in jeopardy of being indicted for capital offenses.[20]

Unlike Hamdi, Mayfield had access to an attorney and to the usual safeguards of our legal system. Independent experts were called in to verify the fingerprint match. "Kenneth R. Moses, Director of Forensic Identification Services, San Francisco, California, was appointed as court expert" and concluded that the latent print was "the left index finger of Mr. Mayfield."[21]

In the meantime, Mayfield's life was turned upside down. Besides keeping him in jail, the government got a search warrant and took files from his office, compromising the confidentiality he owed clients. His arrest was done in public, jeopardizing his reputation. Some potential clients don't want to be represented by a suspected terrorist.

Fortunately for Mayfield, Spanish authorities were skeptical that the fingerprint was Mayfield's. They continued searching and found a match to an Algerian, Ouhnane Daoud. All proceedings against Mayfield were dismissed, he was released from jail, and he could start putting his life together after nineteen nail-biting days in jail.

Imagine if American authorities had decided to consider Mayfield so dangerous and information related to his arrest so sensitive that they refused to let him see an attorney and refused to charge him with any crime, but just kept him locked up for national security reasons until the War on Terrorism is over. They were, after all, 100 percent sure he was an Al Qaeda operative. If they'd chosen this path, we'd never know that fingerprint evidence justified his detention, much less that the evidence was poor.

What an injustice to an American citizen on American soil! Yet, if the government had chosen this path, "Justice" Thomas would deny Mayfield the right to counsel, the right to see evidence against him, and the right to be heard in court. Mayfield would remain in a cell indefinitely. None of us would know about him, but his wife would lack his support, and his three children would grow up without their father.

Utilitarian calculations aimed at promoting the greatest good of the greatest number may demand enormous sacrifice from some people. Utilitarianism gives individuals only the right to have their interests weighed equally with everyone else's in calculations of the greatest good. There are no other individual rights, so the greatest good may justify sacrificing some people. Many consider this a flaw in utilitarianism and in the utilitarian reasoning given by Justice Thomas in his *Hamdi* opinion.

A Contractarian Defense of Individual Rights

Justice O'Connor and Justice Antonin Scalia, writing separately, supported Hamdi's right to legal counsel and to a hearing to determine whether his detention was justified. O'Connor, writing for the plurality, would accept the creation of military tribunals for this purpose, like those already used "to determine the status of enemy detainees who assert prisoner-of-war status under the Geneva Convention."[22] Such tribunals, O'Connor claims, strike a reasonable balance between the individual's right to be free of unwarranted detention and the government's "interests in ensuring that those who have in fact fought with the enemy during a war do not return to battle against the United States."[23]

Scalia, writing in dissent, would accept nothing less than full due process. If an American citizen takes up arms against his country, Scalia reasons, he has committed treason and should be tried for that offense in federal court. If the case can't be proved, he should be set free. There is constitutional provision for such proceedings. In fact, Scalia notes, "The only citizen other than Hamdi known to be imprisoned in connection with military hostilities in Afghanistan against the United States was subjected to the criminal process and convicted upon a guilty plea."[24] Hamdi should be given the same rights and treatment as John Walker Lindh.

Scalia paints a dark picture of government without due process. He quotes Sir William Blackstone, the eighteenth-century British jurist who influenced the founders of our country:

Of great importance to the public is the preservation of . . . personal liberty: for if once it were left in the power of any, the highest, magistrate to imprison arbitrarily whomever he or his officers thought proper . . . there would soon be an end of all other rights and immunities. . . . Confinement of the person, by secretly hurrying him to gaol, where his sufferings are unknown or forgotten; is . . . [a] dangerous engine of arbitrary government.[25]

Yet this is just what the government wanted to do with Hamdi and what Justice Thomas was willing to accept in the name of national security.

Justice Scalia replies to the security issue with quotes from the same author used by Thomas, Alexander Hamilton:

Safety from external danger is the most powerful director of national conduct. . . . The violent destruction of life and property incident to war . . . will compel nations the most attached to liberty to resort for repose and security to institutions which have a tendency to destroy their civil and political rights. To be more safe, they, at length, become willing to run the risk of being less free.[26]

Scalia concludes that the constitutional provision for a trial of treason allows for the simultaneous protection of the country and of individual rights.

Scalia's concerns about tyranny could reflect a different utilitarian calculation than Thomas's did. In the long run, he could be saying, the greatest good for the greatest number requires respect for individual rights even during times of war, because lack of such respect leads to tyranny and misery. Utilitarianism, as we've seen, can often be invoked on more than one side of an issue, because utilitarianism calls for actions that produce the best consequence and predictions of consequences are seldom certain.

Alternatively, Scalia's reasoning may rest not on utilitarianism, but on contractarianism. As noted in chapter 1, this is the view that a state's legitimacy rests on a kind of contract among its citizens. Everyone agrees to live by the same rules, including rules about establishing a government (the constitution) and additional rules enacted later in accordance with the constitution (legislation). All citizens should feel morally bound to obey state laws under this arrangement, because—if only indirectly through their representatives—these laws reflect the will of each and every citizen.

Contractarians recognize that citizens don't actually sign any such contract. And even if a contract were offered, it might not be fair to everyone. The rich and powerful might bribe or coerce people to accept a contract that favors some over others. Finally, some people might reject the contract, making their obligation to obey the laws uncertain.

Contractarians address these issues by saying that state legitimacy rests on a hypothetical contract that's fair to everyone. Twentieth-century philosopher John Rawls, in *A Theory of Justice* and other works,[27] asks us to imagine people who are about to start a new society, like the people on the Mayflower before they landed at Plymouth, or intelligent beings on *Star Trek* about to inhabit a new planet. They discuss the rules of their new society. To make sure that these rules are fair to everyone, Rawls wants us to imagine that the people setting up the rules don't know their own personal identities in the new society. They don't know if they'll be rich or poor, male or female, young or old, tall or short, black or white, extremely intelligent or just above average, and so on.

Star Trek, which Rawls doesn't actually mention, can be helpful here. On *Star Trek*, people are "beamed" from the space ship to any new planet. Their elementary particles and the formulas for their reconstruction on the planet enter a transporter and then the particles are beamed down. People are reconstructed on the planet from their own particles and formulas. But that wouldn't be necessary. Imagine entering everyone's particles and formulas into the beamer and before anyone's beamed down, having a Vanna White spin a wheel of fortune that randomly reassigns elementary particle to formulas for reconstruction. This means that anyone's particles could become anyone else. You don't know who your particles will become. You don't know if you'll be reconstructed as someone who's rich or poor, male or female, old or young, and so on.

When you don't know your personal identity in the new society, you want rules that are fair to everyone, because if anyone's treated unfairly, that person may be you (someone reconstructed from your elementary particles). In this situation, Rawls believes that you'd make individual liberty and basic individual rights your top priorities, qualified by equal employment opportunity and help for the poor. Everyone wants individual liberty and respect for their rights because liberty and rights help people get whatever else they want in life. In addition, in case it turns out you belong to an unpopular minority, you want fair equality of opportunity so your employment prospects won't be limited by unfair prejudice. Finally, in case you're poor, you want the state to help people get out of poverty. What you'd reject completely is the forced sacrifice of some people for the good of society, because you might turn out to be someone who's sacrificed.

The contractarian political philosophy thus calls on the state to protect individual liberty and respect individual rights. Contractarians would endorse the protections of freedom in our Constitution and its Bill of Rights. When you don't know what position you'll occupy in society— you may turn out to be a Muslim or an Arab-American—you want our government to respect individual rights in the War on Terrorism. Unlike Justice Thomas, contractarians would reject a government plan to hold citizens indefinitely without criminal charges or evidence that has withstood cross-examination by competent counsel. Contractarians would agree with Justice Scalia that every citizen deserves due process, even in times of war, the only exception being temporary suspensions of due process authorized by Congress to meet emergencies. In the light of Brandon Mayfield's scary story, this contractarian position will seem attractive to many.

In 2008, with Justice Scalia in the minority, the Supreme Court expanded the right of detainees to contest their indefinite detention. In the case of *Boumediene v. Bush* the Court ruled that even non-citizens of the United States have the right to contest their detention when they are held in a territory—including the military prison camp at Guantanamo Bay, Cuba—that is controlled by the U.S. government.[28] This ruling could represent an expansion of the idea of a social contract to include non-citizens who are subject to our government's power and jurisdiction.

The American Practice of Torture

Rawls's contractarianism applies to a single society. Justice Scalia's reasoning accords with this focus. He stresses that Hamdi was an American citizen on American soil. His opinion two years later regarding due process for non-citizens held as enemy combatants overseas shows that he doesn't extend fundamental rights worldwide. Foreigners on foreign soil, he agrees with Thomas, may be held without due process.[29]

If contractarianism doesn't establish the rights of foreigners in the War on Terrorism, what political philosophy does? The issue is pressing in view of Americans torturing (suspected) enemies in Iraq and elsewhere to gain information. Journalist Mark Danner reported practices found by The International Committee of the Red Cross (ICRC) at the Abu Ghraib prison run by the United States in Iraq in 2003:

Handcuffing with flexi-cuffs, which were sometimes made so tight and used for such extended periods that they caused skin lesions and long-term after-effects on the hands (nerve damage) . . . , as observed by the ICRC;

Beatings with hard objects (including pistols and rifles), slapping, punching, kicking with knees or feet on various parts of the body (legs, sides, lower back, groin . . .);

Being paraded naked outside cells in front of other persons . . . and guards, sometimes hooded or with women's underwear over the head . . . ;

Being attached repeatedly over several days . . . with handcuffs to the bars of their cell door in humiliating (i.e., naked or in underwear) and/or uncomfortable positions causing physical pain. . . .

The ICRC medical delegates [to the prison] examined persons . . . presenting signs of concentration difficulties, memory problems, verbal expression difficulties, incoherent speech, acute anxiety reactions, abnormal behavior, and suicidal tendencies. These symptoms appear to have been caused by the methods and duration of interrogation.[30]

We have photographs of such interrogation techniques, including one "of a hooded man standing naked on a box, arms outspread, with wires dangling from his fingers, toes and penis."[31] Major General Geoffrey Miller developed interrogation methods at Guantanamo Bay that included "the use of harsh heat or cold; withholding food; hooding for days at a time; naked isolation in cold, dark cells for more than 30 days and . . . ; 'stress positions' designed to subject detainees to rising levels of pain."[32] "Waterboarding" is yet another practice. Senator John McCain explains that "a prisoner is restrained and blindfolded while an interrogator pours water on his face and into his mouth—causing the prisoner to believe that he is being drowned."[33]

I won't discuss who was ultimately responsible for these practices—President George W. Bush, General Miller, "bad apple" soldiers, or others. Neither will I investigate issues of legality under American law. Some administration lawyers argued that the president has the right to authorize such practices as commander-in-chief responsible for national security.

I also won't enter debates on whether "unlawful combatants," people fighting without formally attaching to and wearing the uniform of a foreign state, should be treated differently than "lawful combatants," traditional enemy soldiers. The reason is that treatment of the first group influences treatment of the second. Consider the case of Major General Abed Hamed Mowhoush, who was chief of Iraqi air defenses, a traditional enemy soldier. Anthony Lewis reports in the *New York Review of Books*:

He was captured in October 2003 and died on November 26, 2003, in a U.S. detention facility in Iraq. At first the Pentagon released a death certificate saying that he had died of "natural causes." But after a Denver Post story questioned the circumstances of his death, the Pentagon admitted that an autopsy report said General Mowhoush died of "asphyxia due to smothering and chest compression" and said there was "evidence of blunt force trauma to the chest and legs." The Pentagon said a homicide investigation was underway.

Another Iraqi officer, Lieutenant Colonel Kareem 'Abd al-Jalil, died on January 9, 2004, while at an interrogation facility.[34]

Again, natural causes were claimed until investigative reporting forced the Pentagon to reclassify the death as a homicide caused by "blunt force injuries and asphyxia."[35]

Finally, I make no distinction between interrogation techniques called "cruel, inhuman, and degrading," and those classified as torture. Torture is defined by the Convention against Torture, an international treaty that the United States has signed, as "any act by which severe pain or suffering, whether physical or mental, is intentionally inflicted on a person" by or on behalf of any government agent.[36] U. S. law making torture illegal uses similar language. I believe much of the prisoner abuse at issue is torture in this sense. I have two reasons. First, Senator McCain, who was subjected to torture in North Vietnam, considers it torture. He writes regarding waterboarding:

If you gave people who have suffered abuse as prisoners a choice between a beating and a mock execution, many, including me, would choose a beating. The effects of most beatings heal. The memory of an execution will haunt someone for a very long time and damage his or her psyche in ways that may never heal. In my view, to make someone believe that you are killing him by drowning is no different than holding a pistol to his head and firing a blank. I believe that it is torture, very exquisite torture.[37]

Second, people die under U.S. interrogation. Anthony Lewis reported that by the middle of 2004 "the Army admitted that at least thirty-nine prisoners in Iraq and Afghanistan died, and some of them died while being interrogated.[38]

The debate that I'm interested in concerns the legitimacy of torture as a way of extracting information from our enemies to improve national security. American opinion is divided on the issue. *Newsweek* conducted a poll in 2005 and found that "44 percent of the public thinks torture is often or sometimes justified as a way to obtain important information, while 51 percent say it is rarely or never justified. A clear majority—58 percent—would support torture to thwart a terrorist attack."[39]

The Utilitarian Case for Torture

In *Commentary*, Andrew McCarthy argues in favor of legalizing torture:

Seventy percent of Americans, all of whom presumably oppose killing, favor the death penalty. A comparably sizable number who oppose abortion favor its availability in cases of rape, incest, or where the life of the mother is at risk. All sensible people oppose the slaughter of innocent civilians, but an overwhelming number favor war if the evil it seeks to defeat is worth fighting against, even if war will ineluctably lead to the slaughter of innocent civilians.

Torture is not meaningfully different. Considered in a vacuum, it is a palpable moral evil. Moral evils, however, do not exist in a vacuum; they exist in collision with other evils, and sometimes we are forced to choose. . . .

Let us posit a terrorist, credibly believed to have murdered thousands of people. Suppose this terrorist is aware that a radiological bomb will be detonated momentarily in the heart of a major metropolis, but is refusing to impart the details to interrogators. Now, suddenly, black and white becomes gray: perhaps there are worse evils than some forms of torture.[40]

This is a utilitarian argument. Torture is bad, but morally right when needed to avert worse evils. The greatest good for the greatest number sometimes requires choosing the lesser evil. This is why we tolerate "collateral damage" in war. We don't want to kill innocent civilians, but will knowingly do so when failure to fight and win a war promises even worse consequences. Similarly, it's worth torturing one person to get information that spares thousands of others agonizing deaths from radiation poisoning.

McCarthy notes further that we do and will employ torture in these extreme situations. "The consequences of the current system" is that "we mouth opposition to all torture while knowing full well that forms of it are occurring, with greater frequency than should be acceptable to anyone, inside many officially civilized countries that are signatories to the UN convention." The greater good is therefore served by making torture legal so it can be monitored and controlled.

By imposing an absolute ban on something we know is occurring, we promote disrespect for the rule of law in general and abdicate our duty to enact tailored and meaningful regulations. Both of these failings have the juggernaut effect of increasing the total amount of unjustifiable and otherwise preventable torture.[41]

McCarthy proposes ending the current ban on torture by establishing a system of torture warrants that federal judges could issue upon application from high-ranking federal officials. "The warrant would be issued only on a showing of reasonable grounds for believing that a catastrophe was impending, that the person to be subjected to torture had information about this event, that he had been given immunity . . . [so his statements couldn't be used against him in any court], and that he had nevertheless remained silent." Further protections are possible. "There could be limitations on who would be eligible for such treatment: for example, convicted terrorists or those who, even if not previously convicted, could be demonstrated to be terrorists according to some rigorous standard of proof." McCarthy adds: "Since torture would now be permitted, under stricture and with scrupulous judicial monitoring, no excuse would exist for engaging in torture outside the process, and those shown to have done so would be vigorously prosecuted."[42] The end result, McCarthy thinks, passes the utilitarian test—less torture overall and greater protection of innocent people from terrorists.

The Utilitarian Case against Torture

Utilitarian reasoning can be used against as well as for interrogation systems that use torture. Utilitarian opponents of torture deny that torture yields reliable information. Some confessed witches in Salem may have been lying. Senator McCain writes, "In my experience, abuse of prisoners often produces bad intelligence because under torture a person will say anything he thinks his captors want to hear—whether it is true or false— if he believes it will relieve his suffering." When McCain was abused by North Vietnamese who wanted the names of the members of his flight squadron, he "gave them the names of the Green Bay Packers' offensive line, knowing that providing them false information was sufficient to suspend the abuse."[43]

A more recent case relates to the War in Iraq. Ibn Al-Shaykh al-Libi ran Al Qaeda training camps before he was captured in Afghanistan in November 2001. To extract information from him, he was sent to Egypt in a process called "rendition." Evan Thomas and Michael Hirsh write in *Newsweek*:

Under questioning by the Egyptian authorities (techniques unknown, but not hard to imagine), al-Libi confessed that Al Qaeda terrorists, beginning in December 2000, had gone to Iraq to learn about chemical and biological weapons. This was just the evidence the Bush administration needed to make the case for invading Iraq and getting rid of Saddam Hussein.[44]

Colin Powell relied on this intelligence in February 2003 when he claimed erroneously at the UN that he knew Saddam had weapons of mass destruction. Like McCain, al-Libi had told his torturers what they wanted to hear, which helped unleash a war whose consequences include the deaths of many thousands and an uncertain future for Iraq.

The second utilitarian argument against torture is that even if accurate information is extracted, the practice backfires, because it creates enemies. The War on Terrorism requires draining the pool of terrorists faster than it's replenished by new recruits. When torture becomes public knowledge as victims talk, guilty guards confess, and whistleblowers report, it becomes a recruitment tool for terrorists. At the same time, it reduces the support of needed allies. This was France's experience in the 1950s. They got some good intelligence from torture victims in Algiers, but they lost the war, and lost Algeria, because the population turned increasingly against them.

Finally, torture can't be confined to worthy cases, as McCarthy suggests. Attorney Harvey Silverglate writes, "Institutionalizing torture will give society's imprimatur, lending it a degree of respectability. It will then be virtually impossible to curb not only the increasing frequency with which warrants will be sought—and granted—but also the inevitable rise in unauthorized use of torture."[45] It's easy to imagine some judges who can issue torture warrants being torture-friendly. Their hard-line reputation may account for their appointment to the bench in the first place.

The cogency of this slippery slope argument depends on the plausibility of its prediction. Frustration in the War on Terrorism can motivate the use of torture on the mere possibility that a suspect has useful information. When information is not forthcoming, brutality increases. Increasing numbers of detainees die of abuse, as occurred in Israel. After ten Palestinians died in custody, the Israeli high court outlawed torture. The same trend was noted among Americans. After some aggressive interrogation was allowed by U.S. forces, the practice quickly became more common, less professional, and more brutal, resulting in homicides as well as the senseless, counterproductive behavior captured on camera at the Abu Ghraib prison.[46]

Slippery slope arguments are questionable, because people on many issues seem to think the sky will fall if their policy is rejected. But historical evidence makes the slippery slope argument regarding torture among the most plausible, which is important from a utilitarian perspective. When torture becomes brutal and senseless, it produces more bad than good, detracting from—rather than adding to—the overall good.

Cosmopolitanism against Torture

My mother used to say, "What's right is right." She wasn't a philosopher, but she had a point: some moral truths are so obvious that there's no sense arguing about them. Cosmopolitans place condemnation of torture in this category.

Cosmopolitans believe that national borders are not of ultimate moral importance. They're just convenient; they help people organize their political and economic affairs. On basic issues, the humanity we share is more important than any national, ethnic, religious, or racial differences among us. We're all citizens of the world, not just citizens of individual states and members of individual ethnic, religious, and racial groups.

Our common humanity gives us a common moral status. We all possess some basic human rights. These rights are declared from time to time, such as in the United Nation's Universal Declaration of Human Rights. But these legal documents, according to cosmopolitans, do not create human rights; they merely recognize existing rights in order to promote their widespread appreciation and vigorous defense.

The Geneva Convention and the Convention against Torture are in this category. The Convention against Torture is explicit about its basis in human rights.

> Recognition of the equal and inalienable rights of all members of the human family is the foundation of freedom, justice and peace in the world. . . . Recognizing that those rights derive from the inherent dignity of the human person . . . , each State Party shall take effective legislative, administrative, judicial or other measures to prevent acts of torture in any territory under its jurisdiction. No exceptional circumstances whatsoever, whether a state of war or a threat of war, internal political instability or any other public emergency, may be invoked as a justification of torture. . . . No State Party shall expel, return . . . or extradite a person to another State where there are substantial grounds for believing that he would be in danger of being subjected to torture.[47]

Such international agreements, which the United States has joined, treat torture differently than "collateral damage" in war. Generally speaking, war is justified only in national defense. Because an offensive or aggressive war is not morally justified, no actions of the offending party are morally justified, including the killing of enemy soldiers. In a defensive war, by contrast, killing enemy soldiers is justified and killing innocent civilians as an unintended, regrettable by-product of killing enemy soldiers is allowed if reasonable steps are taken to minimize civilian casualties. But even when the war is defensive and justified, torture is not allowed, because it's not an inevitable by-product of waging war. It's an additional tactic to gain advantage.

It's simply not true that all's fair in love and war (well, in war anyway). Your country may gain a tactical advantage, and save soldiers' lives, by raping women in captured cities because that might demoralize the enemy or cause them to use limited resources to relocate their women. But it's obviously wrong. Even if bombing prior to a city's capture had justifiably killed many women, raping survivors is still wrong.

Torture's no different. It's wrong even if it produces intelligence that saves soldiers' lives. If torture were allowed when helpful, there'd be no reason in principle to reject torturing the children and other family members of people thought to have vital information. This would give new meaning to the angry cry, "Torture the mothers!"

Social conservatives tend to side with cosmopolitans on this issue. Social conservative William Safire criticizes torture and all euphemisms designed to disguise it.[48] In general, social conservatives favor basic values common to all great religious traditions. Because they think these religions share a core set of values, they are like cosmopolitans in believing that some values are universal. Unlike cosmopolitans, however, they look to traditions and tend to favor traditions associated with religion. Cosmopolitans are more likely to look to individual and collective conscience regardless of connection to any religion, and to want new, more humane traditions to develop. Cosmopolitans are more open to innovation. In any case, both condemn torture.

But how does this condemnation square with common sense when there's a real ticking bomb, and thousands of lives could reliably be saved by torturing one individual? Some cosmopolitans agree that torture would be appropriate in this situation, but still insist on application of criminal penalties against the torturer. Such penalties maintain the credibility of world condemnation of torture and deter would-be torturers who don't want to risk their own hides and who lack confidence that torture is really necessary. In cases where torture still seems right, the torturer will be placing herself at the mercy of the legal community, similar to those who break the law on grounds of conscience. If the torture really saves many lives, a jury is likely to be sympathetic, but if the torture was unproductive and unnecessary, the torturer will suffer as well as her victim.[49]

Racial Profiling

The clash of individual rights with perceived collective need arises also when authorities use racial profiling in the War on Terrorism. From the Arab perspective, it's obviously degrading and humiliating to be subjected to special searches and delays simply for being Arab. No matter how successful you are, no matter how law-abiding, no matter how kind and considerate, racial profiling follows you. And this could last for as long as the War on Terrorism, which could be for the rest of your life.

Like other forms of racial prejudice, racial profiling is unfair to the individual. It's condemned by cosmopolitans who seek a world where race, ethnicity, nationality, and religion don't affect basic human rights, and by contractarians who want the majority to imagine themselves in the position of a minority subjected to prejudice. The ideals of both groups were expressed well in 1963 by Dr. Martin Luther King Jr., who looked forward to a time in the United States when people would be judged not by the color of their skin but by the content of their character. We've made a lot of progress in race relations since then, but racial profiling in the War on Terrorism may be a step backward.

Against this cosmopolitan and contractarian appeal for individualized justice is a utilitarian argument that the greatest good for the greatest number sometimes requires individual sacrifice. The Justice Department targeted Italian Americans in its successful campaign against the mafia. Similarly, according to Andrew McCarthy, the Department of Homeland Security should target Muslims and Arabs because even though most Muslims and Arabs aren't terrorists, most terrorists are Muslims or Arabs. Chances of success with limited resources increase when you're looking in the right direction.[50]

As usual, utilitarian arguments are given on the other side as well. David Harris testified before the U.S. Commission on Civil Rights that racial profiling targeting African Americans and Latinos in the War on Drugs produced worse results than policing without profiling. He claimed "the 'hit rates'—the rates of successful searches—were actually lower for minorities than they were for whites, who were not apprehended by using a racial or ethnic profile."[51] The reason is that most members of the profiled group were not drug dealers. Profiling resulted in law enforcement wasting a lot of effort investigating law-abiding citizens. Profiling also angers the community whose cooperation with intelligence-gathering is needed to catch the real criminals.

The same is true in the War on Terrorism, Harris claims. We should concentrate on individual behaviors, "like the buying of expensive one-way tickets with cash just a short time before take-off, as some of the World Trade Center hijackers did."[52] Sparing most Arabs humiliating searches and vexing delays will make it easier to enlist their cooperation with needed intelligence-gathering.

As with utilitarian claims generally, it's hard to know who's right. But the anti-profiling logic is strange. It suggests we concentrate intelligence efforts in the Muslim and Arab communities (hence the importance of their cooperation with intelligence gathering) but not apprehension and interdiction efforts (thereby sparing most Arabs humiliating searches and vexing delays). However, the only reason to concentrate intelligence efforts there is belief that members of the community are more involved than most others in terrorist activity, so why not concentrate apprehension and interdiction efforts there as well? I'm no expert, but I can't help thinking that some attention to race or ethnicity, combined with more attention to behavior, would be most effective. Race or ethnicity would be one factor among others to be considered, as in some controversial programs of affirmative action, our next topic.

Conclusion

Racial profiling offends individual rights less than indefinite detention without due process, because an unnecessary search is less harmful than long-term confinement. Similarly, indefinite detention offends individual rights less than torture. Torture tends to produce permanent physical and mental scars, when it isn't fatal. Detainees, by contrast, retain their faculties and health, if they're not tortured, and have at least some hope of release, which usually occurs sooner or later.

I conclude that contractarians and cosmopolitans opposed to indefinite detention and torture generally have a more persuasive case against utilitarian proponents of these practices than against utilitarian proponents of racial profiling. If people find utilitarianism distasteful when it prescribes sacrificing some individuals for the good of the majority, the distaste increases as the sacrifice becomes greater and decreases as the sacrifice becomes less. Yet, affirmative action—which uses racial and ethnic classifications to give preferential treatment to members of certain minority groups—is fought vigorously by many people, even though its Anglo-Caucasian victims suffer no more than reduced opportunities in education and employment. Why do some people find affirmative action more objectionable than racial profiling? Our next chapter considers this question.

6

Affirmative Action: Libertarianism, Utilitarianism, and Social Conservatism

Disappointment at Reverse Discrimination

Jennifer Gratz had her heart set on attending the University of Michigan at Ann Arbor, the flagship university in her state, beginning in the fall of 1995. Coming from a working-class neighborhood in a Detroit suburb—her father was a police sergeant and her mother a hospital lab technician—she would be the first member of her family to complete college. She knew admission standards were high, but she had reason to expect success. She had a 3.8 grade point average, was in the top 5 percent of her class, and had a score of 25 on her ACT (which placed her at the eighty-third percentile among those taking this standardized achievement test nationwide). Her extracurricular activities included cheerleading, helping out at a "prom" for senior citizens, organizing a blood drive, and tutoring in math. Good-looking, blonde, and engaging, she was the prom queen.

Journalist Greg Stohr writes:

Jennifer pictured herself walking to class across the green grass of the "Diag" in the center of campus, making new friends in one of the ivy-covered dormitories, getting decked out in maize and blue for the football weekends that turn Ann Arbor into a daylong, 100,000-person party. The University of Michigan was the essence of college. It would be a perfect fit.[1]

Jennifer took little for granted. She worked on her application essay in between cheerleading at basketball games and submitted her application in early January 1995. She was so set on going to Ann Arbor that her mother had a hard time getting her to apply to two fallback schools, Wayne State and the University of Michigan at Dearborn.

The first signs of trouble came in late January, when she received a letter saying the university wouldn't act on her application before April because, although she was "well qualified," she was "less competitive than the students who have been admitted on first review." She knew others who'd waited until April for admission, but for the sake of additional security, she quickly applied to Notre Dame.

By spring, she was rushing home every day after cheerleading practice to check the mail. Finally, one afternoon in the last week of April, Jennifer burst into the house, picked up the stack of bills and letters, and pulled out the thin envelope. Her father, Brad, sat across from her in the living room and watched. She scanned the first few sentences until she got to the part that said, "I regret to inform you we are unable to offer you admission." Then she burst into tears. . . .

Jennifer was sure something had gone horribly wrong. She understood that Michigan used affirmative action in admissions, though she knew nothing of the specifics. Her thoughts flashed to a Hispanic classmate who had been admitted to Michigan with lower grades than hers.

Finally, Jennifer uttered the first words that came to her.

"Dad," she said, "Can we sue them?"[2]

Jennifer was correct that race may have influenced the admissions decision. The year she applied, admissions officials at the University of Michigan's College of Literature, Science, and the Arts used separate grids for non-Hispanic Caucasians and for minorities (African Americans, Hispanics, and Native Americans). The same high school grades, class rank, and test scores that placed non-Hispanic Caucasians in Jennifer's category of delayed consideration might, on the grid for minorities, lead to a student's immediate acceptance.

By the time Jennifer's case, *Gratz v. Bollinger*, reached the Supreme Court in 2003, the college used a new system that both sides agreed had the same effect of giving preference to minorities. It allowed students to earn a maximum of 150 points: 110 were available for strictly academic matters. A 4.0 high school grade point was worth eighty points, a 3.0 was worth sixty points, and so on. Up to ten points could be added for attending an academically tough high school, and up to eight for taking demanding high school courses. Finally, up to twelve points could be added for high scores on nationwide standardized achievement tests, such as the SAT and ACT.

Up to forty additional points could be added for non-academic factors. State residents received ten points. Two points were available to out-of-state students from underrepresented states. Personal achievement could yield up to five points. Four points were possible for alumni connections and one to three points for a good essay. Finally, twenty points went into a miscellaneous category and were awarded to "underrepresented minorities, other socioeconomically disadvantaged students, scholarship athletes, and other applicants at the discretion of the provost." Greg Stohr explains, "Applicants could receive the twenty points only once. In other words, a poor, black scholarship athlete got twenty miscellaneous points, not sixty."[3]

Applicants with 100 or more points were immediately admitted. Those with 90–99 points were either admitted immediately or postponed. Those with 75–89 points were not admitted immediately but could be put on a waiting list, while those with 74 or fewer points were rejected unless the file was flagged for special consideration.

A black, Hispanic, or American Indian applicant whose score, excluding the miscellaneous category, was 81 would have 20 points added and gain immediate admission, whereas a non-Hispanic Caucasian with 81 points might receive no miscellaneous points, go to a waiting list, and later be rejected. This was the kind of unfairness that Gratz thought about when she recalled the early admission of the Hispanic classmate with lower grades than hers.

Legal and Libertarian Arguments against Affirmative Action

How can such affirmative action be legal? Our law seems to disallow racial discrimination. The Fourteenth Amendment to the Constitution provides that "No State shall . . . deny to any person within its jurisdiction the equal protection of the laws." This Equal Protection Clause was used by the Supreme Court in 1954 to deny states the right to segregate schools by race, because racial segregation denied people equal educational opportunities. Yet the State of Michigan was using racial criteria for admission to its flagship university. Like racial segregation, it seems that some people—whites, this time—are denied equal educational opportunity on account of race.

Just in case the Constitution wasn't clear enough, Congress passed the Civil Rights Act in 1964. Section 601 reads: "No person in the United States shall, on the grounds of race, color, or national origin, be excluded from participation in, be denied the benefits of, or be subjected to discrimination under any program or activity receiving Federal financial assistance."[4] The University of Michigan receives financial assistance from the federal government, as do almost all universities, so it again seems illegal for the university to discriminate among applicants on the basis of race or national origin. Giving people twenty extra points for their race or national origin seems like blatant discrimination in their favor.

Such discrimination seems unjust as well as illegal. Libertarians follow the seventeenth-century philosopher John Locke in believing that all people have natural rights to "life, liberty, and property." Locke inspired Thomas Jefferson to claim in the Declaration of Independence that people have "unalienable rights . . . [to] life, liberty, and the pursuit of happiness."

For Locke and later libertarians, the reference to property, rather than the pursuit of happiness, is important. Libertarians believe that people own their bodies as original, natural property. That's why, for example, we ask people for blood and organ donations; we don't just take their blood and organs for use by others. That's why rape is criminal. People own their bodies, so they should control their use, just as people who own cars decide who can drive them. Many libertarians favor legalized prostitution. What people own they should be able to rent, or, to use the more suggestive British term, "to let."

Because people own their bodies, they naturally own their inborn talents and the fruits of their own labor. Labor's just the use someone makes of her body. For example, in a wilderness where nothing is owned (a condition Locke erroneously attributed to seventeenth-century North America), someone who cuts down trees and makes houses owns those houses because they embody her inborn talent and labor. She can exchange a house for other things she needs from willing home buyers. The ideal free market is a complex mix of such exchanges. People manufacture goods or perform services for willing customers in exchange for money that can be used to buy other things. The free market thus respects everyone's property and freedom. People use what they naturally own—talent and effort—to get money from willing customers without force or fraud. Most Americans find these elements of libertarian thinking attractive.

Libertarians want taxes to be as low as possible, because taxes are forced payments to the state. Money represents labor, so taxes resemble forced labor. Libertarians therefore want the state to be small and frugal, which usually rules out state support of universities. Higher education should be in the free market, they think. But when there is a state university, it should mimic the free market. It should reward talent and effort relevant to the university's educational mission, judging prospective students by high school grades, class rank, standardized test scores, and the like.

If places are limited, as at the University of Michigan, those who perform best on these criteria should be admitted. Racial preferences are unjust—they shouldn't be among the criteria—because race doesn't reflect academic talent, effort or educationally relevant merit. So, it's unjust when universities use race, even when it's just one of several factors, to choose among qualified candidates competing for limited spots. This is the view of Roger Clegg, vice president and general counsel of the Center for Equal Opportunity, a Washington, D.C.–based think tank. He writes:

Always put the shoe on the other foot. Imagine someone told you: "True, I prefer whites over nonwhites, but I use race as only one of many factors. I also consider the person's grades, test scores, economic background; that someone isn't white works against them only in really close cases." Everyone would agree that was still discrimination. If you use race . . . as a factor, even one of many factors, you're discriminating. That's true regardless of which race . . . you're discriminating against.[5]

The fact that minority members are qualified is also irrelevant to the issue of fairness.

Again, put the shoe on the other foot. Imagine someone told you: "I'd never select an unqualified white over a qualified nonwhite. It's just that when there are two qualified applicants and the nonwhite is more qualified than the white, I might select the white despite that." Not very reassuring to a nonwhite, is it? The people who were admitted to law schools when they were segregated [all white] were all "qualified." But this was still discrimination. It was still unfair to those who were discriminated against.[6]

In sum, Jennifer Gratz can object on libertarian grounds to the University of Michigan's admissions policy which used race to put her at a competitive disadvantage. She would find most Americans on her side. *Newsweek* reported in 2003 that its poll found whites oppose preferences for blacks by a 72 to 22 margin, and that blacks opposed such preferences 56 to 38.[7] There's a strong libertarian streak in most of us.

In fact, "Americans of all colors oppose admissions preferences of *all* kinds, whether it's for minorities, athletes, legacies, or the drum line."[8]

Again, this may reflect a libertarian streak. Consistent libertarians object not only to Michigan awarding twenty points for race, but also to its giving twenty points to children of large donors, four points to children of alumni, and twenty points to outstanding athletes. Points should go only for inborn talent and personal effort that result in academic merit. Athletic accomplishment reflects talent and effort, but is irrelevant unless the university is also in the business of developing professional athletes.

Affirmative Action to Rectify Past Discrimination

Affirmative action, a child of the 1960s, can't be understood apart from racial desegregation ordered by the Supreme Court in 1954 in *Brown v. Board of Education*.[9] Before that time, laws in southern states typically required that blacks and whites use separate public facilities, including separate schools. When such forced segregation was declared unconstitutional, because it didn't give blacks and whites equal protection of the laws as the Fourteenth Amendment requires, southern states tried to maintain the status quo. Some school districts, for example, adopted "freedom-of-choice" plans. Parents could choose without regard to race the schools their children would attend. But because blacks were subject to violence if they entered a white school, black parents chose historically black schools for their children and school segregation continued. The Supreme Court was not amused and eventually ordered school districts to adopt plans that effectively integrated their schools.[10]

My school district in Springfield, Illinois, is under such a desegregation order. As a result of a case decided in 1976, Springfield's grade schools must maintain minority (mostly African American) enrollment that's no more than 15 percent higher or lower than the 37 percent minority enrollment in the district. All grade schools must have at least 22 percent and may have no more than 52 percent minority students.

Such desegregation orders are necessary to move desegregation from theory to practice. School districts can't simply stop segregating and expect integration to occur. Residential patterns and social expectations favor the segregated status quo. Schools must take affirmative steps to effect integration. In Springfield, we use bussing.

One lesson from this history, besides the tendency of social momentum to maintain the status quo, is that integration is impossible in a race-blind society. The school district must ask parents to volunteer information about their race or they'll have no way of verifying the percentage of children who are black in the district or in any school.

Affirmative action began in this context. The term was used first by President John F. Kennedy in Executive Order No. 10,925 to protect minorities against blatant discrimination in hiring. Companies receiving federal contracts were to use affirmative action to ensure that minorities have equal employment opportunities.[11] President Lyndon B. Johnson's Executive Order No. 11,246 reiterated the call for affirmative action.

As with school desegregation, the government expected good-faith efforts to yield results. For example, unions dominating the construction industry in Philadelphia had only 1.6 percent minority members, a small fraction of the percentage of minorities in the area. President Nixon issued his "Philadelphia Order" in 1969 to require federal construction contractors to meet specific goals and timetables for increased minority employment.[12] Just as administrators in Springfield Public Schools must consider the race of students, these unions had to consider the race of acceptable applicants in order to verify an increasing percentage of minorities in their unions.

Such affirmative action poses a dilemma. On the one hand, it seems only right to hire the most qualified applicant. Few minority applicants were as qualified as whites for official union training because many whites, whose family members were already in the trades, had grown up expecting to follow their elders' footsteps. They had prepared themselves from childhood, benefiting from informal training in their communities. So, if trade unions continued to admit only the most qualified, blacks and other minorities would continue to be excluded. This practice would perpetuate expectations and systems of early training that mostly kept blacks out, constituting another example of social momentum. Although the best would be hired and given union training, the perpetuation of white dominance doesn't seem fair. It doesn't seem like equal opportunity.

The only way to break the cycle of white dominance, which rested historically on blatant racial discrimination, was to hire people who were not the best qualified but who could, with some extra effort, attain required skills. People can object that this is unfair. Someone who's worked on skills for years expecting to join a union that promises lifelong employment at a reasonable salary is passed over for someone else less skilled, who's admitted to the union only because he's black. But this unfairness no longer seems entirely irrational. How else can the social momentum of past discrimination be stopped so that equal opportunity can flourish in the future?

Rectifying past injustice is a libertarian value. Libertarians believe people should be free to enjoy the fruits of their labors. A key function of the state is to protect people from unjustified interference with this freedom. So, when people are robbed, libertarians endorse government efforts to catch criminals and restore property to rightful owners.[13] The racially motivated exclusion of blacks from good jobs is like theft, an unjustified transfer of wealth from blacks to whites. Many whites got jobs and earned money that blacks should have had. Affirmative action, on this libertarian rationale, transfers wealth in the opposite direction. It's like requiring thieves to return stolen property. Yet, I know of no libertarian who favors affirmative action. They favor government intervention to return stolen property, but not to restore stolen economic opportunities.

One reason why libertarians oppose affirmative action is that it harms innocent people. Whites losing places to blacks aren't like thieves with stolen property. They didn't discriminate in hiring; they were children when other people acted unjustly. But now their education and employment opportunities are impaired.

A second objection is that the beneficiaries of affirmative action aren't the people previously harmed. They, too, were children at the time. The only way to rectify past wrongs is to find people who were wronged and offer them compensation. In this case, however, that wouldn't be practical. Racial discrimination extends back many generations; most of its victims are dead. Many of those still alive wouldn't think of themselves as victims because prevailing employment patterns affected their job-seeking efforts. Knowing the construction trades were all but closed to blacks in Philadelphia, for example, they never tried to join relevant unions. Most earned lower wages throughout their lives as a result of not being union members, but it's impossible to know which individuals would have joined the union if racial discrimination had not been the rule.

Carl Cohen, a philosopher at the University of Michigan, summarizes: "When preference is given flatly by skin color or by national origin . . . , most often, those who benefit did not suffer the wrong for which compensation is supposedly being given; those who are disadvantaged by the preference most often did not do any wrong whatsoever, and certainly not that earlier wrong to a minority group for which the preference is alleged redress."[14] No one accused Jennifer Gratz of engaging in racial discrimination. Considerations like these undercut the libertarian rationale for affirmative action.

Current Racism and White Privilege

The 2003 *Newsweek* poll that shows most Americans oppose racial preferences reveals that "sixty-five percent approve of using affirmative action based on income rather than race to give preferences to people from low-income families."[15] This suggests an understanding of academic merit that's sensitive to students having overcome obstacles to learning. Ordinary merit, reflected in test scores, grades, class rank, and the like, measure students' academic results stemming from talent and effort. But the talent and effort needed for someone raised in poverty to achieve an 81 on Michigan's scale is greater than the talent and effort needed for rich kids to get the same score. If we should reward people for relevant merit stemming from talent and effort, as libertarians propose, it's reasonable to give extra points to children of poverty. This primarily libertarian view may explain why most Americans favor affirmative action for children raised in poverty.

Proponents of race-based affirmative action welcome this view. They claim that African Americans and other minorities must overcome extra obstacles to academic achievement, so they should also benefit from affirmative action on this essentially libertarian rationale. The United States remains a significantly racist society, affecting the school performance of black youth. Mary Francis Berry, while chairing the U.S. Civil Rights Commission during the Clinton administration, reported that

the Federal Reserve Board, drawing on the records of more than nine thousand lending institutions, found that not only were African-Americans more likely to experience discrimination, but the rejection rate of blacks in the highest income bracket was identical to the denial rates of the poorest whites. Housing and

Urban Development secretary Henry Cisneros concluded that the report "tells us that discrimination is still alive and well in America."[16]

The ability to get a home loan affects where people live, which, in turn, affects the quality of schools their children attend.

Other investigators have found pervasive racism. Congressman Robert C. Scott reported in *Insight* about "testing studies" to check for racism.

Identical candidates, with the exception of their race, are sent to apply for credit, rent a house or apply for a job. Guess what? Discrimination uncovered by these testing studies is far greater than even the most ardent supporters of affirmative action ever could have imagined in 1998.

A recent testing study . . . found that minorities are discriminated against 40 percent of the time they attempt to rent apartments or buy homes [and] that African-American and Latino job applicants suffer blatant and easily identifiable discrimination once in every five times they apply for a job.[17]

Bryan Grapes, editor of an anthology on affirmative action observes, "the Federal Glass Ceiling Commission reports that African-American men with a bachelor's degree earn as much as $15,180 less [per year] than their white counterparts."[18]

Whites in our society benefit from white privilege. Robert Jensen, a white professor of journalism at the University of Texas, writes:

When I seek admission to a university, apply for a job, or hunt for an apartment, I don't look threatening. Almost all of the people evaluating me look like me—they are white. They see in me a reflection of themselves—and in a racist world, that is an advantage. I am one of them. I am not dangerous. . . .

White privilege is not something I get to decide whether I want to keep. Every time I walk into a store at the same time as a black man and the security guard follows him and leaves me alone to shop, I am benefiting from white privilege. It is clear that I will carry this privilege with me until the day white supremacy is erased from this society.[19]

This lesson was brought home to me in 2006. My wife Grace and I, along with several colleagues from the school where Grace used to work, attended an elaborate wedding in Chicago. On each of the twenty-eight round tables was a silver picture frame displaying the table's number. A teacher from Grace's old school, the one who's black, saw someone at her table put a silver picture frame in her handbag. Kenyatta immediately got up and told the wedding planner. When Grace asked why, she said, "I'm one of the few black people here, and I didn't want anyone to think I stole the picture frame." An innocent white person would have no such concern.

Psychological predispositions resulting from life in a racist society can affect academic performance. Psychologists Claude Steele and Joshua Aronson found that African Americans who took a standardized achievement test after being asked their race on the test form scored much lower than comparably prepared African Americans taking the same test who weren't asked to indicate their race.[20]

Educational obstacles for blacks come from socialization in many black communities. Actor Bill Cosby created a stir in 2004 at an NAACP gathering celebrating the fiftieth anniversary of the *Brown* desegregation decision. According to Richard Leiby of the *Washington Post*, Cosby said:

Ladies and gentlemen, the lower economic people are not holding up their end in this deal. These people are not parenting. They are buying things for kids—$500 sneakers for what? And won't spend $200 for "Hooked on Phonics."

[The kids are] standing on the corner and they can't speak English. I can't even talk the way these people talk: "Why you ain't," "Where you is." . . . And I blame the kid until I hear the mother talk. And then I heard the father talk. . . . Everybody knows it's important to speak English except these knuckleheads. . . . You can't be a doctor with that kind of crap coming out of your mouth.[21]

Perhaps even worse than this, black kids who want to do better are often ridiculed by their peers. Here's another personal story. My three daughters are adopted. My daughter Felicia, who's a bi-racial African American, mostly identifies herself as black, and so do her two daughters, although they live in a predominantly white suburb of a major American city. Felicia has contacted members of her extended biological family who live in the city and they socialize. One day when Felicia's children and their city cousins were visiting my oldest daughter Ami, who lives in the same suburb, Ami heard one of the cousins say to my oldest grandchild, eleven-year-old Kiahna, "Why you tryin' to talk white?" Kiahna is under social pressure to adopt forms of language that won't help her succeed in life.

This problem is widespread, according to Patrick Hall, instructional services coordinator of the University Libraries at Notre Dame University.

The defining of middle-class values as "white" by both less-educated and educated blacks (who should know better) is perhaps the most insidious factor that continues to hamstring the progress of blacks as a group. If someone is reasonably articulate, motivated, and focused on success, the black community often brings forth a particularly nasty reflex response that interprets this as "being white. . . ." It is not accident that so many black youths chastise their studious peers with the indictment that "it's not cool to study," or "you think you're white."[22]

Children raised in this atmosphere, even in middle-class households, are not competing on a level playing field with Jennifer Gratz. Through no fault of her own, Gratz has white privilege, and that privilege may justify race-based affirmative action on the same libertarian grounds that justify affirmative action for children raised in poverty. Some people who support affirmative action as compensation for white privilege might be surprised to learn that their reasoning could be justified on libertarian grounds.

Utilitarian Arguments for and against Affirmative Action

Utilitarian arguments for affirmative action, stressing social benefits rather than individual justice, were raised in *Grutter v. Bollinger*,[23] the companion case to *Gratz*.

In 1996, Barbara Grutter applied to law school at the University of Michigan. A forty-three-year-old mother of two, she ran her own health-care consulting business. She had a bachelor's degree from Michigan State with a 3.8 grade point average and had an LSAT (Law Scholastic Aptitude Test) score of 161, which placed her at the eighty-sixth percentile nationwide.[24] The law school put Barbara on a waiting list and later rejected her application. She, too, suspected that affirmative action had hurt her chances. She thought minority candidates with poorer records had been admitted in her stead.

She may have been right. The law school had an affirmative action program aimed at increasing "racial and ethnic diversity with special reference to the inclusion of students from groups which have been historically discriminated against, like African-Americans, Hispanics and Native Americans, who without this commitment might not be represented in our student body in meaningful numbers."[25]

Utilitarians favor policies that promise to provide the greatest good for the greatest number. Three different utilitarian justifications for affirmative action programs were put forward in *Grutter*: improving the effectiveness of organizations through their incorporation of a racially diverse workforce; maintaining the legitimacy of major social institutions by showing that power is available to people of all races; and exposing students to a wide variety of perspectives to improve their education.

Improve Effectiveness of Organizations

A friend of the court (amicus) brief filed by Lt. Gen. Julius Becton on be-half of the United States Service Academies and the ROTC (Reserve Officers Training Corps) explains the military's need for affirmative action. The U.S. military was racially segregated until President Harry S. Truman ordered integration in 1948. However,

In 1962, a mere 1.6% of all commissioned military officers were African-American.

The chasm between the racial composition of the officer corps and the enlisted personnel undermined military effectiveness in a variety of ways. For example, military effectiveness depends heavily upon unit cohesion. In turn, group cohesiveness depends on a shared sense of mission and the unimpeded flow of information through the chain of command. African-Americans experienced discriminatory treatment in the military, even during integration, but the concerns and perceptions of the African-American personnel were often unknown, unaddressed or both, in part because the lines of authority, from the military police to the officer corps, were almost exclusively white. . . .

Hundreds of race-related incidents occurred. For example, in the 1960s, racial violence among the Marines at Camp Lejeune was not uncommon. White officers were simply unaware of intense African-American dissatisfaction with job assignments and the perceived lack of respect from the Marine Corps.[26]

These problems affected U.S. fighting capacities in Vietnam, according to Lt. Gen. Frank Peterson Jr., who said, "In Vietnam, racial tensions reached a point where there was an inability to fight."[27] Becton continues, "The painful lesson slowly learned was that our diverse enlisted ranks rendered integration of the officer corps a military necessity." Yet, "in 1973, when the nation instituted its all-volunteer force, 2.8% of military officers were African-American."[28] To rectify the situation, the U.S. Military Academy began race-based affirmative action. By 2003, 8.8 percent of the officer corps was African American, which still trailed significantly the percentage of African Americans in the enlisted ranks—21.7.[29] The military doesn't think it could maintain its current 8.8 percent, much less approach the 21.7 percent, without affirmative action. In sum, the program is needed to maintain and improve the military's effectiveness.

Maintain Legitimacy of Major Social Institutions

In her opinion for the Court in *Grutter*, Justice Sandra Day O'Connor writes, "Effective participation by members of all racial and ethnic groups in the civic life of our Nation is essential if the dream of one nation, indivisible, is to be realized."[30] In other words, just as misunderstanding, mistreatment, and mistrust afflicted the military when its officer corps was predominantly white, leading to debilitating disruption, alienation from established political authority can result when political leaders are almost all white. Just as the military needs racial diversity in the officer corps for organizational effectiveness, society at large needs racial diversity among its leaders for political legitimacy and social health.

Justice O'Connor continues:

Universities, and in particular, law schools, represent the training ground for a large number of our Nation's leaders. . . . Individuals with law degrees occupy roughly half the state governorships, more than half the seats in the United States Senate, and more than a third of the seats in the United States House of Representatives. . . . The pattern is even more striking when it comes to highly selective law schools. A handful of these schools accounts for 25 of the 100 United States Senators, 74 United States Courts of Appeals judges, and nearly 200 of the more than 600 District Court judges.

In order to cultivate a set of leaders with legitimacy in the eyes of the citizenry, it is necessary that the path to leadership be visibly open to talented and qualified individuals of every race and ethnicity.[31]

Affirmative action is needed, O'Connor found, for significant participation by blacks in elite schools. For example, in 1996, before California eliminated affirmative action at its state schools, seventy-five black students were admitted to the law school at UC Berkeley. The next year, without affirmative action, only fifteen were admitted.[32]

Diversity for Improved Education

The only rationale for race-based affirmative action officially endorsed by the Supreme Court was to improve the education of students. According to O'Connor, "The Law School's assessment that diversity will, in fact, yield educational benefits is substantiated by respondents and their *amici*."[33] Inserting quotes from the District Court that first heard the case, O'Connor writes:

The Law School's admissions policy promotes "cross-racial understanding," helps to break down racial stereotypes, and "enables [students] to better understand persons of different races." These benefits are "important and laudable," because "classroom discussion is livelier, more spirited, and simply more enlightening and interesting" when the students have "the greatest possible variety of backgrounds."[34]

O'Connor continues: "Numerous studies show that student body diversity promotes learning outcomes" and, according to the American Educational Research Association, "better prepares students for an increasingly diverse workforce and society, and better prepares them as professionals." O'Connor notes, "Major American businesses have made clear that the skills needed in today's increasingly global marketplace can only be developed through exposure to widely diverse people, cultures, ideas, and viewpoints."[35]

The educational benefits of diversity require a "critical mass" of minority students. O'Connor writes:

Diminishing the force of [racial] stereotypes is both a crucial part of the Law School's mission and one that it cannot accomplish with only token numbers of minority students. Just as growing up in a particular region or having particular professional experiences is likely to affect an individual's views, so too is one's own, unique experience of being a racial minority in a society, like our own, in which race unfortunately still matters.[36]

Affirmative action at elite schools meets a compelling public need for better education, and this need justifies racial classifications that the Constitution otherwise forbids.

All three of these rationales for affirmative action concern the good of a group—an organization's effectiveness, political and social legitimacy, and educational climate. None is based on individual rights to be judged on academic merit alone or to receive the benefits of affirmative action as compensation for others having white privilege. Unlike libertarians, utilitarian proponents of affirmative action say that individual rights have nothing to do with the matter. The point of affirmative action, like the point of all other social programs, is to promote the greatest good of the greatest number.

Utilitarian critics of affirmative action counter that race-blind policies serve society better than race-conscious affirmative action. They say that affirmative action harms blacks and exacerbates racial tensions.

Affirmative action harms blacks, according to Justice Thomas, by casting doubt on the ability of blacks to succeed without special preferences. He writes in *Grutter*: .

It is uncontested that each year, the Law School admits a handful of blacks who would be admitted in the absence of racial discrimination. . . . Who can differentiate between those who belong and those who do not? The majority of blacks are admitted to the Law School because of discrimination, and because of this policy all are tarred as undeserving. . . . When blacks take positions in the highest places of government, industry, or academia, it is an open question whether their skin color played a part in their advancement. The question itself is the stigma.[37]

Linda Chavez, president of the Center for Equal Opportunity, finds that affirmative action exacerbates racial tensions. She reviewed the research of political scientist Paul Sniderman and survey researcher Thomas Piazza. As Chavez writes, they

found that "merely asking whites to respond to the issue of affirmative action increases significantly the likelihood that they will perceive blacks as irresponsible and lazy." In a poll, they asked one group of whites to evaluate certain images of black people in general. They asked another group of whites the same questions, but this group was first asked to give an opinion on a racial preference program in a nearby state. Forty-three percent of whites who were first asked about racial preferences said that blacks in general were "irresponsible," compared with 26% of whites who were not asked about racial preferences.[38]

As mentioned earlier, when Jennifer Gratz wasn't admitted to the University of Michigan, she quickly thought of a Hispanic classmate with lower grades who'd been accepted. She was incensed that a minority member had taken the place she thought she deserved at the University of Michigan. Affirmative action didn't further the cause of sisterly love.

Let's assume that these two utilitarian considerations are correct. Affirmative action casts doubt on the accomplishments of blacks in general and increases racial tension. I still don't know whether these utilitarian negatives outweigh the utilitarian positives—improvements in organizational performance, social legitimacy, and educational climate.

The Supreme Court's Social Conservative Views on Affirmative Action

The Supreme Court seems more socially conservative than libertarian or utilitarian regarding affirmative action. Social conservatives, like utilitarians, favor the greater good, but unlike utilitarians, social conservatives distinguish the good society from what people actually want at any given time. Utilitarians calculate the good of society as the sum total of happiness or satisfaction among society's members, making no judgments about what makes people happy or satisfied. Social conservatives, by contrast, appeal to standards of value based on their understanding of tradition and human nature. Policies designed to make people happy may harm society if they ignore established insights into requirements for long-term success.

One established insight is that racial classifications promote moral catastrophe. Racial classifications resulted in slavery and were reflected in the phrase "The only good Indian is a dead Indian." Racial classifications were used in the South to deny blacks voting rights and good schools for 100 years after the Civil War. Racial classifications were used primarily on the West Coast to deny equal rights to immigrants from Asia. For many years, for example, an Asian couldn't testify in court against a Caucasian. Racial classifications were used when Japanese Americans were locked up during World War II. Racial classifications were used when blacks were denied federal home loans after World War II and when banks restricted black homeownership to certain "red-lined" areas by refusing to write mortgages for black-owned homes outside those areas. In short, racial classifications have proven poisonous to the body politic. Even when they make most people happy, they warp the soul.

Social conservatives are therefore reluctant to allow racial classifications for any purpose. The Supreme Court reflects this social conservative perspective by making race a "suspect classification." This means any law or state rule classifying people by race must withstand "heightened scrutiny" to see whether it's constitutional. Under heightened scrutiny, the law or rule is unconstitutional unless it's "narrowly tailored" (the minimum use of race necessary) to meet a "compelling public need." Justice Thomas includes self-quotation to emphasize the point in his *Grutter* dissent:

The Constitution abhors classifications based on race, not only because those classifications can harm favored races or are based on illegitimate motives, but also because every time the government places citizens on racial registers and makes race relevant to the provision of burdens or benefits, it demeans us all. "Purchased at the price of immeasurable human suffering, the equal protection principle reflects our Nation's understanding that such classifications ultimately have a destructive impact on the individual and our society."[39]

Accordingly, Thomas points out with satisfaction, the Supreme Court has refused to allow racial classifications even when they promised to provide positive racial role models for school children or might have served the best interests of a child involved in a custody dispute.[40] Our history shows that racial classifications are just too hot to handle.

As noted earlier, a libertarian who favors merit-based admissions must object as much to favoritism toward alumni as to favoritism based on race. Thomas speaks for the Supreme Court in general when he rejects this libertarian view. He writes:

Elite institutions utilize a so-called "legacy" preference to give the children of alumni an advantage in admissions. This, and other, exceptions to a "true" meritocracy give the lie to protestations that merit admissions are in fact the order of the day at the Nation's universities. The Equal Protection Clause does not, however, prohibit the use of unseemly legacy preferences or many other kinds of arbitrary admissions procedures. What the Equal Protection Clause does prohibit are classifications made on the basis of race.[41]

Well, it doesn't prohibit them completely; it just requires that they be narrowly tailored to meet a compelling public need. This is where Thomas parts company with the Court majority in *Grutter*. Thomas saw no compelling public need in the University of Michigan's goal of improving the education of its students by having a more racially diverse student body. The Supreme Court majority, by contrast, found a compelling need in the utilitarian benefits of improved education. Like most Americans, they're susceptible to utilitarian considerations that seem particularly strong. So, racial classifications in affirmative action programs are constitutional if narrowly tailored (they're used to the minimum extent possible) to meet that need.

Because education is improved by diversity of many different kinds—geographic, linguistic, occupational, and so forth—the best way to meet the goal of increasing diversity, the Court reasoned, is to look at each candidate individually to determine her potential contribution to diversity. Racial classifications are narrowly tailored only when they're part of such individualized consideration. In this case, race doesn't predominate; it's just one among several diversity factors. Accordingly, the Court decided that the University of Michigan's law school affirmative action program is constitutional, because although it takes race into account, it individualizes its consideration of all candidates. Barbara Grutter, by then about fifty years old, lost her case.

Justice Thomas dissented from this decision upholding affirmative action and Ms. Grutter expressed her disappointment: "Thirty years ago as a young woman, I entered a sexist work environment, empowered and emboldened by the promise of the equal-opportunity statement, and encouraged by the strides being made—only to find myself 25 years later discriminated against on yet another basis—this time by race."[42]

The undergraduate affirmative action program, by contrast, failed the test of individualized consideration. It automatically awarded twenty points to African Americans, Hispanics, and Native Americans without individualized assessments of each candidate's potential contribution to the kind of diversity that improves the university's educational climate. So, four years after she graduated from her back-up school, the University of Michigan at Dearborn, Jennifer Gratz won her case in the Supreme Court. Justice Thomas joined Justice O'Connor in the majority.

There's irony in the social conservative reluctance to classify people by race. Race shouldn't be used, they think, because it was abused in the past. Other kinds of classifications that deviate from strictly merit-based admissions, by contrast, don't carry this baggage of grave injustice and social turmoil, so they're constitutional. The irony is that the unconscionably horrible past treatment of a group disqualifies its current members from receiving benefits. Current members of groups that weren't treated so badly in the past—alumni and athletes, for example—can be treated favorably today.

Another irony concerns Jennifer Gratz's academic credentials and career. Her complaint about preferences for minorities resulted in the University of Michigan's affirmative action program being declared unconstitutional. But a brochure Gratz received with her admission material noted that 63 percent of admitted freshman in fall 1993 had ACT scores of twenty-seven or better, whereas Gratz's best score was only twenty-five. Gratz was turned down by Notre Dame as well as by the University of Michigan. And her performance at Dearborn was erratic. Some semesters she had a 3.7 grade point average, but others only 2.5 or 2.6.[43] These facts cast doubt on Gratz's belief that she was denied a place at Michigan because minorities were preferred.

In fact, William Bowen and Derek Bok, former presidents of Princeton and Harvard, reported in 1998 that affirmative action for minorities has little effect on the prospects for non-Hispanic Caucasians being admitted to elite colleges and universities. With affirmative action, these applicants have about a 25 percent chance of admission. Without affirmative action, their chances increase to only about 26.5 percent.[44] People like

Gratz, who think their rejection was caused by affirmative action, are often mistaken.

The final irony is that, in spite of her marginal record, Gratz could have attended the University of Michigan if she'd been more persistent. Her disappointing letter in April 1995 included an invitation to join an extended waiting list. Gratz thought this futile, so she didn't fill out and mail back the form. Every Michigan resident offered this opportunity who returned a filled-out form was admitted in fall 1995.[45]

Conclusion: Racial Classifications and Racial Politics

According to U.S. Representative Charles Canady (R-Florida), an opponent of affirmative action, "The emphasis on preferences has diverted attention from the task of addressing the root causes of black Americans' disadvantage." What's needed, he argues, is structural reform of the American elementary and secondary education systems.[46]

I don't know what reforms Representative Canady has in mind, but I know of one program designed to prepare children, including black children, for entrance into elite universities without preferences. But it, too, includes racial classifications.

In my town, Springfield, Illinois, there's a public school for gifted children in grades 1 though 5. Admission rests on three factors: parent recommendation, teacher recommendation, and results on a standardized test, the Naglieri, that children can take in kindergarten. Children are admitted if they score 1.5 standard deviations above the mean, placing them in the top five to seven percent of test takers.

Assuming that intelligence in Springfield is unrelated to race—any other assumption seems racist—the school expects to admit a percentage of minority students—predominantly African Americans in Springfield—similar to the percentage of minority students in the school district. However, Springfield's African Americans don't score as well on the Naglieri as do non-Hispanic Caucasians, and no better test has been found. In order to invite the appropriate percentage of minority children to the school, minority children are compared to one another—the top five or seven percent being invited to Iles School—and non-Hispanic Caucasians are compared to one another—with the same percentage being invited. The result is that cut-off scores differ for the two groups. In 2006, for example, the cut-off score for non-Hispanic Caucasians was 133, whereas for minority children it was 114.

Fortunately, minority children do nearly as well at the school as non-Hispanic Caucasians, which may vindicate their preferential admission. The school is developing minority candidates who won't need affirmative action to enter elite universities. But this wouldn't be possible without some race-sensitive admissions at the start.

There have been few complaints, but I can imagine the parent of a child who wasn't invited to the school because she scored 130 on the Naglieri being upset that a minority child who scored 120 was invited. I wonder what Justice Thomas would say.

We saw in the previous chapter that another use of racial classification, advocated by many Americans, is racial profiling to catch criminals and terrorists. Some people might say that affirmative action is unacceptably unjust but that racial profiling is acceptable because the utilitarian benefits of increased public safety outweigh injustices to members of profiled minority groups. Opponents of racial profiling, by contrast, suspect a double standard. When racial classifications harm the majority, they're unacceptable, but when they only harm minority members, they're all right.

Derrick Jackson suggests this in his *Boston Globe* column. He writes, "African-American actor Danny Glover made a big stink about being passed up by taxicabs he tried to hail in New York City. Glover complained to the city's taxi commission after the episode in which five cabs sped past him, his college-age daughter Mandisa, and her roommate at New York University."[47] Mandisa said it was embarrassing that she sometimes had to ask a white person to hail a cab for her. But taxicab drivers, most of them minority members, were generally unsympathetic, citing occasions when a black person had skipped out on a fare or robbed them. The general sentiment seemed to be, according to Jackson, that black people will just have to put up with being judged by the color of their skin and stranded on street corners while trying to get a cab. "But many of the people who imply this take the opposite perspective when white people complain about being passed up. Take affirmative action. . . . America is deciding that no individual white person should be stranded on the corners of fairness."[48] He concludes:

The forces that say that no individual white person should pay a price for institutionalized racism show their hand when they tell black folks to calm down about cabs. The "color-blind" America, where individuals bear nothing on their backs as they compete for school slots, jobs, and cabs, is reserved for white people. Black people are told to carry the weight of all black criminals on their back.[49]

From this perspective, it's part of white privilege to determine which injustices are unacceptable. Whether it's getting a cab, borrowing money, renting an apartment, buying a car, or getting a job, blacks face documented discrimination, much of it illegal, but there's no great public outcry or debate, and law enforcement is lax. But when whites are harmed by affirmative action, the issue becomes contentious. The huge controversy over affirmative action may reflect white self-interest rather than principled concern about racial classifications.

This response to the affirmative action debate is double-edged. It belittles the concerns of people opposed to affirmative action but at the same time seems to concede that all racial classifications are unjust, a matter on which utilitarians and libertarians remain divided. Social conservatives are more consistently opposed to or wary of racial classifications and affirmative action.

7

Pornography, Child Pornography, and the Internet: Feminism, Social Conservatism, Libertarianism, and Utilitarianism

The Many Faces (and Cheeks) of Pornography

Pornography is a hot-button issue for many people, so I wanted to discuss it. But I didn't have examples of "it" to discuss. I was too embarrassed to linger near the "men's interest" magazine rack at the book store, much less buy anything, so I Googled "pornographic literature" for recommendations. Among them was *Crash*, a novel by J. G. Ballard published in 1973, which was in stock at my local Barnes and Noble.

Our hero James killed a man in a car crash and developed a sexual relationship with the man's widow Helen, who was also injured in the crash. The new lovers have sex in cars. James recalls:

The passenger compartment enclosed us like a machine generating from our sexual act an homunculus of blood, semen and engine coolant. My finger moved into Helen's rectum, feeling the shaft of my penis within her vagina. These slender membranes, like the mucous septum of her nose which I touched with my tongue, were reflected in the glass dials of the instrument panel, the unbroken curve of the windshield.[1]

The book associates sex with violence. James's friend Vaughan is obsessed with killing himself and Elizabeth Taylor in an erotic car crash.

In his vision of a car-crash with the actress, Vaughan was obsessed by many wounds and impacts . . . , by the compound fractures of their thighs impacted against their handbrake mountings, and above all by the wounds to their genitalia, her uterus pierced by the heraldic beak of the manufacturer's medallion, his semen emptying across the luminescent dials that registered for ever the last temperature and fuel levels of the engine. . . . Vaughan . . . dreamed of dying at the moment of her orgasm.[2]

In addition to adult pornography, child pornography concerns many Americans. *New York Times* reporter Kurt Eichenwald writes of child pornography on the Internet:

In the photograph, the model is shown rising out of a bubble bath, suds dripping from her body. Her tight panties and skimpy top are soaked and revealing. She gazes at the viewer, her face showing a wisp of a smile. . . .

In just over seven months, the model has become an online phenomenon. She has thousands of fans from around the world, membership lists show, who pay as much as $30 a month to see images of her. . . .

The model's online name is Sparkle. She is—at most—9 years old.[3]

"Call 911 before viewing!!!" proclaims the site for Sparkle, which shows her in a thong so revealing that she appears to be naked below the waist. . . . "Only 9 years old! Hot!"[4]

This is one of more than two hundred online sites found by the *Times* featuring children who appear to be between the ages of two and twelve.

The Internet has helped youngsters generate pornography, too, Eichenwald reports. Thirteen-year-old Justin Berry hooked up his webcam to his computer hoping to find friends over the Internet. "Instead, he heard only from men who chatted with him by instant message as they watched his image on the Internet." One afternoon in 2000, a

member of his audience sent a proposal: he would pay Justin $50 to sit barechested in front of his webcam for three minutes. The man explained that Justin could receive the money instantly and helped him open an account on PayPal .com, an online payment system.

"I figured, I took off my shirt at the pool for nothing," he said. . . . "So, I was kind of like, what's the difference?"

Justin removed his T-shirt. The men watching him oozed compliments.

So began the secret life of a teenager who was lured into selling images of his body on the Internet over the course of five years.[5]

Gradually the requests became bolder, the cash offers larger: More than $100 for Justin to pose in his underwear. Even more if the boxers came down. The latest request was always just slightly beyond the last, so that each new step never struck him as considerably different. . . .

Unknown to Justin, [these adults] honed their persuasive skills by discussing strategy online, sharing advice on how to induce their targets to go further at each stage.[6]

Who are these adults? "A majority [are] doctors and lawyers, business men and teachers, many of whom work with children on a daily basis."[7]

Justin interacted with other teens online as well. He "sometimes persuaded the girls to masturbate on camera while he did the same."[8] You can't beat that for safe sex.

However, physical molestation followed. "Gilo Tunno, a former Intel employee, gave [Justin] thousands of dollars to visit him in a Las Vegas hotel. . . . There, Justin said, Mr. Tunno began a series of molestings."[9] Other patrons did the same.

But most of Justin's sex work was online. In the course of five years, "this soccer-playing honor roll student was drawn into performing in front of the webcam—undressing, showering, masturbating and even having sex—for an audience of more than 1,500 people who paid him, over the years, hundreds of thousands of dollars."[10]

Paper routes can't compete.

Libertarian and Utilitarian Arguments for Free Speech and Free Press

Pornography worries many people. Yet it's essentially a form of communication, and our political culture generally protects our right to communicate as we wish. The First Amendment to the Constitution says, "Congress shall make no law . . . abridging the freedom of speech, or of the press. . . ."

Justifications for these freedoms are primarily libertarian and utilitarian. Because libertarians champion individual freedom, they reject limitations on what people can think and say. Nineteenth-century English philosopher John Stuart Mill explains in his classic essay "On Liberty": "The sole end for which mankind are warranted individually or collectively, in interfering with the liberty of action of any of their number, is self protection."[11] Mill believed that opinions, and their expression in speech and writing, don't threaten others, so people should be free to think, say, and write what they want. Mill concludes: "If all mankind minus one were of one opinion, and only one person were of the contrary opinion, mankind would be no more justified in silencing that one person, than he, if he had the power, would be justified in silencing mankind."[12]

To these libertarian thoughts, Mill quickly adds a utilitarian consideration:

The peculiar evil of silencing the expression of an opinion is, that it is robbing the human race, posterity as well as the existing generation. . . . If the opinion is right, they are deprived of the opportunity of exchanging error for truth: if wrong, they lose, what is almost as great a benefit, the clearer perception and livelier impression of truth, produced by its collision with error.[13]

In the long run, free speech serves the greatest good of the greatest number.

General distrust of government is an additional libertarian justification of the freedoms of speech and press. Libertarians are wary of government because governments operate through laws that compel obedience, thus reducing individual freedom. They think it's essential that all governments be challenged so people aren't oppressed by unnecessary laws or corrupt officials. Investigation and challenge require the freedoms of speech and press, which help to preserve everyone's liberty.

Again, there's a utilitarian element here. Corrupt, oppressive governments not only trample the individual freedoms that libertarians consider universal human rights, they also lead to unhappiness and unfulfilled desires. The greatest good of the greatest number requires investigative reporting to keep government officials honest.

The Supreme Court's view of the freedoms of speech and press also combine libertarian and utilitarian elements. In 1943, the Court found unconstitutional a West Virginia law that required all school children to pledge allegiance to the flag. Jehovah's Witnesses refused on religious grounds. Justice Robert Jackson, writing for the Court, didn't find the issue of religion as important as the freedom to be different. He wrote:

We can have intellectual individualism and the rich cultural diversities that we owe to exceptional minds only at the price of occasional eccentricity and abnormal attitudes. . . . Freedom to differ is not limited to things that do not matter much. That would be a mere shadow of freedom. The test of its substance is the right to differ as to things that touch the heart of the existing order.

If there is any fixed star in our constitutional constellation, it is that no official, high or petty, can prescribe what shall be orthodox in politics, nationalism, religion, or other matters of opinion or force citizens to confess by word or act their faith therein. If there are any circumstances which permit an exception, they do not now occur to us.[14]

Jackson's reference to the social benefits stemming from "exceptional minds" when we tolerate "eccentricity and abnormal attitudes" is basically utilitarian. Who knows, for example, what beneficial insights into the human condition will flow from sexualized accounts of car crashes? The position Jackson advocates also gives libertarians what they want: the freedom to be different, which they consider a basic human right.

Feminist Arguments against Pornography

Some feminists would nevertheless ban all pornography. Feminists believe that no one should be disadvantaged simply because she's a woman. Many feminists believe pornography harms women, so they would ban it. But they differentiate pornography from what they call *erotica*. Gloria Steinem explains:

> "Erotica" is rooted in "eros" or passionate love, and thus in the idea of positive choice, free will, the yearning for a particular person. . . . "Pornography" begins with a root "porno," meaning "prostitution" or "female captives"; . . . the subject is not mutual love, or love at all, but domination and violence against women. . . .
>
> Perhaps one could simply say that erotica is about sexuality, but pornography is about power and sex-as-weapon—in the same way we have come to understand that rape is about violence, and not really about sexuality at all.[15]

Feminists advocate the right of women to control their lives and enjoy sex. Erotic depictions of sex can foster women's self-expression. Most feminists therefore reject social conservative views that seem prudish, such as Attorney General John Ashcroft's staff using drapes to cover a statue, "Spirit of Justice," that has stood in the Great Hall at the Justice Department since 1936. One breast of the female statue is bare.[16] Feminist philosopher Helen Longino writes:

> I define pornography as *verbal or pictorial explicit representations of sexual behavior that,* in the words of the Commission on Obscenity and Pornography, *have as a distinguishing characteristic "the degrading and demeaning portrayal of the role and status of the human female . . . as a mere sexual object to be exploited and manipulated sexually."* In pornographic books, magazines, and films, women are represented as passive and as slavishly dependent upon men. The role of female characters is limited to the provision of sexual services to men. . . . While the sexual objectification of women is common to all pornography, women are the recipients of even worse treatment in violent pornography, in which women characters are killed, tortured, gang-raped, mutilated, bound, and otherwise abused, as a means of providing sexual stimulation or pleasure to the male character.[17]
>
> What is wrong with pornography, then, is its degrading and dehumanizing portrayal of women (and *not* its sexual content). . . . Pornography lies explicitly about women's sexuality, and through such lies fosters more lies about our humanity, our dignity, and our personhood.[18]

On this understanding, I'm uncertain if depictions of sex in the novel *Crash* are pornographic. The book is written from a male perspective, sex goes with violent car crashes that sometimes kill women, and the only three-dimensional aspects of female characters are their orifices. But no one is raped.

Longino would object to *Crash* if, like pornography in general, in her view, it inspires violence against women. She disagrees with the 1970 Presidential Commission on Obscenity and Pornography, which found no link between pornography and criminal behavior. She claims "a growing body of research is documenting . . . a correlation between exposure to pornographic materials and the committing of sexually abusive or violent acts against women."[19]

Writer Andrea Dworkin gives examples in *Letter from a War Zone* of what she considers pornography-generated rape. One concerns a thirteen-year-old girl.

Three deer hunters, in the woods, looking at pornography magazines, looked up and saw the blond child. "There's a live one," one said. The three hunters chased the child, gang-raped her, pistol-whipped her breasts, all the while calling her names from the pornography magazines scattered at their campsite—Golden Girl, Little Godiva, and so on.[20]

Dworkin writes also of a Native American woman whose rape, like many others, she claims, was modeled on the pornographic video game *Custer's Revenge*. The men referred explicitly to the video as they raped her.

Ted Bundy, who was executed in 1989 for the sexually related killing of twelve-year-old Kimberly Leach said: "I take full responsibility for whatever I've done and all the things that I've done. The question and the issue is how this kind of [pornographic] literature contributed and helped mold and shape these kinds of violent behavior." He claimed pornography broke down his "last vestiges of restraint."[21]

In 2006, journalist John Hughes reported in the *Christian Science Monitor* that Craig Roger Gregerson, accused of luring five-year-old Destiny Norton to his property, suffocating her and then abusing her dead body, blamed pornography. Hughes considers this evidence that "violent material in magazines and books, on videos and television . . . foster violence, child molestation, and sex crimes in those exposed to it." He points to

serious research that proves this to be the case. For instance, the Rand Corp. in Pittsburg has just published in . . . *Pediatrics* the results of a survey indicating that teens who listen to music full of raunchy, sexual lyrics start having sex sooner than those who prefer other songs. . . . Corydon Hammond, codirector of the Sex and Marital Therapy Clinic at the University of Utah says: "I don't think I've ever yet seen an adult sex offender who was not involved with pornography."

Judith Reisman, author of "The Psychopharmacology of Pictorial Pornography," sees a direct causal link between pornography and sex crimes.

"In many cases I don't think we have any problem saying pornography caused [the sex offense]. We have tons of data," she writes. . . . "It's not that pornography acts like a drug. It is a drug."[22]

In light of the dangers, especially to women, posed by pornography, some feminists advocate legal penalties for its production, sale, and dissemination. Texas Law School Professor Michael Weiss and Cato Institute policy analyst Cathy Young explain:

In 1983, the City of Minneapolis contracted with [Catharine] MacKinnon and [Andrea] Dworkin to draft a . . . pornography code . . . that would make "pornography" a violation of women's civil rights. Any materials in which "women's body parts . . . are exhibited such that women are reduced to their parts" or "women are presented as whores by nature" were defined as pornographic. Essentially, the law allowed any woman who felt that certain "degrading" sexually explicit materials violated her civil rights to sue the producers and distributors of pornography for monetary damages or to seek an injunction on the distribution of the materials. In addition, it gave women who had appeared in pornographic materials the right to sue for "coercion into pornography."[23]

Feminist Arguments for Pornographic Freedom

Feminists for pornographic freedom opposed this anti-pornography ordinance on four grounds. First, censorship to protect women has in the past contributed to their subordination. Second, pornography can help women's self-expression and self-realization. Third, anti-pornography feminists treat many women like children, which is degrading. Finally, pornography doesn't cause violence.

Nadine Strossen, law professor and president of the ACLU, makes the first point—censorship to protect women has contributed to their subordination. Censorship tends to harm people who lack power, and women lack power compared to men.

All censorship measures throughout history have been used disproportionately to silence those who are relatively disempowered and who seek to challenge the status quo. Since women and feminists are in that category, it is predictable that any censorship scheme—even one purportedly designed to further their interests—

would in fact be used to suppress expression that is especially important to their interests.[24]

The history of feminist struggles illustrates this point. After the Civil War, a purity campaign led by women reformers and physicians was designed to protect women from the ravages of men's insatiable appetite for sex. Banning contraceptives as obscene materials was part of their program, historian Sheila Rothman tells us:

> The social purity legislation presupposed . . . that the male was a savage beast who would subvert and corrupt women in order to satisfy his animal impulses. Contraceptive practices were so reprehensible precisely because they separated sexual activity from procreation, thus enabling the male to indulge all his lusts while free of the responsibility of rearing children. Contraception would turn woman into a "slave to her husband's desires."[25]

These women were joined in their crusade by Anthony Comstock who pushed through the enactment in 1873 of legislation, soon called the Comstock Act, which categorized all birth control information and devices as obscene and mandated their seizure. Comstock raids impeded the early twentieth-century work of feminist birth-control advocate Margaret Sanger.

More recent events illustrate the same tendency, Strossen claims. In 1992, Canada adopted restrictive legislation using a definition of pornography like that advocated by MacKinnon and Dworkin. It outlaws "sexually explicit expression that is 'dehumanizing' or 'degrading' to women. The Canadian authorities have seized upon this powerful tool," Strossen contends, "to suppress lesbian and gay publications and feminist works, and to harass lesbian and gay bookstores and women's bookstores."[26]

Indianapolis adopted the ordinance originally drafted for Minneapolis. In the ensuing court challenge, the Feminist Anti-Censorship Task Force claimed that pornography opens new possibilities for women's self-expression and self-realization: "The range of feminist imagination and expression in the realm of sexuality has barely begun to find voice. Women need the freedom and the socially recognized space to appropriate for themselves the robustness of what traditionally has been male language. Laws such as the one under challenge here would constrict that freedom."[27]

Author Sallie Tisdale also reproaches anti-pornography feminists, writing:

I take this personally, the effort to repress material I enjoy—to tell me how wrong it is for me to enjoy it. Anti-pornography legislation is directed at me: as a user, as a writer. Catharine MacKinnon and Andrea Dworkin . . . look down on me and shake a finger: Bad girl. Mustn't touch. That branch of feminism tells me my very thoughts are bad. Pornography tells me the opposite: that none of my thoughts are bad, that anything goes. . . . The message of pornography . . . is that our sexual selves are real.[28]

The ACLU's Strossen suggests reconsidering one of the depictions that anti-pornography feminists would outlaw as degrading to women:

the "come shot," in which a man ejaculates on a woman's body. In many such scenes, the woman then smears the sperm over her body and licks it. Although pro-censorship feminists routinely cite these as archetypal images of female degradation . . . , Canadian writer Wendy McElroy has suggested . . . that makers of commercial erotic films often insert "come shots" simply to prove that the male *did* ejaculate, that he was "into" the sex. Likewise, the woman's response of spreading the sperm over her body or tasting it would simply demonstrate that she, too, was fully, enthusiastically involved in the sexual encounter.

Many women viewers may be particularly interested in seeing come shots because men's ejaculations are usually hidden from them, occurring inside the woman's own body. As McElroy observes, to such women, the sight of male ejaculation "is as elusive as a glimpse of breast or lace panty must be to a pubescent boy."[29]

Women show their interest in pornography, according to Strossen, by constituting, either singly or as part of a couple, "more than 40 percent of the adult videotape rental audience." Strossen continues, "In 1987 two social scientists conducting a survey of over 26,000 female readers of *Redbook* magazine found that nearly half the respondents said they regularly watch pornographic films."[30]

Some pro-pornography feminists complain also that the model ordinance drafted by Dworkin and MacKinnon for Minneapolis and Indianapolis is paternalistic and condescending toward women. Women appearing in pornography are presumed to have been coerced, and none of the following will count as disproving coercion:

That the person knew that the purpose of the acts or events in question was to make pornography; or . . . that the person showed no resistance or appeared to cooperate actively in the photographic sessions or in the sexual events that produced pornography; or . . . that the person signed a contract, or made statements affirming a willingness to cooperate in the production of pornography; or . . . that no physical force, threats, or weapons were used in the making of the pornography; or . . . that the person was paid.[31]

Wendy McElroy, former president of Feminists for Free Expression/ Canada, comments:

Consent by the woman was rendered impossible. The author of the Ordinance . . . , Catharine MacKinnon, later explained that "in the context of unequal power (between the sexes), one needs to think about the meaning of consent— whether it is a meaningful concept at all." A male-controlled society made it impossible for women to consent. Women who thought they agreed were so damaged by male society that they were not able to give true consent.[32]

In case that's not enough, the model ordinance also states: "Children are incapable of consenting to engage in pornographic conduct, even absent physical coercion, and therefore require special protection. By the same token, the physical and psychological well-being of women ought to be afforded comparable protection."[33]

There's the smoking pop-gun of paternalism.

Feminist defenders of a woman's right to choose pornography dispute claims that link pornography to violence against women. McElroy writes the following on studies alleged to show that pornography causes violence:

The standards used and the conclusions drawn usually depend on the bias of researchers and those who commission the research.

For example, in 1983, the Metropolitan Toronto Task Force on Violence Against Women commissioned Thelma McCormack to study pornography's connection to sexual aggression. McCormack's study indicated that pornography might be cathartic and, so, it might reduce the incidence of rape. Her report was discarded and reassigned to David Scott, a non-feminist committed to anti-pornography, who produced more palatable conclusions.[34]

The catharsis idea was expressed in plainer language by Mathew Gever, writing in *Daily Bruin*, a student newspaper at UCLA. He asks, "Who is going to sexually assault a person after they have just masturbated in their living room?"[35]

Skepticism about research linking pornography to sexual violence comes also from Feminists for Free Expression. They refer to the Meese Commission mandated by Ronald Reagan to study pornography in 1985. Unlike a similar commission in 1970, the Meese Commission claimed some link between pornography and violence. Yet one of the commissioners said, "I've been working with sex offenders for 10 years, and have reviewed the scientific literature and I don't think a causal link exists." The Feminists for Free Expression continue:

No research, including the Surgeon General's report, finds a link between "kinky" or "degrading" images and violence. . . . The derailed impulses of child abusers and rapists are caused by childhood traumas. "They are not," wrote leading researcher John Money, "borrowed from movies, books or other people."[36]

In the light of anti-pornography claims, I conclude there are dueling experts on this issue.

The Court's Utilitarian/Social Conservative View of Obscenity

Although adult pornography is legal in the United States—hence the attempt to ban it in Indianapolis—obscenity is not. Justice William Brennan explained the Court's view in 1957: "All ideas having even the slightest redeeming social importance—unorthodox ideas, controversial ideas, even ideas hateful to the prevailing climate of opinion—have the full protection of the guaranties" of free speech and free press. This echoes the views of John Stuart Mill and Justice Jackson. It sounds libertarian, but Brennan adds qualifications that highlight utilitarian considerations. He claims that obscene speech, because it's "utterly without redeeming social importance," is not protected, and has never been protected, by the First Amendment. Rather than vindicate the absolute right to free speech favored by libertarians, Brennan endorses freedom only to such speech as may be socially useful, a somewhat utilitarian position. Obscenity is defined as speech without social importance, so it's not protected.

Brennan identified obscenity as "material which deals with sex in a manner appealing to the prurient interest . . . , i.e., material having a tendency to excite lustful thoughts." He endorsed the American Law Institute's Model Penal Code definition of "prurient interest" as "a shameful or morbid interest in nudity, sex, or excretion [that] goes substantially beyond customary limits of candor in description or representation of such matters."[37] Clarifying the Court's position in 1966, Brennan wrote:

three elements must coalesce: it must be established that a) the dominant theme of the material taken as a whole appeals to a prurient interest in sex; b) the material is patently offensive because it affronts contemporary community standards relating to the description or representation of sexual matters; and c) the material is utterly without redeeming social value.[38]

Confined to matters of sex but otherwise reiterated in 1973 by Chief Justice Warren Burger in *Miller v. California*,[39] this three-part test for obscenity is known as "the *Miller* test." It's not exactly utilitarian, because the slightest chance of social value makes the speech protected, even if that value is outweighed by social harm, and the speech reduces overall good in society. The bias of the *Miller* test is toward, but not all the way to, the libertarian ideal of free speech as an inherent right.

When Justice Brennan abandoned this three-part formula in favor of full libertarian First Amendment protection of speech, including obscene material, Chief Justice Burger appealed to social conservative thought to justify states outlawing obscenity. He noted that the Court has never endorsed the libertarian proposal to allow consenting adults to do whatever they want so long as no one else is directly harmed.

The state statute books are replete with constitutionally unchallenged laws against prostitution, suicide, voluntary self-mutilation, brutalizing "bare fist" prize fights, and duels, although these crimes may only directly involve "consenting adults. . . ." As Professor Irving Kristol has observed: "Bearbaiting and cockfighting are prohibited only in part out of compassion for the suffering animals; the main reason they were abolished was because it was felt that they debased and brutalized the citizenry who flocked to witness such spectacles."[40]

Burger writes that states are free to "conclude that a sensitive, key relationship of human existence, central to family life, community welfare, and the development of human personality, can be debased and distorted by crass commercial exploitation of sex."[41]

It's unclear if anti-pornography feminists, focused on depictions of women subjected to violence and degradation, would agree to ban all "crass commercial exploitation of sex," as some of this may be erotica, not pornography. More reliable allies of the social conservative view are anti-pornography theocrats. For example, Section 2354 of the Catechism of the Catholic Church reads:

Pornography consists in removing real or simulated sexual acts from the intimacy of the partners, in order to display them deliberately to third parties. It offends against chastity because it perverts the conjugal act, the intimate giving of spouses to each other. It does grave injury to the dignity of its participants (actors, vendors, the public), since each one becomes an object of base pleasure and illicit profit for others. . . . It is a grave offense. Civil authorities should prevent the production and distribution of pornographic materials.[42]

The Catholic Church seems to want legislation outlawing erotica and pornography as well as obscenity. Other theocrats may agree.

Lined up against free speech, then, are feminists, social conservatives, and theocrats whose views overlap, but don't coincide. Some theocrats would ban all explicit depictions of sex but some feminists only depictions that degrade women. Social conservatives are divided. Irving Kristol might have agreed with theocrats to ban all explicit depictions of sex, but Chief Justice Burger uses Kristol's social conservative insight to argue only against legalized obscenity. He doesn't think erotica and pornography smear the body politic enough to justify prohibition.

The Court's Libertarian Approach to Pornography

In contrast to their view of obscenity, the Supreme Court's approach to pornography, like their approach to free speech in general, combines libertarian and utilitarian elements. Even depictions of sex that are violent, degrading, and disgusting are protected by the First Amendment if they're not obscene—that is, if they have some artistic merit or social value taken as a whole.

The Indianapolis Anti-Pornography Ordinance drafted by Dworkin and MacKinnon doesn't follow this standard. Federal Circuit Judge Frank Easterbrook wrote for the United States Court of Appeals, Seventh Circuit:

The Indianapolis ordinance does not refer to the prurient interest, to offensiveness, or to the standards of the community. It demands attention to particular depictions, not to the work judged as a whole. It is irrelevant under the ordinance whether the work has literary, artistic, political, or scientific value.[43]

In short, the ordinance doesn't pass the Supreme Court's *Miller* test for censorship. Worse yet, Easterbrook points out:

The ordinance discriminates on the grounds of the content of the speech. Speech treating women in the approved way—in sexual encounters "premised on equality"—is lawful no matter how sexually explicit. Speech treating women in the disapproved way—as submissive in matters sexual or as enjoying humiliation—is unlawful no matter how significant the literary, artistic, or political qualities of the work taken as a whole. The state may not ordain preferred viewpoints in this way. The Constitution forbids the state to declare one perspective right and silence opponents.[44]

The judge actually agreed with MacKinnon that pornography harms women as a group, but such harm makes no difference. It's still protected speech. He writes:

Depictions of subordination tend to perpetuate subordination. The subordinate status of women in turn leads to affront and lower pay at work, insult and injury at home, battery and rape on the streets. . . . Yet this simply demonstrates the power of pornography as speech. . . . If the fact that speech plays a role in a process of conditioning were enough to permit governmental regulation, that would be the end of freedom of speech.[45]

Instead, it was the end of the Indianapolis ordinance.

Contrast this 1985 pornography case with the 1991 public nudity controversy, also in Indiana, discussed in the introduction. Darlene Miller wanted to dance nude at the Kitty Kat Lounge in South Bend, but was required by a state law barring public nudity to wear pasties and a G-string. In light of the 1985 pornography ruling it seems that if Ms. Miller had danced nude for the camera, no one could object. Her dancing was not called obscene, and in works of art, nudity by itself doesn't make something obscene. So, captured images of her nude dancing would be at worst pornography, which is protected by the First Amendment. Does this mean that if she were to dance nude on closed-circuit TV out of the direct sight of Kitty Kat patrons, her dancing could legally be delivered to patrons on huge TV screens? Inquiring minds want to know.

Children Appearing in Pornography

Although pornography of adults, by adults, and for adults, shall not perish for lack of First Amendment protection, child pornography enjoys no such benefit. Children can't legally appear in pornography or view pornography.

Consider first children who appear in pornography. "Paul Ferber," Supreme Court Justice Byron White wrote in 1982, was "the proprietor of a Manhattan bookstore specializing in sexually oriented products [who] sold two films to an undercover police officer. The films are devoted almost exclusively to depicting young boys masturbating." Ferber challenged the constitutionality of the New York statute prohibiting the sale and distribution of child pornography, claiming the works were not obscene and were therefore constitutionally protected under the *Miller* test. However, the Supreme Court upheld his conviction because the state has a right to protect its children, and children visually depicted in such works are liable to be harmed. White writes:

The distribution of photographs and films depicting sexual activity by juveniles is intrinsically related to the sexual abuse of children in at least two ways. First, the materials produced are a permanent record of the children's participation and the harm to the child is exacerbated by their circulation. Second, the distribution network for child pornography must be closed if the production of material which requires the sexual exploitation of children is to be effectively controlled.[46]

White's second point is that outlawing the distribution of pornography reduces incentives to produce it. Less child pornography produced means fewer children abused in the production process. The *Miller* test doesn't apply because children are involved.

No major political philosophy objects to such protections for children. Libertarian freedom is for adults; child pornography is assumed by utilitarians to cause more harm than good; and feminists of all kinds are as interested as others in protecting children from abuse. Pornographic images of Sparkle and Justin Berry are illegal.

Technological developments since 1982 complicate matters. Children can't appear in pornography. But what if, through digital magic, they only appear to appear? Congress answered this question in 1996 with the Child Pornography Prevention Act (CPPA). Supreme Court Justice Anthony Kennedy explains:

The CPPA extends the federal prohibition against child pornography to sexually explicit images that appear to depict minors but were produced without using any real children. The statute prohibits . . . possessing or distributing these images, which may be created by using adults who look like minors or by using computer imaging. The new technology, according to Congress, makes it possible to create realistic images of children who do not exist.[47]

For the Court majority, the issue was whether children are directly harmed by such pornography as they are harmed when appearing actually, not just virtually, in pornographic works. One virtual technique, all agreed, harms children directly. Images of actual children engaged in age-appropriate behavior can be electronically morphed to make it appear the children are engaged in sexual activity. Such a record of apparent sexual activity can follow children and harm them psychologically and socially. The CPPA is constitutional insofar as it bans such virtual child pornography.

Other virtual techniques, however, don't harm children directly. One technique is to use older actors whose images are electronically morphed to make them look like juveniles. Another is to generate images of children out of thin silicon without any human subjects at all. Such works don't harm children directly, because no children are involved in production and no real children are depicted. The reasoning in *New York v. Ferber* doesn't apply. Does the First Amendment protect such works?

The CPPA can ban them if they're obscene, but Justice Kennedy thinks the CPPA outlaws material that passes the *Miller* test. "The materials [banned by the CPPA] need not appeal to the prurient interest. . . . The CPPA applies to a picture in a psychology manual, as well as a movie depicting the horrors of sexual abuse."[48] Kennedy also cites the movie *Traffic*, Academy Award nominee for Best Picture in 2001. It

portrays a teenager, identified as a 16-year-old, who becomes addicted to drugs. The viewer sees the degradation of her addiction, which in the end leads her to a filthy room to trade sex for drugs. The year before, *American Beauty* won the Academy Award for Best Picture. . . . In the course of the movie, a teenage girl . . . yields herself to the gratification of a middle-aged man. . . . Whether or not [these] films . . . violate the CPPA, they explore themes within the wide sweep of the statute's prohibitions.[49]

Kennedy concludes: "The CPPA cannot be read to prohibit [only] obscenity," and works directly harming children.[50]

Defenders of the statute claim that protecting children is so important that even nonobscene material can be banned if it harms children indirectly. Kennedy explains the alleged indirect harms of virtual child pornography, quoting from congressional findings:

Pedophiles might use the materials to encourage children to participate in sexual activity. "[A] child who is reluctant to engage in sexual activity with an adult, or to pose for sexually explicit photographs, can sometimes be convinced by viewing depictions of other children 'having fun' participating in such activity. . . ." Furthermore, pedophiles might "whet their own sexual appetites" with the pornographic images, "thereby increasing the creation and distribution of child pornography and the sexual abuse and exploitation of children. . . ." In addition. . . , computer generated images . . . can make it harder to prosecute pornographers who do use real minors. . . . As imaging technology improves. . . , it becomes more difficult to prove that a particular picture was produced using actual children.[51]

The Court majority found these rationales unpersuasive. Regarding pedophiles using virtual child pornography to seduce children, Kennedy writes: "There are many things innocent in themselves . . . , such as cartoons, video games, and candy, that might be used for immoral purposes, yet we would not expect those to be prohibited because they can be misused."[52] Regarding virtual child pornography encouraging pedophiles "to engage in illegal conduct," Kennedy states:

The mere tendency of speech to encourage unlawful acts is not a sufficient reason for banning it. . . . First Amendment freedoms are most in danger when the government seeks to control thought or to justify its laws for that impermissible end. The right to think is the beginning of freedom, and speech must be protected from the government because speech is the beginning of thought.

To preserve these freedoms, and to protect speech for its own sake, the Court's First Amendment cases draw vital distinctions between words and deeds, between ideas and conduct.[53]

Finally, if virtual images become indistinguishable from real images of children, Kennedy reasons, the crime of child pornography will diminish as people avoid prosecution by preferring virtual to real children in their pornographic works. This might complicate prosecution of genuine child pornography, but it's good on the whole.

In sum, pornography in which images of children don't correspond to any real children is protected by the First Amendment along with adult pornography.

Congress responded in 2003 to this Court opinion with the Protect Act, which outlaws *pandering* child pornography. According to the act, whether the child pornography is virtual (and no children were involved in its production), real, or non-existent (but advertised as existing), it is illegal to offer or request child pornography. Under this statute, "a person offering material as child pornography can be convicted on either of two grounds: for believing that the material depicts real children, or for intending to convince a would-be recipient that it does."[54] In 2008 the Supreme Court declared this statute constitutional.[55] The First Amendment still protects the generation and possession of virtual child pornography that involves no real children, but it does not allow soliciting or offering such works, or any other works, as if they depicted *real* children engaged in sexual behavior. The additional restrictions of speech in the Protect Act concern not the content of depictions of child sexuality but the content of speech concerning these depictions. Trade in virtual child pornography is still legal so long as it is clear in all discussions of it that it is merely virtual.

Children's Access to Pornography

Children are harmed, many people believe, by access to pornography. They can be excluded from adult bookstores rather easily, but the Internet poses greater problems. Mark Laaser, a recovering sex addict and executive director and cofounder of the Christian Alliance for Sexual Recovery, testified before the House of Representatives in 2000 about the problem of children's access to pornography over the Internet. He said:

Recently, for example, parents that I know told me the story of how their 8-year-old daughter was researching the fairy tale Cinderella on the web. She entered Cinderella in the search engine of her on-line service provider. She was given a number of options. One of them included the title, "See Cinderella for Yourself." This little girl of course wanted to see Cinderella, so she clicked in. She was immediately confronted with the picture of a nude female using an artificial penis to stimulate herself.[56]

I wonder if the prince knows.

Congress addressed this problem with the Communications Decency Act (CDA) in 1996. It criminalized sending "obscene or indecent" material over the Internet "knowing the recipient . . . is under 18 years of age." It also criminalized "the knowing sending or displaying of patently offensive messages in a manner that is available to a person who is under 18 years of age." Finally, it outlaws anyone knowingly allowing telecommunications equipment under his control to be used in the above ways.[57]

The Supreme Court found this law unconstitutional. First, the terms "indecent" and "patently offensive" aren't defined clearly enough to give people fair notice of what the act prohibits. For example, Justice John Paul Stevens wrote for the Court:

Under the CDA, a parent allowing her 17-year old to use the family computer to obtain information on the Internet that she, in her parental judgment, deems appropriate could face a lengthy prison term. . . . Similarly, a parent who sent his 17-year-old college freshman information on birth control via e-mail could be incarcerated even though neither he, his child, nor anyone in their home community, found the material "indecent" or "patently offensive," if the college town's community thought otherwise.[58]

Second, the CDA would interfere with communication among adults that's protected by the First Amendment. There's no way to ensure that a "patently offensive" message, whatever that may be, will not reach a minor, and every sender knows this. Therefore, Justice Stevens concludes, "the sender must be charged with knowing that one or more minors will likely view . . . [any] indecent message" she might send. This "would surely burden communication among adults."[59]

Third, parents can protect their children without limiting free speech among adults. Stevens quotes the District Court's finding that "currently available *user based* software suggests that a reasonably effective method by which *parents* can prevent their children from accessing sexually explicit and other material which *parents* may believe is inappropriate for their children will soon be widely available."[60] Solveig Bernstein, assistant director of telecommunications and technology studies at the libertarian Cato Institute, writes: "Products such as CyberSitter, CyberPatrol, and SurfWatch . . . restrict the type of Web searches that a child can perform and restrict visits to unrated content by watching for words and phrases typical of sexually explicit material."[61]

Stevens concludes: "The Government may not 'reduce the adult population . . . to . . . only what is fit for children'. . . . 'Regardless of the strength of the government's interest' in protecting children, 'the level of discourse reaching a mailbox . . . cannot be limited to that which would be suitable for a sandbox.'"[62]

Some Success in Fighting Pornography

Although obscenity is not protected by the First Amendment, pornography is protected; even pornography that depicts children, if no real kids were involved in production. Nevertheless, pornography can be fought within constitutional limits. One example is the Children's Internet Protection Act (CIPA). Chief Justice William Rehnquist explains. "Under CIPA, a public library may not receive federal assistance to provide Internet access unless it installs software to block images that constitute obscenity or child pornography, and to prevent minors from obtaining access to material that is harmful to them."[63] Rehnquist and the Court majority found this limitation on federal funding to be constitutional.

First, Congress isn't constitutionally obligated to fund pornography.[64] Second, libraries remain in control of their collections, both traditional and electronic. If they want to give easy Internet access to all material, they can do so, but without federal money. Third, libraries don't create what the Court calls a public forum where limits on the content of speech are unconstitutional. Libraries exist for the benefit of patrons, not for the benefit of people wanting to communicate ideas to others. This is why libraries violate no one's rights when they exercise their traditional function of choosing what to include in their collections. Most exclude pornography anyway, so excluding it from their Internet access raises no First Amendment issues.[65] Finally, any adult patron can have any library unblock a Web site for her, no questions asked. Adult patrons are therefore not denied information they seek.[66] Anti-pornography won this battle.

Jay Nordlinger, writing in *National Review* in 2001, explains some additional ideas to reduce the negative influence of Internet porn. He writes:

Some anti-porn activists [suggest] a separate "domain" for Internet porn. . . . The domain would be ".xxx." So, just as we have ".edu" for educational websites. . . , we would have the triple X for pornography. This would be sort of an Internet zoning law, according to which all porn sites would be ghettoized.[67]

Another idea is to pressure corporations. Nordlinger agrees with Pat Trueman—"late of the Justice Department, now with the American Family Association"—that "Yahoo is home to thousands of sex 'clubs' that disseminate manifestly illegal pornography." Trueman wants prosecution, but in the meantime public pressure is having some effect. "The company had planned to sell porn videos over the Net, but changed its mind in the wake of negative publicity and a letter campaign."[68]

Nordlinger cites Bob Rowling as a hero of the anti-porn community because he banned pornography from the Omni Hotels when he bought them in 1996. Unfortunately for him, "that action cost him dearly in revenues." This tells us something about consumers. "Ultimately," Nordlinger writes,

our country probably needs to be "re-moralized". . . . And Americans need to care about this "pervasive presence." Think what happened to smoking in America when people generally, and elites in particular, became interested: It is now almost a pariah activity. . . . Illegal porn can be prosecuted, and legal porn can be discouraged. In this realm, a little stigmatizing can go a long way.[69]

In 2006, the *Times* reported pedophile dismay at the disappearance of Web sites featuring nude children, which is progress in the fight against illegal child pornography.[70] Although she is clothed, images of Sparkle are also illegal, because they emphasize sexuality.[71] The same legal attention to sites like that one may reduce their presence.

Conclusion

Pornographic images of children are illegal. Justin Berry was convinced by reporter Kurt Eichenwald to turn over incriminating material to the FBI to assist their pursuit of adult offenders. Unfortunately, Sparkle's identity and future remain unknown.

Some dangers to children posed by the Internet can't be eliminated. Eichenwald reports that pedophiles, who used to be isolated individuals, now gather at Internet chat rooms to champion the view that having sex with adults is good for kids and to exchange tips on getting close to children. Although these groups condemn forcible rape, "acts of molestation are often celebrated as demonstrations of love." Consider this case:

"My daughter and I have a healthy close relationship," a person with the screen name Sonali posted. "We have been in a 'consensual sexual relationship' almost two months now."
    The daughter, Sonali wrote, is 10. Whatever guilt Sonali felt for the relationship was eased by the postings of other pedophiles. "I am so happy to find this site," Sonali wrote. "I thought having a sexual attraction to my daughter was bad. I now do not feel guilty or conflicted."[72]

Sonali can be prosecuted for raping his daughter if he's caught, but given our free-speech heritage, it's really inconceivable that conversations encouraging such actions could be illegal. We're too libertarian to give the state power over what perspectives can be put into words. Banned views are too likely to include some associated with oppressed groups or the political party out of power.

Tensions remain between the values of free speech and clean speech, endangering the uncommon alliance of some feminists with social conservatives. For example, some blocking software parents can buy to shield their families from pornography incorporate anti-feminist bias. Langdon Winner, professor in the Department of Science and Technology Studies at Rensselaer Polytechnic Institute, writes:

Cybersitter . . . makes it impossible for computers to access the home page of the National Organization for Women. Cybersitter was developed by SolidOak Software in close cooperation with Focus on the Family—a right-wing organization. . . . Thus, Cybersitter is actually an extension of Focus on the Family's anti-feminist, antigay, anti-abortion rights agenda.[73]

Still, social conservatives, along with some feminists and theocrats, would outlaw all pornography to promote traditional morality and to improve safety for women and children, whereas libertarians, some feminists, and most utilitarians oppose legal enforcement of traditional sexual norms and favor freedom over safety.

But how far should freedom extend? If no one should be disadvantaged simply because she's a woman, as feminists claim, and many women want freedom to express themselves sexually in deeds as well as in words, what options should be available to women who have unwanted pregnancies? Abortion is our next topic.

8

Abortion: Libertarianism, Feminism, Communitarianism, Theocracy, and Social Conservatism

Abortion Stories

It was February 1936 when they got the news. Married only five months, she was pregnant. They wanted children eventually, but it was the middle of the Great Depression, and they couldn't afford a place of their own. They stayed some months with his parents and some with her mother, recently widowed. Trained as a commercial artist, Alberta painted ties; trained as an engineer, Irv worked for his older brother selling auto parts. Each earned $15 to $25 per week.

Lucky for them, Alberta had an aunt whose third husband was a doctor practicing in Toronto. Alberta took the train alone to visit her aunt; Irv stayed home working; husbands weren't welcome companions or observers. When she came back, Alberta was no longer pregnant and the couple continued their search for the American dream. My older brother was born two-and-a-half years later.

My parents agreed on most political matters because my father had strong opinions and my mother didn't. She was passionate only about abortion. She'd say, "A woman's abortion is nobody else's damn business." (Ladies didn't say "damn" very loud.)

Here's a more recent abortion story by Eliza:

I'm not sorry about the abortion, but I am sorry for the conception. I was 19 years old, a sophomore in college, and searching for love and acceptance in men. Looking back, I think mostly I wanted to feel attractive and sexy. An old friend came into town, Dan. . . . We had unprotected intercourse, but he pulled out. It was the mentality of "it'll never happen to me."

Weeks after he had left town, I had to leave one of my classes to violently throw up outside. That was when I first had fears. . . . A few days later . . . one of my closest friends . . . drove me to Safeway and bought the tests for me and then we holed up in a bathroom stall of our church—both tests were positive.

So important to my experience is my family and how blessed I am to have them. I went to my sister and we sat on her front porch and cried together. And then we went home to our parents' house and told them. . . . All I could do was bury my face in my mother's chest and tell her how sorry I was.

In the coming days, I felt numb. Dan was still calling and writing letters, but I was short with him each time he called until he finally stopped contacting me at all. It was my burden, my decision. . . . I have never spoken to him again and I never want to.

I knew I was supposed to make a decision, but I felt numb and scared and separated from all my peers. Looking back, I realize now how rare and amazing it is that I have a family who I always knew would support my decision, whatever it might be. . . . My mother researched clinics and she and my sister went with me to the appointment. I remember that the clinic seemed scary and that my doctor had kind, sad eyes. . . . Afterward, the three of us drove home in the sunshine and my mother bought matching necklaces for us, so that we would always remember what we had gone through as a family.

I left the church I was attending because they pronounced abortion as a sin. The spiritual aspects of my abortion were only between myself and God and it angered me that the church thought they were entitled an opinion also. I returned to the open and affirming church I was raised in and found a hero in the pastor. I told him my story and later that year he officiated over my marriage. The man I married became my boyfriend at the end of the same year I had my abortion. We had only been dating a month when I told him, and when he held me while I cried, I knew he might be someone I could marry.

I made my choice and I do not regret it and I know I never will. I am a better, more empathetic person because of it. . . . I have a college degree and a career, a happy and fulfilling marriage, and the promise that the conception of our first child will be a joyous occasion. I made my choice and because I know the importance of that freedom, I will . . . fight for others to have that same choice.[1]

Eliza's view could be justified on feminist grounds. Feminists believe no one should be disadvantaged for being a woman. Because the burdens of pregnancy directly affect only women, if women can't unburden themselves through abortion, they're disadvantaged relative to men. Abortion rights promote equality between the sexes.

Another view, compatible with feminism on this issue, is libertarian. Adults should be able to choose their path of life with minimal interference from others, especially the state. The state interferes with individual rights when it outlaws abortion. Because no one else is directly involved, state interference with abortion denies women the right to self-determination owed all people as a basic human right.

Both of these rationales, feminist and libertarian, champion individual rights.

The Rights of the Unborn

Many pro-life opponents of abortion rights accept the libertarian premise that individuals should be self-determining so long as they're not harming others. But abortion harms others. Eliza's unborn was a person, they think, killed by abortion.

Philosopher John Noonan argues that humanization begins at conception.

The positive argument for conception as the decisive moment of humanization is that at conception the new being receives the genetic code. It is this genetic information which determines his characteristics, which is the biological carrier of the possibility of human wisdom, which makes him a self-evolving being. A being with a human genetic code is a man.[2]

Noonan considers and rejects a later starting point for what he calls "humanization" and others call "personhood." Viability is when the unborn can survive independently of the pregnant woman. Before that time, owing to its dependence on her, some people claim the unborn has no independent existence and therefore is not yet a person.

Noonan counters that "the perfection of artificial incubation may make the fetus viable at any time: it may be removed and artificially sustained." Although that technology doesn't yet exist, its scientific possibility makes viability an unstable standard. Also, it seems strange to say that the unborn goes from nonperson to person depending on its physical location. What is more, Noonan notes, "dependence is not ended by viability. The fetus is still absolutely dependent on someone's care."[3] If independence from needed care is the criterion for personhood, newborns are not persons and infanticide should be permitted along with abortion. A major theme of those attributing personhood to the unborn is that withholding protection from the unborn logically requires withholding it from newborns as well.

Pro-life law professor Robert George also finds viability an inappropriate criterion for a right to life. He writes:

Independence should not be confused with distinctness. From the beginning, the newly conceived human being, not its mother, directs its integral organic functioning. It takes in nourishment and converts it to energy. Given a hospitable environment, it will, as Dianne Nutwell Irving says, "develop continuously without any biological interruptions, or gaps, throughout the embryonic, fetal, neo-natal, childhood and adulthood stages—until the death of the organism."[4]

On this logic, the unborn has a right to life from the moment of fertilization (when the genetic code is fixed).

Law professor Richard Stith rejects the alternative of birth as the beginning of a right to life. Rights depend on a being's nature. All that changes at birth is location. Stith writes, "The birth-wall thesis . . . claims that what something is depends upon where it is."[5] This is obviously false. If the newborn has a right to life, so must the unborn. If the unborn lacks a right to life, so must the newborn, and infanticide should be legal.

On the other hand, abortion-rights advocates claim, many changes in the unborn take place between fertilization and birth, and these may account for the newborn having rights that the unborn lacks. For example, at about eight weeks the unborn can respond to stimuli, which may indicate the beginning of experience. We usually treat sentient beings with more respect than the non-sentient. It's no crime to bash a rock or carrot against a stone wall, but it is to bash a puppy, because the puppy can experience life. Perhaps the unborn, like the rock or carrot, has no rights before it's capable of experience, so abortion should be allowed during the first eight weeks of pregnancy.

Perhaps it should be allowed even later in pregnancy because mere sentience doesn't confer a right to life, as many animals learn on their first trip to a slaughterhouse. The distinctively human capacities for reason and language are what confer a right to life. Charles Gardner points out in the *Nation* that a "mature brain cell pattern" associated with these traits "is not seen until the sixth or seventh month."[6] Accordingly, if the mind is the basis for our right to life, late-term fetuses have such a right along with newborns and all other human beings, but abortion violates no right of the unborn in the first two thirds (the first two trimesters) of pregnancy.

Right-to-life advocates reject this reasoning, because they reject associating rights with capacities. They claim that the right to life inheres in a certain kind of being. The being that becomes a baby, child, and adult is the being created at fertilization. If newborns have a right to life, so must fertilized eggs.

Abortion-rights advocates, by contrast, claim that traits are always the bases for rights. Americans get the right to vote when they turn eighteen and the right to drink hard liquor at twenty-one. Most places, they must complete driver's education and be sixteen years old to get a driver's license. A license to practice medicine or law takes more training and time. Assuming that newborns have a right to life, the unborn has the same right when it differs from newborns only in ways that clearly don't matter, such as location. Pro-lifers are correct that birth makes no difference. But having the distinctively human traits possessed by newborns is required, and these don't develop until at least the seventh month of gestation.

Right-to-life advocates counter that we do sometimes attribute rights on the basis of potential. Children have a right to education to develop their potential. Children with special intellectual gifts or disabilities usually have the right to appropriate special educational attention. The unborn has the potential and tendency from the moment of fertilization to develop all distinctively human traits that confer a right to life, so it should be nurtured, just as we nurture school children, to make that potential a reality.

In sum, the two sides agree that individual rights are the proper basis for resolving questions about abortion's permissibility. But one side concentrates on the woman's right and the other on the right of the unborn. Against the right of the unborn, pro-choice (pro-abortion-rights) thinkers claim that at least through the first two trimesters, the unborn lacks traits necessary for human rights. Pro-life thinkers counter that it's the same being throughout pregnancy, birth, and later life, and that a right to life inheres in the kind of being it is—human—not in the traits it possesses at any given time.

It seems neither side has an irresistible argument. Reasonable people can differ about the unborn's right to life, at least before the third trimester of pregnancy.

Social Status of the Unborn

Another approach to abortion rights concerns social perceptions and norms. The pro-choice side notes that current modes of thinking and acting differentiate between the unborn early and late in pregnancy. Novelist Mary Gordon writes:

We habitually consider, for example, a seven-week-old fetus to be different from a seven-month-old one. We can tell this by the way we respond to the involuntary loss of the one against the other. We have different language for the experience of the involuntary expulsion of the fetus from the womb. . . . If it occurs early in the pregnancy, we call it a miscarriage; if late, we call it a stillbirth. . . .

Our ritual and religious practices underscore the fact that we make distinctions among fetuses. If a woman took the bloody matter—indistinguishable from a heavy period—of an early miscarriage and insisted upon putting it in a tiny coffin and marking its grave, we would have serious concerns about her mental health. By the same token, we would feel squeamish about flushing a seven-month-old fetus down the toilet.[7]

Polls back up Gordon's observations. An ABC News/*Washington Post* poll conducted in January 2003 found that whereas 57 percent of Americans favored legalized abortion in "All or Most Cases," and 42 percent thought abortion should be legal "To End Unwanted Pregnancy," only 23 percent thought a late-term procedure called "partial-birth abortion" should be legal and even fewer, 11 percent, approved of abortions after six or more months of pregnancy.[8] It seems most Americans find abortion early in pregnancy less troubling than abortion later, as if the unborn's right to life increases with age.

John Noonan rejects reliance on popular opinion.

Feeling is notoriously an unsure guide to the humanity of others. Many groups of humans have had difficulty in feeling that persons of another tongue, color, religion, sex, are as human as they. . . . Any attempt to limit humanity to exclude some groups runs the risk of furnishing authority and precedent for excluding other groups. . . . To decide who is human on the basis of the sentiments of a given society has led to consequences which rational men would characterize as monstrous.[9]

There are two themes here. One associates protecting the unborn from abortion with protecting Jews from Nazis and blacks from slaveholders. Society is wrong in all these cases when it fails to recognize humanity in others. The second theme is a slippery slope argument. If we don't protect the unborn now, the elderly, the ill, the outcast, and others will eventually be considered expendable as well.

Gordon addresses fears of a slippery slope.

Many anti-choice people fear [a] slippery slope toward a brave new world where handicapped children are left on mountains to starve and the old are put out in the snow. But if we look at the history of abortion . . . , excepting . . . the People's Republic of China (which practices forced abortion), there seems to be a real link between repressive anti-abortion stances and repressive governments. Abortion was banned in Fascist Italy and Nazi Germany. . . . It is paid for by the governments of Denmark, England, and the Netherlands, which have national health and welfare systems that foster the health and well-being of mothers, children, the old and the handicapped.[10]

Technological developments since Noonan wrote in 1970 may also allay fears of a slippery slope. The unborn have increasing social visibility. Debra Rosenberg writes in *Newsweek*, "new high-tech fetal ultrasound images allow prospective parents to see tiny fingers and toes, arms, legs and a beating heart as early as 12 weeks. . . . These images . . . pack such an emotional punch that even the most hard-line abortion-rights supporters may find themselves questioning their beliefs."[11] To the extent that abortion rights depend on social perceptions and norms, fetuses twelve weeks or older may receive increased protection, owing to their increased visibility.

Abortion Rights as Religious Freedom

The increasing visibility of and empathy toward the unborn worries the pro-choice camp. They argue that social perceptions should not impair the fundamental right of women to control their own bodies. A major reason we have our Bill of Rights is to protect individuals from popular perceptions and electoral majorities that would deny fundamental rights and curtail basic freedoms.

The First Amendment protects religious freedom. It begins: "Congress shall make no law respecting an establishment of religion, or prohibiting the free exercise thereof." This statement contains what are called the Establishment Clause and the Free Exercise Clause. Although not the original understanding, the Establishment Clause now means that no government agency—local, state, and federal—may show preference for one religion over another or for religious over secular views. So, for example, a publicly funded Christmas display at the courthouse may unconstitutionally establish religion. Adding a Chanukah menorah, Kwanza welcome, and model Stonehenge may convert the display into a constitutional celebration of the season.

Some people believe that restrictions on abortion violate the Establishment Clause. They accuse abortion opponents of being theocrats attempting to confine everyone's behavior to what their religion finds acceptable. The Catechism of the Catholic Church, for example, states: "Human life must be respected and protected absolutely from the moment of conception."[12] The Church wants to impose this religious view on everyone: "The inalienable right to life of every innocent human individual is a *constitutive element of a civil society and its legislation*.[13] Another staunch

opponent of abortion rights is the Christian Coalition. Imposing their religious morality on everyone seems to violate the Establishment Clause.

This reasoning is flawed. Faith-based advocacy for a social cause doesn't
turn government action for that cause into an establishment of religion.
Catholics, for example, advocate feeding the hungry, healing the sick, and
housing the homeless. They run soup kitchens, hospitals, and shelters to
meet people's needs. The government can do these things as well, without establishing religion, because there are secular justifications. Secular
utilitarians, for example, may believe that such programs promote the
greatest good for the greatest number. Although taxes needed to provide
low-cost housing may reduce taxpayers' well being, that reduction is less
than the increase in well being among poor people provided decent places
to live, utilitarians might think. Whether they're right or wrong, their reasoning is entirely secular.

Similarly, government action to curtail abortions doesn't become religious and violate the Establishment Clause simply because religious
groups concur.

On the other hand, there must be a secular justification for government
action. We saw that both pro-life and pro-choice advocates appeal to
secular political philosophies that emphasize individual rights—one side
concentrating on the rights of women, the other on rights of the unborn.
But the unborn have rights only if they are persons—hence the centrality
of the debate on the personhood of the unborn.

Good reasons based on solid science and respectable analogies are
given on both sides of this debate. Pro-life supporters emphasize the integrity of the individual from fertilization through adulthood. Pro-choice
supporters point out differences concerning distinctively human traits
between an embryo and a newborn. The pro-life people claim, correctly,
that the embryo will (most likely) develop such traits if given the chance.
The other side counters that rights generally correspond to actual traits,
not potentials. Pro-lifers note that the right to education is an exception
to this rule.

No argument by either side would convince neutral observers, because
remaining differences don't depend on facts but on unarguable judgments
about the importance of certain facts and the strength of competing
analogies. Our intellectual resources make the personhood of the unborn
(in nearly the first two-thirds of gestation) impossible to decide upon.

The pro-life comparison of protecting the unborn from abortion with protecting blacks from slavery breaks down, because we can prove to neutral observers that people of different races share common human biological traits. Blacks and whites can have children together, which makes them the same species. Blacks and whites can speak the same languages and do other species-specific tasks, such as write and do math. Genetics adds additional proof. There's no stalemate here.

The stalemate regarding the unborn resembles religious disagreements. Some people believe that God exists; others don't. Some believe that Jesus is the son of God sent to Earth to redeem sinners; others don't. Some believe that there's life after death; others don't. Some believe that there's a heaven and hell; others don't. As with the rights of the unborn, reasons are given on both sides, some of them based on science, but neither side can convince neutral observers. That's why we say these are matters of faith.

People are free in the United States to live by their faiths and to attempt to convert others, so long as they respect the right of everyone else to do the same. This is guaranteed by the Free Exercise Clause of the First Amendment. But the Establishment Clause prohibits people using the law to impose their faith on others. If belief in the personhood of the unborn is a matter of faith—like belief in the existence of God, as the intractability of disagreement suggests—the Establishment Clause would forbid using the law to impose this religious-like belief on others. Legislatures violate the Establishment Clause when they forbid abortion on the rationale of protecting the unborn (in the first two-thirds of pregnancy). This kind of reasoning may account for the persistent belief among pro-choicers that pro-lifers are theocrats unconstitutionally imposing their religion on an unwilling public.[14]

Abortion opponents reply that when abortion is legal, the shoe's on the other foot. If both beliefs are religious-like, legalized abortion is the imposition on society in general of the religious-like belief that the unborn is not a person with a right to life.

But this reasoning is flawed. The Establishment Clause requires the law to avoid taking sides on matters of faith. Decisions are left up to individuals. Abortion is legal in this situation because everything is legal unless the state has a secular reason to make it illegal. Abortion is legal by default.

A better objection to the pro-choice Establishment Clause argument concerns the relevance of "religious-like beliefs" to First Amendment analysis. Like many religious beliefs, beliefs about the unborn's personhood can't be proved. But the subject matter, rights of the unborn, is different from religious subjects—God, Jesus, life after death, and so on. Pro-lifers could claim this difference is crucial to application of the Establishment Clause, which uses the word "religion," not the term "religious-like belief."

On the other hand, perhaps the essential point of the Establishment Clause is to avoid the civil discord that often accompanies government attempts to impose some people's beliefs on others, when the beliefs in question are not central to our way of life or our ability to interact harmoniously and productively. People can interact well while disagreeing about God, Jesus, heaven, and the afterlife, but discord ensues when some try to impose their views on others. If the point of the Establishment Clause is to avoid such discord, civil strife surrounding the abortion debate suggests that religious-like beliefs about the unborn should be treated as religious beliefs for Establishment Clause purposes.

In any case, when individual rights are the sole focus of debate, the pro-choice side has an advantage. Women seeking abortions are definitely individuals with rights, whereas the rights of the unborn are uncertain.

Communitarian Opposition to Abortion, But Not to Abortion Rights

Law professor Mary Ann Glendon contrasts the individual-rights approach to abortion common in the United States to the more communitarian approach in Western Europe. Communitarians emphasize that individuals are products of social interaction. Religion, for example, is important to many people. For the most part, individual religious commitment presupposes that preceding generations had religious insights, shared those insights, and started organizations featuring those insights. Most religious people were raised in regular contact with a religious group and are sustained in their commitment by continued fellowship with co-religionists. In short, the individual makes a religious commitment, but the soil in which commitment sprouts and grows is social.

The same is true of those whose life stories center on baseball, physics, architecture, philosophy, or politics. Society makes individuals more than individuals make society, because although in our society individuals have many paths to choose from, those paths are socially created and maintained. In the vast majority of cases, social paths set limits to individual aspiration and commitment.

Communitarians are interested in the social paths that society creates and maintains. For example, Glendon notes, in 1975 the West German Constitutional Court considered the issue of abortion and decided the unborn has a right to life after fourteen days. But the court "chose to emphasize the character of this right as a value of the community rather than as something that belongs to the fetus. The court was more concerned with the obligation of the state to promote the public value than it was with any rights the value might give to individuals." This explains why "the West German court . . . held that the legislature need not impose penal sanctions for abortion when continuation of the pregnancy would constitute an insupportable hardship for the woman concerned." Rather than vindicate one individual right at the expense of another, the court showed "a commitment to an order of values."[15] An order of values is the mainstay of the socialization process that forms individuals, so the state must take care, on communitarian premises, to maintain it and improve it where possible.

Like communitarians, social conservatives recognize the limits of individualism and individual rights. They, too, advocate maintaining an order of values. The two philosophies differ, however, in their estimates of human flexibility. Social conservatives appeal to tradition because they fear that innovations unleash human tendencies toward misbehavior. Communitarians, by contrast, are more accepting of change, because they are less fearful of human immorality.

The Spanish high court's abortion ruling, like the West German, reflected communitarian commitment to evolving public values. The Spanish court advanced

the notion that what the pregnant woman can be required to sacrifice for the common value is related to what the social welfare state is ready and able to do to help with the burdens of childbirth and parenthood. For example, the Spanish court, reluctantly upholding the exception for a defective fetus, takes note of the hardship involved in raising a disabled child and the very limited degree of public assistance presently available in Spain.[16]

Compassion for the pregnant woman and her family tempers concern for fetal life in the evolving order of public values.

American values may resemble Western Europe's communitarian thinking more than pro-choice or pro-life views that concentrate on the individual rights of women or the unborn. For example, when abortion was illegal, the crime was never treated as murder, as it logically should have been if the unborn has a right to life equal to that of other people. More recently, the ABCNEWS/*Washington Post* poll conducted in 2003 found that 81 percent of Americans think abortion should be available in cases of rape or incest. But the same poll finds that only 42 percent favor legal abortion to terminate an unwanted pregnancy. On an individual-rights basis, 39 percent of respondents—81 percent minus 42 percent—seem confused. They think the unborn has a right to life, so it shouldn't be killed at a woman's whim, but if pregnancy results from rape or incest, the unborn somehow loses its right to life.

I think these poll results show support for something like the communitarian order of values found in Western European law. The life of the unborn is an important value, but not the only important value. Glendon writes, "All of the West European laws, while permitting abortion on a wide variety of grounds, communicate that fetal life is an important interest of the society and that abortion is not a substitute for birth control."[17] Allowing abortion for trivial reasons, on this communitarian analysis, can erode the social solidarity needed for human flourishing, but so could ignoring the plight of women whose unborn results from rape or incest.

This communitarian analysis suggests that a good society helps pregnant women and working mothers in order to reduce the burdens of pregnancy and motherhood. Countries that do this have lower abortion rates. Glendon points out that the United States has a poor record of obtaining child support payments from absent parents. "Countries like Denmark, Norway, and Sweden," by contrast,

have long had mandatory paternity actions that do in fact result in determining paternity for nearly all children born to unmarried mothers. Several countries now use standard formulas and tables for calculating realistic amounts of child support and have extremely efficient collection mechanisms, including direct deduction of child support from the noncustodial parent's wages.[18]

Most European countries also have laws requiring employers to give pregnant women a maternity leave of six months, followed by "the right to an additional year of unpaid leave, with full job protection and fringe benefits." Typically in the United States, a woman is lucky to get several weeks off. In addition, Western European countries provide "day care for children ages three to five within the public educational system."[19]

Most American must pay for day care, and affordable, quality day care is hard to find.

The fact that Western Europe has a lower abortion rate than the United States suggests that people who want to minimize the incidence of abortion here should imitate Europe's communitarian model of social solidarity. Europeans have universal health care and generous unemployment benefits that reduce the burden of having a child. Freelance writer Nina Kohl claims that in the United States, "rising unemployment and soaring healthcare costs are directly connected to the abortion rate. . . . Of women who abort, two-thirds say they can't afford a child. Half say they don't have a responsible mate and co-earner."[20]

Comprehensive sex education can also help, Kohl maintains: "Belgium, a country where abortion is legal, has achieved the lowest abortion rate in the world, with sex education that recommends abstinence but stresses responsibility and teaches teens how to use contraception."[21] In sum, the way to reduce the abortion rate, according to Kohl, is to protect women "from poverty, inadequate healthcare coverage, jobs without flexible schedules, lack of affordable daycare, limited access to contraception and sex education, and fathers who don't take financial and emotional responsibility for their children."[22]

This communitarian approach may find support among feminists because it ties the abortion issue to a host of feminist concerns, such as childcare, flexible working hours, payments from missing fathers, and other programs needed for women to fulfill maternal duties without looming poverty and competitive disadvantage in the workplace.

Theocratic and Social Conservative Opposition to Abortion Rights

Theocrats and social conservatives, like communitarians, emphasize social good rather than individual rights and relate the abortion issue to a vision of society transformed. However, while communitarians envision new government programs and mandates that protect women and children, theocrats and social conservatives envision a society rededicated to the nuclear family and the simple pleasures of home life.

The theocratic and social conservative vision has endured over decades. Sociologist Kristin Luker's study in the early 1980s found opposition to abortion related by theocrats and social conservatives to belief that the nuclear family is grounded in natural differences between men and women. One of her interviewees said:

What is natural for human life and what will make people happy? The feminist movement has wanted to . . . turn women into men or to kind of de-sex them. . . . [What] I find so disturbing [about] the whole abortion mentality is the idea that family duties—rearing children, managing a home, living and caring for a husband—are somehow degrading to women. And that's an idea which is very current in our society—that women are not going to find fulfillment until they get out there and start competing for a livelihood with men.[23]

Another pro-life activist said: "I believe there's a natural mother's instinct. . . . I believe men and women are very different, and beautifully different, and that they're complementary in their nature to one another."[24]

The traditional nuclear family, because it reflects natural differences between men and women and gives children the support they need to assume adult responsibilities is the basic building block of healthy societies. Anything that jeopardizes the nuclear family should be resisted. Married women working outside the home jeopardizes the nuclear family, according to some pro-life activists interviewed by Luker.

When you start . . . competing in the marketplace for what you can do and how you can get one-up or whatever, then I think we get into problems. It's harder to come down off that plane [of activity] and come home to a life where everything is quite mundane, and the children are way beneath you.[25]

Another activist adds: "I think [pro-choice] people help destroy the family because they want to make it so free for the woman to go to work, like with the childcare centers and all the rest of it."[26] From this perspective, the subsidized daycare that communitarians promote is bad because it encourages women to work outside the home and neglect their primary duties as wife and mother. This weakens the nuclear family.

Women's outside employment also reflects a materialistic mind-set that devalues children. One pro-life activist put it this way:

There has been a very strong attitude that the child represents an obstacle to achievement [and] an obstacle to a lifestyle that will include the yacht and weekend skiing. . . . A great many couples are opting not to have any children at all because of the portrayal of the child as an obstacle, especially to a woman's career and a two-salary family.[27]

Materialism, the loss of traditional roles in the nuclear family, the marginalization of children in families, and the availability of abortion to end unwanted pregnancies all tend to oppress rather than liberate women, according to pro-life activists. They create pressure for women to have sex outside marriage, an activist explains:

I think having abortion as an alternative—as a way out, I guess—makes it easier for men to exploit women than ever before. I think they are less inclined probably to take responsibility for their actions or to anticipate the consequences of their actions as long as abortion is available. And I think it makes it harder for women who do not choose to engage in premarital sex to say no.[28]

One self-identified Catholic among the pro-life activists interviewed by Luker believed that sex should take place only between married couples, thereby strengthening the nuclear family, because procreation is the natural goal of sex. He said: "You're not just given arms and legs for no purpose. . . . There must be some cause [for sex] and you begin to think, well, it must be for procreation ultimately . . . , in addition to fostering a loving relationship with your spouse."[29] Luker comments:

Values that define sexuality as a wholesome physical activity, as healthy as volley-ball but somewhat more fun, call into question everything that pro-life people believe in. Sex is sacred because in their world view it has the capacity to be something transcendent—to bring into existence another human life. To rou-tinely eradicate that capacity through . . . contraception or abortion is to turn the world upside down.[30]

Journalist Russell Shorto, writing in the *New York Times Magazine* in 2006, found the same view among twenty-first-century pro-life activists. He quotes Dr. Joseph B. Stanford:

Sexual union in marriage ought to be a complete giving of each spouse to the other, and when fertility (or potential fertility) is deliberately excluded from that giving I am convinced that something valuable is lost. A husband will sometimes begin to see his wife as an object of sexual pleasure who should always be avail-able for sexual gratification.[31]

Judie Brown, president of the American Life League, told Shorto: "The mind-set that invites a couple to use contraception is an antichild mind-set. So when a baby is conceived accidentally, the couple already have this negative attitude toward the child. Therefore seeking an abortion is a natural outcome. We oppose . . . contraception."[32]

Dr. R. Albert Mohler, president of the Southern Baptist Theological Seminary, applies this insight to the contraception pill.

I cannot imagine any development in human history, after the Fall, that has had a greater impact on human beings than the pill. It became almost an assured form of contraception. . . . Prior to it, every time a couple had sex, there was a good chance of pregnancy. Once that is removed, the entire horizon of the sexual act changes. I think there could be no question that the pill gave incredible license to everything from adultery and affairs to premarital sex and within marriage to a separation of the sex act and procreation.[33]

The pill, like abortion, promotes pleasure-oriented, materialistic values in place of family-oriented commitment to spouse and children. It helps wives control fertility so they can work outside the home in pursuit of material gain, and it helps men and women gratify hedonistic impulses through sex that's degraded through dissociation from procreation. Kristin Luker summarizes:

If one values material things too highly, one will be tempted to try to make detailed plans for acquiring them. If one tries to plan too thoroughly, one will be tempted to use highly effective contraception, which removes the potential of childbearing from a marriage. Once the potential for children is eliminated, the sexual act is distorted . . . and husbands and wives lose an important bond between them. Finally, when marriage partners who have accepted the logic of these previous steps find that contraception has failed, they are ready and willing to resort to abortion in order to achieve their goals.[34]

People with this anti-abortion view don't oppose abortion primarily because anyone's rights are violated. They oppose contraception even if it violates no rights. They promote an ideal of human sexuality and social interaction that's incompatible with widespread use of contraception and abortion. If their views are based on religious texts, they're theocrats. Others are social conservatives who think contraception and abortion endanger the nuclear family and valuable social traditions regarding male and female roles. They think the nuclear family and traditional roles have served humanity well, because they reflect natural differences between men and women.

Central to this outlook is belief that people tend to act immorally, contrary to their own long-term interests. Most seek immediate pleasure and material rewards, using contraception and abortion to gain pleasure from sex while avoiding responsibility for children. The resulting lifestyle is spiritually impoverished. The goal of public policy should be moral renewal. Communitarian proposals to reduce abortion through programs that educate the young about contraceptives and help women with children work outside the home are misguided, according to these theocrats and social conservatives. Equally, whether or not abstinence-only programs of sex education are the most effective, or effective at all, is beside the point.[35] The point is that more comprehensive sex education that teaches youngsters how to use birth control furthers society's moral decline.

Legal Restrictions on Abortion

The Supreme Court decided in *Roe v. Wade* (1973)[36] that women have a privacy right to get abortions from willing providers with no government restrictions during the first trimester of pregnancy. During the second trimester, states can impose restrictions aimed at safeguarding the woman's health. Only during the third trimester may states impose restrictions aimed at preserving the life of the unborn, but these restrictions mustn't jeopardize the life or health of the pregnant woman. *Planned Parenthood v. Casey* (1992)[37] modified *Roe* by allowing at all stages of pregnancy state restrictions that don't overly burden a woman's fundamental right to have an abortion. The central decision in *Roe* was upheld. Women have a right to abortions, and no state may restrict abortion at any stage of pregnancy in ways that jeopardize a woman's life or health.

Since 1992, states have experimented with many abortion restrictions. One that the Supreme Court found unconstitutional was Nebraska's ban on what pro-life advocates call partial-birth abortion.

Partial-Birth Abortion

According to the organization Religious Tolerance, based in Ontario, Canada, the procedure, officially called "dilation and extraction,"

is usually performed during the fifth month of gestation or later. The woman's cervix is dilated, and the fetus is partially removed from the womb, feet first. The surgeon inserts a sharp object into the back of the fetus' head, removes it, and inserts a vacuum tube through which the brains are extracted. The head of the fetus contracts at this point and allows the fetus to be more easily removed.[38]

Critics of the procedure claim that because the fetus is no longer fully in the uterus, killing it is technically murder, not abortion.[39] A less-technical concern is that after about twenty-four weeks of gestation, the unborn may reasonably be considered a person with a right to life. It has all the major systems and organs, including distinctively human sections of the brain. It differs from a healthy newborn, whose right to life is undisputed, only in ways that generally don't make a difference in our law and culture.

It's smaller, weaker, and more dependent on a particular life-support system (the maternal uterine environment) than a healthy newborn, but size, strength, and temporary dependence on a life-support system aren't usually considered relevant to decisions about personhood.

The Supreme Court viewed matters differently, finding two flaws in Nebraska's prohibition of partial-birth abortion.[40] First, the procedure outlawed is often used earlier in pregnancy, during the second trimester, when—according to the *Roe* decision—states may not limit abortions to preserve the life of the unborn. (I'd prefer saying that Nebraska banned abortions when the personhood of the unborn is just a religious-like belief.)

Second, although the law allowed exceptions to protect the woman's life, it didn't allow exceptions to protect her health, as *Roe* requires. Feminists might support *Roe*'s requirement this way: even if the unborn is a person with a right to life, denying women the right to abortions needed to preserve their health is unfair. Men are never required to jeopardize their health to save the life of a child. Suppose a child needs a liver or kidney transplant to survive, and the father is the only person with enough tissue match for successful donation. He isn't required to donate. Because people have the right to decide what medical risks they'll undertake, the law gives everyone the right to decline medical operations no matter the consequences for others, even their own children. If women were denied the right to abortions late in health-jeopardizing pregnancies, they'd be the only category of patients required to risk their health for others. This goes against the feminist principle that no one should be disadvantaged for being a woman.

On the other hand, consider this case:

My name is Elena and I am 39 years old. I am single and childless. After many many years of working full time and attending college part time I am finally living my dreams and attending medical school. . . . I am through my first year and so happy to be here. I am peri-menopausal; for the last 3 years my periods have been quite irregular. I can easily go for several months without a period. . . . I always use condoms, so when I found out I was pregnant I couldn't believe it. I went out and bought 3 more pregnancy tests; every one came up positive. I cried, it just couldn't be so. There was no way I was going to have that child. My partner already had 4 kids and a horrible relationship with his ex-wife. I was not willing to toss my dreams aside so I could raise an unplanned child in that environment. Besides . . . , I had worked too hard to get where I was in my life, and I didn't want to just throw that away. I decided that I would terminate the pregnancy.

I scheduled a surgical abortion with Planned Parenthood in between my crazy school schedule and multiple exams. . . . But during the ultrasound portion of my scheduled abortion I discovered that I was . . . in my 23rd week of pregnancy. I was completely devastated and I felt like an idiot. . . . There was only one place that could help me at that stage and it was hundreds of miles away in Wichita, KS. My partner went with me. . . . It took almost 16 hours to drive to the clinic in Wichita. . . . I could feel the fetus moving inside me, kicking me. That made me cry even more. I was certain I was making the right choice for me, but it was so difficult and I felt so alone in my situation. . . . The clinic was not what I expected, everyone was extremely warm and supportive. (Well, except of course the bitter protestors cursing at me outside the clinic, while they clutched their small children.)[41]

The pregnancy interfered with Elena's plans and dreams, not with her physical health. What would Elena have thought and done if she'd discovered the pregnancy two or three weeks later, when the unborn was arguably a person with a right to life? What if she still wanted the abortion? An exception for women's health might have been used to spare her the mental anguish of coping with grave disappointment. That's one kind of loophole to bans on late abortions that Nebraska was trying to close by refusing to allow exceptions for maternal health.

Parental Consent and Other Requirements
One way of cutting down on abortions, many pro-life advocates believe, is to require parental approval before minors can have abortions. Any reduction of abortions is good, from the individual-rights perspective of those who think the unborn is a person. Theocrats and social conservatives who champion family values also want to encourage family interaction.

However, in 2006, the Supreme Court didn't allow a New Hampshire parental consent law to go into effect, because the law requires a forty-eight-hour waiting period after parents are notified of their daughter's abortion plans. The waiting period could jeopardize the minor's health in cases of medical emergency.[42]

Also out of concern for the minor's welfare, the Court requires that laws mandating parental notification or consent make provision for exceptions in cases where the minor convinces a judge that she's either mature enough to make her own decision or that abortion without parental involvement would be in her best interest. *New York Times* correspondent John Leland reports that such provisions for judicial bypass make it easy for minors to get abortions without parental notification or consent. He tells the story of seventeen-year-old Alicia, who sought abortion in Arkansas, which requires parental consent.

Alicia, who was 17 or 18 weeks pregnant, said she did not have the abortion earlier because she was afraid to confront her parents. . . .

"But I can't give the baby a life it should have financially," she said. "My boyfriend didn't want me to go through with it, but he realized he couldn't support a baby either. . . ."

Getting judicial bypass was not difficult. . . . "If you go to the judge and say, 'I'm afraid to tell my parents because they might harm me,' that's all you need to say," said Dr. Tom Tvedten, who has been performing abortions in Arkansas for 20 years. . . . "It doesn't have to be true, because how would anybody know?"[43]

Parental notification requirements in more than thirty states have little effect on rates of teen pregnancy or abortion, according to the *New York Times.*

The *Times* analysis of the states that enacted laws between 1995 and 2004—most of which had low abortion rates to begin with—found no evidence that the laws had significant impact on the number of minors who got pregnant, or, once pregnant, the number who had abortions. . . .[44]

Providers interviewed in 10 states with parental involvement laws said that of the minors who came into their clinics, parents were more often the ones pushing for an abortion even against the wishes of their daughters.

"I see far more parents trying to pressure their daughters to have one," said Jane Bovard, owner of the Red River Women's Clinic in Fargo, N.D., a state where a minor needs consent from both parents.[45]

Various states have other requirements designed to discourage abortion. Some states require abortion providers to offer to show women who are at least twelve weeks pregnant a sonogram of the unborn. Some require providers to read scripts that inform patients of such information as the father's legal duty to help support his child. Required waiting periods of twenty-four or forty-eight hours (with exceptions for medical emergencies) are also meant to discourage women from having abortions. These roadblocks are constitutional, so long as they don't place too great a burden on a woman's right to choose abortion.

Conclusion

Most pro-choice advocates appeal to individual rights. Their political philosophy is either libertarian or feminist. If they don't see the unborn as a person, they're not dismayed by abortion and don't see it as tragic. Many communitarians, by contrast, are concerned about public morality and fear that widespread, casual abortions are morally degrading. Some consider the unborn a person. Others are unsure of the unborn's personhood or want to show respect for people who think the unborn is a person. In any case, communitarians propose reducing abortion through sex education and child-friendly government policies, while retaining abortion's legal availability.

Pro-life advocates may also appeal to individual rights, but they stress the right to life of the unborn. This position is no less libertarian, except that the unborn's rights are less certain than a woman's rights. Alternatively, pro-life advocates may adopt a theocratic or social conservative view that considers abortion to be just one aspect among many of our society's moral decline. Abortion is wrong and should be stopped, not so much to vindicate the unborn's right to life as to start reversing the general trend of Western civilization toward irresponsible hedonism. Evidence of this lamentable trend, according to many theocrats and social conservatives, are increasing individualism, materialism, sexual promiscuity, divorce, contraception, and homosexuality. Keeping the focus on what such people view as moral degradation, homosexuality, same-sex marriage, and polygamy are discussed in the next chapter.

9

Homosexuality, Same-Sex Marriage, and Polygamy: Social Conservatism, Theocracy, Natural Law, Libertarianism, Contractarianism, and Multiculturalism

Wedding Announcements

The *New York Times* included this special wedding announcement in 2004:

Hillary Smith Goodridge and Julie Wendrich Goodridge, the lead plaintiffs in the case that led the Massachusetts Supreme Court to extend marital rights to same-sex couples in the state, were themselves married on Monday [May 17] in Boston. The Rev. William G. Sinkford, the president of the Unitarian Universalist Association, officiated.[1]

Hillary Goodridge (formerly Hillary Ann Smith) met Julie (formerly Julie Nell Wendrich) in 1985 at a seminar at Harvard on disinvestment from South Africa. Both in their late twenties, the issue drew them together, owing to their interest in socially responsible investing.

Like most couples, Julie and Hillary have stories of meeting and pursuing. Julie remembers, "For two years I pursued Hillary, but she would have nothing to do with me." When the two were working late at Hillary's place in 1987, writing a speech for a conference at Radcliffe, Julie tried to make a good impression by offering to cook dinner. "When she told me that all she had in her refrigerator was raw chicken and some beer, I said, 'That's no problem.' I threw it together in an aluminum baking pan. Of course it was disgusting. We went out for ice cream instead."[2] Their relationship blossomed a few months later at a gay pride parade.

Just before Julie gave birth to their daughter Annie in 1996, both women changed their names to Goodridge. The *UU World: The Magazine of the Unitarian Universalist Association* explains how Annie's birth sparked their desire for marriage:

Annie's birth provided them with their first real encounter with the consequences of not being legally married. After problems developed following a planned Caesarian birth, Annie was rushed to the neonatal intensive-care ward. But when Hillary tried to see her, she was told she wasn't allowed. Hospital staff also barred her from visiting Julie in the post-op room. That wouldn't have been the case if they had been legal spouses. "It was really jarring," she recalls.[3]

Interviewed on their wedding day, Hillary added:

If either of us dies, becomes disabled, it's all things mostly that happen when you're older or things none of us want to think about—but disability, death, bad things, accidents—it's in those times that you realize, "I have no relationship to this person." If Julie were to die, it's possible that I would have to sell the house because I would have to pay tax on the inheritance, which most spouses would not have to do, and we have a child to protect.[4]

The couple didn't act on these concerns until Annie was five years old and they were discussing love with her, pointing out married couples they knew. Annie didn't understand why Julie and Hillary weren't married. She said: "You don't love each other. If you loved each other, you'd be married!"[5] That's when they and six other same-sex couples initiated a lawsuit to force the state to allow them to marry.

They lost their case in Superior Court but won a 4–3 ruling in the Massachusetts Supreme Court. Justice Margaret Marshall, writing for the majority, noted that marriage in Massachusetts is a civil matter, not a religious one. "No religious ceremony has ever been required to validate a Massachusetts marriage." Because "the government creates civil marriage . . . , who may marry and what obligations, benefits, and liabilities attach to civil marriage . . . are set by the Commonwealth."[6] However, there are two conditions. The state constitution requires that all laws "apply equally to persons in similar situations" and that they respect individual liberty in personal matters. The Court majority found that denying marriage to same-sex couples violates both of these requirements.

Consider liberty first. Justice Marshall writes:

Civil marriage is at once a deeply personal commitment to another human being and a highly public celebration of the ideals of mutuality, companionship, intimacy, fidelity, and family. . . . Because it fulfils yearnings for security, safe haven, and connection that express our common humanity, civil marriage is an esteemed institution, and the decision whether and whom to marry is among life's momentous acts of self-definition. . . . The liberty interest in choosing whether and whom to marry would be hollow if the Commonwealth could, without sufficient justification, foreclose an individual from freely choosing the person with whom to share an exclusive commitment in the unique institution of civil marriage."[7]

Powerful justifications would be needed to justify state intrusion into so intimate an area as marriage and to justify treating some who aspire to marriage differently than others.

Marshall found unconvincing the rationales put forward by the Department of Public Health for denying marriage to same-sex couples. The first rationale is that marriage exists to provide a "favorable setting for procreation." Marshall comments:

Our laws of civil marriage do not privilege procreative heterosexual intercourse between married people above every other form of adult intimacy and every other means of creating a family. General Laws c. 207 contains no requirement that the applicants for a marriage license attest to their ability or intention to conceive children by coitus. Fertility is not a condition of marriage, nor is it grounds for divorce. People who have never consummated their marriage, and never plan to, may be and stay married. . . . People who cannot stir from their deathbed may marry.[8]

The state's second rationale is that marriage exists to provide an optimal setting for childrearing. Marshall didn't see how "restricting marriage to opposite-sex couples" furthers this goal.

The department has offered no evidence that forbidding marriage to people of the same sex will increase the number of couples choosing to enter into opposite-sex marriages in order to have and raise children. There is thus no rational relationship between the marriage statute and the Commonwealth's proffered goal of protecting the "optimal" child rearing unit. Moreover, the department readily concedes that people in same-sex couples may be "excellent" parents. . . . [In sum,] excluding same-sex couples from civil marriage will not make children of opposite-sex marriages more secure, but it does prevent children of same-sex couples from enjoying the immeasurable advantages that flow from the assurance of "a stable family structure in which children will be reared, educated and socialized."[9]

Besides Julie and Hillary, three other couples among the plaintiffs were parents.

Marshall concludes, "Here, the plaintiffs seek only to marry, not to undermine the institution of marriage." Recalling opposition to interracial marriage in centuries past, she adds, "Recognizing the right of an individual to marry a person of the same sex will not diminish the validity or the dignity of opposite-sex marriage, any more than recognizing the right of an individual to marry a person of a different race devalues the marriage of a person who marries someone of her own race."[10]

Failing to find a rational reason for the ban on same-sex marriage, Marshall identifies what she believes to be the real reason. "The marriage restriction is rooted in persistent prejudices against persons who are (or who are believed to be) homosexual."[11]

Against Homosexuality

Marshall's suspicion was confirmed by Russell Shorto when he investigated the issue for the *New York Times Magazine* in 2005. He writes:

I found no one among the people on the ground who are leading the anti-gay-marriage cause who said in essence: "I have nothing against homosexuality. I just don't believe gays should be allowed to marry." Rather, their passion comes from their conviction that homosexuality is a sin, is immoral, harms children, and spreads disease. Not only that, but they see homosexuality itself as a kind of disease, one that afflicts not only individuals but also society at large and that shares one of the prominent features of a disease: it seeks to spread itself.[12]

Most of the anti-gay-marriage activists Shorto spoke to related their negative view of homosexuality to religion, making their opposition to gay marriage largely theocratic. Brian Racer, pastor of the Open Door Bible Church, told Shorto, "The Hebrew words for male and female are actually the words for the male and female genital parts. The male is the piercer; the female is the pierced. That is the way God designed it."[13] Historian Dennis Prager noted in 1990 that the Bible declares homosexuality to be an abomination. "If a man lies with a male as with a woman, both of them have committed an abomination; they shall be put to death, their blood is upon them."[14] "Abomination" is the Bible's strongest negative evaluation. Prager writes that the Bible

lists homosexuality together with child sacrifice among the "abominations" practiced by the peoples living in the land about to be conquered by the Jews. . . . They both characterized a way of life opposite to the one that God demanded. . . .
The Bible adds a unique threat to the Jews if they engage in homosexuality and the other offenses of the Canaanites: "You will be vomited out of the land" just as the non-Jews who practice these things were vomited out of the land.[15]

Protestant Pat Robertson voiced similar faith-based opposition to homosexuality on the program *The 700 Club* when he warned the city of Orlando, Florida, about allowing Gay Days flags on city streetlamp poles.

The Apostle Paul made it abundantly clear in the Book of Romans that acceptance of homosexuality is the last step in the decline of Gentile civilization. . . . I would warn Orlando that you're right in the way of some serious hurricanes, and I don't think I'd be waving those flags in God's face if I were you. . . . It'll bring about terrorist bombs; it'll bring earthquakes, tornadoes, and possibly a meteor.[16]

Additional arguments against homosexuality come from the natural law tradition. Natural law philosophers support what's natural against (what they consider) perversions of nature. They're often allied with theocrats who believe that God made nature and likes it, so perversions of nature thwart God's will. For the most part, what natural law advocates consider perversions of nature, theocrats consider affronts to God. However, a strictly natural law perspective doesn't appeal to revelations from God, such as those in the Bible. Natural law can be discovered, they claim, by reason and science alone.

Consider this natural law argument against homosexuality:

We know by reason that the natural law tells us that, for example, food is for sustenance. . . . Now suppose someone were going to eat for pleasure alone and, not wanting to experience the natural result of such activity, deliberately induced vomiting to keep from gaining weight. Such an activity is not ordered towards the natural process of eating and digestion. This fact is recognized by mental health professionals and known as an eating disorder called bulimia. . . . Food is meant to go on a one-way trip. The organs of digestion are designed for this process.

In the same way the sexual organs are designed for certain functions. . . . The male and female bodies . . . are different. By the light of reason alone we can tell that the male and female organs are made for different purposes. We can also determine by reason alone what those purposes are. When someone uses his or her sexual organs for purposes other than those for which they are specifically designed, such actions are disordered.[17]

From this viewpoint, homosexuality is as futile as trying to put a square peg in a square peg.

History is also invoked against homosexuality. Prager writes:

Yet another reason for Judaism's opposition to homosexuality is homosexuality's negative effect on women. . . . There seems to be a direct correlation between the prevalence of male homosexuality and the relegation of women to a low societal role. . . . The emancipation of women has been a function of Western civilization, the civilization least tolerant of homosexuality.[18]

Ancient Athens, for example, "elevated homosexuality to an ideal." Correspondingly:

Classicist Eva Keuls describes Athens at the height of philosophical and artistic greatness as "a society dominated by men who sequester their wives and daughters, denigrate the female role in reproduction, erect monuments to the male genitalia, [and] have sex with the sons of their peers."[19]

Prager thinks the same denigration of women accompanied homosexuality in eleventh-century France, in Arab society, and in traditional Chinese culture. He's surprised that feminists haven't noticed this and objected to gay rights as bad for women's rights. But Prager's objections aren't feminist. When he's not a theocrat, he's a social conservative worried about the baleful social effects of widespread homosexuality.

If homosexuality is bad, whether for theological, natural law, or social conservative reasons, same-sex marriage shouldn't be allowed, because it encourages homosexual unions by giving them legal recognition and corresponding benefits.

Homosexuals Gain Ground

Recent legal trends favor homosexuality on libertarian grounds. Aspen and Boulder, Colorado, had outlawed discrimination based on sexual orientation. Restaurants, stores, hotels, landlords, employers, and others couldn't discriminate against gays or lesbians simply because of their sexual orientation, just as they can't discriminate on the bases of race, religion, age, or national origin. But in 1992, the state passed Amendment 2, which, in the words of Supreme Court Justice Anthony Kennedy, "prohibits all legislative, executive or judicial action at any level of state or local government designed to protect . . . homosexual persons or gays and lesbians."[20]

Proponents of the amendment claimed they were just removing special protections from gays and lesbians. Justice Kennedy wrote in 1996:

The amendment withdraws from homosexuals, but no others, specific legal protection from injuries caused by discrimination, and it forbids reinstatement of these laws and policies. . . .[21] These are protections taken for granted by most people either because they already have them or do not need them; these are protections against exclusion from an almost limitless number of transactions and endeavors that constitute ordinary civic life in a free society.[22]

The primary rationale the State offers for Amendment 2 is respect for other citizens' freedom of association, and in particular the liberties of landlords or employers who have personal or religious objections to homosexuality.[23]

To Kennedy and the Court majority, however, Amendment 2 served no legitimate purpose and unconstitutionally deprived gays and lesbians of the "equal protection of the laws." Quoting a prior case, Kennedy put it this way:

Laws of the kind now before us raise the inevitable inference that the disadvantage imposed is born of animosity toward the class of persons affected. "[I]f the constitutional conception of 'equal protection of the laws' means anything, it must at the very least mean that a bare . . . desire to harm a politically unpopular group cannot constitute a *legitimate* government interest."[24]

Justice Antonin Scalia disagreed. He claimed that people should be free to act upon their moral (social conservative) disapproval of certain conduct: "I had thought that one could consider certain conduct reprehensible—murder, for example, or polygamy, or cruelty to animals—and could exhibit even 'animus' toward such conduct. Surely that is the only sort of 'animus' at issue here: moral disapproval of homosexual conduct."[25]

In a later case (2003), the Court declared unconstitutional all laws against homosexual acts between consenting adults. Again writing for the Court majority, Kennedy believes laws against homosexuality attempt "to control a personal relationship that . . . is within the liberty of persons to choose without being punished as criminals."[26] "Adults may choose to enter upon this relationship in the confines of their homes and their own private lives and still retain their dignity as free persons."[27]

Scalia again wrote in dissent:

The Texas statute undeniably seeks to further the belief of its citizens that certain forms of sexual behavior are "immoral and unacceptable"—the same interest furthered by criminal laws against fornication, bigamy, adultery, adult incest, bestiality, and obscenity. . . . The Court today . . . effectively decrees the end of all morals legislation.[28]

The Court majority's logic, as Scalia sees it, threatens to make unconstitutional all citizen attempts to enact laws that merely express popular revulsion—the "yuck!" factor. If people can't criminalize homosexual sex simply because they find it revolting, Scalia wonders why they can criminalize other behaviors the majority finds repulsive. Consider necrophilia, sex with a corpse, which is currently illegal. Imagine that it's sex with a consenting corpse, that is, the body of someone who specified in her will that she'd like her corpse made available for sex with some specified individual or, if the corpse is a slut, with just anyone. Necrophiliacs indulging in this freebie could be prosecuted for having sex with a corpse. How could anti-necrophilia laws remain constitutional when the Constitution forbids legislation based on the "yuck!" factor? Scalia imagines that the Court majority will abandon logic and allow laws to stand that criminalize behavior they agree with most Americans is too yucky to tolerate.

In the meantime, homosexuality seems to get less yucky to most Americans all the time. Russell Shorto quotes anti-gay-marriage activist Bryan Simonaire:

We have to recognize that they [homosexuals] have a strategy to propagate their lifestyle. Think back 10 or 20 years ago, when you had the first openly homosexual person on TV. It was shocking to a lot of people. Now it's the norm on television, so you don't have the shock factor. Then they had two men with a passionate kiss on TV. That's the road they're heading down.[29]

Another activist, Don Dwyer, adds: "They are attempting through the public school system to teach not only that homosexuality is O.K. but that it's normal." Shorto reports that Maryland state officials favor a "value-neutral approach." However, "to conservative Christian activists, homosexuality is anything but value-neutral."[30]

Philosopher Kwame Anthony Appiah summarizes:

Over the last thirty or so years, instead of thinking about the private activity of gay *sex,* many Americans started thinking about the public category of gay *people.* Even those who continue to think of the sex with disgust now find it harder to deny these people their respect and concern (and some of them have learned, as we all did with our own parents, that it's better not to think too much about other people's sex lives anyway).[31]

Gains for homosexuality in popular culture follow gains in acceptance among psychiatrists. Until about 1970, homosexuality was considered a psychiatric illness or personality disorder. Then some psychiatrists designed a test of this belief. They had both gay and straight people take personality profiles that reveal all kinds of psychiatric illnesses and personality disorders. They asked experts who didn't know which profiles were of gay and which of straight people to discern from the profiles who was gay and who was straight. They couldn't do it. No known psychiatric illness or personality disorder is reliably associated with homosexuality. For this reason, theologians Patricia Jung and Ralph Smith report, "The American Psychiatric Association removed homosexuality from its list of mental illness in 1973. . . . This judgment has received global confirmation [from] the World Health Organization."[32]

Although law, popular culture, and science all increasingly consider homosexuality normal for some people, rather than a sickness or moral failure, proponents of same-sex marriage are still a minority. Russell Shorto reports that in 2004, "all 11 states that had anti-gay-marriage amendments to their state constitutions on the ballot saw those amendments pass. . . . And polls on the issue reinforce the point. Only about a quarter of voters surveyed in the national exit poll following the election favored same-sex marriage, and interestingly enough, only about half of gay and bisexual voters did."[33]

Unlike some theocrats and social conservatives, most people seem opposed to same-sex marriage for reasons other than opposition to homosexuality itself. This is shown in "the fact that civil unions, as well as efforts to extend specific rights and benefits to gay couples, receive significant support in polls."[34] In other words, Massachusetts Supreme Court Justice Margaret Marshall may be wrong when she concludes that laws against same-sex marriage merely reflect prejudice against homosexuality. Perhaps many Americans identify with social conservative arguments against same-sex marriage that center on marriage, not homosexuality.

Social Conservatism against Same-Sex Marriage

Maggie Gallagher, writing in the *Weekly Standard* in 2003, presents an eloquent case against same-sex marriage based on the importance of marriage for raising children. She quotes research from *Child Trends*:

Research clearly demonstrates that family structure matters for children, and the family structure that helps children the most is a family headed by two biological parents in a low-conflict marriage. Children in single-parent families, children born to unmarried mothers, and children in stepfamilies or cohabiting relationships face higher risks of poor outcomes. . . . There is thus value for children in promoting strong, stable marriages between biological parents.[35]

Gallagher sees two different conceptions of marriage at war in contemporary culture. One conception views marriage as a way of expressing profound connection between two individuals. Justice Marshall articulates this idea in her Massachusetts Supreme Court opinion that allowed Julie and Hilary Goodridge to marry. "The decision whether and whom to marry is among life's momentous acts of self-definition." So, the state shouldn't, "without sufficient justification, foreclose an individual from freely choosing the person with whom to share an exclusive commitment in the unique institution of civil marriage."[36] Marshall emphasizes individual choice and self expression. Concerning this conception of marriage, Gallagher writes, marriage is

a kind of Good Housekeeping Seal of Approval that government stamps on certain registered intimacies. . . . In this view, endorsement of gay marriage is a nobrainer, for nothing really important rides on whether anyone gets married or stays married. Marriage is merely individual expressive conduct, and there is no obvious reason why some individuals' expression of gay love should hurt other individuals' expressions of non-gay love.

There is, however, a different view . . . radically opposed to this: Marriage is the fundamental, cross-cultural institution for bridging the male-female divide so that children have loving, committed mothers and fathers. Marriage is inherently normative: It is about holding out a certain kind of relationship as a social ideal, especially when there are children involved.[37]

The marriage idea is that children need mothers and fathers, that societies need babies, and that adults have an obligation to shape their sexual behavior so as to give their children stable families in which to grow up.[38]

Gallagher emphasizes individuals meeting preset norms of behavior appropriate to marriage and raising their children to do the same. Marriage is not merely a contract between two people. It bonds the couple to a tradition that spans generations, because it meets the need of our species and society to raise children responsibly.

Gallagher claims that bonding the couple to a tradition—not just to one another—is necessary because many distractions and temptations threaten marriage:

Many of the things men and women have to do to sustain their own marriages, and a culture of marriage, are hard. Few people will do them consistently if the larger culture does not affirm the critical importance of marriage as a social institution. Why stick out a frustrating relationship, turn down a tempting new love, abstain from sex outside marriage, or even take the pains not to conceive children out of wedlock if family structure does not matter?[39]

The results of viewing marriage as merely formal recognition of two people's love is evident in the weakening hold that marriage has in society. Gallagher writes:

Marriage is in crisis. . . . High rates of divorce and illegitimacy have eroded marriage norms and created millions of fatherless children, whole neighborhoods where lifelong marriage is no longer customary, driving up poverty, crime, teen pregnancy, welfare dependency, drug abuse, and mental and physical problems.[40]

The ideal of marriage so crucial to responsible procreation and child-rearing does not require that every couple have children or even try to have children. Still, the traditional concept of marriage protects children.

Even today, in our technologically advanced contraceptive culture, half of all pregnancies are unintended: Sex between men and women still makes babies.[41] Every marriage between a man and a woman is capable of giving any child they create or adopt a mother and a father. Every marriage between a man and a woman discourages either from creating fatherless children outside the marriage vow. . . . Even when a man marries an older woman and they do not adopt, his marriage helps protect children. How? His marriage means, if he keeps his vows, that he will not produce out-of-wedlock children.[42]

Rejecting same-sex marriage also protects children put up for adoption, social conservative William Bennett writes. If gays could marry, "homosexual couples would . . . have equal claim with heterosexual couples in adopting children." Bennett acknowledges that "the research on this matter is very sparse," but still claims, "we know . . . that it is far better for a child to be raised by a mother and a father than by two homosexuals."[43] (He doesn't explain how "very sparse" research leads to knowledge.)

In sum, same-sex marriage shouldn't be allowed, because it assumes that marriage is an expression of individual attachment, rather than the joining of a couple to a multigenerational tradition that protects children and perpetuates culture. Gallagher writes:

Same-sex marriage would enshrine in law a public judgment that the desire of adults for families of choice outweighs the need of children for mothers and fathers. It would give sanction and approval to the creation of a motherless or fatherless family as a deliberately chosen "good." It would mean the law was neutral as to whether children had mothers and fathers. Motherless and father-less families would be deemed just fine.[44]

This judgment will further erode adherence to the marriage ideal that protects children. It will harm individual children and impair our culture's ability to pass on to future generations all the moral and civic ideals that children learn first and best from dutiful parents.

Gallagher's social conservative critique of same-sex marriage, unlike some others, doesn't rest at all on disapproval of homosexuality.

William Bennett believes that same-sex marriage will degrade traditional marriage because gay men tend to be promiscuous. He writes:

Advocates of same-sex marriage concede that at least among male homosexuals, promiscuity *is* a problem—but, they say, it is a problem only because access has been denied to the institution of marriage and would recede once access were granted. This is, at best an untested hypothesis. . . .

There is also this: men are in general much more inclined than women to want sex without commitment or restraint—which suggests . . . that it is not marriage that domesticates men; it is women . . . and . . . children. . . . Yet both women and (for the most part) children would be missing in male homosexual marriages. . . .[45]

My own guess is that . . . instead of marriage radically tempering homosexual promiscuity, same-sex marriage in practice would lead to the further legitimation of "extramarital outlets" for all.[46]

Because Bennett here concentrates on the problem of promiscuity, which is less prominent among lesbians, the argument is aimed at same-sex marriage for men.

Social Conservative Arguments for Same-Sex Marriage

Social conservative Jonathan Rauch agrees with fellow social conservatives Gallagher and Bennett that marriage is an essential institution currently in trouble, but thinks same-sex marriage will strengthen the institution.

He writes, "marriage serves three essential social needs: providing a healthy environment for children (one's own and other people's), helping the young (especially men) settle down and make a home, and providing as many people as possible with caregivers."[47] Consider these in order.

Rauch agrees with other social conservatives:

Marriage is uniquely good for raising children. Children need stability, security, affection, socialization, resources, moral instruction. Marriage does a better job of providing those than does any other arrangement we know. . . . A single-parent home is (on average) a more financially and emotionally vulnerable environment for kids than is a two-parent home, and no amount of welfare money can change that. . . . Marriage is the surest way to keep food on the table, to ensure against disasters and shocks, to weave your family into a supportive community, and to keep both parents involved in your upbringing.[48]

Marriage helps children of same-sex parents as much as other children. The 2000 census recorded between 166,000 and 300,000 children parented by same-sex couples. Given continuing reticence to reveal same-sex partnerships, the real figure may be over a million. Rauch asks the rhetorical question: "If you were the child of a same-sex couple, would you feel more secure with legally married parents, or less secure?"[49] The presence of children in same-sex unions argues for same-sex marriage.

Children can't be the only reason for marriage, however. Rauch, being a social conservative, looks to tradition: "No society denies marriage to the infertile; no society requires couples to promise they will have children; no society nullifies marriage if children don't turn up."[50] There must be other reasons for marriage besides children.

Society promotes marriage also to help young men settle down. Rauch quotes social conservative James Q. Wilson: "In every known society, men are more likely than women to play roughly, drive recklessly, fight physically, and assault ruthlessly, and these differences appear early in life. . . . Of all the institutions through which men may pass—schools, factories, the military—marriage has the largest [stabilizing] effect."[51] Rauch thinks marriage will have the same stabilizing effect on gay as on straight men. "Some people argue that women and children, more than just the fact of marriage, socialize and settle men. That may be true," Rauch acknowledges.

But that hardly means that the settling effect of marriage on gay men would be negligible. . . . In American gay-male life, it's a cliché that men in relationships vanish from the clubs and the parties. "Haven't seen you out in ages," people say. "You must have found someone." Because of the realities of stitching two lives together, couples simply do not have as much time or energy for getting around, or as much desire to do so. . . .

And marriage stabilizes relationships. . . . You get the binding power of legal entitlements and entanglements, of caterers and in-laws, of the publicly acknowledged fact that the two partners are a couple. Even without kids or women, abandoning a marriage is much harder than abandoning a relationship.[52]

Finally, besides providing for children and helping to settle men down, marriage provides partners with caregivers.

From society's point of view, an unattached person is an accident waiting to happen. The burdens of contingency are likely to fall, immediately and sometimes crushingly, on people—relatives, friends, neighbors—who have enough problems of their own, and then on charities and welfare agencies. . . .

If marriage has any meaning at all, it is that when you collapse from a stroke, there will be another person whose "job" it is to drop everything and come to your aid. Or that when you come home after being fired, there will be someone to talk you out of committing a massacre or killing yourself. To be married is to know there is someone out there for whom you are always first in line.[53]

This care-giving aspect of marriage is reflected in traditional marriage vows. Take out the part about obeying and this oath still expresses what we expect in marriage: "To have and to hold from this day forward, for better for worse, for richer for poorer, in sickness and in health, to love, cherish, and to obey, till death us do part."[54]

The three social benefits of marriage apply to same-sex marriages. Children get more secure homes, young men are tamed, and partners have caregivers. So it's not just that the same-sex couple benefits from their marriage, society benefits.

But what about the corrosive effect of same-sex marriage on traditional marriage? Rauch argues that same-sex marriage will strengthen rather than weaken traditional marriage. He notes first that same-sex couples are here to stay. "The days when homosexual unions—marital or nonmarital—were invisible are gone, and gone for good. Homosexual relationships will enjoy increasing social recognition and respect even outside marriage."[55] Evidence for this view comes from increasing calls for same-sex couples to be granted civil unions instead of marriage. Russell Shorto reports: "In April [2005] Connecticut passed a law recognizing same-sex civil unions, which have been legal in Vermont for five years. The fact that civil unions, as well as efforts to extend specific rights and benefits to gay couples, receive significant support in polls suggests that many who object to gay marriage nevertheless see an underlying civil rights issue."[56] The realistic choice, as Rauch sees it, isn't between same-sex marriage and gay relationships disappearing from view, but between same-sex marriage and civil unions.

Civil unions and domestic partnership status for same-sex couples will erode traditional marriage, Rauch claims. Same-sex couples are increasingly given some benefits, such as health coverage, by employers who see the exclusion of gays as unfair and bad for morale. Unmarried heterosexual couples then want the same. It's none of the company's business why they've chosen not to marry. "Gay groups figure the surest way to get and keep partner programs is to give the straight majority a stake in them," so they support extension of the programs to straight couples.

As of the end of 2002, nine states, the District of Columbia, and 140 municipalities and other local government agencies offered domestic-partner benefits (including at least health insurance); 70 percent of those programs were open to both gay and straight couples. Among the *Fortune* 500 companies, 154 offered domestic-partner programs, of which just over 60 were open to straight couples.[57]

Domestic partnership is becoming a kind of marriage-lite.

The same is true of civil unions. Rauch asks us to consider: "Why do we see marrying as one of life's epochal decisions? What gives the institution such mystique, such force? I believe the answer is, in two words, *social expectation*."[58] "Marriage is not merely a contract between two people. It is a contract between two people *and their community*."[59] Civil unions, like domestic partnerships, promise to give people many of the practical benefits of marriage without all the social expectations of life-long mutual support. It's another form of marriage-lite that commitment-phobic straight couples may find convenient and attractive.

Cohabitation is the greatest competitor to marriage.

According to the 2000 census, during the 1990s the number of unmarried-partner households in the United States increased by 72 percent. . . . Now the number [is] more than 5 million cohabiting couples, the vast majority of them heterosexual. . . . Marriage, meanwhile, is headed in the other direction. The marriage rate (defined as the annual number of weddings per thousand single women age fifteen or older) fell by 40 percent from 1970 to 2000.[60]

As people become increasingly used to same-sex couples cohabiting because they can't get married, cohabitation as an alternative to marriage for straight couples is reinforced.

The proliferation of alternatives to marriage weakens the institution of marriage. Rauch writes:

Already in America, if you want to get together with someone, and depending on where you live or work, you can have cohabitation, employer domestic-partner benefits, public domestic-partner benefits, marriage, or even covenant marriage (. . . which is harder to get into and out of). At this rate, marriage may become merely an item on a mix-and-match menu of lifestyle options.[61]

Rauch concludes:

Same sex-marriage, then, clarifies and reinforces the key message to people who are embarking on coupledom: marriage is for everybody, marriage is unique—no exceptions, exclusions, or excuses. In doing so, gay matrimony bolsters marriage's status as the gold standard for committed relationships, at a time when marriage's competitors are gaining ground.[62]

Polygamy

Social conservative William Bennett counters that legalizing same-sex marriage will put us on a slippery slope leading to legalized incest and polygamy.

There are no principled grounds on which advocates of same-sex marriage can oppose the marriage of two consenting brothers. Nor can they (persuasively) explain why we ought to deny a marriage license to three men who want to marry. Or to a man who wants a consensual polygamous arrangement. . . . Any of these people may desire to enter into a lifetime of loving, faithful commitment; may believe that without marriage their ability to love and to be loved is incomplete, that society is preventing their happiness, and that they deserve to be treated equally by the government.[63]

Bennett realizes that leading proponents of same-sex marriage, like most people, reject polygamy. Nevertheless, Bennett argues:

Having just rewritten the central rule of the marriage bond, proponents of same-sex marriage are hardly qualified to dictate to others what constitutes its central meaning, or why it can be felt only between two human beings, and not more than two. What arguments would they invoke? Tradition? Religion? The time-honored definition of the family? These are the very pillars they have already destroyed. No, once marriage has been detached from the natural, complementary teleology of the sexes, it becomes nothing more than what each of us makes of it. This way, chaos follows: social chaos no less than intellectual and moral chaos.[64]

Like Bennett, Rauch considers polygamy morally odious, but doesn't think accepting same-sex marriage leads to accepting polygamy. On the contrary, he claims same-sex marriage will help defend society against polygamy.

Rauch recognizes that "most cultures, throughout history, have been polygamous. One man marries several women, at least in society's upper echelons."[65] But such societies are not worth emulating. "As far as I can tell not a single one of those polygamous societies has ever been a liberal democracy. . . . To the contrary, they tend to be authoritarian rather than liberal, hierarchical and male-supremacist rather than egalitarian, and closed rather than open. Examples begin with the biblical patriarchs and extend through Brigham Young's Mormons down to Saudi Arabia today. Why?"[66]

In polygamous societies, plural wives are status symbols. "A yacht or a Lamborghini can't hold a candle to a harem. With elite men taking more than their share, low-status men have trouble finding mates, and some can't marry at all."[67] This leads to the problem of bad behavior endemic among single men.

Whether in the Third World or in inner-city America, a good way to create an angry and restless underclass is to create a population of unmarriageable, low-status men. . . . [In our society] young unmarried men are three times more likely than are comparable married men to commit murder, and they are also more likely to rob and rape. To worsen the problem . . . , make these young men not only unmarried but unmarriageable. . . . I suspect . . . that such a society can keep a lid on its marriageless underclass only by repressing it. Every man needs to know his place and be kept in it, by convention if possible, by force if necessary.[68]

Rauch speculates: "Without equal opportunity in marriage, anything like today's social mobility and political equality would be unthinkable. Women, especially, would be losers, because in polygamous marriages they often become more like their husband's rival concubines than his full equals."[69]

This argument against polygamy would appeal to contractarians. Contractarians think that state laws and social rules should be fair to everyone, and one sign of fairness is acceptability to all people, regardless of their social position. Everyone should be able to endorse the laws and rules without knowing their own positions in society. Only rules that allow for equal opportunity pass this test.

Marriage laws allowing polygamy don't pass this test, if Rauch is correct that they lead to many men being unmarriageable and many women being oppressed by husbands and harassed by co-wives. No one would want to be among the unmarriageable males or oppressed females, so polygamy doesn't pass the contractarian test of fairness. It doesn't allow for equal opportunity in marriage.

Same-sex marriage is completely different. From a contractarian perspective, marriage laws, to be fair to everyone, should accommodate gays, because no one wants automatic and permanent exclusion from such a valuable institution. Only by allowing same-sex marriage will gays be given equal opportunity. Rauch writes:

Homosexual love is natural and essential *for homosexuals,* just as heterosexual love is natural and essential for heterosexuals. . . . Sex, love, and marriage go together. . . . Sex without love and love (at least romantic love) without sex both tend to be hollow, unstable, and difficult to integrate into a healthy emotional life. And marriage is just as important as the other two. . . . Every kiss, every passion, from the first crush and the first date, has a different, deeper meaning in the context of possible marriage.

Marriage gives love a direction, a calling. It promises that love can lead somewhere, to a purpose higher than oneself. It also gives purpose to sex by making it potentially a union of lives rather than just of bodies.[70]

If you didn't know if you were gay or straight, you'd want same-sex marriage to be legal so that you wouldn't be denied an important aspect of human fulfillment.

Male polygamists might also want what they consider fulfillment—several wives—but their desire, Rauch thinks, conflicts with equal opportunity for all, whereas the homosexual desire for marriage allows everyone equal opportunity.

Rauch's argument against polygamy is also socially conservative. Polygamy, unlike same-sex marriage, fails to fulfill two important social roles of marriage. One role is domesticating young men so that they aren't socially disruptive. Same-sex marriage promises to do this, whereas polygamy promises to unleash onto society a host of permanently unattached men. Another social role of marriage is securing caregivers for everyone. Same sex-marriage furthers this goal, but polygamy doesn't. First, all those unattached men would lack reliable caregivers. Second, Rauch reasons,

if I were to marry three or four people, the pool of potential caregivers would be larger, but the situation would, perversely, make all of them less reliable: each could expect one of the others to take care of me (and each may be reluctant to do more than any of the others are willing to do. . .). The pair bond, one to one, is the only kind which is inescapably reciprocal, perfectly mutual. Because neither of us has anyone else, we are there for each other.[71]

Finally, polygamy undermines traditional marriage. Rauch, as we've seen, argues that having a single standard of marriage for all people, gay and straight, protects marriage against competition from civil unions, domestic partnerships, and cohabitation. Polygamists, by contrast, could get their foot in the door for plural marriage by strengthening domestic partnerships, Rauch thinks.

The polygamist would say, "Look, this [domestic partnership] program isn't marriage anyway—that's why it exists. I have two equally important women in my life, and we share a home. . . . So have a heart and sign up both of my girlfriends for domestic-partner benefits." To whatever extent society bestows recognition and legitimacy and prerogatives on group arrangements, the path would be eased for the law to follow suit. Group marriage might come to seem . . . less shocking. . . . A generation on, adjusting legal marriage to allow groups might seem a natural thing to do.[72]

Rauch considers this possible criticism of his reasoning:

Aha! Rauch has just inadvertently explained why it is so important to leave the definition of marriage alone. Marriage is hard to change. . . . The thing to do is leave it that way. . . . Rauch depends on marriage's tamper resistance to stop polygamy, even as he calls for just the sort of radical redefinition which would make marriage less tamper resistant. He's really saying: "One unprecedented, dramatic change—then no more." But that's not how things work. In the real world, break one taboo, and others follow.[73]

This imagined criticism could have been written by William Bennett. Rauch answers that equal treatment for gays—based on what I've labeled contractarian arguments—will prevail. People increasingly realize that "everyone should have a reasonable chance of marrying somebody."[74] But we must also protect marriage.

Gay marriage . . . aligns with the one-person-one-partner rule. . . . It clarifies rather than smudges marriage's boundaries by confirming marriage as *the* one-to-one lifelong commitment of choice. . . . I don't think the American public will have much trouble distinguishing the principle of same-sex marriage (one for everybody—the principle of monogamy itself) from the principle of traditional polygamy (many for some, none for others). . . .[75]

Polygamy has its defenders, however. Although some communities are under investigation for forcing underage girls to marry older men who already have several wives,[76] Centennial Park, Arizona, is home to a community of polygamists who marry only as adults. They broke away from the mainstream Church of Jesus Christ of the Latter Day Saints and claim the right to plural marriage on grounds of religious freedom. They pride themselves on providing individual freedom to both women and men and first-rate education for both girls and boys. Mindelle Jacobs, reporting in the *Edmonton Sun*, quotes one woman, "I am a plural wife . . . and we feel that we are much more empowered than our monogamous counterparts." Another, Anne Wilde, spoke of her plural marriage of thirty-three years to a man who died in 2002. She didn't live with her husband, preferring to stay in the community with her children from a traditional marriage that ended in divorce. "He'd come here one night and then maybe the next night he'd be with somebody else and that was fine. . . . I just had a great marriage. We were very happy."[77]

LeAnne Timson, administrator of Centennial Park's Masada Charter School told Jacobs that most of the school's 380 children in kindergarten through ninth grade are from the polygamous community.

The school is a "performing plus" school, meaning the children exceed both state and county averages on test scores. More than 90% finish high school and many go on to college and university. About one-third of the teachers, who are from Centennial Park's polygamous community, have master's degrees. There are no underage marriages and no one is forced into polygamy. If they would like to leave the community, they can. There are no walls and gates that keep them here. The lifestyle and these kinds of families are not for everyone. We don't encourage our children to enter these relationships naively.[78]

Linda Valdez, writing in the *Arizona Republic*, reported after visiting Centennial Park: "The children I met there are well-spoken and praise an 'awesome' lifestyle of growing up with a father, mothers and many siblings. . . . [Adults] tout the educational attainment and career accomplishments of women whom they say thrive in the 'liberating' and 'uplifting' lifestyle of plural marriage."[79]

Some Centennial Park women whom Valdez met acknowledged that problems exist in their community, but think this argues for legalizing polygamy.

The women pointed out that the secrecy into which polygamists were driven by laws against the way of life practiced by early Mormons is a breeding ground for . . . problems. . . . By making polygamy a crime, a society that professes a belief in religious freedom has denied them the opportunity to take advantage of law enforcement, child welfare agencies and other resources that can deal with the evils that occur whenever humans live with other humans.[80]

The argument here is the same as the contractarian equal opportunity argument for legalizing same-sex marriage. The state should not pick and choose among lifestyles, helping some and hindering others, without good reason. Legal marriage confers many benefits that should be available to everyone who's not harming others. Jonathan Rauch rejects stereotyping homosexuality but seems to rely on stereotypes of polygamy.

Alternatively, the argument for polygamy could rest on multiculturalism, the view that the state should accommodate as many different cultural traditions as can peacefully coexist. The premise is that no culture has a monopoly on the best way to live, so people should be allowed to retain cultural traditions that differ from mainstream society, and experiments in different social arrangements should be allowed. Regarding marriage, multiculturalists deny the ideal, shared by social conservatives on both sides of the same-sex marriage debate, of a single model for everyone in society.

Conclusion

The argument for legalizing homosexuality is purely libertarian. Consenting adults should be free to engage in private acts that harm no one else. Homosexuals just want to be left alone to do their own thing; they're not seeking any government help.

The arguments against legalizing homosexuality are primarily theocratic (God disapproves of homosexuality, as the Bible makes clear) or natural law (observation and reason reveal that the human body is constructed only for heterosexual sex).

The arguments for same-sex marriage are either contractarian or social conservative. The contractarian argument for same-sex marriage is the same as the argument for polygamy. Legal marriage confers benefits and, absent compelling reasons to the contrary, all people should have equal opportunity to reap those benefits. This is the argument of Massachusetts Supreme Court Justice Margaret Marshall whose opinion allowed Julie and Hillary Goodridge to get married. The same basic rationale was given by a majority of the California Supreme Court in 2008 when they declared laws against same-sex marriage to violate the state constitution.[81] Jonathan Rauch emphasizes social conservative arguments as well. Marriage helps society: it provides good environments for child-rearing; tames men; and supplies caregivers to those in need. Giving gays an alternative to marriage, such as civil unions or domestic partnerships, will undermine traditional marriage much more than allowing same-sex marriage.

The arguments against same-sex marriage are theocratic and natural law insofar as they're just extensions of arguments against legalizing homosexuality. If homosexuality should be illegal, so should same-sex marriage. The major arguments against same-sex marriage that don't rest on arguments against homosexuality are social conservative. Marriage is a precious social institution in jeopardy from many causes. Any deviation from tradition could be a mortal blow, especially a deviation as momentous and unprecedented as acceptance of same-sex marriage.

In any case, marriage doesn't solve all problems. The *Boston Globe* reported two years after their wedding that Julie and Hillary Goodridge had officially separated. Some people will note that half of all marriages in the United States end in divorce. Others may consider this particular divorce to vindicate the claim that same-sex marriages are unnatural, immoral, and/or against God's law. People in this latter category are likely to object on similar grounds to genetic engineering, especially when it is used to design children to meet parental specifications. This is our next topic.

10

Genetic Engineering and Designer Children: Libertarianism, Utilitarianism, Contractarianism, Environmentalism, Natural Law, and Social Conservatism

The Utilitarian Promise of Genetic Engineering

Genetic engineering includes all procedures aimed at health or improvement using knowledge of how specific genes can affect certain traits. Here we consider applications to human beings, as in this *Newsweek* account: "The patient is in the bloom of her early 30s, blessed by good health and cursed by a bleak future. Thanks to a rare genetic mutation—a single misplaced nucleotide among the billions that constitute a chromosome—she is almost sure to develop Alzheimer's disease by 40."[1]

Alzheimer's disease produces dementia. According the *American Medical Association Family Medical Guide*:

Most characteristic of dementia at the onset is the gradual loss of memory, especially for recent events. You may notice that the person cannot remember what has happened a few hours (or even moments) earlier, although he or she can recall what happened many years ago.

Dementia often culminates in emotional and physical instability. Many people swing between apathy and aggression, tears and laughter, at the slightest provocation. . . . Table manners may deteriorate, personal cleanliness is sometimes neglected, and usual politeness abandoned. Some people may even become violent if impulsive behavior is frustrated. . . . .

In the advanced stages of dementia, there is generalized stiffness of the muscles. . . . Toward the end, the affected person may have lost all ability to perceive, think, speak or move. . . . This gradual collapse . . . may linger on for ten years or more.[2]

This fate almost surely awaits the woman described in *Newsweek*, who wanted to leave a child for her husband. But she didn't want their child to suffer as she will. So,

using a procedure called pre-implantation genetic diagnosis, or PGD, specialists in Chicago helped her bear a child who will escape her awful fate. . . .

The woman at the center of this story had seen her father and two siblings stricken at young ages. And when researchers linked the family curse to a genetic anomaly, she discovered she was a carrier. Knowing that her own decline was imminent—and that any child she conceived naturally would have a 50 percent chance of inheriting the bad gene—she consulted specialists [who] proposed using in vitro fertilization [IVF] to create a child who wouldn't share her fate.[3]

IVF requires a woman to take drugs to stimulate ovulation, making many ova available for harvesting instead of just one a month. The harvested ova are fertilized outside the woman. As Amy Harmon explains in the *New York Times*:

When the resulting embryos are three days old, doctors remove a single cell from each and analyze its DNA. Only embryos without the defective gene are then considered candidates to implant in the mother's uterus. . . . Because embryos are selected for their genetic status, rather than solely by which look the healthiest, the chance that they will fail to develop after implantation is higher. And despite the birth of thousands of apparently healthy babies after P.G.D., there is still concern that the long-term effects of removing a cell from an eight-cell embryo have not been studied enough.[4]

Embryos found to have undesirable genes are usually destroyed. The woman discussed in *Newsweek*, for example, required two cycles of egg harvesting. "An initial cycle yielded only two mature [fertilized] eggs, and tests showed that both carried the mutation. But a second cycle yielded thirteen, including six that were unaffected. Doctors placed four of the six in the woman's uterus, and one of them took. The result was a healthy baby girl, now nearly a year and a half old."[5] At least nine fertilized eggs will never be allowed to develop. Two others, with no known genetic defects, may eventually be destroyed. People who believe that personhood begins at fertilization oppose PGD on the same grounds as they oppose abortion. Yet the technique promises to free people from some devastating diseases, such as cystic fibrosis and Huntington's disease, and to reduce risks of colon, breast, and other cancers among children of high-risk parents.

Philosopher Bonnie Steinbock describes a life-saving application of PGD:

Molly Nash was born on July 4, 1994, with multiple birth defects due to Fanconi anemia, a deadly genetic disease that causes bone marrow failure, eventually resulting in leukemia and other forms of cancer. Her best chance for survival was a bone marrow transplant from a perfectly matched sibling donor. Lisa and Jack Nash had considered having another child [but] had decided against it because there was a one-in-four chance that the infant would have the same illness as Molly, and aborting an affected fetus was not an option Mrs. Nash would consider. Then they learned about . . . PGD, which would enable them to screen embryos for the disease, and implant only the healthy ones. Moreover, the embryos could also be tested to find which one shared Molly's tissue type.[6]

After three failed attempts, involving a few dozen embryos, during which time Molly was slowly approaching death, Lisa became pregnant with a healthy, matching embryo. Adam Nash was born on August 29, 2000, and his umbilical cord blood prevented Molly from developing leukemia. Molly's healthy now, but remains at great risk for many other medical problems, such as future cancers of the mouth and neck.

The utilitarian benefits of these medical interventions are obvious. Much pain and suffering is avoided and great joy provided by saving lives and ensuring that genetic diseases don't afflict future generations.

Libertarians for Sex Selection and Genetic Enhancement

PGD can also be used for sex selection, as Claudia Kalb and Karen Springen explain in *Newsweek*: "Sharla Miller of Gillette, Wyo., always wanted a baby girl." After she had three sons, she had her tubes tied and considered adopting a girl. "I'm best friends with my mother. . . . I couldn't get it out of my mind that I wanted a daughter." She learned about PGD through an Internet search.

PGD could guarantee—with almost 100 percent certainty—the sex of her baby. Price tag: $18,480, plus travel. Last November [2003] Sharla's eggs and Shane's sperm were mixed in a lab dish, producing 14 healthy embryos, seven male and seven female. [The doctor] transferred three of the females into Sharla's uterus, where two implanted successfully. If all goes well, the run of Miller boys will end in July with the arrival of twin baby girls. "I have three wonderful boys," says Sharla, "but since there was a chance I could have a daughter, why not?"[7]

Some people worry about where all this is going; how techniques based on knowledge of the human genome will be used in the future. Kalb and Springen write: "If couples can request a baby boy or girl, what's next on the slippery slope of modern reproductive medicine? Eye color? Height? Intelligence?"[8] Are we headed to an era of designer children and, if we are, is this bad?

Lee Silver, who teaches molecular biology at Princeton University, thinks designer children are definitely in our future. "Parents are going to be able to give their children genes that increase athletic ability, genes that increase musical talents and ultimately genes that affect cognitive abilities."[9] And they won't have to use PGD, which allows parents to choose only among embryos whose genetic profile has already been determined by parental genes and chance. Instead, they'll be able to have desired genes, including ones not present in the family line, inserted directly into an embryo. This is genetic enhancement. In a *Frontline* interview, Silver said: "The reason I'm sure it's going to happen is because we have already perfected this in animals. It's something that we do in mice in this building every day. We put genes in these mouse embryos and the mice grow up with these new genes."[10] Dinesh D'Souza reports in *National Review*: "In 1999, neurobiologist Joe Tsien boosted the intelligence of mice by inserting extra copies of a gene that enhances memory and learning; these mouse genes are virtually identical to those found in human beings."[11]

Inserting genes can enhance an embryo either by giving the resulting child extra protection against disease or by conferring other advantages, such as greater height, memory, intelligence, or strength. Silver supports parental rights to help their children through genetic enhancements of both sorts. "I don't see why it is problematic for parents to want to give their children . . . advantages, because after birth they provide all sorts of advantages to their children. Before birth, they're going to want to do the same."[12]

The four bioethicists who wrote *From Chance to Choice*, Allen Buchanan, Dan Brock, Norman Daniels, and Daniel Wikler, agree with Silver that genetically enhancing children is just a new way of parents trying to get what's best for their kids.

Parents are generally regarded as having permission, and some would say an obligation, to produce the "best" children they can. They are expected, for example, to keep their children as healthy as possible. . . , by moderating their fat intake . . . and restricting their access to "junk" foods. . . .

Parents also pursue the best for their children—as they see it—through exercise and sports. Some children are enrolled in Little League baseball, soccer, basketball, football, or hockey. They get tennis and swimming lessons. . . .

Of course, parents who have the means often . . . give their children violin or piano or ballet lessons, enroll them in chess clubs and tournaments, or encourage their computer skills or interest in math teams.[13]

In all these cases, "there is a presumption in favor of not interfering with parents."[14]

Like Silver, Buchanan et al. think that parents should be able to use genetic as well as traditional means of improving their children's future. They note that opponents of genetic enhancement say parents using traditional means "are only 'bringing out the best in them,' or developing 'the potential' that is already there. In contrast, the use of genetic information and intervention . . . suggests parents are changing their children in some fundamental way."[15] But this is incorrect, they claim. Ordinary interventions alter children in fundamental ways, too. A vaccination "permanently affects the ability of the immune system to respond to particular bacteria or viruses." In addition:

How the child is fed, for example, will affect height, strength, and resistance to illness. How the child exercises will affect body shape, muscle development, strength, and physical capabilities and even neurological development. How the child is spoken to, read to, and interacted with will affect the development of cognitive and emotional capabilities. There is no pre-existing ("essential") "best" in the child that is brought out.[16]

In sum, libertarian freedom includes the right of parents to genetically enhance their children if they want to.

Some people object to designing children because they consider it a form of eugenics. "Eugenics," a term coined in 1883 by Francis Galton, a cousin of Charles Darwin, means good inheritance. The idea was to improve the human species by encouraging mating among people of superior qualities while discouraging procreation among inferiors. Buchanan et al. explain, "In both the United Kingdom and the United States, a long list of social ills, including poverty, prostitution, drunkenness, and crime, were attributed to the [biologically] 'unfit.'"[17] In 1914, for example, eugenics enthusiast Charles Davenport wrote:

We hear a great deal about infant mortality and child saving that appeals to the humanity and the child-love in us all. . . . But the daughters of prostitutes have hardly one chance in two of being able to react otherwise than their mothers. Why must we start an expensive campaign to keep alive those who, were they intelligent enough, might well curse us for having intervened on their behalf? Is not death nature's great blessing to the race?[18]

Buchanan et al. comment:

These views betray an almost visceral hatred (parading as concern for the victims who would curse us for their rescue). The first step toward atrocity is the objectification, vilification, and ridicule of the victim. The comparison of "feeble-minded" people and others in the underclass to feces, waste, and animals made it thinkable to deprive hundreds of thousands of people of their civil rights, first through institutionalization, then by involuntary sterilization, and, in the singular instance of Nazi Germany, through murder.[19]

Current proposals for genetic engineering, whether PGD or enhancement, differ from eugenics programs, the ethicists point out. Eugenics programs empowered the state to curtail individual liberties for the greater good of society, whereas current proposals for genetic engineering empower parents to do what they consider best for their children. There's no official stereotyping of groups as inferior, no involuntary sterilization, no loss of liberty. Instead, the freedom of parents to influence their children's future for the better is increased. The libertarian value of parental autonomy coincides with the utilitarian goal of providing the greatest good for the greatest number, proponents argue.

Others, however, resist such parental prerogatives on utilitarian and feminist grounds. Imagine, for example, if sex selection becomes cheap and widely available. Bioethicist Bonnie Steinbock writes in *Hastings Center Report* about sex selection in China where "the population has been so drastically skewed (through abortion and infanticide) that at one point there were 153 boys to every 100 girls."[20] In 2001 in India's most prosperous provinces, ethicist Dan Brock reports, there were about 130 boys to 100 girls.[21] The normal ratio at birth is 105 boys for every 100 girls. The result of too many boys could be young men without any prospect of marriage wreaking havoc on society. This utilitarian concern explains some opposition to polygamy.

Most people in the United States want both a boy and a girl, so problems of sex-ratio imbalance may not develop here. "Nevertheless," Steinbock tells us,

a study . . . at Cleveland State University found that of those Americans who would use sex selection, 81 percent of the women and 94 percent of the men would want their firstborn to be a boy. Lori Andrews has commented that this finding is troubling in light of research on birth order, which "consistently finds that first-borns are more aggressive, more achieving, of higher income and education than later-borns. We'll be creating a nation of little sisters."[22]

This is a concern for feminists who worry that associating women with subordinate roles will impair equal opportunity.

What is more, fashions may change. Americans may start wanting more girls than boys or more boys than girls. If sex selection were easy and cheap, fashion trends in children could result in skewed sex ratios and attendant social problems.

Another objection to parental genetic selection arises from disagreement with parental choices. Consider, as ethicist Dan Brock puts it, "the preference of some deaf persons to have a deaf child."[23] Philosopher Robert Sparrow explains that "deaf persons who identify with Deaf culture . . . [believe] it is perfectly possible to lead a happy and productive life without hearing or spoken language."[24] They think deafness is a disability for social reasons only. All obstacles could be removed, such as by replacing all telephones with telex machines. In addition, Sparrow explains:

A loss of capacities in one area is often accompanied by a gain in capacities in another. People who are deaf often have skills and abilities that hearing people lack. First and foremost of these is the ability to communicate in Sign as a natural first language. But deaf persons may also have superior consciousness of subtlety of gesture and of the movement of bodies through space than do hearing persons. More generally, the differences which in existing social contexts appear to us as disabling may sometimes be better thought of as constituting a different way of being, and one which is not necessarily inferior.[25]

Many deaf people want their children to be deaf so they can participate in Deaf culture, just as many Irish-Americans want their children to participate in Irish culture, and many Jews want their children to be culturally Jewish. It's common in America to honor parental aspirations of cultural continuity. For example, school attendance policies were modified to help Amish parents retain the Amish way of life among their children.[26]

The deaf have good reason to think they have a culture of their own, Sparrow claims:

Deaf people possess their own distinct language(s), each with a unique vocabulary and grammar. Deaf people also have a shared set of experiences, relating to the consequences of deafness in a hearing culture, a shared history and distinct set of institutions. They have their own schools, clubs, meeting places and even sporting competitions. The combination of the possession of a language and a set of institutions makes the claim of Deaf culture a particularly strong one.[27]

Believing that deafness isn't a disability and that hearing impairs participation in Deaf culture, it's no surprise that many deaf parents want their children to be deaf. They could use PGD to ensure deafness, just as others use it to determine sex.

Dan Brock finds this troubling. He thinks that if it's all right for parents to use PGD to ensure deafness, "it would also seem justified for parents to stick a pin in the ears of a child, under anesthesia (to avoid the child's experiencing pain) and while the child is very young (to avoid any subjective experience of loss)."[28] Because, he suggests, the pin idea is child abuse, so is using PGD to ensure that one's child is deaf.

Brock neglects one factor, however, that distinguishes using the pin from using PGD. If a pin were used to make a hearing infant deaf, a person who could hear would be deprived of hearing. If PGD were used to ensure birth of a deaf child, on the other hand, deafness would be secured by choosing an appropriate embryo among those available after in vitro fertilization. Deafness would result from the embryo's own genetic makeup. The embryo chosen for implantation never had the potential to be born hearing. Parental preference for deafness was this embryo's only chance to live. Most people think living deaf is better than not living at all, so designing a child for deafness benefits, rather than hurts the resulting child. Of course, other embryos won't get the chance to live, because they aren't chosen, either because they lack the gene for deafness or because there were just too many embryos for all to be implanted. But it's common in IVF and PGD that more embryos are created than will develop and live.

Perhaps some people will qualify their libertarian belief in parental choice when confronted with deaf parents using PGD to have deaf children.

Communitarian and Contractarian Critiques of Genetic Engineering

As a communitarian, Michael Sandel is concerned with the moral tone of society, especially with shared commitments to social excellence, not just individual excellence. We are all products of society, encumbered with obligations stemming from the contingencies of our birth, communitarians claim. For example, most of us feel special obligations to help parents and siblings, even though we didn't choose these relationships. Communitarians emphasize that individual self-definition consists largely in decisions about group membership, because we're social animals. We join groups, becoming members of different communities, when we choose our professions, our places of work, our places of residence and, if we're religious, our places of worship. All these communities have a call on our energies and talents.

In a good society, people recognize their various community memberships and honor attendant obligations because they value collective goals, not just individual advancement. They want to promote progress in their profession, success for their colleagues, and improvement of their town, state, and nation, because they value all these communities. They have a sense of solidarity across all divisions in society and identify with the success of their country, not just with that of their family, church, or business. President John F. Kennedy's call for people to "Think not of what your country can do for you, but of what you can do for your country" is a communitarian appeal.

Sandel argues in *Atlantic* that genetic engineering threatens communitarian values by replacing chance with choice. When our genetic endowments are a matter of chance, we receive our talents as gifts and therefore can't take full credit for our achievements. We can take credit for our effort, but not for the inborn talents which, combined with effort, produce success. The genetic engineering project attempts to substitute human effort for what is now a matter of chance, enabling people more fully to take credit for success. This could reduce people's tendency to share with those less fortunate than themselves. Sandel writes:

The more alive we are to the chanced nature of our lot, the more reason we have to share our fate with others. Consider insurance. Since people do not know whether or when various ills will befall them, they pool their risk by buying health insurance and life insurance. As life plays itself out, the healthy wind up subsidizing the unhealthy, and those who live to a ripe old age wind up subsidizing the families of those who die before their time. Even without a sense of mutual obligation, people pool their risks and resources and share one another's fate.[29]

The contractarian political philosophy also relies on ignorance of individual fates to promote justice. According to contractarians, people should view state laws and policies as if they don't know who they are in society to ensure government is treating everyone fairly. In my variation of John Rawls's thought experiment about people deciding what basic rules to adopt in a society they're about to establish, I had Vanna White spin the Wheel of Fortune to reassign identities before people enter their new society. This element of chance introduced ignorance of personal fate which, as in Sandel's insurance example, motivates self-interested people to protect everyone's rights.

But Sandel's communitarian point goes beyond self-interest. He doesn't think self-interest is a proper or sufficient basis for morality. In a good society, people really care about others. Sandel thinks genetic engineering that enables people to reduce the element of chance in their genetic makeup undercuts the rationale for caring and sharing.

Why, after all, do the successful owe anything to the least-advantaged members of society? The best answer to this question leans heavily on the notion of giftedness. The natural talents that enable the successful to flourish are not their own doing, but rather their good fortune—a result of the genetic lottery. If our genetic endowments are gifts, rather than achievements for which we can claim credit, it is a mistake and a conceit to assume that we are entitled to the full measure of the bounty they reap in a market economy. We therefore have an obligation to share this bounty with those who, through no fault of their own, lack comparable gifts.[30]

Without this sense of giftedness, Sandel believes that "the successful would become even more likely than they are now to view themselves as self-made and self-sufficient, and hence wholly responsible for their success. Those at the bottom of society would be viewed not as disadvantaged, and thus worthy of a measure of compensation, but as simply unfit, and thus worthy of eugenic repair."[31]

Sandel could more accurately compare genetically engineered talents to property inheritance from parent. Genetically engineered people don't choose their own genetic makeup; their parents choose for them. Still, Sandel's point remains. Just as people now don't want to share much of their financial inheritance with the state—hence the exemption of almost everyone from inheritance taxes—they wouldn't feel morally compelled to share the enrichment that flowed from talents their parents had engineered into them. This would undercut the moral motivation to engage in the contractarian thought experiment. Why try to set up rules that are fair to everyone, when your parents have ensured that you're among the financially and genetically well endowed?

Communitarianism and Environmentalism against Genetic Engineering

If Sandel's first argument relates communitarian concerns to contractarianism, his second relates communitarian concerns to environmentalism. Attempts to engineer our children's genes reflects the general tendency in society to master nature, making it conform to our design. Success tends to diminish humility. It's better to accept what nature offers as a gift, Sandel thinks.

To appreciate children as gifts is to accept them as they come, not as objects of our design or products of our will or instruments of our ambition. Parental love is not contingent on the talents and attributes a child happens to have. We choose our friends and spouses at least partly on the basis of qualities we find attractive. But we do not choose our children. Their qualities are unpredictable, and even the most conscientious parents cannot be held wholly responsible for the kind of children they have.[32]

The problem with genetically engineering children

lies in the hubris of the designing parents, in their drive to master the mystery of birth. Even if this disposition did not make parents tyrants to their children, it would disfigure the relation between parent and child, and deprive the parent of the humility and enlarged sympathies that an openness to the unbidden can cultivate.[33]

Sandel's view could easily be confused with the notion, popular among some theocrats, that contraception manipulates nature too much in the service of human desires. Such theocrats want people making love to have "an openness to the unbidden" child that may result. But this is not Sandel's view; he doesn't go that far. He advocates moderation, a compromise between surrender to nature and control of nature. In child-rearing, it's a compromise between "accepting love" and "transforming love." "Accepting love affirms the being of the child." It appreciates children as gifts. But parents also "have an obligation to cultivate their children, to help them discover and develop their talents."[34] This is transforming love.

Some people argue that if parents can confer a host of advantages on their children by "enrolling them in expensive schools, hiring private tutors, sending them to tennis camp, providing them with piano lessons" and so forth, they should be allowed to confer genetic enhancements as well. Sandel agrees that a parallel exists but thinks the best course is for parents to back off of both projects.

The defenders of enhancement are right to this extent: improving children through genetic engineering is similar in spirit to the heavily managed, high-pressure childrearing that is now common. But this similarity does not vindicate genetic enhancement. On the contrary, it highlights a problem with the trend toward hyperparenting. One conspicuous example of this trend is sports-crazed parents bent on making champions of their children. Another is the frenzied drive of overbearing parents to mold and manage their children's academic careers.[35]

Valuing acceptance and appreciation in place of discontent and modification aligns Sandel with some environmentalists. Environmentalists believe that we need to protect nature, because current technologies enable people pursuing short-sighted goals to upset natural systems on which all life depends. Long-term human survival and well being depend on people rejecting many attempts to improve on nature. Environmentalist Bill McKibben, for example, discussing genetic engineering, contrasts the mind-sets of engineers and environmentalists:

The human instinct that looks at a free-flowing river and sees something that could be dammed to make power (or money) collides with the human instinct that values, deeply . . . the very free-flowingness of that water. The engineering impulse to tinker, bend, twist, patent, sell comes up against the environmental impulse to appreciate, preserve, protect, cherish. And that impulse, on both sides, extends to the human genome as surely as it does to the Colorado River, the Arctic National Wildlife Refuge, the grassland Savannas of Africa.[36]

Like Sandel regarding parental intervention in children's lives, McKibben takes a moderate view of human intervention in nature. We should respect nature by refraining from efforts to tame it completely, but we can use technologies that improve human life—so long as they're compatible with appreciating and sustaining nature.

Appreciating nature is part of popular culture. Many products are advertised as free of artificial colors and preservatives because consumers are thought to prefer what's natural to what's artificial.

Lee Silver, however, rejects this preference for what's natural. He told *Frontline,* "I don't think that natural is good. Natural brings us AIDS, natural brings us polio. We go against nature all the time."[37] Additionally, "Every time we use medicine to cure a disease or prevent death, we are going against nature. And most people do it gladly because they want to live longer."[38] He adds, "So I don't think we should put natural onto a pedestal and that is not the reason that we should regulate reproductive technologies."[39]

Silver disagrees with those, like Sandel and McKibben, who think we should be content with children whose genetic makeup results from chance.

I reject the luck of the draw argument against the use of the technology, because it was the same argument that people used against medicine 200 years ago. People said, "Well, some people get infected and die and other people don't and that is just the way it is. That is the way God intended it to be."

Now we reject that notion. We use medicine to overcome the unlucky draw. I don't understand why we should stop people from wanting to use medicine at an earlier time.[40]

Silver fails to note here the distinction that many people make between using genetic technology to avoid or cure illness, on the one hand, and using it to make their children taller, smarter, faster, and better looking, on the other. Like Buchanan et al., Silver generally favors moving us from chance to choice, even if that means designer children.

Social Conservative Critique of Genetic Engineering

Social conservatives, like communitarians, value social cooperation and cohesion. But they differ from communitarians in their greater concern about human moral frailties. They think that people have tendencies to misbehavior that traditions, often religious traditions, help to keep in check. They therefore prefer to preserve traditions, even imperfect ones, rather than redesign society, fearing that without traditional dos and don'ts, the new society will be worse than the old one.

Genetic engineering is particularly troublesome, according to social conservative Francis Fukuyama, because it could deprive humanity of its basic moral compass—human emotion allied with reason. He writes in *Our Posthuman Future*:

Human values are intimately bound up, as a matter of empirical fact, with human emotions and feelings. . . . There is scarcely a judgment of "good" or "bad" that has been pronounced by a human being that has not been accompanied by a strong emotion, whether of desire, longing, aversion, disgust, anger, guilt, or joy. . . . When we unearth the tortured body of a political prisoner in an authoritarian dictatorship, we pronounce the words *bad* and *monstrous* because we are driven by a complex gamut of emotions: horror at the decomposed body, sympathy for the victim's sufferings and those of family and friends, and anger at the injustice of the killing.[41]

Our emotions set limits to political forms. People tend to feel more altruistic toward a small circle of intimates than toward anonymous others in society, and this is why communism was never a real possibility for human beings. Human emotions make some state coercion necessary, because emotions produce violence born of jealousy and spite. Social control of violence is as universal as violence itself in human societies, Fukuyama points out.[42] In the modern world, family and other social training combines with government coercion to reduce violence.

Genetic engineering could aim at the laudable goal of reducing violence by reducing human tendencies toward aggression, but Fukuyama cautions against this. In the first place, the human genome is like an ecosystem. Genes interact with one another in complex ways we don't understand just as plants and animals do in ecosystems. Fukuyama quotes evolutionary biologist Edward O. Wilson: "In heredity as in the environment, you cannot do just one thing. When a gene is changed by mutation or replaced by another gene, unexpected and possibly unpleasant side effects are likely to follow."[43] Fukuyama notes: "The mouse whose intelligence was genetically boosted by neurobiologist Joe Tsien . . . seems also to have felt greater pain as a result."[44] Reducing the human tendency toward aggression might change people in some very negative ways.

Even if we could get the genetic result we wanted without unwanted side effects, there would still be unintended consequences. For example, there are good reasons, Fukuyama thinks, for human tendencies toward aggression and violence:

In evolutionary history, human beings learned . . . to cooperate in order to compete. That is, the vast panoply of human cognitive and emotional characteristics that enable such an elaborate degree of social organization was created not by the struggle against the natural environment but rather by the fact that human groups had to struggle against one another. . . . Human competitiveness and cooperation remain balanced in a symbiotic relationship. . . . If the balance shifts too far away from aggressive and violent behavior, the selective pressures in favor of cooperation will also weaken. Societies that face no competition or aggression stagnate and fail to innovate; individuals who are too trusting and cooperative make themselves vulnerable to others who are more bloody-minded.[45]

In general, Fukuyama thinks genetic engineering will try to simplify human nature, which, at present, "cannot be reduced to the possession of moral choice, or reason, or language, or sociability, or sentience, or emotions, or consciousness, or any other quality. . . . It is all of these qualities coming together in a human whole."[46] These several factors interact in complex ways that modify one another.

Human reason, for example, is not that of a computer; it is pervaded by emotions, and its functioning is in fact facilitated by the latter. Moral choice cannot exist without reason, needless to say, but it is also grounded in feelings such as pride, anger, shame, and sympathy. Human consciousness is not just individual preferences . . . , but is shaped intersubjectively by other consciousnesses and their moral evaluations. We are social and political animals not merely because we are capable of game-theoretic reason, but because we are endowed with cer tain social emotions. Human sentience is not that of a pig or a horse, because it is coupled with human memory and reason.[47]

One danger of genetic engineering is "the attempt to reduce a complex diversity of natural ends and purposes to just a few simple categories like pain and pleasure." Other things being equal, the utilitarian goals of more pleasure and less pain are laudable, Fukuyama thinks, but they shouldn't become our only goals.

This will be the constant trade-off that biotechnology will pose: we can cure this disease, or prolong this person's life . . . , at the expense of some ineffable human quality like genius, or ambition, or sheer diversity. We will be constantly tempted to think that we understand what "good" and "bad" emotions are, and that we can do nature one better by suppressing the latter, by trying to make people less aggressive, more sociable, more compliant, less depressed.[48]

If we succeed in eradicating suffering we will decimate some of "the highest and most admirable human qualities," which are brought out in how "we react to, confront, overcome, and frequently succumb to pain, suffering, and death. In the absence of these human evils there would be no sympathy, compassion, courage, heroism, solidarity, or strength of character."[49]

Social conservatives rely on emotions of disgust to protect us from innovations that could upset the social equilibrium. Consider, for example, using genetic engineering to create headless human bodies whose organs would be available for transplant. Social conservative Charles Krauthammer asked Lee Silver if he thought this was acceptable. Silver said most people would find this disgusting, but it's still a good idea, and he wouldn't mind helping people overcome their disgust.[50] Social conservatives, by contrast, think such disgust signals that a dangerous line is being crossed. Leon Kass and James Q. Wilson write, "Repugnance is the emotional expression of deep wisdom, beyond reason's power fully to articulate it. . . . Shallow are the souls [of scientists] that have forgotten how to shudder."[51] Silver quotes McKibben to the same effect: "Our gut revulsion at the coming 'enhanced' world is consciousness trying to save itself."[52]

Natural law thinkers may also rely on disgust, believing that dangerous violations of natural law appear disgusting to most people. Smearing human feces on the body, for example, is naturally disgusting. Science explains that it's also dangerous; it exposes people to microorganisms that cause disease. Sex with a parent or sibling is disgusting. Science reveals the genetic risks of incest. In general, natural law thinkers agree with social conservatives and environmentalists that disgust is a self-protective instinct. All three object to genetic engineering on this basis.

Silver, by contrast, doesn't attribute saving wisdom to "gut revulsion." He could find support from Kwame Anthony Appiah, who notes that disgust is culturally relative.

Many Americans eat pigs but won't eat cats. It would be hard to make the case that cats are . . . dirtier or more intelligent than pigs. And since there are societies where people *will* eat cats, we know that it is possible for human beings to eat them with pleasure and without danger. Most American meat eaters who refuse to eat cats have only the defense that the very thought of it fills them with disgust.

Psychologists . . . think that this capacity for disgust is a fundamental human trait, one that evolved in us because distinguishing between what you will and will not eat is an important cognitive task for an omnivorous species like ours. . . . But that capacity for disgust . . . can be built on by culture. Is it the *same* capacity that makes some men in many cultures feel polluted when they learn they have just shaken hands with a menstruating woman? Or that makes most Americans squirm in disgust at the thought of incest?[53]

Appiah thinks so. The danger of taking our revulsion too seriously is that we may unjustifiably curtail other people's activities. For example, homosexual activity between consenting adults used to be illegal because most citizens thought it disgusting. Some may have considered their disgust a sign that homosexuality violates natural law. Social conservatives on the Supreme Court, such as Justice Antonin Scalia, would allow citizen preference in this matter to carry the day, but the Court majority declared laws against homosexuality unconstitutional.[54] The majority thought revulsion isn't a rational basis for public policy. Social conservative, natural law, and environmentalist appeals to disgust as a basis for rejecting genetic engineering may similarly lack rational grounding and needlessly curtail vital freedoms, such as the freedom of parents to use genetic engineering to give their children enhancements that will improve their lives.

Genetic Engineering and (In)Justice

Social Discrimination

Applying genetic engineering to some people may cast others in a negative light. For example, some carriers of a genetic mutation making them particularly susceptible to breast cancer oppose using PGD to select only embryos for implantation that lack the mutation. They told Amy Harmon of the *Times* that they

take particular offense at the selection procedure, which they say implies that they themselves, and many members of their family, should never have existed. It raises the specter of eugenics, they say, in the most personal terms.

"It's like children are admitted to a family only if they pass the test," said Denise Toeckes, 32, a teacher who tested positive for a BRCA mutation. "It's like, 'If you have a gene, we don't want you; if you have the potential to develop cancer, you can't be in our family.'"[55]

In the future, if people use PGD extensively to avoid Down syndrome, Huntington's disease, and deafness, those with these conditions may be considered unfortunate products of prenatal parental neglect. Their parents should have ensured they didn't exist. That view leads easily to the kind of contempt that early twentieth-century eugenicist Charles Davenport had for prostitutes and their children. Social inclusion of disabled people may decline and their suffering increase.

Positional Goods

Other problems arise when people use genetic technologies to alter embryos for competitive advantage. As Buchanan et al. point out, "In the United States and other 'developed' societies, the most basic cooperative framework consists . . . of the competitive market system."[56] Genetic endowments, such as height, can be advantageous, especially to men, in competition. The taller presidential candidate usually wins. Suppose that an inexpensive technology is developed that allows parents to add four inches of height to their children. Most parents will want this for their children to give them a competitive edge.

But height is a positional good. It's not advantageous to be any particular height. The advantage is in being taller (up to a point) than the competition. So, if the height-increasing genetic procedure is cheap and available to everyone, the bioethicists tell us, "it may be self-defeating: no one gains a height advantage if everyone increases in height."[57] Height increase will be an exercise in futility.

What is more, freedom would decrease. Technology is often promoted as increasing freedom by increasing our choices, but Dean Clancy, writing in *National Review*, agrees with ethicist Daniel Callahan, who asks rhetorically: "How much choice do we really have about driving automobiles?

Do women have about using prenatal diagnosis? Do we have for ignoring e-mail, the Internet, and television?" Clancy adds: "The truth is: not much. Perhaps the motto of the 1933 Chicago World's Fair was correct: 'Science finds, Industry applies, Man conforms.'"[58] Height enhancement would fit this bleak model. Parents initially unenthusiastic about it would have to go along to avoid their children suffering competitive disadvantage. Children whose parents, for religious or other reasons, refused to have them enhanced, would suffer. It seems utilitarians would oppose enhancement of height and other traits that confer merely positional advantage.

Unequal Opportunity

Contractarians object when genetic enhancements aren't available to everyone. Buchanan et al. invite us to

suppose that advances in immunology based on increased knowledge of genes make it possible to enhance resistance to common illnesses, including the common cold, flu, depression, and cardiovascular diseases.

Suppose also, as now is the case, that most people in this country have access to health insurance and hence to these beneficial interventions but, as is also the case, that a significant segment of the population—say 15 percent—lack insurance and cannot afford the interventions. Under these [realistic] conditions, standard employment contracts . . . might come to be geared to the health needs of those who have benefited from these enhancements. The number of sick days allowed to employees without loss of wages might decrease significantly, reflecting the lower risk of illness that now characterizes the "enhanced" majority.

In these circumstances, those who lack access to the interventions in question . . . would be disabled relative to their social environment in the way that people with chronic illnesses are in our present social environment.[59]

Lee Silver makes the same point: "What I see is the problem is really conflict between liberty and justice. On the one hand, people should have the liberty, which we care a lot about in this country, to be able to do things to help their children. On the other hand, this technology is so powerful that if we leave it in the hands of the marketplace, the parents who don't get to use it will have their children at a disadvantage."[60] As he suggests, libertarians will not be troubled by this development, but contractarians will object to loss of fair equal opportunity.

Buchanan et al. respond that such problems of justice could be overcome in a just society. A just society would, for example, make enhancements available to everyone to promote equal opportunity. But the United States has never been so committed to justice. More than 15 percent of

Americans lack health insurance, which impairs equal opportunity. Publicly supported preschool education is the exception, not the rule in the United States, and K–12 public education is funded largely by property taxes, resulting in unequal per pupil expenditures. All of this impairs equal opportunity. Medical ethicist Glenn McGee writes: "It is amazing that we are willing to spend millions of dollars on the search for genes that code for calculative efficiency, while Head Start programs go unfunded, teachers are underpaid and overworked, and even smart kids graduate ill prepared for the job market and uninspired by democracy."[61]

Evident gaps in serious commitment to equal opportunity in the United States mean that we can't employ a technology that could harm poor people and expect public programs to come to the rescue. What is more, if communitarian Michael Sandel is correct, genetic enhancement will weaken the moral motivation of haves to share with have-nots. Instead of viewing their genetic advantages as undeserved products of chance, they'll see their genetic profile as inherited property to which they have a right.

This implies that genetic enhancement should be illegal if fair equal opportunity is important. Although writing in favor of developing genetic technologies, Buchanan et al. provide powerful contractarian reasons against genetic enhancement.

Evolutionary Trends

Lee Silver believes that human beings are about to direct their own evolutionary development: "This is a revolutionary, evolutionary point in our history as a species. I really believe, very strongly, that our species will change. . . . We have taken control over our own evolution as a species. We have no idea of where we are going to end up. But we're going to control our evolution—not nature, not the environment. We are going to control the evolution of our species."[62]

Silver does have some concrete ideas about probable developments, and they aren't reassuring. He thinks gaps will continue to grow between haves and have-nots. Children of social elites who have been enhanced "will take those genetic enhancements and automatically give them to their children and add extra ones in. And . . . generation after generation after generation of accumulating these genetic enhancements could lead to a group of people who are genetically distinct from the naturals who are us."[63] Silver told the BBC:

Ultimately you could end up with human beings splitting into two different groups of people who can actually no longer breed with each other, at which point they would be different species. . . .

I don't think those people would be able to interact very well and so they will stay apart from each other socially. . . . This I think is actually quite horrible. I think it's going to be a disaster because one group of people who is a different species to the other group of people will no longer have the desire or need to treat that second group of people with dignity and respect. And I think that's a pretty bad outcome, although I don't see how we can stop it from happening.[64]

Buchanan et al. worry about the same thing.

We can no longer assume that there will be a single successor to what has been regarded as human nature. We must consider the possibility that at some point in the future, different groups of human beings may follow divergent paths of development through the use of genetic technology. . . . For all we know, it might turn out that if differences among groups . . . became pronounced enough, they would not treat each other as moral equals. History is replete with instances in which human beings have failed to empathize with their fellows simply because of quite superficial differences in physical appearance or even in customs and manners.[65]

Surprisingly, both Silver and Buchanan et al. support development and use of a technology they envision leading to genocide. Buchanan et al. conveniently but unrealistically imagine society becoming so morally enlightened that rich people, unlike now, won't use their wealth to give their already advantaged children additional advantages. This makes equal opportunity compatible (in their dream) with genetically enhanced children. Silver doesn't even do that. He's sad about future oppression, but sees no alternative. The rest of us might consider outlawing genetic enhancements.

Conclusion

Libertarians favor the freedom of individuals to design their children if they want to. Utilitarians, as usual, can be on either side, depending on expected consequences. The most negative consequences, such as injustice, oppression, and genocide—strong utilitarian reasons against designing children—are predicted by proponents of genetic enhancements. Taking these predictions seriously makes enhancing embryos wrong for contractarians as well as utilitarians, owing to drastic losses in equal opportunity. Communitarians oppose designing children, because it emphasizes individual control and assertiveness that erode the bases for mutual caring in society. Social conservatives, environmentalists, and proponents of natural law oppose genetic engineering, because it gives people more power over nature—including human nature—than they think humanity can handle. Theocrats would agree, cautioning people against "playing God." They might all hope that technological difficulties will stand in the way. Not every bad idea succeeds.

But Sharla and Shane Miller were happy to play God. After having three boys, Sharla gave birth to two healthy girls in July 2004.

Even without successful genetic engineering, controversies about injustice abound. Many of these controversies concern appropriate levels of wages and taxes, the topic of our next chapter.

11
Wages and Taxes: Libertarianism, Free-Market Conservatism, and Contractarianism

The Growing Gap between Rich and Poor

The gap between rich and poor has been growing since the 1970s in the United States. Here's an example reported in the *New York Times* in 2006:

In 1977, James P. Smith, a shaggy-haired 21-year-old known as Skinny, took a job as a meat grinder at what is now a ConAgra Foods pepperoni plant. At $6.40 an hour, it was among the best-paying jobs in town for a high school graduate.

Nearly three decades later, Mr. Smith still arrives at the same factory, shortly before his 3:30 a.m. shift. His hair has thinned; he has put on weight. Today, his union job pays him $13.25 an hour to operate the giant blenders that crush 3,600-pound blocks of pork and beef.

His earnings, which total about $28,000 a year, have not kept pace even with Omaha's low cost of living. The company eliminated bonuses about a decade ago. And now, almost 50, Mr. Smith is concerned that his $80,000 retirement nest egg will not be enough—especially since his plant is on a list of ones ConAgra wants to sell.[1]

The company's former CEO, Bruce C. Rohde, by contrast, retired in September 2005 with a compensation package that sets him up for life.

All told, Mr. Rohde, 57, received more than $45 million during his eight years at the helm, and was given an estimated $20 million retirement package as he walked out the door.

Each year from 1997 to 2005, when Mr. Rohde led Con Agra, he was awarded either a large cash bonus, a generous grant of stock or options, or valuable benefits, such as extra years' credit toward his guaranteed pension.[2]

Many workers' incomes decline as our country goes from a manufacturing to a service economy. Here's an example from central Illinois, where I live:

For almost 10 years, Clinton Lay—a Springfield native with a high-school equivalency diploma—could afford new cars, vacations and cross-country outings with his family, all because of his $70,000-a-year job at Decatur's Bridgestone/ Firestone plant. . . .

The 12-hour shifts at the factory were monotonous and exhausting, but Lay planned to stay until retirement. . . .

But Lay and more that 1,500 other people lost their jobs when the plant closed in fall 2001.

Lay has been retrained through a program at Springfield's Capital Area Career Center and now works as a home health-care nurse. But in the job turmoil, his car and his wife's were repossessed. They can't afford to buy a home. They live paycheck-to-paycheck, Lay said. . . .

Lay isn't alone. Data from the U.S. Census Bureau . . . confirmed [that] median household income—the point at which half of households had higher incomes and half lower—was $46,115 in Sangamon County in 2005. . . . That compares with a median (after adjusting for 17 percent inflation) of $50,320 in 1999. . . . Mean real household income has declined . . . 5.8 percent nationally . . . , 8.4 percent in Sangamon County, and almost 7 percent in Springfield since 1999.[3]

The rising economic tide of President Bush's second term lifted average, but not median income. The average can go up, while ninety percent of household income stagnates or declines, because enormous gains by those at the very top—people like former ConAgra CEO Bruce Rohde— pull up the average.

The *New York Times* reported in 2005:

The people at the top of America's money pyramid have so prospered in recent years that they have pulled far ahead of the rest of the population. . . .

Call them the hyper-rich . . . the top 0.1 percent of income earners—the top one-thousandth. Above that line are about 145,000 taxpayers, each with at least $1.6 million in income and often much more.

The average income for the top 0.1 percent was $3 million in 2002, the latest year for which averages are available. That number is two and a half times the $1.2 million, adjusted for inflation, that group made in 1980. No other income group rose nearly as fast.

The share of the nation's income earned by those in this uppermost category has more than doubled since 1980, to 7.4 percent in 2002. The share of income earned by the rest of the top 10 percent rose far less, and the share earned by the bottom 90 percent fell.

Next, examine the net worth of American households. The group with homes, investments and other assets worth more than $10 million comprised 338,400 households in 2001, the last year for which data are available. The number has grown more than 400 percent since 1980, after adjusting for inflation, while the total number of households has grown only 27 percent.[4]

One aspect of the trend to super wealth is the steady increase of CEO salaries, bonuses, and stock options. *USA Today* reported in 2006: "Even after a decade of sharply rising CEO pay, 2005 proved a watershed for a select group of executives. . . . Median 2005 pay among chief executives running most of the nation's 100 largest companies soared 25% to $17.9 million, dwarfing the 3.1% average gain by typical American workers."[5]

Average workers are borrowing more because their pay isn't keeping pace with inflation. In 2006, Steven Greenhouse reported in the *New York Times*:

Debt payments now consume 19.4 percent of the income of the average American family. . . . Household debt rose to 132 percent of disposable income last year, partly because many Americans have pushed their credit card debt to the max and . . . have piled on the mortgage interest debt. Last year, for the first time since the Depression, the personal savings rate for the nation fell below zero, meaning that Americans are spending more than they are earning (and are saving no money on a net basis).

"There are really two types of households out there," . . . said Mark M. Zandi, chief economist at Moody's Economy.com. . . . High-income households have balance sheets about as good as I've ever seen, while lower-income households have balance sheets about as bad as I've ever seen them—complete tatters. These households are on the financial edge, and if there's any slight disruption, like a car breaking down, it can be a real disaster for them financially.[6]

Libertarians and Free-Market Conservatives against State Intervention

Libertarians recognize that the situation is troublesome for families in precarious financial straights, but they deny it's a problem that government should address. States exist to protect natural rights, they believe. People's natural right to their own bodies gives them a natural right to the fruits of their labor. For example, if you use your own tools to make a statue from a piece of driftwood, the artwork is yours. You can do whatever you want with it—smash it, put it in your basement, display it in your home, give it away, or sell it. So long as you don't deprive other people of their rights, it's none of the state's business. At the same time, as guarantor of rights, the state ensures that no one deprives you of the statue through force, such as theft, threat of force, such as an offer you can't refuse, or fraud, such as paying for the statue with a phony check.

When people create property without infringing on anyone else's rights and exchange property without force, threat of force, or fraud—that is, when they conform to the free market system—the resulting distribution of property is none of the state's business. Some people become much richer than others owing to talent, effort, and luck, but state interference with the results of free market exchange violates individual liberty and property rights. Suppose, for example, that the state raised taxes from rich people to provide welfare for the poor. Because taxes are forced payments, the state would be using force to extract property from some people to give it to others. This violates the natural right to property. The state would be doing exactly what it's supposed to prevent.

Libertarian philosopher Robert Nozick recognized that some taxation is necessary because the state needs money to protect people's rights—to pay for police, courts, prisons, homeland security, and national defense. These are legitimate domains of state activity and people should be forced through taxation to pay their fair share. But taxes should be kept to a minimum, Nozick claims.

Taxation of earnings from labor is on a par with forced labor. . . : taking the earnings of n hours of labor is like taking n hours from the person; it is like forcing the person to work n hours for another's purpose. . . .[7] They decide . . . what purposes your work is to serve apart from your decisions. This . . . makes them a *part-owner* of you; it gives them a property right in you.[8]

On this libertarian understanding, taxation is akin to slavery.

Free-market conservatives also caution against government intervention in markets. They're not concerned with the state infringing anyone's natural right to property because they believe property exists by convention, not by nature. Milton and Rose Friedman give this example in *Free to Choose*: "I own a house. Are you 'trespassing' on my private property if you fly your private airplane ten feet over my roof? One thousand feet? Thirty thousand feet? There is nothing 'natural' about where my property rights end and yours begin."[9] Free-market conservatives think the state should use its power to define property to promote affluence through free-market activity. If people could fly planes ten feet over a house, property values would plummet, so the state should give people property rights empowering them to prevent such low flyovers. But if homeowners' rights extended to forty thousand feet, transcontinental air traffic would become impossible owing to illegal trespass on so many people's property.

Intellectual property rights promote economic growth by giving entrepreneurs incentive to be creative. As far as we know, Matthew, Mark,

Luke, and John didn't make a penny on the Gospels, whereas J. K. Rowling made millions on the Harry Potter books. The difference is that stories weren't property in biblical times. Now they are property, because governments have copyright laws. Such property is real, but not natural. New forms of property have been created in recent decades. For example, the patent office now allows patents on species created in the laboratory, giving scientists and investors in science financial incentives to create bacteria that eat oil spills and mice that serve as improved models for cancer research. By allowing inventors and investors to gain from this new form of property, free-market conservatives expect society in general will gain in the long run. The oceans will be cleaner and more cancers will be cured.

In short, according to free-market conservatives, the state doesn't exist to protect property rights, as libertarians imagine, because property rights don't exist except by government decision, which should be guided by the goal of promoting prosperity through free-market exchanges.

In spite of this difference, many free-market conservatives agree with libertarians that governments shouldn't intervene in the market to promote greater equality, because even if a rising economic tide doesn't lift all boats financially, it lifts them materially. In his 1997 *Commentary* article, Christopher DeMuth writes, "The much-noticed increase in measured-income inequality is in part a result of the increase in real social equality." The free-market has spurred innovation that helps everyone.

First, progress in agriculture, construction, manufacturing, and other key sectors of economic production has made the material necessities of life—food, shelter, and clothing—available to essentially everyone. . . . The problem of poverty, defined as material scarcity, has been solved. . . .

Second, progress in public health, in nutrition, and in the biological sciences and medical arts has produced dramatic improvements in longevity, health, and physical well-being. Many of these improvements . . . have affected entire populations, producing an equalization of real personal welfare more powerful than any government redistribution of income.[10]

DeMuth claims that another sign of increased affluence at all levels of society is reduction of time at work. According to one estimate, men averaged 61.6 hours per week at work in 1880, but only 33.6 in the 1990s. What is more, much reduction of work hours is now voluntary: "longer periods of education and training for the young; earlier retirement despite longer life spans; and, in between, many more hours devoted to leisure, recreation, entertainment, family, community and religious activities."[11] In addition, technological innovations spurred by free-market incentives make more entertainment available to the masses.

Television, videocassettes, CD's, and home computers have brought musical, theatrical, and other entertainments (both high and low) to everyone, and have enormously narrowed the differences in cultural opportunities between wealthy urban centers and everywhere else. Formerly upper-crust sports like golf, tennis, skiing, and boating have become mass pursuits . . . and health clubs and full-line book stores have become as plentiful as gas stations.[12]

Government reducing its control of the market has helped. "For example," DeMuth writes, "deregulation . . . since the 1970s . . . has democratized air travel. Low fares and mass marketing have brought such luxuries as foreign travel, weekend getaways to remote locales, and reunions of far-flung families—just twenty years ago, pursuits of the wealthy—to people of relatively modest means."[13]

In sum, the free market has improved the lives of just about everyone and, as the case of air travel illustrates, it does more when government reduces economic regulation. Regulations and taxes tend to impede market activity and should therefore be kept to a minimum. Raising the minimum wage or taxing the rich to give money to the poor would impair the free market, injuring the goose that laid the golden egg. Although their reasoning is entirely different, many free-market conservatives agree with libertarians that the state should not concern itself with growing differences of income and wealth between rich people and most Americans.

Problems of the Working Poor

Writer Barbara Ehrenreich gives a different perspective in *Nickel and Dimed*, the story of her year-long attempt to live on the wages of the working poor. As a waitress, house cleaner, and Wal-Mart associate in the late 1990s, she found she had little leisure time and couldn't make ends meet. In Key West, Florida, she was a waitress for $2.43 an hour plus tips. Waitresses can be paid less than the $5.15 minimum wage on the theory that tips make up the difference. The wage made housing a problem for her co-workers.

Gail is sharing a room in a well-known downtown flophouse for $250 a week. Her roommate, a male friend, has begun hitting on her, driving her nuts, but the rent would be impossible alone.[14]

When Gail and I are wrapping silverware in napkins . . . she tells me she is thinking of escaping from her roommate by moving into the Days Inn herself. I am astounded: how can she even think of paying $40 to $60 a day . . . ? She squints at me in disbelief: "And where am I supposed to get a month's rent and a month's deposit for an apartment . . . ?" In poverty, as in certain propositions in physics, starting conditions are everything. . . .

If you can't put up the two months' rent you need to secure an apartment, you end up paying through the nose for a room by the week. If you have only a room, with a hot plate at best, you can't save by cooking up huge lentil stews that can be frozen for the week ahead. You eat fast food or the hot dogs and Styrofoam cups of soup that can be microwaved in a convenience store.[15]

Ehrenreich avoided these problems by allowing herself some startup money to put down on a $500 per month efficiency apartment. Still, she found that her minimum-wage income was not enough to pay the rent. She made her own lunch almost every day and didn't see how she could cut down on expenses. A single person can't make ends meet on a single minimum-wage income, even when she has no additional expenses related to health care or car repair, both of which are bound to arise sooner or later. At minimum wage, a second job is necessary for a single person.

Ehrenreich moved to Portland, Maine, where she worked cleaning houses. If you've ever hired a cleaning service—my wife hired me, but now I'm writing this book—you know it's expensive. The company that Ehrenreich worked for, The Maids, charged customers $25 an hour for her work, but paid her only $6.65 an hour. Even at that, the workers were cheated. They weren't paid for the first half hour, between 7:30 and 8 in the morning, or for the last half hour of the day, both of which they spent in the office.

In any case, the pay wasn't enough for women with children, Ehrenreich learned from Maddy,

a single mom of maybe twenty-seven or so, [who] has worked for only three months and broods about her child care problems. Her boyfriend's sister, she tells me on the drive to our first house, watches her eighteen-month-old for $50 a week, which is a stretch on The Maids' pay, plus she doesn't entirely trust the sister, but a real day care center could be as much as $90 a week.[16]

The woman whose house they were cleaning, by contrast, a graduate of a prestigious college, occupied herself "monitoring her investments and the baby's bowel movements." For the latter she had "special charts . . . with spaces for time of day, most recent fluid intake, consistency, and color." She also had "a whole shelf of books on pregnancy, breastfeeding, the first six months, the first year, the first two years." Ehrenreich wondered "what the child care-deprived Maddy makes of all this."[17]

Although she was earning $6.65 an hour, $1.50 an hour above the minimum wage, Ehrenreich couldn't make ends meet and took a second job on the weekends in the food service at a nursing home. So much for the extra leisure that Christopher DeMuth thinks the free market has brought to everyone. In fact, the time crunch has hit large segments of the working population, not just the working poor. Kevin Phillips reports in *Wealth and Democracy*, "Among women with children under six, the percentage who worked rose from 19 percent in 1960 to 64 percent in 1995." (Maddy's difficulties with childcare are widespread.) Another sign of less leisure and more work is the number of hours on the job by the average American worker. It increased from 1,795 hours in 1960 to 1,919 hours in 1990 to 1,966 hours in 1999. "Between 1990 and 1995 the average annual hours worked in the United States finally passed those of workaholic Japan, leading the International Labor Organization to report in 1999 that Americans toiled the longest hours in the industrial world."[18]

Double shifts, second jobs, and longer hours to make ends meet is not the norm in the industrial world, Phillips writes. "American pay must be placed alongside its inflation-adjusted equivalents in more relaxed Britain, France, Germany, and Japan. Wages in those places *rose* in the eighties and nineties while working hours *shortened*."[19]

Ehrenreich was working at least eight hours a day, seven days a week. She writes, "I wonder what the two-job way of life would do to a person after a few months with zero days off . . . ? If you hump away at menial jobs 360-plus days a year, does some kind of repetitive injury of the spirit set in?"[20]

Spiritual injury isn't the only hazard of cleaning houses. The work produces many physical injuries as well, Ehrenreich tells us.

If I don't know how my coworkers survive on their wages or what they make of our hellish condition, I do know about their back pains and cramps and arthritic attacks. Lori and Pauline are excused from vacuuming on account of their backs, which means you dread being assigned to a team with them. Helen has a bum foot. . . . Marge's arthritis makes scrubbing a torture; another woman has to see a physical therapist for her rotator cuff.[21]

These are all women in their twenties and thirties. Ehrenreich concludes: "So ours is a world of pain—managed by Excedrin and Advil, compensated for with cigarettes and, in one or two cases and then only on weekends, with booze. Do the owners have any idea of the misery that goes into rendering their homes motel-perfect?"[22]

It seems that by working seven days a week and risking her health Ehrenreich could make ends meet in Portland, so long as her car and body held out. She moved next to the Twin Cities, where she learned from the St. Paul–based Jobs Now Coalition, that "a 'living wage' [in 1997] for a single parent supporting a single child . . . was $11.77 an hour. This estimate was based on monthly expenses that included $266 for food (all meals cooked and eaten at home), $261 for child care, and $550 for rent." Rents increased greatly in 2000, but the cost of living estimate remained the same for some time. Ehrenreich eventually got a job at Wal-Mart for about $7 an hour. Her rent was much more than the estimated $550 a month, so she failed to make ends meet as a single, healthy, low-wage earner.

Millions of people working full-time or even two jobs are trapped in poverty, Ehrenreich finds, and this cuts into "that web of expectations that make up the 'social contract.'" She notes a poll "conducted by Jobs for the Future, a Boston-based employment research firm, [that found] 94 percent of Americans agree that 'people who work full-time should be able to earn enough to keep their families out of poverty.'" Growing up, Ehrenreich heard that if you work hard you'll get ahead. "No one ever said that you could work hard—harder even than you ever thought possible—and still find yourself sinking ever deeper into poverty and debt."[23]

The Minimum Wage and Earned Income Tax Credit

One way of addressing problems of the working poor is to raise the minimum wage, which was set at $5.15 an hour in the 1990s. But economist Thomas Rustici argued as a free-market conservative in 1985 for just the opposite course. We should eliminate the minimum wage altogether. He writes, "It is well known that the minimum wage creates unemployment among the least skilled workers by raising wage rates above free market levels."[24] In a free market, Rustici believes, workers command wages that reflect the value of their work to their employers. If the state requires employers to pay more than that wage, employers will fire workers and replace them with technology.

As a production input, low-skilled labor is often in direct competition with highly technical machinery. A Whirlpool dishwasher can be substituted for low-skill manual dishwashers in the dishwashing process, and an automatic elevator can take the place of a nonautomatic elevator and a manual operator. This [is] not to imply that automation "destroys jobs," a common Luddite myth. . . . Automation shifts the *kinds* of jobs to be done in society but does not reduce their total number. Low-skill jobs are done away with, but higher-skill jobs are created simultaneously.[25]

These observations seem unwittingly to support increase of the minimum wage, rather than its elimination. A major argument for the free market system is that competition for customers sparks technological change that enables more and better products to be produced at lower prices. Rustici's argument is that the higher the minimum wage, the greater the pressure on employers to seek and develop technological innovations in production. But on free-market principles, this is good. Low-skilled workers lose their jobs but, because "automation shifts the *kinds* of jobs to be done in society but does not reduce their total number," displaced workers can be retrained for the new, higher-skilled jobs available in a high-tech world. Thus, a high minimum wage is good, because it sparks technological innovations that enrich society without creating unemployment.

Rustici errs also when he claims that wage levels reflect the value of labor to employers. In that case, wages would rise with increases in worker productivity. But just the opposite has occurred in recent years. The *New York Times* reported in 2006:

The median hourly wage for American workers has declined 2 percent since 2003, after factoring in inflation. The drop has been especially notable, economists say, because productivity—the amount that an average worker produces in an hour and the basic wellspring of a nation's living standards—has risen steadily over the same period.[26]

CEO compensation also indicates that financial rewards can diverge from productivity, but at this top end, rewards exceed productivity. Bruce Rohde's enormous compensation from ConAgra came after eight years, during which

ConAgra routinely missed earnings targets and underperformed its peers. Its share price fell 28 percent. The company cut more than 9,000 jobs. Accounting problems surfaced in every one of Mr. Rohde's eight years.

Even when ConAgra restated its financial results, which lowered earnings in 2003 and 2004, Mr. Rohde's $16.4 million in bonuses for those two years stayed the same.[27]

If productivity isn't the only factor determining compensation at either end of the income spectrum, what other factors are involved? Labor economist Charles Craypo, writing in 2002, explains that in the blue-collar world, low wages reflect the power of employers in labor negotiations, not the value of the work being done.

Individual workers find there are far more workers than there are good jobs and they take what they can get on the terms that are offered. Additionally, employers . . . can hold out much longer financially than can workers in the event of differences over wages and working conditions. Finally, and importantly, because they own the plant and equipment upon which the worker's livelihood depends, they can threaten to relocate the workplace or to replace workers with machines or other workers.[28]

Craypo has two replies to the claim that increasing the minimum wage increases unemployment among society's least-skilled workers. First, empirical studies show that in the past this has not always be case.[29] Second, on free-market principles, if employers can't stay in business paying a living wage, they should be allowed to fail.

In brief, if a job pays less than enough to sustain workers and their dependents at the customary standard of living, then that job is not paying its way in a productive economy because it is being subsidized by some household, charitable organization, or government transfer payment. The beneficiary is either the employer paying the low wage and making a profit by doing so, or the customer paying a low price for the good or service. Fast-food restaurant fare, for example, is cheap in part because fast-food workers earn poverty wages. . . .

This subsidization does not have to occur. In Australia, for example, restaurant workers, "bag boys" in grocery stores, bartenders in taverns, and other workers who are generally low paid in the United States are paid in excess of $12 an hour. Nevertheless, McDonald's hamburgers and Pizza Hut pizzas still abound in Australia. In the United States unionized waitresses in Las Vegas also earn $12 an hour, before tips. . . . Waitresses in other parts of the country commonly receive about half the level of the minimum wage, before tips.[30]

These figures show that there's economic leeway for substantial increases in the minimum wage without jeopardizing viable enterprises or creating unemployment.

A free-market conservative's reason for increasing the minimum wage, in addition to sparking innovation, is that higher wages put money into the hands of consumers, and consumption is the engine that drives economic growth and prosperity.

Many free-market conservatives agree with Craypo that the minimum wage should be increased. Some suggest a $2 an hour increase to $7.15 an hour. But I don't find anyone advocating an increase large enough to make full-time employment at the minimum wage sufficient for a decent life. The reason is that in many places, the minimum wage would have to triple. We learn from Ehrenreich that in 1997 the wage needed to live decently in the Twin Cities was almost $12 an hour, and the budget at that wage was skimpy, at best. With general inflation averaging about 3 percent a year and housing and health care costs rising much faster, the equivalent in 2007 might be $17 an hour. In Springfield, Illinois, where I live, perhaps $12 or $13 an hour would buy the same package of goods. I don't know any economist who suggests that the economy could accommodate such drastic increases in the minimum wage without significant disruption.

An alternative way of helping the working poor make ends meet is the Earned Income Tax Credit (EITC). It began in 1975 under President Ford and was praised by Presidents Reagan and Clinton. People earning the lowest wages get back from the Federal Treasury not only the income tax withheld during the year, but additional dollars as well. For example, a single parent of one child who earned the minimum wage, about $10,000 a year, got back withheld income plus $2,747 after filing federal taxes for 2005.[31] In effect, her hourly wage, assuming that she worked 2000 hours in the year (40 hours a week for 50 weeks), increased by about $1.35 an hour. The $5.15 per hour minimum wage becomes $6.50 an hour.

The minimum wage could be raised that much, most economists think, without economic disruption. But the EITC can allow much larger increases, whatever the taxpayers will allow, without altering basic economic relationships in society. For example, adding the $100 billion dollars spent on the War in Iraq in 2006 to the money already spent that year on the EITC would go a long way toward giving the working poor a decent income. The basic idea, called a "negative income tax," was first proposed by free-market conservative Milton Friedman in the early 1960s.

Contractarians would also like the minimum wage raised and the EITC increased to give all working people decent incomes. Contractarians put themselves in other people's shoes and want public policies to meet everyone's needs. Imagining themselves as working poor people, contractarians want work to be rewarded with decent incomes. My father used to say: "People deserve a good day's pay for a good day's work."

Income and Estate Taxes: Libertarian and Free-Market Views

The Tax Burden
American taxpayers would have to fund an increased EITC. Before the tax cuts of 2001, total taxation in the United States (federal, state, and local) was low compared to that of most other industrialized nations. It was 28.5 percent of gross domestic product (GDP—the value of goods and services sold in the country during the year); the European Union average was 42.4 percent of GDP and the average for twenty-nine industrial countries in Europe, North America, and Asia was 37.7 percent.[32]

Federal income taxes are progressive; in general, the more people earn, the higher the percentage of their income goes to the federal government. When all exemptions, deductions, and credits are figured in, Citizens for Tax Justice finds that in 2000

taxpayers in the middle 20 percent pay only 6 percent of their income in personal income taxes. Due to the EITC, the poorest 20 percent actually have a *negative* tax rate of –3.8 percent. On the other hand, taxpayers in the wealthiest one percent of the income scale—those with an average income of $195,000—pay 24.6 percent of their income in federal personal income tax.[33]

By contrast, federal payroll taxes, which fund Social Security and Medicare, are not progressive. The wealthiest 1 percent pay only 2.3 percent of their income in payroll taxes, whereas the middle 20 percent pay 10.9 percent and the poorest 20 percent pay 8.1 percent. Federal excise taxes, such as on gasoline and cigarettes, are more regressive. The top 1 percent of taxpayers pay 0.2 percent of income in excise taxes, while the middle fifth pay 1.5 percent and the lowest fifth 3.7 percent. But the estate tax is extremely progressive, applying in 2000 to bequests of only the wealthiest 2 percent of taxpayers with estates worth more than $1.2 million.[34] Politicians who label it the "death tax" must think that 98 percent of people don't die.

This was the tax system that Congress revised in 2001 under the presidential leadership of George W. Bush. David Johnston, writing for the *New York Times*, took issue in 2005 with Bush's claim that his tax cuts went mostly to low- and middle-income Americans. "In fact," Johnston reports, "most—53 percent—will go to people with incomes in the top 10 percent over the first 15 years of the cuts. . . . And more than 15 percent will go to the top 0.1 percent . . . , 145,000 taxpayers." What is more:

The 400 taxpayers with the highest incomes—a minimum of $87 million in 2000, the last year for which the government will release such data—now pay income, Medicare, and Social Security taxes amounting to virtually the same percentage of their incomes as people making $50,000 to $75,000.

Those earning more than $10 million a year now pay a lesser share of their income in these taxes than those making $100,000 to $200,000.[35]

The Bush tax cuts also include phasing out the estate tax, which disappears in 2010. But because almost all the 2001 tax cuts were temporary, lasting only until 2011, the original estate tax will reappear unless altered by new legislation. In the 1990s, this tax raised about 1.5 percent of federal revenue, which is 0.3 percent of GDP. This may not seem like much, but according to *The Economist*, it's about half the amount needed to fix Social Security from projected shortfalls in the middle of the century.[36]

In sum, the Bush tax cuts helped the rich and super-rich the most. Still, even after the Bush tax cuts, people with a lot of money generally pay much, much more in taxes than people with little money. How should we evaluate this situation?

Libertarian Concerns

Libertarians who believe that people have natural rights to their property, because it results from their labor, want to minimize taxes for everyone, believing that all taxes are forced transfers of property that risk violating natural rights. Taxing some more than others is particularly suspect.

But philosophers Liam Murphy and Thomas Nagel disagree. Like free-market conservatives, they believe that there's no natural right to property. They emphasize that ownership is embedded in a host of legal rules that include tax laws. People really own only what they retain after taxes, not before.

I own my car, for example, not because—as libertarians would have it—I made it with my own labor from unowned steel, plastic, and microchips, but because in 1995 I paid the previous owner, Saturn of Springfield, the price they asked. The money I used was legally mine, because I had taught philosophy under a legal contract. I could use my salary to buy the car only because laws and banking rules of Illinois and of the United States decree that the electronic deposits in my account can be transformed into the kind of currency that retailers must accept in payment for merchandise. State law decrees also that 3 percent of my salary belongs to the state to cover its expenses, and 8 percent is sequestered in the State Universities Retirement System. Federal law decrees that much of my salary goes to income tax. My property rights exist in the context of all these laws—the tax laws as much as the others. Many arrangements in business and personal finance, in fact, are made primarily for tax reasons.

In this context, Murphy and Nagel claim, it's an illusion for people to think their salaries and investments are really theirs, but taxes are an outside imposition, because salaries and investments are embedded in a system of laws that includes taxes. Take away that system of laws and you have no legal title to your car or your investments. Someone could take your car and you'd have no legal recourse. Ownership of stocks would be impossible because corporations and their stocks exist only through a legal system that includes laws of incorporation. Murphy and Nagel put it this way:

> The tax system . . . is not an incursion on a distribution of property holdings that is already presumptively legitimate. Rather, it is among the conditions that *create* a set of property holdings, whose legitimacy can be assessed only by evaluating the justice of the whole system, taxes included. Against such a background, people certainly have a legitimate claim on the income they realize through the usual methods of work, investment, and gift—but the tax system is an essential part of the background which creates the legitimate expectations that arise from employment contracts and other economic transactions, not something that cuts in afterwards.[37]

The question to be asked about taxes, they think, isn't whether a particular tax is good or fair, but whether the economic system as a whole is good or fair and how this tax contributes to or detracts from the goodness or fairness of the whole system.

Free-Market Conservative Concerns

Free-market conservatives worry that taxing the rich too much might weaken their entrepreneurial drive. If tax rules allocate too much money to government, business people may lack the motivation of financial gain to compete and innovate. The economy could stagnate and affluence decline.

There seems no doubt that after a certain point, rich people would have insufficient financial motive to work hard to make more money. But what tax rate would trigger such a response? The top income tax bracket has varied widely in the United States without any apparent effect on rich people trying to get richer. It was 39.5 percent during much of the Clinton administration before the Bush tax cuts lowered it to 35 percent. But these figures don't establish the ballpark of what's possible. The top income tax bracket was 70 percent in the 1950s, a time of great economic growth and improved standards of living for almost everyone.

Some free-market conservatives favor a stiff inheritance tax to promote economic growth. Economist Joseph Stiglitz asks: "How many of the dot-com billionaires would have said, I will not create my company if the government takes, say, 40 percent of my wealth [when I die] in excess of $10 million?"[38] Stiglitz doesn't think a stiff inheritance tax reduces entrepreneurial motivation. In fact, some entrepreneurs worry that failure of the government to tax large legacies might lead to a concentration of wealth that could diminish American innovation, David Johnston reports:

Some of the wealthiest Americans, including Warren E. Buffett, George Soros, and Ted Turner, have warned that such a concentration of wealth can turn a meritocracy into an aristocracy and ultimately stifle economic growth by putting too much of the nation's capital in the hands of inheritors rather than strivers and innovators.[39]

Another free-market reason for high marginal tax rates on high incomes is that it allows greater government support of poorer people through the earned income tax credit. This increases incentives for poorer people to work hard. Also, because poorer people spend money quickly, putting money in their hands helps to stimulate the economy. Finally, greater government tax receipts made possible by high taxes on the rich would allow the state to maintain and improve the physical infrastructure on which commerce depends—roads, canals, and bridges—while also improving the human infrastructure—health care and schools. A growing economy needs healthy, educated workers.

Contractarian Views on Progressive Taxation and Equal Opportunity

Progressive Taxation

Contractarians agree with free-market conservatives that allowing some people to be richer than others is necessary to make society in general affluent through free-market entrepreneurial activity. Thus, economic inequality is acceptable, they think, so long as everyone benefits, including the poorest members of society. They reason from their thought experiment about people not knowing their personal identities: if you didn't know your identity, you wouldn't know whether you were rich or poor. You wouldn't mind some people being much richer than you are, so long as you would benefit as much as possible from their extra riches. This creates a win-win situation. If it turns out that you're rich, you have advantages from being richer than most other people. But if it turns out that you're poor, your poverty is reduced as much as possible by programs or payments from rich people. These programs and payments reduce, but don't eliminate inequality. However, they give you as much affluence as possible. The alternative of greater equality would impair free-market incentives and make everyone poorer.

By this reasoning, taxes on rich people should be as high as possible without discouraging entrepreneurial innovation. This could easily be a tax on large incomes and estates of 50 percent or more, because history shows that such rates have not impaired economic growth. The additional tax receipts could be used largely to raise the effective wage of poorer people through an expanded EITC so that everyone working full-time has the material means for a decent life. Contractarians favor this.

Taxing the rich much more than others seems the only way to accomplish this goal, because, as Willie Sutton replied when asked why he robbed banks: "That's where the money is." Middle-income people simply don't have the means to pay higher taxes. One of my daughters, for example, is a single parent of two children and lives in a suburb of a major American city. She earned $48,000 per year from her regular job in 2006, which was very close to the median household income. Here was her monthly budget in 2006:

$800	rent
$630	daycare (for her two-year-old)
$100	hot lunches, after-school enrichment, and intersession fees (for her five-year-old in kindergarten)
$80	Internet and cable (she uses the Internet for work)
$50	electricity (water and gas are included in the rent)
$100	cell phone (a bad deal that lasts for another year)
$120	college loan repayment
$150	other debt payments
$150	gas (she has a long commute)
$40	car insurance
$2,220	total

My daughter takes home $1,300 every other Friday, after deductions for taxes and health insurance. In a typical month, therefore, she takes home $2,600. Given the above expenses, she has only $380 per month for toiletries, car repair (or car payments, when she needs to replace her car), clothes, food, toiletries, Christmas presents, birthday parties and presents, lessons for her children, entertainment, and so on. She'll be in better financial shape in a few years when both children are in school and she gets a better cell phone deal. At the moment, this budget doesn't work, even with two additional infusions of $1,300 during the course of a year (the two months with three Fridays). So, in 2006, she took an extra job for several months delivering about 230 newspapers a day for an additional $720 a month before taxes. Between her main job, commuting to her main job, picking up and delivering kids, and doing the paper route, she didn't sleep much. Her case may be extreme, but sleep deprivation is common in the United States.[40]

No contractarian would suggest raising my daughter's taxes to help the working poor when rich folks are getting richer as a result of corporate profits, stock market increases, inflated salaries in upper management, and tax cuts.

Equal Opportunity

Another use for increased tax revenues from rich people is to ensure the equal opportunity that everyone would want if they didn't know their position in society. They'd want a fair chance to move up the socioeconomic ladder. In the United States, however, educational opportunities are currently quite unequal, owing in part to public schools being financed largely by local property taxes. Some communities can afford much better schools than others.

The suburb where my daughter lives has excellent schools, which is why a very small two-bedroom apartment costs $800 a month. In some other communities in the state, the same apartment might cost only $500 a month. Steeply progressive federal taxes could be used to provide more equal funding for schools, which would help the working poor (whose communities seldom can afford the best schools), and the middle class (whose rents and mortgages are inflated when they crowd into areas with good schools).

Lack of equal opportunity afflicts higher education as well, writes Dorothy Wickenden in the *New Yorker*: "According to the Century Foundation, only three percent of students at the hundred and forty-six most competitive colleges come from families . . . in the bottom socioeconomic quarter. Seventy-four percent come from the top quarter."[41] Federal grants and loans to help poor kids attend college have diminished, as has tax support of state universities, resulting in tuition increases at formerly affordable schools. "All of this has had a predictable effect . . . : during the current decade, up to two and a half million qualified students, stricken by the costs of higher education, either will be forced to drop out or won't enroll at all."[42]

What's needed for greater equality of opportunity is more public support of at least public universities so that tuitions can be lowered. Also needed are increased grant and loan opportunities so that poor people can attend these and other quality schools. Contractarians would look to rich people for required finances.

Democracy

Democracy suffers when great disparities exist between rich and poor. David Johnston reported in the *Times* in 2005: "Speaking of the increasing concentration of incomes, Alan Greenspan, the Federal Reserve chairman, warned in congressional testimony a year ago: 'For the democratic society, that is not a very desirable thing to allow it to happen.'"[43] Political writer Kevin Phillips explains that some reasons for concern relate to the influence of money on politics through campaign contributions.

Compared to the overall size of the American economy, political campaign expenditures are modest. Phillips writes, "One notable Republican called politics underfunded (by private contributions) because Americans spent more on antacids alone."[44] Total expenses in a presidential election cycle, including primaries and the fall election for president, for 435 members of the house, and for 33 or 34 senate seats may amount to no more than $4 or $5 billion. That's not much compared the federal budget of about $2,800 billion. Still, the amount of money required to run an effective campaign keeps increasing and is far more than the average American can afford. Phillips notes: "In 1976, winning Senate incumbents laid out an average of $610,000 on their races. By 1986, the figure had grown to $3 million. By 2000, the average figure for all Senate incumbents was $4.4 million, while the average winner in all races raised $7.3 million."[45]

Because few Americans have $3 or $4 or $8 million to spend on a political campaign, either elected officials will be wealthy people who can fund their own campaigns, or wealthy people will choose candidates and thereby influence public policies by deciding which campaigns to finance. Both trends exist. Phillips includes the following satire from the 2000 presidential race to explain the drawbacks of politicians relying on rich people for campaign contributions. A group calling itself "Billion airesforBushorGore.com" used real facts and figures.

While you may be familiar with stocks and bonds, currency speculation, IPOs and all the rest, there's a new investment arena you should be aware of: *legislation*. If a mutual fund returns 20% a year, that's considered quite good, but in the low-risk, high-return world of legislation, a 20% return is positively lousy. There's no reason why your investment dollar can't return 100,000% or more.

Too good to be true? Don't worry, it's completely legal. With the help of a professional legislation broker (called a Lobbyist), you place your investment (called a Campaign Contribution) with a carefully selected list of legislation manufacturers (called Members of Congress). These manufacturers then go to work, crafting industry-specific subsidies, inserting tax breaks into the code, extending patents or giving away public property for free.

Just check out these results. The Timber Industry spent $8 million in campaign contributions to preserve the logging road subsidy, worth $458 million—a return on their investment was 5,725%. Glaxo Wellcome invested $1.2 million in campaign contributions to get a 19-month patent extension on Zantac worth $1 billion—their net return 83,333%. The Tobacco Industry spent $30 million in contributions for a tax break worth $50 billion—a return on their investment: 167,000%. For a paltry $5 million in campaign contributions, the Broadcasting Industry was able to secure free digital TV licenses, a give-away of public property worth $70 billion—that's an incredible 1,400,000% return on their investment.[46]

Free-market conservatives oppose government expenditures that serve special interests. They believe that people should earn money in the marketplace, not through political manipulation, because the market fosters efficiency that enriches society, whereas political manipulation fosters inefficiency and enriches only a privileged few. Contractarians also oppose the extra influence gained through campaign contributions, because such influence interferes with equal opportunity in politics and often results in public policies that favor the rich over the poor. We see the effects of campaign contributions on political debate when reducing taxes on the wealthiest 2 percent of estates is taken more seriously than state-supported preschool for all. My mother used to say: "Rich or poor, it's nice to have money."

Conclusion

Dramatic differences in wealth and income between the rich and poor are of no concern to libertarians, because they think people's property and earnings depend on individual physical and mental effort to which everyone has a natural right. The government violates natural rights when it forces the rich, through high taxes, to pay for services or opportunities for the poor.

Free-market conservatives want the economy to work efficiently according to free-market principles. Although they prefer low to high taxes, because taxes take money out of the free market, which generally allocates resources most efficiently, they recognize some problems with increasing gaps between rich and poor. Disparities in opportunity threaten to leave the economy with insufficient human capital, and the ability of the rich to dominate politics encourages wasteful government spending. On the other hand, they want labor costs and inflation to be low, and don't want taxes so high that they discourage entrepreneurial activity. Therefore, depending on their understanding of the particular facts, some free-market conservatives would support a more progressive tax structure to increase government support of wages and educational opportunities for the poor, and others would not.

Contractarians think that government should redistribute income from rich to poor to the greatest extent possible without discouraging entrepreneurial activity. This suggests a steeply progressive tax structure to pay for increases in government funding of the EITC and of education at all levels.

One of the areas of greatest concern to many people as they assess their financial situation is health care. They wonder if they will be able to afford health insurance, be able to keep health insurance if they become seriously ill, and be able to pay for an expensive operation or long-term care should they need it. This is the topic of our next chapter.

12

Health Care in America: Free-Market Conservatism, Contractarianism, and Communitarianism

Lethal Conditions

Between forty-five and fifty million Americans lack health insurance. Here's an example, given by philosopher Robert Munson, of the human reality behind that statistic:

Robert Ingram (as I'll call him) was fifty-two years old and very worried about himself, a result of two months of having episodes of sharp, stabbing pains on the left side of his chest. When the pains came, he felt cold and sweaty, and although he tried to ignore them, he found he had to stop what he was doing and wait until they passed. . . .

He operated Bob's Express, which picked up car and truck parts from the smaller supply houses and delivered them to mechanics and garages within a twenty-mile radius. He'd founded the business only a year ago, after working as a mechanic himself for almost thirty years.

He was making enough money to pay the operating expenses and the rent, but not much more.[1]

Upon learning about the pain, Robert's wife Jeri convinced him to see a doctor.

Dr. Tran asked about Robert's parents and grandparents. Robert told him both grandfathers had died of heart attacks in their late fifties. One of his grandmothers was still alive, but the other had also died of a heart attack. . . .

Dr. Tran finished his examination [and said], "I'm worried that you may be on the verge of a heart attack. . . . Your coronary arteries may be significantly blocked by plaque, and if that's so, the outcome could be devastating."

"You mean I could die."

"Exactly," Dr. Tran said. "We need to know what shape your heart's in, so I want you to have a coronary angiogram. I'm referring you to a cardiologist. . . . Don't worry. Angiography is quite safe, really. And the ultrasound amounts to nothing at all."

"But what will that *cost?*"

"I'm not sure exactly," Dr. Tran said. "Probably in the neighborhood of $5000 to $7000."

"Then it's out of the question," Robert said. "I don't have the money."

"Your insurance will cover both procedures."

"I don't have insurance, Doctor." Robert shook his head. "I run my own business, and I put all my money into keeping it going. . . ."

"If the tests show what I think they might," Dr. Tran said, "you'll need coronary artery bypass surgery. That will cost in the neighborhood of $30,000. Perhaps as much as $50,000, depending on complications and hospital stays."

"That's just laughable," Robert said. "No way I could raise $30,000. Not even if my life depended on it."

"I suspect it does," Dr. Tran said. "But selling your truck would have the advantage of qualifying you for Medicaid. In this state, if you have assets under $3000, you qualify."

"But if I sold my truck, I'd have to go out of business," Robert said. "I wouldn't have any way to earn a living, and my wife's sickly. She can't work a regular job because of her headaches. . . . I'll just have to take my chances until I'm either rich enough or poor enough to get the right treatment."[2]

The number of uninsured has increased in the United States because fewer employers offer health insurance. The United States is unique in its reliance on employment-based health insurance. After World War II, there was a labor shortage, but wage and price controls limited the ability of employers to attract workers with higher salaries. So employers attracted workers with fringe benefits, such as health insurance, which they could deduct from federal taxes. Now employers are abandoning that role. Economists Paul Krugman and Robin Wells write: "The share of nonelderly Americans with employment-based health insurance was 67.7 percent as recently as 2000." By 2004 it was down to 63.1 percent.[3] Jennifer Lee reports in the *New York Times* that it "dropped to 60 percent in 2005."[4] Krugman notes another indication of quickly decreasing coverage. A survey conducted "by the Commonwealth Fund, a nonpartisan organization that studies health care . . . , found that 41 percent of nonelderly American adults with incomes between $20,000 and $40,000 a year were without health insurance for all or part of 2005. That's up from 28 percent as recently as 2001."[5]

Cost is the reason for employers reducing health coverage for employees. "Today," Krugman and Wells report, "the annual cost of coverage for a family of four is estimated by the Kaiser Family Foundation at more than $10,000. . . . That's roughly what a worker earning minimum wage and working full time earns in a year. It's more than half the annual earnings of the average Wal-Mart employee." They add:

Now that health costs loom so large, companies that provide generous benefits are in effect paying some of their workers much more than the going wage—or, more to the point, more than competitors pay similar workers. . . . This creates pressure to reduce or eliminate health benefits. And companies that can't cut benefits enough to stay competitive—such as GM—find their very existence at risk.[6]

These economic fundamentals will likely cause additional reductions in coverage.

The effects are deadly. Krugman and Wells write: "Among Americans diagnosed with colorectal cancer, those without insurance were 70 percent more likely than those with insurance to die over the next three years."[7] The Institute of Medicine reported in 2004: "Lack of insurance . . . leads to delayed diagnoses, life-threatening complications, and 18,000 premature deaths in the United States every year."[8]

The United States compares unfavorably to other industrialized countries in health care. We spend more money per capita and as a percentage of GDP and get poorer health outcomes. In 2002, for example, per capita health care spending was $5,267 in the United States, but only $2,931 in Canada, $2,736 in France, and $2,160 in Great Britain. We had comparable numbers of doctors, nurses, and hospital beds per 1,000 people, yet life expectancy in the Unites States was lower than in these other countries and infant mortality higher.[9] Our system seems to be uniquely inefficient.

Free Markets and Health Care: Moral and Practical Concerns

Our system is more free-market-based than the others. The public pays from 70 to more than 80 percent of health-care costs in these other countries, but only 45 percent in the United States.[10] This raises questions about relying on the free market in health care.

Moral Concerns about a Free Market in Health Care

Some issues are moral in nature. Is the free-market allocation of health care services morally appropriate? We don't allow the free market to allocate organs needed for transplant, even though such organs are in short supply. "In 1996," writes the United Hospital Fund's Carol Levine, "Almost 4,000 people on waiting lists died while waiting to receive an organ."[11]

More organs would be available for transplant, allowing many people to ensure that a matching kidney, heart, liver, or lung was available if and when they needed it, if free trade were allowed in organ futures. The system could work this way. Many thousands of potential donors could receive regular payments on condition that they donate their organs to a certain for-profit organ distributor, should they die with organs fit for transplant. These payments would encourage organ donations, thereby increasing the supply available for transplant. The payments would come from subscribers assessed large fees to be among those eligible to receive the organs. No purposeful deaths would be required for rich people to secure vital organs, including hearts, in this way. But under current law, the system would be illegal. Why?

Congress outlawed commercial organ traffic in 1984, Levine claims, "because it was concerned that traffic in organs might lead to inequitable access to donor organs with the wealthy having an unfair advantage."[12] But why shouldn't money influence access to organs when it influences access to so many other things, such as large houses and fancy cars? Communitarians might say that where life and death are concerned, we remember our common humanity. Distinctions of income, race, national origin, and the like appear trivial in the face of death, which appropriately elicits sentiments of human solidarity.

Contractarians would also oppose commercialization if it meant additional advantages for the haves in society without corresponding advantages to the have-nots. But they wouldn't be as absolute as communitarians, because some commercialization arrangements could help have-nots. Suppose the above-mentioned subscription system was revised so that every other organ procured under subscription was donated from the subscription system to the ordinary network, with the result that more organs were available for transplant and half of this increase was available without regard to income or wealth. Contractarians might well favor such a system.

The point is that regarding organs for transplant, Americans generally oppose allowing rich people to use money to gain advantage. Yet we tolerate rich people using money to gain advantage in life-and-death situations through purchase of private health insurance that many other people lack, resulting in eighteen thousand preventable deaths a year among the uninsured. Robert Ingram is probably headed for a life-threatening cardiac event. How can we make sense of this? Why do we leave Mr. Ingram uncovered?

Free-market conservatives assume that a free market in health care will help everyone in the long run. The pressures of competition in a free market force providers of health care services to be efficient. With greater efficiency, everyone is ultimately better served. Unfortunately, this doesn't seem to be working in health care.

Efficiency and Insurance

Some free-market conservatives blame insurance for at least part of the problem. Health insurance, they think, drives up health care costs and makes health care unavailable to many people. Insurance typically allows people to get services without paying most of the cost out of pocket. Patients who have insurance often pay only 20 percent of the cost of medical services they receive. In 2004, the *Economic Report of the President* included this parable about the clothing industry:

Suppose, for example, that an individual could purchase a clothing insurance policy with a "coinsurance" rate of 20 percent on the dollar for all clothing purchases. An individual with such a policy would be expected to spend substantially more on clothes—due to larger quantity and higher quality purchases—with 80 percent discount than he would at the full price. . . . The clothing insurance example suggests an inherent inefficiency in the use of insurance to pay for things that have little intrinsic risk or uncertainty.[13]

The report suggests that insurance shouldn't cover predictable, routine, and low-risk medical procedures, such as routine dental care, annual medical exams, vaccinations, and visits to the doctor for a sore throat. People overconsume these services when insurance pays 80 percent of the cost. The alternative, called "consumer-directed health care," is for people to pay for such services out of pocket.

But out-of-pocket payment can't be the answer to soaring health care costs in the United States. First, people in other developed countries don't pay out of pocket for routine and low-risk health interventions. They're all covered by some form of universal, national health insurance. If insurance were a major source of inefficiency, those countries should have higher costs than we do. But they don't. They have lower costs.

Second, many routine medical services, such as immunizations and annual physicals, are cost-effective, saving health care dollars by avoiding problems or finding them before they become severe and more expensive to treat. Without insurance, fewer people would get preventive care and the nation's health care bill would increase.[14]

Finally, Krugman and Wells point out, inefficient use of routine services can't be a major source of increasing health care costs in the United States, because these services constitute only a small fraction of health care expenditures. The big-ticket items needed by a small percentage of people are driving up total costs. They write:

> In 2003, health spending roughly followed the "80–20 rule": 20 percent of the population accounted for 80 percent of expenses. Half the population had virtually no medical expenses; a mere 1 percent of the population accounted for 22 percent of expenses. . . .[15] [So], when you think of the problem of health care costs, you shouldn't envision visits to the family physician to talk about a sore throat; you should think about coronary bypass operations, dialysis, and chemotherapy. Nobody is proposing a consumer-directed health care plan that would force individuals to pay a large share of extreme medical expenses, such as the costs of chemotherapy, out of pocket.[16]

With the median family income less than $50,000 a year, few people could afford $50,000 heart surgeries or $100,000 cancer treatments if they had to pay out of pocket. Most people would be in Robert Ingram's unfortunate position, and technological developments in medicine and surgery would go to waste for lack of use.

Private Insurance

Private insurance is the free-market backup alternative to paying for services out of pocket. A major problem for all private health insurance plans, however, is adverse selection. The costs of the plan are geared to the average cost of medical care of the group being covered. Healthy people pay more than their medical costs would be without insurance, giving the insurance company enough money to pay for the health care of sicker people and still make a profit. But healthy people seldom want to subsidize the health care of sickly strangers using the same insurance company, so they drop their coverage or don't sign up in the first place. This behavior raises the average cost to cover those who remain in the plan, raising the price of insurance. This makes the next healthiest group among those covered by the insurance realize that they're now paying more than their costs without insurance, so they drop out. The pool of the insured becomes smaller, the cost of insurance increases, and more people lack insurance, because it costs more than it's worth to them, or more than they can afford. Krugman and Wells write:

Insurance companies deal with these problems, to some extent, by carefully screening applicants to identify those with a high risk of needing expensive treatment, and either rejecting such applicants or charging them higher premiums. But such screening is itself expensive. Furthermore, it tends to screen out exactly those who most need insurance.[17]

Another problem with private insurance is that less than 80 cents of every dollar, Krugman writes, "is paid out to doctors, hospitals and other health care providers. . . . The other 20 cents go into profits, marketing and administrative expenses. . . . And here's the thing: most of those 20 cents spent on things other than medical care are unnecessary. . . . Medicare manages to spend about 98 percent of its funds on actual medical care."[18]

Doctors and hospitals waste money as well when forced to deal with many different private insurance companies. Krugman notes that Benjamin Brewer, a doctor who writes for the *Wall Street Journal*, has to deal with 301 different insurance companies. "He currently employs two full-time staff members for billing, and his two secretaries spend half their time collecting insurance information. Brewer thinks he could go from four people to one if we had a single-payer system like Canada's."[19]

Private insurance tied to employment, as most private insurance is in the United States, has additional problems. First, it has the effect of keeping some people in jobs that they detest because they fear losing insurance coverage. Unenthusiastic workers aren't maximally productive. Second, people staying in jobs for security reduces the entrepreneurial activity that creates innovation and sparks economic growth.

Third, employment-based insurance limits job opportunities for people with health problems as employers shun applicants whose use of the medical plan will drive up the company's rates. Yet, these are among the people who need jobs the most.

Finally, employment-based insurance hurts the international competitiveness of American industry. Fareed Zakaria pointed out in *Newsweek* in 2005: "This year, General Motors will pay about $5.2 billion in medical and insurance bills for its active and retired workers. That adds $1,500 to the cost of every GM car. For Toyota, whose products are manufactured in many countries abroad, these costs add just $186 per car."

Health insurance costs are only about $200 per car in Canada, owing to Canada's single-payer, government-run health care system. As a result, American manufacturers have been moving to Ontario, where more cars are now made than in Michigan.[20]

Managed Care Organizations

Private health insurance in the United States, including insurance provided by employers, is dominated now by managed care organizations (MCOs), which were designed to combat increasing health care costs. Here's how they try to do that:

1. The MCO contracts with certain doctors, called "preferred providers," to get reduced rates for services.

2. Primary care physicians are used as gatekeepers who decide when patients can see specialists, whose services tend to be more expensive.

3. Payments are geared to diagnostically related groups (DRGs). For example, an appendectomy should, on average, cost a certain amount of money in a given part of the country, so the MCO holds doctors and hospitals accountable (in every sense of the word) for meeting this average cost.

4. Certain services, such as magnetic resonance imagery (MRI) and surgery, require preauthorization from the MCO to ensure that these high-priced items are provided only when truly necessary.

5. Whenever possible, someone with less training and lower salary is substituted for someone with more training working at a higher salary. Registered nurses, for example, may not check patients' blood pressure and temperature if a nurse's assistant can so with competence.

6. Physicians are given financial incentives to keep costs down. These include, bioethicist Allen Buchanan writes, "year-end bonuses or holdbacks of payments that physicians receive only if they do not exceed specified utilization limits."

7. "Managed care increasingly employs data from outcome (efficacy) studies to develop practice guidelines."[21]

Some of these methods of saving money upset patients. When a company changes MCOs, or the MCO changes its list of preferred providers, patients may be denied insurance coverage to visit their favorite doctors. Also, patients wanting to see a specialist may dislike waiting for required authorization from a primary care physician.

The MCO system can upset doctors as well. Regarding preauthorization, they often resent having to convince a non-physician MCO employee that a certain test or procedure is genuinely necessary for a patient. MCO practice guidelines similarly put doctors on the spot to justify what they think is right for patients when the guidelines suggest less expensive alternatives.

More controversial is the apparent conflict of interest that physicians have when their own income is affected by the level of care they offer patients. This was typical of the old fee-for-service system that MCOs replaced. Physicians were paid for services rendered, so they had a financial incentive to provide services—possibly more services than patients needed, which may have contributed to increases in health care costs. MCOs, by contrast, attempt to save money by giving physicians the opposite incentive. Dr. Norman Levinsky writes: "Some doctors may . . . increase their incomes by reducing the time they spend with patients to less than what they themselves consider to be optimal." Or doctors may prescribe cheaper, but possibly less effective, drugs.[22]

Levinsky addresses a more troubling case of cost containment. A hospital was losing money on hip replacements because Medicare, which funds most hip replacements, paid less than the devices cost. A cheaper prosthesis was available which was expected to work just as well over a ten-year period, after which it was more likely to fail. The hospital's CEO recommended using the less-expensive device in patients at least eighty years old, reasoning that they'd less likely need the prosthesis more than ten years. "If the chief of orthopedic surgery did not agree," Levinsky writes, "the CEO would limit the number of patients who could undergo hip-replacement surgery at the hospital. The chief of orthopedic surgery and his colleagues were community practitioners wholly dependent on clinical fees for their professional incomes."[23]

The kicker is that the CEO didn't want elderly patients affected by this cost-cutting measure to be told that a more durable prosthesis was available at other hospitals. He didn't want the hospital to lose business, which is a normal response in the free market. Levinsky finds such secrecy morally unacceptable, but notes: "Very few physicians to whom I presented the case over the past several years thought that the surgeons were obligated to inform their elderly patients that they would receive the less durable hip prosthesis."[24] Thus, cost containment often involves some morally questionable practices, including secrecy and physician conflicts of interest.

What is more, MCOs lack incentive to use preventive care to avoid long-term health costs. Employers change MCOs as they look for more coverage at lower cost. MCOs have little incentive to cover preventive care, because by the time current subscribers need major medical attention, they'll likely be covered by different insurance. But preventive care is one of the best ways to hold down overall costs.[25] One reason medical costs grow much more quickly in the United States than in other countries is that fewer Americans have regular, preventive health care.

In sum, it seems that health care is the exception to the rule that free markets are the most efficient way to allocate services. A multitude of private insurance companies, including MCOs, tend for several reasons to promote inefficiency, which explains why countries with state-run programs all have more efficient (and thus less expensive and more effective) health care systems than ours.

The Cost of Drugs

Another factor driving up health care costs in our system is the price of drugs. Marcia Angell, former editor of the *New England Journal of Medicine*, writes in her 2004 article in the *New York Review of Books*:

Drugs are the fastest-growing part of the health care bill. . . . The increase in drug spending reflects, in almost equal parts, the facts that people are taking a lot more drugs than they used to, that those drugs are more likely to be expensive new ones instead of older, cheaper ones, and that the prices of the most heavily prescribed drugs are routinely jacked up, sometimes several times a year.[26]

For example, before its patent ran out, the price of the anti-allergy drug Claritin was raised thirteen times in five years, "for a cumulative increase of more than 50 percent—over four times the rate of general inflation. . . . In 2002, the average price of the fifty drugs most used by senior citizens was nearly $1,500 for a year's supply."[27] The percentage of the American GDP going to drugs tripled between 1980 and 2000. By 2002, Americans were spending about $200 billion a year on prescription drugs, which doesn't include "the large amounts spent for drugs administered in hospitals, nursing homes, or doctors' offices (as is the case for many cancer drugs)."[28]

Steeper price increases affect people taking drugs that serve few patients, making it uneconomical to have competing production facilities. In February 2006, for example, Ovation Pharmaceuticals raised the wholesale price of the cancer-fighting medication nitrogen mustard, whose patent protection expired decades ago, about tenfold. Joyce Elkins, who bought a two-week supply for $77.50 at the beginning of the month, paid $548.01 for the same prescription later in the month, Alex Berenson reports in the *New York Times*. Although long used as an ointment for certain cancers, nitrogen mustard was never officially approved for that purpose, so most insurance, including Medicare Part D, won't cover the cost increase. Ms. Elkins said she and her husband would pay $7,000 over a six-month course of treatment by cutting down on utilities and food.[29]

This is not an isolated case, Berenson writes. "In 2003, Abbott Laboratories . . . raised the price of Norvir, an AIDS drug introduced in 1996, from $54 a month to $265 a month. AIDS groups protested, but Abbott refused to rescind the increase." Neither company identified increased costs to justify increased prices.[30]

Drug companies often claim that they need to charge high prices for their drugs in order to fund research designed to discover better drugs, but Angell points out flaws in this claim. She writes, "The pharmaceutical industry is not especially innovative. . . . Only a handful of truly important drugs have been brought to market in recent years, and they were mostly based on taxpayer-funded research at academic institutions, small biotechnology companies, or the National Institutes of Health (NIH)." Instead of seeking health-improving innovation, drug companies make minor changes in existing drugs and market them as innovations. This is why we now have six different (but not very different) statins to help lower cholesterol. Angell quotes Dr. Sharon Levine, associate executive director of the Kaiser Permanente Medical Group: "If I'm a manufacturer and I can change one molecule and get another twenty years of patent rights, and convince physicians to prescribe and consumers to demand the next form of Prilosec, or weekly Prozac instead of daily Prozac, just as my patent expires, then why would I be spending money on a lot less certain endeavor, which is looking for brand new drugs?"[31]

Angell adds:

Of the seventy-eight drugs approved by the FDA in 2002, only seventeen contained new active ingredients, and only seven of these were classified by the FDA as improvements over older drugs. The other seventy-one drugs approved that year were variations of old drugs or deemed no better than drugs already on the market. In other words, they were me-too drugs. Seven of seventy-eight is not much of a yield. Furthermore, of these seven, not one came from a major U.S. drug company.[32]

Instead of doing research, drug companies allocate their income to profit, marketing, and lobbying. Drug manufacturers' profits are huge by corporate standards. "In 2001, the ten American drug companies in the Fortune 500 list . . . ranked far above all other American industries in average net return, whether as a percentage of sales (18.5 percent), of assets (16.3 percent), or of shareholders' equity (33.2 percent). These are astonishing margins. For comparison, the median net return for all other industries in the Fortune 500 was only 3.3 percent of sales." In 2002, the most startling fact was that "the combined profits for the ten drug companies in the Fortune 500 ($35.9 billion) were more than the profits for all the other 490 businesses put together ($33.7 billion)."[33]

Drug company executives are lavishly rewarded for returning such profits, Angell writes: "According to a report by the non-profit group Families USA, the former chairman and CEO of Bristol Myers Squibb, Charles A. Hombold Jr., made $74,890,918 in 2001, not counting his $76,095,611 worth of unexercised stock options. The chairman of Wyeth made $40,521,011, exclusive of his $40,629,459 in stock options. And so on."[34] Drug companies could lower the price of drugs and pay for more research by reducing profit and upper-management compensation.

Instead, they use their wealth on campaign contributions to get additional favors from government. For example, Congress modified laws governing patent extensions. "The result is that the effective patent life of brand name drugs increased from about eight years in 1980 to about fourteen years in 2000. For a blockbuster—usually defined as a drug with sales of over a billion dollars a year (like Lipitor or Celebrex or Zoloft)—those six years of additional exclusivity are golden. They can add billions of dollars to sales."[35]

Another effect of drug company lobbying was the 1987 law that prohibits Americans going to Canada to buy prescription drugs at lower prices. Prices are lower in Canada, because government agencies bargain effectively with drug companies. When drug prices in the United States became so high that political pressure from senior citizens was irresistible, Congress passed Medicare Part D, a prescription drug benefit. The drug companies gained because the new law makes it illegal for the American government to do what keeps drug prices lower in Canada—bargain for lower prices. Angell notes: "Drug companies have the largest lobby in Washington, and they give copiously to political campaigns. Legislators are now so beholden to the pharmaceutical industry that it will be exceedingly difficult to break its lock on them."[36]

In effect, the growing gap between haves and have-nots in society, which allows some to wield so much political power through campaign contributions, can be harmful to your health. As prescription drugs become more expensive, employers offer less drug coverage and employees must pay more for drugs out of pocket. Angell writes:

Many of them simply can't do it. They trade off drugs against home heating or food. Some people try to string out their drugs by taking them less often than prescribed, or sharing them with a spouse. Others, too embarrassed to admit that they can't afford to pay for drugs, leave their doctors' offices with prescriptions in hand but don't have them filled. Not only do these patients go without needed treatment but their doctors sometimes wrongly conclude that the drugs they prescribed haven't worked and prescribe yet others.[37]

In sum, the pharmaceutical industry is a major part of the difficulties besetting health care in the United States.

Government-Run Systems and Political Philosophy

Free-market conservatives favor free-market solutions to problems of resource allocation, because they think the free market spurs efficiency and technological improvement that benefit everyone in the long run. They're usually right. However, health care seems to be an exception. Private drug companies, insurance companies, and employer-provided health care have resulted in U.S. aggregate outcomes worse than in countries with state-run systems providing universal access to health care. Americans pay more money per capita, representing a larger percentage of GDP, than other countries, and have poorer outcome regarding insurance coverage, average life span, and infant mortality. The superiority of the government-run model in the United States is apparent in the lower administrative costs in Medicare and the better preventive care, service, and cost containment in health care provided by the Veterans Administration.

These facts put free-market conservatives in a bind. They favor both efficiency and the free market. Here, it seems the free market doesn't promote efficiency. When Milton Friedman, perhaps the most famous free-market conservative of the twentieth century, considered property rights to interfere with efficiency, he advocated the corrective modification of property rights. Perhaps in the face of conflicts between the free market and efficiency, evident in the efficiency gap between the United States and other countries, he would favor a government-run plan that promises greater efficiency.

In any case, free-market conservatism shouldn't be confused with a business perspective. In a free market, according to Adam Smith in *The Wealth of Nations* (the free-market Bible), business people should seek profit. But if the system is working correctly, their profits are low. "In a country fully stocked in proportion to all the business it had to transact . . . , competition . . . would everywhere be . . . great, and consequently the ordinary profit as low as possible."[38]

In their attempts to increase profit, business people seek government favors, such as grants of monopoly. Monopoly allows business people to charge higher prices, which is good for them, but not for the public who are paying higher prices for no improvement in the product. Smith writes, "In every country it always is and must be the interest of the great body of the people to buy whatever they want of those who sell it cheapest."[39] Monopoly circumvents the free market system and reduces the social benefits of trade by allowing producers to evade the competition that keeps prices and profits low. Smith would look at patent extensions on lucrative drugs as a perfect example of business gaining extra profit at the expense of the public through government-granted monopoly.

Another popular way for business to gain monopoly profits is for the state to outlaw importation from foreign competitors. Smith writes, "In the restraints upon the importation of all foreign commodities which can come into competition with those of our own growth, or manufacture, the interest of the home-consumer is evidently sacrificed to that of the producer."[40] Smith would see restrictions on reimporting prescription medications from Canada as such a reduction in foreign competition.

Because high profit depends on circumventing the free-market system and overcharging the public, Smith finds, "the rate of profit does not . . . rise with the prosperity, and fall with the declension, of the society. On the contrary, it is naturally low in rich, and high in poor countries, and it is always highest in the countries which are going fastest to ruin,"[41] a judgment confirmed by subsequent history, according to political analyst Kevin Phillips in *Wealth and Democracy* and *American Theocracy*.[42] Smith concludes of business people that their "interest is never exactly the same with that of the public. . . . [They] have generally an interest to deceive and even to oppress the public, and . . . accordingly have, upon many occasions, both deceived and oppressed."[43] Smith would probably see Medicare Part D restrictions on government bargaining with drug companies for lower prices as an example of oppression.

A free-market conservative steeped in the tradition of Adam Smith would be skeptical of business claims that private enterprise is the answer to problems of health care coverage when profits are high, prices are soaring, and service to the public is inferior to what exists in other countries. Executives and stock holders in health care and pharmaceutical companies may believe they represent a free-market approach, but Smith would likely disagree. Accordingly, a free-market conservative might see health care as that odd area where efficiency requires government control.

Libertarians, by contrast, less interested in efficiency, would rely on the free market even if outcomes are poor, because they want to defend private property rights. Contractarians would favor some government-run system, such as in Great Britain, Canada, Italy, or France, because poor people are much better served under those systems. Communitarians would favor a government-run system for the same reasons.

However, efficiency is not the only issue besetting health care. Another matter, which government-run systems can't entirely overcome, is that of rationing. No country or system can afford to fund every medical procedure that may benefit patients.

Last-Chance Therapies and Health Care Rationing

Consumer expectations are part of the problem. When threatened by grave illness or death, people want the right to all possibly helpful measures, regardless of cost. Christine deMeurers, for example, went all out to defeat her breast cancer, diagnosed in August 1992. She was a married, thirty-two-year-old teacher with two children. After a radical mastectomy and radiation treatments, she discovered in May 1993 that the cancer had spread and was now at Stage IV. Her doctor said her best chance for survival was high-dose chemotherapy with autologous bone marrow transplant, or HDC/ABMT. Philosopher Alex London explains the theory behind the procedure:

There is a direct correlation between the dose of chemotherapy a patient receives and its effect on the targeted cancer. The problem, however, is that there is a natural limit to the amount of these toxic agents the body can endure. In HDC/ABMT physicians remove stem cells from a patient's bone marrow, purify them of cancer cells, and then freeze them for later use. Patients are then exposed to near lethal doses of chemotherapy, up to 10 times the normal level. In addition to killing cancer cells, however, such concentrated amounts of these potent chemicals inevitably kill much of the patient's remaining bone marrow. So after receiving this high dose of chemotherapy the harvested and purified stem cells are transplanted back into the patient.[44]

Like many Americans, Christine and her husband had health insurance through a managed care plan they had chosen at work. Theirs was called Health Net. It didn't cover experimental therapies. Although an accepted form of treatment for Hodgkins disease and leukemia, HDC/ABMT was experimental for breast cancer and Health Net decided not to cover Christine's treatment. London writes: "A 1992 review article by the respected health policy expert Dr. David Eddy had concluded that there were no data to support the claim that this procedure was in any way superior to the standard dose of chemotherapy when treating women with metastatic breast cancer."[45] The cost was too great for the low probability of patient benefit, a Health Net committee had decided.

The deMeurers were desperate. Christine saw a second oncologist, who also recommended HDC/ABMT. They contacted a lawyer to write an appeal of the Health Net decision and started trying to raise the $100,000 the treatment would cost. One of Christine's physicians, Dr. John Glaspy, was in a bind, because he had been on the committee that decided the plan wouldn't cover this treatment for Stage IV breast cancer, yet he wanted to help his patient. Dr. Glaspy's boss, Dr. Dennis Slamon, tried

to salvage as much of the medical center's relationship with the deMeurers and with Health Net as possible. . . . He decided that UCLA would absorb the costs of Christine's procedure, thus relieving Health Net of any obligation to pay and enabling Christine to receive the health care she so desperately wanted. On September 23, 1993, Christine was admitted to UCLA to begin the first phase of treatment. According to her husband, she experienced four disease-free months after recovering from the severe chemotherapy, but by the Spring of 1994 she was ill again and on March 10, 1995 Christine deMeurers succumbed to her cancer.[46]

This case raises the issue of rationing health care in a world of fiscal limits where desperate patients seek unproven, last-chance, high-cost therapies. Can we blame them? Would we act differently if we or our loved ones were in Christine deMeurers's position? On the other hand, we can't afford to give people every therapy that might possibly be helpful, even in life-and-death situations. London asks: "Should we pay for costly medical procedures of unknown therapeutic benefit when there are people struggling to get access to a host of genuinely effective therapies?" Recall that Robert Ingram will likely experience a life-threatening cardiac event that could probably be avoided if he had access to health care resources. London also asks: "Are four disease-free months in the life of a terminally ill person worth the $100,000 to $200,000 it takes to secure them? Could this money be better spent somewhere else? If we do not draw the line on medical expenses in front of cases like this, then where do we draw it?"[47]

The American health care system is troubled in part because few Americans want to draw the line anywhere. London gives this example:

In 1993 Health Net lost a lawsuit filed by Jim Fox, the husband of Nelene Fox, a Health Net subscriber who had been denied HDC/ABMT for her Stage IV breast cancer on the grounds that it was experimental. . . . The jury awarded Nelene's estate $14 million in actual damages and $77 million in punitive damages, although Health Net later agreed to pay only $5 million in exchange for their right to appeal the verdict. Nevertheless, the members of the jury were eager to send a message to health care companies. "You cannot substitute profits for good-quality health care," one juror was quoted as saying.[48]

Dr. Norman Levinsky writes:

Groups of patients and public officials have resisted most open efforts to ration care. Some health insurance plans that initially would not pay for some kinds of organ transplantation have changed their policy in response to public outcry. There is public and political pressure to require health maintenance organizations (HMOs) and insurance companies to relax restrictions on the use of hospital emergency departments, referrals to specialists, and the length of hospital stays after normal deliveries. It seems reasonable to conclude that, thus far, Americans are willing to pay the price necessary to avoid undisguised rationing of the medical care they receive.[49]

But some rationing is inevitable, because there's no end to the variety and cost of therapies that may give people a last chance at continued life. Ethicist Leonard Fleck gives the example of the totally implantable artificial heart (TIAH). He writes:

To concretize the issue a bit, there's a potential annual need of 350,000 TIAHs at an aggregate cost of $52 billion. If this number seems high, the reader should know that we currently perform about 650,000 bypass surgeries in the United States each year and another 600,000 coronary angioplasties. Projections are that the TIAH will provide an average of five extra years of life expectancy, although the range around that average could be quite large.[50]

Fleck adds: "These are the 'early' last-chance therapies. There will be many more, and there will be no morally or rationally obvious place to draw a line."[51] If we give people with insurance access to such therapies, it becomes harder to fund less costly treatments for the growing number of Americans without insurance. Fleck concludes that we have an obligation to ration health care in the most equitable and just manner possible.

Rationing Care of the Elderly and Hopeless

In the 1980s, serious debate began about rationing health care to the elderly. Bioethicist Daniel Callahan, founder and director of the Hastings Center, argued that intergenerational justice requires the elderly to consume fewer health care resources so that more is left for younger people. He took issue with the idea, increasingly popular, that the longest life is the best life.

Our culture has worked hard to redefine old age as a time of liberation, not decline, a time of travel, of new ventures in education and self-discovery, of the ever-accessible tennis court or golf course and of delightfully periodic but thankfully brief visits from well-behaved grandchildren. That . . . picture . . . arouses hopes that spur medicine to wage an aggressive war against the infirmities of old age. [But] the costs of such a war would be prohibitive. No matter how much is spent the ultimate problem will still remain: people will grow old and die. Worse still, by pretending that old age can be turned into a kind of endless middle age, we rob it of meaning and significance for the elderly.[52]

Callahan thinks "the future goal of medical science should be to improve the quality of old people's lives, not to lengthen them."[53] He urges acceptance of what he calls a "natural life span."

We should think of a natural life span as the achievement of a life that is sufficiently long to take advantage of those opportunities life typically offers and that we ordinarily regard as its prime benefits—loving and "living," raising a family, engaging in work that is satisfying, reading, thinking, cherishing our friends and families. People differ on what might be a full natural life span; my view is that it can be achieved by the late 70s or early 80s.[54]

Living longer doesn't guarantee a better life, and "no matter how long medicine enables people to live, death at any time—at age 90 or 100 or 110—would frustrate some possibility, some as-yet-unrealized goal." Callahan proposes, therefore, that "medicine . . . have as its specific goals . . . relief of suffering [and] . . . averting . . . premature death." He thinks that the elderly need most of all "a sense of the meaning and significance of their stage in life, one that is not dependent on economic productivity or physical vigor."[55]

Communitarian social critic Amitai Etzioni opposes this view completely, writing: "Callahan . . . suggests turning off life-extending technology for all those above a certain age, even if they could recover their full human capacity if treated. . . . Look at the list of technologies he would withhold: mechanical ventilation, artificial resuscitation . . . , and artificial nutrition and hydration."[56]

Etzioni claims the elderly need not be the burden that Callahan imagines. "Many of the 'elderly' can contribute to society . . . by continuing to work in the traditional sense of the term. . . . There is also evidence that people who continue to have meaningful work will live longer and healthier lives, without requiring more health care, because psychic well-being in our society is so deeply associated with meaningful work."[57]

In addition, if justice is the issue, justice between the rich and poor is as important as justice between the young and old. Callahan would remove public support of health care for the elderly. But only the poor depend on public support. Richer people would still be able to buy health care designed to extend their lives beyond the limit that Callahan thinks reasonable.

What is more, Etzioni contends, if money needs to be saved, why pick on the elderly? Money could be saved, Etzioni suggests, by stopping interventions whose benefits are questionable, such as psychotherapy.

Why not take the $2 billion or so from plastic surgery dedicated to face lifts, reducing behinds and the like . . . ? Another important area of saving is the exorbitant profits made by the nondoctor owners of dialysis units and nursing homes.

If we dare ask how many years of life are enough, should we not also be able to ask how much profit is "enough"? This profit, by the way, is largely set not by the market but by public policy.[58]

Finally, Etzioni worries that any proposal to limit care to the elderly will result in a slippery slope.

Once the precept that one should do "all one can" to avert death is given up, and attempts are made to fix a specific age for a full life, why stop there? If, for instance, the American economy experiences hard times . . . , should the "maximum" age be reduced to 72, 65—or lower? And should the care for other so-called unproductive groups be cut off, even if they are even younger?[59]

But in the light of current and developing last-chance therapies, we can't afford always to "do 'all one can' to avert death." Also, doing everything possible isn't always reasonable. Consider the case of Helga Wanglie, an eighty-five-year-old woman admitted to Hennepin County Medical Center (HCMC) on January 1, 1990, for shortness of breath. Attempts to wean her from the respirator failed. She was conscious for awhile and may have recognized family, but then her heart stopped. After resuscitation she remained unconscious, and doctors determined in June that she was in a persistent vegetative state. They recommended allowing Mrs. Wanglie to die by discontinuing ventilation.

The family insisted that she would want everything done to preserve her life, writes Steven Miles, a clinical ethicist consulted on the case.

They stated their view that physicians should not play God, that the patient would not be better off dead, that removing life support showed moral decay in our civilization, and that a miracle could occur. . . . In June, an ethics committee consultant recommended continued counseling for the family. The family declined counseling, including the counsel of their own pastor, and in late July asked that the respirator not be discussed again. In August, nurses expressed their consensus that continued life support did not seem appropriate.[60]

Insurance covered the $700,000 bill. Still, the medical center went to court to gain permission to stop ventilator support. The Minneapolis Star Tribune editorial included the following on the eve of the trial: "The hospital's plea is born of realism, not hubris. . . . It advances the claim that physicians should not be slaves to technology—any more than patients should be its prisoners. They should be free to deliver, and act on, an honest and time-honored message: 'Sorry, there's nothing more we can do.'"[61] Miles concurs:

The proposal that this family's preference for this unusual and costly treatment, which is commonly regarded as inappropriate, establishes a right to such treatment is ironic, given that preference does not create a right to other needed, efficacious, and widely desired treatments in the United States. We could not afford a universal health care system based on patients' demands. . . . I believe there is a social consensus that intensive care for a person as "overmastered" by disease as this woman was is inappropriate.[62]

Philosopher Felicia Ackerman disagrees. The issue is not a medical matter upon which physicians have particular expertise. All parties agree that continued ventilation will prolong Mrs. Wanglie's life.

They disagree about whether her life is worth prolonging. This is not a medical question but a question of values. . . . It is as presumptuous and *ethically* inappropriate for doctors to suppose that their professional expertise qualifies them to know what kind of life is worth prolonging as it would be for meteorologists to suppose their professional expertise qualifies them to know what kind of destination is worth a long drive in the rain.[63]

In short, we are back to the basic issue in the Terri Schiavo case. Who is allowed to decide what kind of life is worth living? The difference here is recognition that allowing some people to use a lot of medical resources for modest benefits indirectly deprives others of health insurance by making premiums too high. People like Robert Ingram are then denied access to desperately needed and highly effective medical care.

One reason Americans haven't embraced a more efficient, government-run system may be that setting up such a system requires confronting values implicit in budget priorities. How much should go to last-chance therapies; to innovative therapies; to cutting-edge drugs that are only marginally better than generic drugs; to routine checkups; to expensive but possibly life-saving operations? A single-payer system can solve matters of inefficiency, but not matters of value. People will still want more health care, especially when their lives depend on it, so there will still be pressure for health care costs to increase.

We see this in countries with government-run programs. In 2006 in Great Britain, for example, "An appeals court . . . declared . . . that a local health service had acted illegally in withholding a potentially life-saving drug from a woman with breast cancer," Sarah Lyall reports in the *New York Times.* "Mrs. Rogers, 54, went to court when her local health service, Swindon Primary Care Trust, refused to treat her breast cancer with Herceptin even after her doctor had prescribed it." The reason was cost. "Herceptin costs $36,000 to $47,000 a year."[64] The court's decision means that the health service will have to come up with additional money for Mrs. Rogers' care.

In Canada, cost containment has meant long waits for some operations, prompting some health care providers to set up shop in the private sector, which had long been considered illegal in Canada. Dr. Brian Day, owner of one of these new clinics, thinks that it's not illegal and says, "This is a country in which dogs can get a hip replacement in under a week and in which humans can wait two to three years."[65] The basic problem is that the public needs or wants more medical care than it's willing to fund through taxes.

Health care costs per capita and as a percentage of GDP, although low by American standards, have continued to rise in countries with relatively efficient, state-run systems, showing that two distinct kinds of health care problems face the United States. First, there's the problem of efficiency created by trying to provide health care through the free market. Second, there's the problem the United States shares with other countries of setting limits to otherwise limitless desires for expensive, innovative treatments. Solving the second problem requires deep discussions of values.

Conclusion

Libertarians would oppose all government-run health care systems, preferring to protect property rights than to attain efficiencies. Free-market conservatives could go either way, but those most influenced by Adam Smith would seek an alternative to a system that yields high profits and poor service. Contractarians and communitarians would welcome a government-run system that affords better health care to poor people, but communitarians may resist the hard choices about priorities needed in such a system.

Integral to issues of wages, taxes, and health care are issues regarding the size and demographic composition of the population. Health care demands and costs tend to increase as the population ages. One way to infuse our economy with healthy workers in the prime of life, people whose work can help the country pay for health care and its other needs, is to allow increased immigration. But such immigration may depress the wages of poor Americans. This is our next topic.

13

Immigration: Cosmopolitanism, Communitarianism, Multiculturalism, Free-Market Conservatism, Contractarianism, and Environmentalism

Immigrants Then and Now

She was standing on deck as they approached New York Harbor on a balmy day. It was mostly sunny, with beautiful cumulus clouds. Esther and Abram had left Poland together and settled in London for a time, but Abram wanted the better life he was sure was available in America. Esther waited more than two years in London before she had enough money to join her husband in New Jersey. Now their reunion was at hand. Standing with her three young children as the ship approached the Statue of Liberty, Esther heard another couple talking in Yiddish.

The woman said: "It's so wonderful up here on deck. The air is fresh; the wind is pure; the water is beautiful. We should have enjoyed these things during the whole trip. Instead, we were stuck below deck in third class. Why did we go third class?"

Her husband shot back quickly: "Because there wasn't a fourth class."

Abram and Esther were poor, and their English wasn't good. Abram was an anarchist, which justified evading service in the Czar's army by emigrating to England, and a silk worker, which brought him to Paterson, New Jersey, a center of silk manufacturing. During the silk workers' strike in 1913, my Aunt Sadie, the youngest of the three children born in England, was sent to live with wealthy New Yorkers to conserve money.

My father and his two younger brothers were born in the United States. Abram and Esther were so intent on becoming American that they spoke only English in the home, except when they didn't want the children to understand. Then they used Yiddish, until the older children started catching on, at which point they switched to Polish.

My father's siblings went into business. The oldest brother, my Uncle Dave, had an auto-parts store in Paterson, where the youngest brother, Uncle Rich, worked. Aunt Sadie married a furrier who later opened a gift shop in Orlando, Florida. Uncle Harry had a small soda bottling plant in upstate New York until he bought a small hotel in Miami Beach. They struggled financially, but all eventually owned their own homes and considered themselves middle class. Aunt Anna and her husband Sam were so wealthy that Sam gave me fifty cents for shining his shoes at a family gathering when I was charging only a dime.

Although they were all well-read, only my father, who became an engineer, finished high school. During my formative years, he owned a small hardware store on Long Island. The next generation, my generation, is filled with college-educated professionals and business people.

Esther and Abram could come freely to the United States because there were no immigration restrictions for Europeans until 1924, when Congress passed numerical quotas for people of different national origins. According to immigration historian Mae Ngai, "The 'national origin' quotas were aimed against Italians, Slavs, and Jews, whom old-line American Protestants blamed for the social ills of the time: urban slums, class conflict, and political radicalism." Ngai points out: "Mass European immigration had enabled an enormous expansion in manufacturing capacity in the late 19th and early 20th centuries. But by 1920 increases in productivity came from technological advances rather than sheer increases in the size of the work force. That is why business interests did not oppose restrictions on immigration from Europe."[1] Technological advances that threatened jobs helped provoke the silk workers' strike.

Matters were different in the agricultural West, Ngai reports: "The new 'factories in the field' needed a big work force, and a mobile and seasonal one at that. Ideally, growers wanted a surplus supply to keep wages low and harvest time short. During the '20s the southwestern migratory agricultural work force drew large numbers of new immigrants from Mexico as well as more established immigrants and Mexican-Americans."[2]

Accordingly, limits on immigration didn't apply to Mexico and Canada, although means were found to regulate the flow from Mexico. Four hundred thousand Mexicans were deported during the Depression by county welfare bureaus and then four million imported in the bracero program, which was started during World War II to combat labor shortages and lasted until 1964.

In 1965, Congress passed immigration legislation that eliminated the ethnically insulting "national origins quotas" of the earlier law and "instituted a policy based on individual qualifications (with preferences for professionals and family members of citizens and permanent residents) and with a maximum of 20,000 annual admissions for every country."[3] Mexico and Canada were allowed 40,000 each until 1976. "With western and southwestern agriculture still drawing labor from Mexico, the effect was immediate and severe: In 1976, when Congress applied the 20,000-per-country quota rule to Mexico and Canada, the U.S. expelled 781,000 Mexicans. By comparison, the total number . . . for all other parts of the world combined remained below 100,000 a year."[4]

Largely in response to the number of illegal immigrants from Mexico, Congress passed new legislation in 1986 that combined amnesty for 2.7 million illegal immigrants with improved border enforcement. In addition, hiring illegal workers was made a crime. But because the crime was *knowingly* hiring illegal workers, employers could usually evade prosecution by claiming they were fooled by forged documents. As a result, illegal immigrants given amnesty in the 1980s were replaced by new waves of illegal immigrants. Arian Campo-Flores writes in *Newsweek*: "According to studies by the Pew Hispanic Center, the illegal population living in the United States has grown from 5 million in 1996 to as many as 12 million today [2006]. Of the total, 78 percent came from Mexico and the rest of Latin America—the vast majority of whom were fleeing poverty."[5]

Miguel Carvajal falls into this category. "Mr. Carvajal works evenings for $6.50 an hour at a small parking garage in Manhattan," as Corey Kilgannon explains in the *New York Times*:

He knows just enough English to tell customers how much they owe and for how many hours. . . .

Mr. Carvajal, 40, left behind his family and a solid job as a traffic police officer and bought a round-trip plane ticket to New York, as if taking a vacation. He [found] he could make more money at a minimum-wage job in New York than he could directing traffic in Medellin. . . .

He tries to send $300 a month to his parents and his wife and daughter in Colombia, he said. The money has helped buy a house for them and paid the private school tuition for his daughter, Veronica, 16, whose voice on the telephone no longer sounds like that of the 11-year-old girl he left behind. . . .

Having illegal status means a precarious life, he said. He is nervous in public and refrains from socializing for fear of getting involved in anything that could lead to an encounter with people bearing badges. . . .

Mr. Carvajal said that since coming to New York from Colombia in October 2001, he has paid taxes on his earnings each year, hoping it will help him apply for citizenship so that he can bring over his wife and daughter, who have been unable to win visas to settle in the United States.

He held out his 2005 tax form and pointed to his gross income—$23,487—. . . from working seven days a week and all the overtime he could get.[6]

Much controversy surrounds illegal immigration, but almost twice as many legal as illegal immigrants live in the United States, for a total immigrant population of about 35 million. Deciding what to do about illegal immigration requires deciding why immigration should or shouldn't be encouraged in the first place.

Cosmopolitans for Open Immigration

Cosmopolitans believe that moral values are universal; they don't change from time to time or place to place. That's why, for example, raping women during war to demoralize the enemy is always wrong. It's a crime against humanity that merits prosecution regardless of the country or context. So is torturing children to get their parents to reveal military secrets (which they may or may not possess). Similarly, stuffing ballot boxes to win elections is always wrong, as is imprisoning candidates to stifle criticism of the government. Rules against such activities are universally recognized (although not universally observed) because they're self-evident.

Our Declaration of Independence contains a sweeping generalization of this kind: "We hold these truths to be self-evident, that all men are created equal, that they are endowed by their Creator with certain unalienable Rights, that among these are Life, Liberty and the pursuit of Happiness." We criticize other countries on this basis for human rights violations, holding them to the same standards of respect for human rights as we expect among ourselves. This is cosmopolitanism; one set of moral rules governs everywhere. As philosopher Nigel Dower puts it, "National boundaries do not, with this approach, have any ultimate moral significance."[7]

The rights pronounced in the Declaration of Independence include liberty, which encompasses freedom of movement. People shouldn't be held as slaves or confined to their countries of origin. During the Cold War, Americans criticized the Soviet Union for violating human rights by failing to allow their citizens to emigrate. But the freedom to emigrate is hollow without a corresponding freedom to immigrate. On this cosmopolitan logic, immigration should be limited only to control the spread of crime (including terrorism) and disease. Like my grandparents, Miguel Carvajal should be allowed to move to the United States legally and bring his family with him. Just as globalization increasingly allows the free movement of goods across national borders, it should allow the free movement of people. Philosopher Michael Walzer notes, "The same writers who defended free trade in the nineteenth century also defended unrestricted immigration."[8] Economist John Isbister puts the cosmopolitan argument this way:

As a mental exercise, one could ask how a law passed by the residents of New York City that restricted the permanent entry of Americans who were not city residents would be judged. Leaving aside the fact that it would be unconstitutional, would it be morally justified? The people of New York could offer some good reasons for the law. New York is already crowded and cannot tolerate further population growth, they might argue. The sanitation system is close to breaking down, the schools are crowded, the welfare system is bankrupt, the homeless shelters are inadequate, and the unemployment rate is rising.

These sorts of arguments would not prove convincing to most Americans, who would find the restrictions on personal freedom too onerous. . . . The interests that New Yorkers have in restricting entry, although perhaps meritorious, are not of sufficient weight to permit such massive violations of the rights and interests of outsiders. New York cannot justify its own immigration policy, morally.

Reasoning by analogy, it is hard to find an ethical justification for the United States' restricting entry across its borders. In fact, it is harder, since the people of the United States are privileged, vis-à-vis the rest of the world, in a way that the residents of New York are not, in comparison to other Americans. New Yorkers could argue plausibly that [Americans] denied entry could find comparable amenities in other cities. [However,] the great majority of immigrants and potential immigrants hope to enjoy a significantly higher standard of living in the United States than they experienced in their home countries.[9]

In sum, if being born Iraqi, French, or Bolivian has no bearing on a person's fundamental rights, and freedom of movement is a fundamental right, the freedom to move to any country should also be a fundamental right. Immigration quotas violate that right as clearly as would quotas on Wisconsinites moving to New York.

Communitarians for Immigration Restrictions

Communitarian philosopher Michael Walzer replies to such cosmopolitans as Isbister that people are cultural beings. Meaning in our lives depends largely on our fulfilling expectations created by an evolving culture that influences the way we dress, the kind of housing we desire, the sorts of jobs available and preferred, the number of children we think it appropriate to have, the sports we enjoy, and myriad other aspects of our lives, including everything touched by language. Most people want to interact predominantly with those who share their culture, and also want their children and future generations to continue cultural traditions.

Walzer believes that the importance of cultural integrity and continuity justify limiting entry into the country of people who don't share the same cultural heritage.

The distinctiveness of cultures and groups depends upon closure and, without it, cannot be conceived as a stable feature of human life. If this distinctiveness is a value, as most people . . . seem to believe, then closure must be permitted somewhere. At some level of political organization, something like the sovereign state must take shape and claim the authority to make its own admissions policy, to control and sometimes restrain the flow of immigrants.[10]

Walzer notes that when the United States allowed unlimited immigration, cultural separation was achieved by people gathering in ethnic enclaves that successfully resisted encroachment by people from different ethnic groups. There were Italian, Irish, Polish, and Jewish neighborhoods in large American cities such as New York and Chicago. We now believe people should be free to move to any neighborhood regardless of religion, national origin, or race. But we can sustain such freedom only because fellow Americans dominate the pool of people who might move in. We're not overly threatened—we don't feel compelled to take up arms against newcomers—because they share the American culture. But this sense of cultural and physical safety is available only because we don't permit unlimited immigration from other countries. If we were ever again to have open immigration, Walzer thinks, "It is likely that neighborhoods will become little states. Their members will organize to defend the local politics and culture against strangers."[11]

Sharing a culture involves sharing history, because history, writes historian Arthur Schlesinger Jr., "is to the nation rather as memory is to the individual. As an individual deprived of memory becomes disoriented and lost, not knowing where he has been or where he is going, so a nation denied a conception of its past will be disabled in dealing with its present and its future."[12] History illustrates and reminds us of our common values. Celebrating the civil rights movement reinforces the value of non-discrimination. Remembrance of World War II reminds us to oppose tyrants with force, but the history of Japanese-American internment during the war shows that our own freedom from racism is never guaranteed. Schlesinger summarizes:

> Above all, history can give a sense of national identity. We don't have to believe that our values are absolutely better than the next fellow's or the next country's, but we have no doubt that they are better *for us,* reared as we are—and are worth living by and worth dying for. For our values are not matters of whim and happenstance. History has given them to us.[13]

Political entities are units of sharing. They pool tax money and disburse it according to the dictates of a central legislature. Emotional identification with people makes sharing more attractive. That's why it's usually easier to convince people to share with family members than with strangers, and to share with fellow countrymen than with foreigners. Professor of social policy Christopher Jencks worries that too much immigration will impair the willingness of taxpayers to fund programs for the poor: "Political support for both public education and the welfare state requires some sense of solidarity between haves and have-nots. Support for public education has already collapsed in California, at least in part because so many white California voters see the children in the schools as 'them' and not 'us.'"[14]

In short, from a communitarian perspective, the state has a right to limit immigration to preserve cultural integrity and a community of sharing bound together by a common history that supports common values. The ability of the country to assimilate immigrants should therefore constrain the amount of immigration allowed.

Jencks worries that Latin Americans won't assimilate as well as previous immigrants. Writing about my father's generation, Jencks notes:

> One reason second-generation Southern and Eastern Europeans almost all became fluent in English was that while they were very numerous, they had no common language. No linguistic minority dominated any large American city the way Spanish speakers now dominate Miami. Furthermore, while the new immigrants often lived in ethnic neighborhoods, they still needed some English at work, and they could see that their children would need even more English if they were to get ahead economically. As a result, they almost all sent their children to schools conducted entirely in English.[15]

The contrast between my grandparents and Miguel Carvajal seems to illustrate Jencks's point. My grandparents learned English as quickly as possible and used it in the home. Mr. Carvajal has learned only as much English as he needs for his work, which isn't much. His cultural world is Spanish only. Jencks thinks this is typical.

One reason Latinos know less English . . . is probably that some employers in cities like New York and Los Angeles hire only Spanish speakers for certain tasks. [Workers] in such settings have little reason to improve their English.

Many Mexicans also see themselves as sojourners who will return home once they have made some money. The typical Mexican male earns about half what a non-Latino white earns, so if he compares himself to other Americans he is likely to feel like a failure. But if he compares himself to the Mexicans with whom he grew up, he is likely to feel quite successful. So he clings to his Mexican identity, sends money back to his parents . . . , and retains his Mexican citizenship. Among Mexican immigrants legally admitted to the United States in 1982, only 22 percent had become American citizens by the end of 1997, compared to about 40 percent of those who came here from the Caribbean and well over half of those from Asia.[16]

In contrast to Jencks, Schlesinger is encouraged by the rate of Latino assimilation into American society.

As for Hispanic-Americans, first-generation Hispanics born in the United States speak English fluently, according to a Rand Corporation study; more than half of second-generation Hispanics give up Spanish altogether. A 1996 survey reported that among five educational goals, 51 percent of Hispanic parents regarded learning English as most important as against 11 percent for Spanish and 4 percent for "learning about Hispanic culture." Asked how soon Hispanic-American children should be taught English, 63 percent said as soon as possible; only 17 percent felt their children should be taught Spanish first.[17]

Sociologist Richard Alba also thinks that Jencks worries too much about Latinos failing to assimilate into American society. He points out in a reply to Jencks: "Only in the last few decades has the assimilation of the descendants of pre–World War I immigrants been adequately recognized—the blinkered view that Italians, for example, were stuck in the working class (to say nothing of crime) persisted well after substantial upward mobility had begun. Perhaps the view of the contemporary scene is equally clouded."[18]

In sum, different views among communitarians about how many immigrants to allow into the country turn on beliefs about how well those immigrants will assimilate to mainstream American culture; how quickly and thoroughly they will adopt the English language and see the history and values of the United States as their history and values. Communitarian concerns diminish as confidence in assimilation increases.

Multicultural Reasons for Immigration

Multiculturalists champion the diversity of cultures, because they think no one culture holds all the keys to human flourishing. By learning from one another, cultural groups can evolve toward better solutions to life's persistent difficulties. Immigrants provide cultural pluralism that can be helpful, but only if they don't assimilate so thoroughly as to become indistinguishable from previous residents. So, while communitarians worry that immigrants might not assimilate enough, multiculturalists worry that they might assimilate too much.

Philosopher Michael Walzer is a multiculturalist as well as a communitarian. Though believing a nation must protect its borders to ensure the social compatibility of immigrants with citizens, he thinks that immigrants should retain some distinctiveness. He reasons that society flourishes when it has strong individuals. But individual strength requires experience in voluntary groups and associations—Little League, the PTA, church groups, unions, political parties, and ethnic associations. He writes, "It is only in the context of associational activity that individuals learn to deliberate, argue, make decisions, and take responsibility."[19]

Ethnic groups are particularly important, because they give people a needed sense of rooted identity that combats social isolation in a lonely crowd of ineffectual people. If democracy needs strong individuals to question the status quo, engage in productive debate about the common good, and bargain effectively for interests they represent, it needs ethnic groups that nurture such individuals. He calls upon schools to teach about different cultures and thinks they should strive "to produce hyphenated citizens, men and women who will defend toleration within their different communities while still valuing and reproducing (and rethinking and revising) the differences."[20] He concludes: "Multiculturalism as an ideology is a program for greater social and economic equality. No regime of toleration will work for long in an immigrant, pluralist, modern, and postmodern society without some combination of these two: a defense of group differences and an attack upon class differences."[21]

Schlesinger agrees with Walzer that communitarian concerns about the compatibility of newcomers with established residents should be tempered with appreciation for group differences. He writes:

The interplay of diverse traditions produces the America we know. "Paradoxical though it may seem," Diane Ravitch has well said, "the United States has a common culture that is multicultural." That is why unifying political ideals coexist so easily and cheerfully with diversity in social and cultural values. Within the overarching political commitment [to American democracy], people are free to live as they choose, ethnically and otherwise.[22]

This is why, for example, although the United States is certainly not a Muslim nation, most people think it would be un-American to deny Muslim girls the right to wear headscarves in school. A concern about such scarves arose in France because communitarian concerns about assimilation are not tempered there, as they are here, with a tradition of multicultural appreciation of ethnic and religious differences.

In sum, multiculturalists favor immigration because it furthers the American tradition of multiculturalism.

Free-Market Conservative Reasons for Immigration

Free-market conservatives favor economic growth, which some economists think requires an increasing pool of labor with appropriate skills. According to Frank Sharry, executive director of the National Immigration Forum, the United States'

labor market demands an estimated 500,000 full-time low-skilled service jobs a year. . . . More than half the new jobs created in the American economy require hard work, not multiple diplomas. . . . Young native-born workers are smaller in number, better educated than ever, and more interested in office work than manual labor. Consequently, much of the nation's demand for housekeepers, childcare workers, landscapers, protein processors, busboys, cooks, janitors, dry wallers, and construction workers is met by a steady flow of some 500,000 undocumented migrants who enter and settle in America each year.[23]

The immigrants are undocumented—illegal—because our quotas for legal immigrants are too low. Sharry quotes Dan Griswold of the libertarian Cato Institute:

Demand for low-skilled labor continues to grow in the United States while the domestic supply of suitable workers inexorably declines—yet U.S. immigration law contains virtually no legal channel through which low-skilled immigrant workers can enter the country to fill that gap. The result is an illegal flow. . . . American immigration laws are colliding with reality, and reality is winning.[24]

On this view, the only way to stem the flow of illegal immigration is to either allow more legal immigration of poorly educated workers or encourage more red-blooded Americans to drop out of school (about as attractive as more people becoming disabled to fill unused parking spaces) so that they'll be happy cleaning toilets. Thus, many free-market conservatives favor increased immigration to promote economic growth. President Bush agrees, which is why the immigration reform he supported in 2006 included increased legal avenues for foreigners to work in the United States.[25]

Not everyone accepts this economic reasoning. Mark Krikorian, executive director of the Center for Immigration Studies, believes that current levels of illegal immigration have nothing to do with economic need. He writes:

If we examine the four years before and after 2000, we see that the first period, 1996–2000, was a time of dramatic job growth and rapid expansion, while 2000–2004 saw slower economic growth and weaker labor demand. Immigrant unemployment grew significantly during that period. . . . And yet immigration actually increased slightly, from 5.5 million arrivals [both legal and illegal] during the first period and 6.1 million new immigrants during the second.[26]

Krikorian believes that a major factor boosting current immigration is past immigration. "Migration takes place by way of networks of relatives, friends, acquaintances, and fellow countrymen, and few people immigrate to a place where these connections are absent." This explains why immigration to the United States is much greater from the Philippines than from Indonesia, countries with similar cultures and economic needs. "The ties between the United States and the Philippines are numerous and deep, our having ruled the country for 50 years and maintained an extensive military presence there. . . . On the other hand, the United States has very few ties to Indonesia, whose people tend to migrate to the Netherlands, its former colonial ruler."[27]

Immigration is so great from Mexico today, Krikorian thinks, because the bracero program created the kinds of links that facilitate later immigration. Our country doesn't need their labor. Rather, they are poor people seeking a better life where pre-existing social connections give them a reasonable chance of success. Roger Lowenstein, writing in the *New York Times Magazine*, agrees that as a result of legal changes in the 1960s and the collapse of the Mexican economy in the 1970s, "so many Mexicans settled here that it became easier for more Mexicans to follow."[28]

So, Krikorian claims, increasing legal immigration isn't economically necessary. What is more, it doesn't reduce illegal immigration by substituting legals for illegals. "If increased admission of foreign workers served to limit illegal immigration, how can it be that all three—legal immigration, 'temporary' work visas, and illegal immigration—have all mushroomed together? In 1974, legal immigration was less than 400,000; in 2004, it was nearly 1 million."[29] Yet the flow of illegals was greater in 2004 than in 1974.

Another reason to doubt that immigrants, both legal and illegal, meet America's need for labor is that immigrants often create the jobs that they fill. Lowenstein notes that when Canadian economist David Card "moved [to Berkeley] in the mid-90s . . . , he noticed that everyone in Berkeley seemed to have a gardener, 'even though professors are not rich.' In the U.S., which has more unskilled labor than Europe, more people employ housecleaners. The African-American women who held those jobs before the war, like the Salvadorans . . . of today, weren't taking jobs; they were creating them."[30]

Another example concerns the wine industry in California, Lowenstein writes: "I talked to half a dozen vintners. . . . If Mexicans weren't available, some of the grapes would be harvested by machine. This is what economists mean by 'capital adjusting.' If the human skills are there, capital will find a way to employ them."[31]

The presence of immigrants also creates jobs because immigrants have their own needs for housing, food, and services that require labor.

Contractarian Concerns about Immigration

Contractarians worry that immigrant workers depress the wages of America's working poor. Many business people welcome low labor costs, because—other things being equal—cheaper labor means higher profits. Low labor costs help many others as well. By holding down the cost of goods and services, cheap labor improves consumers' standard of living and combats inflation. But contractarians focus on the plight of the poor, because they believe society should rest on a social contract that everyone finds reasonable, including the poor. Contractarians don't think that the working poor would find it reasonable that employers avoid paying them a living wage by turning to immigrants willing to work for less. Eduardo Porter gives this example in the *New York Times*:

Starting about 30 years ago, as illegal immigration began to swell, building maintenance contractors in big immigrant hubs like Los Angeles started hiring the new immigrant workers . . . to drive down labor costs. Unions for janitors fell apart as landlords shifted to cheaper nonunion contractors to clean their buildings. Wages fell and many American-born workers left the industry.

Between 1970 and 2000, the share of Hispanic immigrants among janitors in Los Angeles jumped from 10 percent to more than 60 percent. . . .

The pattern repeated itself as immigrants spread throughout the rest of the country. By 2000, Hispanic immigrants made up nearly 1 in 5 janitors in the United States. . . . Janitors' median earnings fell by 3 percent in real terms between 1983 and 2002. . . . Meanwhile, earnings across all occupations rose by 8 percent, after accounting for inflation. . . .

In New York City, janitors cleaning commercial buildings make $19 an hour. . . . The union never lost ground in the city, and it is still unusual to find illegal immigrants cleaning office buildings there.

In Southern California, by contrast, unions were decimated in the 1980s, and [now] unionized janitors earn between $8.50 and $11 an hour.[32]

New York Times columnist Nicholas Kristof also finds that immigrant labor hurts America's working poor.

The most careful study of this issue, done by George Borjas and Lawrence Katz and published by the National Bureau of Economic Research, found that the surge of immigration in the 1980s and 1990s lowered the wages of America's own high school dropouts by 8.2 percent.

Another study, by Steven Camarota of the Center for Immigration Studies, reached similar conclusions. Between 2000 and 2005, he found, immigrant workers with a high school degree or less rose by 1.5 million, while employment of native workers at that education level fell by 3.2 million.[33]

Camarota's figures suggest that the United States had enough workers to take the jobs filled by immigrants, but that employers preferred immigrants to native-born workers. *New York Times* reporter John Broder picks up on this point:

It is asserted both as fact and as argument: the United States needs a constant flow of immigrants to perform jobs Americans will not stoop to do.

But what if those jobs paid $50 an hour, with benefits, instead of $7 or $10 or $15?

"Of course there are jobs that few Americans will take because the wages and working conditions have been so degraded by employers," said Jared Bernstein, of the liberal Economic Policy Institute. "But there is nothing about landscaping, food processing, meat cutting or construction that would preclude someone from doing these jobs on the basis of their nativity. Nothing would keep anyone . . . from doing them if they paid better, if they had health care."[34]

Steven Camarota agrees: "The idea that there are jobs that Americans won't do is economic gibberish. All the big occupations that immigrants are in—construction, janitorial, even agriculture—are overwhelmingly done by native Americans."[35]

Economist James Galbraith examined the immigration issue in response to Christopher Jencks's articles in the *New York Review of Books*. He accepts the correlation between increased immigration and lower wages, but doesn't think the arrival of immigrants drives wages down. First, he thinks, employers drive wages down through

outsourcing, or an anti-union campaign, say, or perhaps a legislative maneuver that blocks a rise in the minimum wage and so causes its real value to fall. Now for native workers the worst jobs no longer provide adequate pay. Immigrants may *then* be recruited, directly or through the grapevine, to fill them. They will flood the regions (Los Angeles, Texas) where sweatshops flourish, while remaining scarce in union towns like Detroit. And they will come from low-wage countries, like Mexico.[36]

In sum, employers drive wages down to a point where native-born Americans won't take them and then claim immigrants are needed to take jobs Americans won't do.

The way to discourage immigration, on this understanding of the situation, is for the minimum wage to be high and unions to be strong. When wages are high, American-born workers take the jobs that need to be done. Immigration isn't encouraged, because given union contracts and a high minimum wage, immigrants don't have the opportunity to work for less than native-born Americans. Galbraith writes: "It is no coincidence that in 1970 there was no immigrant-native wage differential and yet no migrant wave. The real value of the federal minimum hourly wage, back then, exceeded seven dollars in today's [2002] values, and a much higher fraction of the workforce belonged to unions."

Galbraith offers the example of Harvard University, which lowered average custodial pay after 1994 from $11 an hour to $9.55. "This is not because immigrants have forced down 'market' wages in Cambridge; just two subway stops away, MIT pays a starting custodial wage of $14.39 per hour."[37] Only as Harvard lowered its pay, Galbraith claims, did it start hiring more immigrant custodians.

Evidence for Galbraith's view comes from lax enforcement of the 1986 ban on hiring illegal immigrants. The law made it illegal *knowingly* to hire illegal immigrants. Eduardo Porter writes: "Employers are not expected to distinguish between a fake ID and the real thing." Porter adds:

Companies have little to fear. The penalty for knowingly hiring illegal immigrants includes up to six months in jail—or up to five years in particularly egregious cases—and fines that range from $275 to $11,000 for each worker. Yet fines are typically negotiated down, and employers are almost always let off the hook. Only 46 people were convicted in 2004 for hiring illegal immigrants; the annual number has been roughly the same for the last decade.[38]

Mark Krikorian writes:

Enforcement of the ban on hiring illegal aliens . . . has been all but abandoned. We might date the abandonment from INS [Immigration and Naturalization Service] raids in Georgia during the Vidalia onion harvest in 1998, which caused large numbers of illegal aliens . . . to abandon the fields to avoid arrest. By the end of the week, both of the state's senators and three congressmen had sent an outraged letter to Washington complaining that the INS "does not understand the needs of America's farmers," and that was the end of that.

So . . . , rather than conduct raids on individual employers, Operation Vanguard in 1998–99 sought to identify illegal workers at all meat-packing plants in Nebraska through audits of personnel records. The INS then asked to interview those employees who appeared to be unauthorized—and the illegals ran off. The procedure was remarkably successful, and was meant to be repeated every two or three months until the plants were weaned from their dependence on illegal labor.

Local law enforcement officials were very pleased . . . , but employers and politicians vociferously criticized the very idea of enforcing the immigration law. Gov. Mike Johanns organized a task force to oppose the operation; in Washington, Sen. Chuck Hagel (R-Neb.) pressured the Justice Department to stop. They succeeded, the operation was ended, and the senior INS official who had thought it up in the first place was forced into early retirement.[39]

Another example of opposition to law enforcement concerns Social Security Administration actions that inadvertently identified undocumented workers. Most illegal immigrants present employers with Social Security numbers so employers can claim they aren't knowingly hiring illegals. Consequently, most illegal workers pay federal taxes and contribute to the social security system. But mismatches occur between the names of these employees and the names associated with their Social Security numbers on file at the SSA. Mismatches occur for many other reasons as well, such as marriage, divorce, misspellings, and typographical mistakes. Not intending to target illegals, the SSA

in 2002 sent out almost a million "no-match" letters to employers. . . . Most of the problem was caused by illegal aliens lying to their employers, and thousands of illegals quit or were fired when they were found out. The effort was so successful at denying work to illegals that business and immigrant-rights groups organized to stop it and won a 90 percent reduction in the number of letters to be sent out.[40]

It seems that powerful groups, including business interests, favor immigration, even if it's illegal, to hold down the cost of labor. Christopher Jencks writes:

Creating a system for identifying people with a legal right to be in the United States is not technically difficult. Banks disburse billions of dollars in cash every day to customers who identify themselves with a piece of plastic and a code number. The federal government could create a similar system for identifying legal residents. The obstacle is not technical but political: employers, Latino activists, and some advocates of civil liberties all prefer a country in which employers can hire anyone they like, legal or illegal.[41]

Some employers may even prefer illegal to legal immigrants. Abby Goodnough and Jennifer Steinhauer reported in the *New York Times* that some employers were wary of provisions in an unsuccessful 2006 Senate immigration bill that would have allowed many illegal immigrants eventually to become U.S. citizens. Citizenship, they worried, "might have encouraged them to quit or be less productive. 'The illegals are probably better workers than the legal ones,' said Mike Gonya, who farms 2,800 acres of wheat and vegetables near Fremont, Ohio. 'The legal ones know the system. They know legal recourse. The illegal ones will bust their butts.'"[42]

Environmental and Other Burdens of Immigration

While contractarians worry that immigration drives down the cost of labor and jeopardizes the American way of life for many people, some environmentalists worry about environmental degradation caused by population increase. Jencks wrote in 2001: "If immigration keeps growing by about three percent a year, as it has since 1965 . . . , America's total population in 2050 will be over half a billion."[43] In 2006, the American population surpassed 300 million, on pace to exceed half a billion by mid century.

American population increase is environmentally more destructive than population increases elsewhere because the American way of life is the most wasteful. On average, per capita American use of fossil fuels is twice that of prosperous Western Europe and Japan. Using fossil fuels adds carbon dioxide to the atmosphere, causing environmentally harmful climate change. Population increase exhausts needed resources as well. Already, writes philosopher Robert Chapman,

the pressures on farmers to produce more have led, in many instances, to unsustainable practices. Soil from U.S. croplands erodes at an annual rate of approximately 3 billion tons. . . . Increased use of chemical fertilizers is poisoning our groundwater and wiping out coastal fisheries. Increased water use for irrigation is [causing] the depletion of groundwater aquifers. . . . The Ogallala aquifer that supplies water to many of our western states, including California, will, if current consumption rates continue, be depleted in 25 years . . . ; likewise, the High Plains aquifer will probably be exhausted within the next 50 years.[44]

Politician and commentator Pat Buchanan added in 2002: "With endless immigration, America is going to need an endless expansion of its power sources—hydroelectric power, fossil fuels (oil, coal, gas), and nuclear power. The only alternative is blackouts, brownouts, and endless lines at the pump."[45]

Until 1996, the Sierra Club, the nation's largest environmental organization, took the position that immigration should be limited to achieve zero population growth.[46] They changed their policy in 1996, it seems, out of concern for the welfare of people in desperate circumstances seeking entry into the United States and possibly to dissociate themselves from some critics of immigration, including Pat Buchanan, whose views many people considered racist. Today, in spite of the environmental damage caused by immigration, many environmentalists favor immigration, perhaps because, besides being environmentalists, they are also cosmopolitans for whom national borders have little meaning, or contractarians concerned about the welfare of poor foreigners.

Immigrants are blamed not only for harming the environment by causing population increase, but for harming ordinary taxpayers by straining the public infrastructure and social safety net. Pat Buchanan's complaints in 2002 are typical:

• A third of the legal immigrants who come to the United States have not finished high school. . . .

• Over 36 percent of all immigrants, and 57 percent of those from Central America, do not earn twenty thousand dollars a year. . . .

• Of immigrant households in the United States, 29 percent are below the poverty line, twice the 14 percent of native born.

• Immigrant use of food stamps, Supplemental Social Security, and school lunch programs runs from 50 percent to 100 percent higher than use by native born.[47]

Immigrants are overrepresented in federal prisons and constitute an increasing percentage of people arrested in Los Angeles and Miami, Buchanan contends. But, he hastens to add, "None of the above statistics . . . holds for emigrants from Europe."[48]

Roger Lowenstein claims, to the contrary, that immigrants, including illegal immigrants, are not a major burden on others in society.

With the exception of a few border states . . . , the effect of immigration on public-sector budgets is small. . . . Since many illegals pay into Social Security (using false ID numbers), they are actually subsidizing the U.S. Treasury. And fewer than 3 percent of immigrants of any stripe receive food stamps. Also, and contrary to popular wisdom, undocumented people *do* support local school districts, since, indirectly as renters or directly as homeowners, they pay property taxes. Since they tend to be poor, however, they contribute less than the average. One estimate is that immigrants raise state and local taxes for everyone else in the U.S. by a trivial amount in most states, but by as much as $1,100 per household per year in California. They are certainly a burden on hospitals and jails but, it should be noted, poor legal workers, including those who are native born, are also a burden on the health care system.[49]

Guest Workers and Amnesty

One proposal to deal with immigration is to meet the (alleged) need for workers without permanently increasing the U.S. population by inviting an appropriate number of guests to work in the United States. Guest workers would be expected to leave after a few years, possibly to be replaced by a different set of guest workers. Immigration critic Peter Brimelow writes: "It may be time for the United States to consider moving to a conception of itself more like that of Switzerland: tolerating a fairly large foreign presence that comes and goes, but rarely if ever naturalizes."[50] The Senate bill sponsored by Senators John McCain and Ted Kennedy in 2006 provided for 400,000 guest workers per year.[51]

Free-market conservatives who think our economy needs more uneducated workers find this approach attractive, because guests would not bring children to be educated in our schools or parents to be treated in our hospitals. We'd have sufficient labor with no responsibilities for phases of the life cycle when people need most help from society. This keeps taxes low and health costs down.

One objection to the guest-worker proposal comes from immigration critic Mark Krikorian who thinks, as we've seen, that the more foreigners we have in the country, the more will be attracted through informational networks, social ties, and family connections. Whereas Brimelow mentions the bracero guest-worker program that secured workers from Mexico during and after World War II as an alternative to permanent immigration, Krikorian sees it as a catalyst of permanent immigration.

A more fundamental objection to guest-worker programs comes from communitarians. Michael Walzer finds community cohesion and the democratic processes that enable diverse people to live together in harmony are jeopardized by guest-worker programs, because the guests are denied the full range of civil liberties and civic participation essential in a democracy. Walzer writes of such guests in Europe: "Neither citizens nor potential citizens, they have no political rights. The civil liberties of speech, assembly, association—otherwise strongly defended—are commonly denied to them, sometimes explicitly by state officials, sometimes implicitly by the threat of dismissal and deportation."[52] Such conditions degrade the kind of democracy needed in a multicultural society.

No democratic state can tolerate the establishment of a fixed status between citizen and foreigner. . . . Men and women are either subject to the state's authority, or they are not; and if they are subject, they must be given a say, and ultimately an equal say, in what that authority does. Democratic citizens, then, have a choice: if they want to bring in new workers, they must be prepared to enlarge their own membership; if they are unwilling to accept new members, they must find ways within the limits of the domestic labor market to get socially necessary work done.[53]

Political columnist Fareed Zakaria adds national security concerns to the debate. Europe has many guest workers, and that's why they have so many alienated individuals, some of whom are willing terrorists. Zakaria notes that "post 9/11 America . . . has not had a subsequent terror attack—even a small backpack bomb in a movie theater—while there have been dozens in Europe. . . . American immigrant communities, even

Arab and Muslim ones, are not very radicalized," because their members look forward to becoming full-fledged Americans. This tells us how to handle foreign workers in this country: "These people must have some hope, some reasonable path to becoming Americans. Otherwise we are sending a signal that there are groups of people who are somehow unfit to be Americans, that these newcomers are not really welcomed and that what we want are workers, not potential citizens. And we will end up with immigrants who have similarly cold feelings about America."[54] Zakaria's concerns about guest-worker programs, like Walzers', are communitarian.

Another issue is what to do about the twelve million people already in the United States illegally. It isn't practical to round them all up and deport them, but strict enforcement of rules against hiring them would encourage their voluntary departure. On the other hand, free-market conservatives who think that the economy needs these workers favor an amnesty that allows illegals to become legal, as in this editorial from the *Wall Street Journal*: "What are restrictionists proposing? Mass arrests, raids on job-creating businesses, or deportations? . . . . Those who wave the 'no amnesty' flag are actually encouraging a larger underground illegal population. The only reform that has a chance to succeed is one that recognizes the reality that 10 or so million illegal aliens already work in the U.S. and are vital to the economy."[55]

Contractarians might also favor amnesty, because legal workers can bargain more effectively for higher pay and therefore don't drag down everyone's wages quite so much. Frank Sharry writes: "When 3 million undocumented immigrants became legal immigrants some 20 years ago, their wages increased by 14% over 5 years—they were no longer afraid to speak up or to change jobs—and their productivity increased dramatically—they studied English and improved their skills through training."[56]

Writing in the *New York Times*, Peter Salins gives communitarian reasons for amnesty: "Clearly, the 11 million to 12 million undocumented immigrants now here can never assimilate, whether they want to or not. Their illegal status will keep them from being accepted by their American neighbors, regardless of their virtue or utility. Thus legalizing their status is essential."[57]

Safety is another communitarian reason for supporting amnesty. I watch enough prime-time television to know that people here illegally are often unwilling to cooperate with police investigations, which jeopardizes everyone but criminals.

However, amnesty rewards illegal behavior and is no guarantee, absent new policies which discourage people from coming to the United States illegally, of fewer illegal immigrants in our midst. Amnesty may be followed by a new increase of illegal residents, as it was after the amnesty in 1986, unless employers are prosecuted for employing illegal workers. With the exception of some communitarians and contractarians, people generally opposed to immigration are likely to oppose amnesty if they think it will lead to additional illegal immigration. Those generally favorable to immigration, by contrast, such as libertarians, free-market conservatives, and multiculturalists, are likely to favor amnesty.

Conclusion

Some free-market conservatives favor continuing immigration to meet our country's (supposed) need for labor. But, as explained in chapter 12, free-market conservatives shouldn't be confused with business people, even though business people often think they are free-market conservatives. Regarding immigration, business people tend to favor immigration to keep wages down. Many free-market conservatives, by contrast, favor wage increases that promote technological improvements in production, because such improvements are needed for maximum productivity. These free-market conservatives might oppose immigration if it depresses wages.[58]

Contractarians would also oppose immigration if it keeps wages low. They favor immigration only if it's conjoined with policies that improve wages for the working poor.

Communitarians who believe that new immigrants won't assimilate oppose immigration, whereas those more confident about assimilation welcome immigration. In any case, communitarians oppose guest-worker programs and want legal status for all immigrants because guest status and illegal status impede assimilation.

Many environmentalists oppose immigration unless it's conjoined with basic changes in the American lifestyle that make it more eco-friendly.

Multiculturalists, by contrast, generally welcome immigration, because they find it culturally enriching. Cosmopolitans think immigration should be legal, because it's a basic human right.

Finally, those opposed to increased immigration have reason to care about economic development in the Third World, because most immigrants, both legal and illegal, come to the United States for economic opportunity. Globalization is supposed to promote economic opportunity in the Third World. That's our next topic.

14

Globalization: Libertarianism, Free-Market Conservatism, Cosmopolitanism, Contractarianism, Social Conservatism, and Environmentalism

Conflicting Faces of Globalization

New York Times political columnist Thomas Friedman, who doubles as globalization's cheerleader-in-chief, writes enthusiastically in *The World Is Flat* about developments in India. He visited the secluded campus of Infosys Technologies Limited, a world leader in information technology, about forty miles from downtown Bangalore.

The Infosys campus is reached by a pockmarked road, with sacred cows, horse-drawn carts, and motorized rickshaws all jostling alongside our vans. Once you enter the gates of Infosys, though, you are in a different world. A massive resort-size swimming pool nestles amid boulders and manicured lawns, adjacent to a huge putting green . . . and a fabulous health club.[1]

Nandan Nilekani, the company's CEO, explained how the world became flat. "What happened . . . was a massive investment in technology . . . , in putting broadband connectivity around the world, undersea cables, all those things." Combine this with cheaper home computers, the Internet, and search engines like Google, and you have "a platform where intellectual work, intellectual capital, could be delivered from anywhere. It could be disaggregated, delivered, distributed, produced, and put back together again—and this gave a whole new degree of freedom to the way we do work."[2]

People can collaborate on projects worldwide and serve customers through call-in centers. I know when I have a problem with my computer, a question about Internet service, or a concern about an airline booking, the helpful person on the other end of an 800 number most often has a gentle Indian accent. Friedman writes: "Clearly, it is now possible for more people than ever to collaborate and compete in real time with more other people on more different kinds of work from more different corners of the planet and on a more equal footing than at any previous time in the history of the world. [This] could usher in an amazing era of prosperity and innovation."³

Swedish economist Johan Norberg celebrates improvements that India and China have made through global commerce. He is struck by two photographs.

In the old one, taken in 1976, a 12-year-old Indian girl named Satto holds up her hands. They are already furrowed and worn, prematurely aged by many years' hard work. The recent picture shows Satto's 13-year-old daughter Seema, also holding up her hands. They are young and soft, the hands of a child whose childhood has not been taken away from her.

The biggest change of all is in people's thoughts and dreams. Television and newspapers bring ideas and images from the other side of the globe, widening people's notions of what is possible. . . . Why must a woman be forced to have children early and sacrifice her career? Why must marriages be arranged—and the untouchables excluded from them—when family relations in other countries are so much freer?⁴

Both Friedman and Norberg see globalization as promoting individual empowerment. People can increasingly choose their path and make their mark regardless of race, gender, national origin, or social status.

Anita Roddick exposes a different face of globalization in her 2004 report in *The Ecologist* on garment workers in Bangladesh. She writes:

The workers live in one-room, dirt-floored huts, which measure about eight feet by twelve feet and are made of scrap metal, wood and plastic. Four or more people live in each hut. Everyone sleeps on a hard, wooden platform raised about a foot off the ground. When it rains, these huts drip with water. During the monsoon the workers' neighborhoods flood, and filth and sewage washes right into their homes.

In these neighborhoods, up to 60 people . . . share one outdoor water pump: the water is filthy. There are also two or three shared gas burners for cooking and only one outside toilet—really just a hole in the ground. Early in the morning and late at night there are long lines as people wait their turn to use these facilities.

One worker said: "We feel like prisoners. There is no value in our lives. . . . Our hands are bound and our mouths are stopped." Every worker said that if their employer knew they were meeting with me, they would be fired.⁵

In one sweater factory, one young employee asked the manager if he and his colleagues could have some replacement food, as what they had been given was rotten. The manager responded by beating the young man, locking him in a room, and calling the police.

One girl told me she had to sew a pocket every 36 seconds; 100 each hour.

Women sewing clothing for some of the best-known labels in Europe and the U.S. repeatedly told us that they needed permission—a "gate pass"—in order to use the factory toilet, and could only do so twice a day.[6]

The personal empowerment promised by global trade had not yet penetrated this factory, it seems. Yet it's part of globalization, Roddick tells us: "Two thousand new garment factories opened in Bangladesh between 1994 and 2003. In that period apparel exports from the country grew by more than 300 percent—exploding from $1.5 billion in 1994 to $4.9 billion in 2003."[7] Increasing trade doesn't, in Roddick's view, lead to greater social justice or improved lives for workers.

The truth is that as unfettered corporate power grows, workers suffer. Consider Wal-Mart, the largest company and worst sweatshop abuser. . . . Three years ago, it paid its contractors in Bangladesh $38 per dozen sports shirts they produced, or $3.17 a shirt. That represents the total cost of production, including all materials, labour, overheads and profit to the contractor. Today, for the exact same shirts, Wal-Mart pays just $26 per dozen, or $2.17 each . . . , more than 30 per cent less.

Companies like Wal-Mart . . . all across the developing world [are] telling their contractors either to accept constantly lower prices or to lose their contracts. Behind Wal-Mart's everyday low prices are workers trapped in slave labour conditions, paid starvation wages and living in utter misery.[8]

Yet my compassionate daughter whose inadequate income was described in chapter 11 shops regularly at Wal-Mart. She tells me she loves Wal-Mart because its low prices enable her to buy items she otherwise couldn't afford.

Jobless Americans are another face of globalization. Clothing, electronics, automobiles, and other items are increasingly manufactured overseas as part of global trade, resulting in the loss of manufacturing jobs in the United States. Dean Olsen reports in my local newspaper that a Central Illinois man, John Bergschneider,

tried to be optimistic at first after losing his job in a downsizing at EMI Group's Jacksonville plant in 2004.

"When it happened, I thought, 'Heck, I shouldn't have any trouble getting a job,'" said Bergschneider, 59, who had worked at the plant for 33 years. He earned about $35,000 a year.

But he tried unsuccessfully to find another factory job. . . .

Ronald McNeil, dean of the College of Business and Management at the University of Illinois at Springfield, [said:]

"When you start losing manufacturing and switch to a service industry, you're going to lose. You're losing jobs that really base-load the economy. Where do these people go to work? Starbucks? Menards? The mall? Those jobs don't pay much."[9]

Globalization Theory

Libertarians and free-market conservatives endorse the theory that globalization helps everyone by improving efficiency. Economist Douglas Irwin writes:

The traditional case for free trade is based on the gains from specialization and exchange. These gains are easily understood at the level of the individual. Most people do not produce for themselves even a fraction of the goods they consume. Rather, we earn an income by specializing in certain activities and then using our earnings to purchase various goods and services—food, clothing, shelter, health care—produced by others. In essence, we "export" the goods and services that we produce with our own labor and "import" the goods and services produced by others that we wish to consume. . . . Specialization allows us access to a greater variety and better quality of goods and services.

Trade between nations is simply the international extension of this division of labor. For example, the United States has specialized in the production of aircraft, industrial machinery, and agricultural commodities (particularly corn, soybeans, and wheat). In exchange for exports of these products, the United States purchases, among other things, imports of crude oil, clothing, and iron and steel mill products. Like individuals, countries benefit immensely from this division of labor and enjoy a higher real income than countries that forgo such trade. Just as there seems no obvious reason to limit free exchange of goods within a country without a specific justification, there is no obvious reason why trade between countries should be limited in the absence of a compelling reason for doing so.[10]

Even if one country does everything better than another country, they are still both enriched by trade. This is the theory of comparative advantage developed by London stockbroker David Ricardo at the beginning of the nineteenth century. Norberg illustrates the theory with a simplified scenario:

Imagine . . . two people . . . stranded on a desert island, where each needs to eat a fish and a loaf of bread every day in order to survive. To achieve this, Julia has to spend two hours baking and one hour fishing. John needs two and one-half hours to bake and five hours to fish. . . . Julia is best at both jobs. But she still gains by swapping with John, because then she can devote her time to what she is absolutely best at—fishing. She can then catch three fish in that same three hours, while John in the course of his same seven and one-half hours can bake three loaves. They then exchange the surplus, getting one and a half each. Thus, without working an iota harder or a minute longer, John and Julia have increased their daily output from two fish and two loaves to three fish and three loaves.[11]

Free trade promotes additional efficiency as well. Philosopher John Stuart Mill observed in the middle of the nineteenth century "the tendency of every extension of the market to improve the processes of production. A country which produces for a larger market than its own can introduce a more extended division of labour, can make greater use of machinery, and is more likely to make inventions and improvements in the processes of production." "In other words," Irwin comments, "trade promotes productivity growth. The higher is an economy's productivity level, the higher is that country's standard of living."[12] Trade improves efficiency also by introducing new, more efficient capital goods into the economy and by subjecting domestic producers to foreign competition.

With these thoughts in mind, most nations have joined the World Trade Organization (WTO), which is dedicated to lowering barriers to international trade. Under the aegis of the WTO, countries agree to mutual reductions of tariffs and other impediments to trade. The WTO hears disputes and can require a country found in violation of trade rules to change its trade-restraining policy or face trade barriers to its own exports equivalent in value to the imposition it has placed on others.

The Effects of Globalization on Poor Countries

Douglas Irwin believes that the net effect of globalization on poor countries is overwhelmingly positive. "Over the past decade," he writes,

study after study has documented this phenomenon. After the Côte d'Ivoire reformed its trade policies in 1985, overall productivity growth tripled, growing four times more rapidly in industries that became less sheltered from foreign competition. . . . Detailed studies of India's trade liberalization in 1991 and Korea's in the 1980s reached essentially the same conclusion: trade not only disciplines domestic firms and forces them to behave more like a competitive industry, but helps increase their productivity.[13]

Different firms in an industry have different levels of productivity. The more productive firms win contracts to supply overseas markets and therefore grow, while less productive firms contract or go out of business. Although some workers lose their jobs, overall productivity increases and the standard of living improves.

Surit Bhalla, head of a New Delhi hedge fund, claims that world trade reduces poverty. He writes: "In 1980, the poverty head count ratio in

India and China was 50 and 60 percent, respectively. By 2000, the poverty ratios in both economies were in the range of 10 to 25 percent. The number of people moved out of [absolute] poverty [earning less than a dollar a day] in these two countries alone was about a billion."[14] Inequality between rich and poor nations has decreased for the first time: "Over the . . . period from 1820 to 1980, developing world inequality increased . . . ; only in the last twenty years has it shown some decline. . . . Inequality started declining when average per capita growth in the poorest countries (such as India and China) started exceeding average growth in the rich countries around 1980."[15]

These improvements are the result of trade: "The share of trade in developing economies expanded: this share (fraction of GDP accounted for by exports and imports) was 20 percent in 1960, 30 percent in 1980 and 53 percent in 2000." At the same time, "with development, fertility rates (number of children ever born per woman) decline, and labor force participation of women increases, and both fuel each other. This is indeed what has happened in China, India, and . . . poor Bangladesh."[16]

This picture of progress seems at odds with sweatshop conditions in Bangladeshi garment factories that Anita Roddick reported in *The Ecologist*. But development economist Jeffrey Sachs claims in *The End of Poverty* that such sweatshops are actually good for economic development and eventual prosperity in Bangladesh. (Sachs is no apologist for exploitation; Bono wrote the forward to his book.) Although less colorful, Sachs's description of sweatshop work largely agrees with Roddick's. He writes:

Arriving at seven or seven-thirty, they may be in their seats for most of the following twelve hours. They often work with almost no break at all or perhaps a very short lunch break, with little chance to go to the lavatory. Leering bosses lean over them, posing a threat of sexual harassment. . . .

These sweatshop jobs are the targets of public protest in developed countries; those protests have helped to improve the safety and quality of the working conditions. The rich-world protesters, however, should support increased numbers of such jobs, albeit under safer working conditions, [because] the sweatshops are the first rung on the ladder out of extreme poverty.[17]

Sachs came across an English-language newspaper with interviews of these workers telling their life stories. Sachs doesn't consider the possibility that these stories are influenced by what the women think their employers would want them to say.

What was most striking and unexpected about the stories was the repeated affirmation that this work was the greatest opportunity that these women could ever have imagined, and that [it] changed their lives for the better.

Nearly all of the women interviewed had grown up in the countryside, extraordinarily poor, illiterate and unschooled, and vulnerable to chronic hunger and hardship in a domineering, patriarchal society. Had they . . . stayed in the villages, they would have been forced into a marriage arranged by their fathers, and by seventeen or eighteen, forced to conceive a child. . . .

The Bangladeshi women told how they were able to save some small surplus from their meager pay, manage their own income, have their own rooms, choose when and whom to date and marry, choose to have children when they felt ready, and use their savings to improve their living conditions and especially to go back to school to enhance their literacy and job-market skills. . . .

Some rich-country protesters have argued that Dhaka's apparel firms should either pay far higher wage rates or be closed, but closing such factories as a result of wages forced above worker productivity would be little more than a ticket for these women back to rural misery. . . . These Bangladeshi women share the experience of many generations of immigrants to New York City's garment district and . . . other places where their migration to toil in garment factories was a step on the path to a future of urban affluence in succeeding generations.[18]

This worked for my family, with my immigrant grandfather working in the silk-manufacturing industry just outside New York City. And it seems to be working for Bangladesh, with fertility rates down and economic growth exceeding 5 percent per year.

Norberg explains why the Bangladeshi women don't feel exploited. "In the poorest developing countries, the average employee of an American-affiliated company makes eight times the average national wage! In middle income countries, American employers pay three times the national average."[19] When comparing similar jobs, foreign firms in poor countries pay considerably more than local employers.

The same marked difference can be seen in working conditions. The International Labor Organization (ILO) has shown that the multinationals, especially in the footwear and garment industries are leading the trend toward better workplace and working conditions. . . . Nike is one of the companies offering employees the best conditions . . . because . . . they are more responsive to popular opinion. Nike, consequently, has demanded a higher standard of its suppliers, and native firms have to follow suit.[20]

Norberg even defends child labor. When Wal-Mart was pressured to eliminate child labor from its textile suppliers in Bangladesh, follow-up studies showed that "many of the children had moved to more dangerous, less well-paid jobs, and in several cases had become prostitutes. A similar boycott of the Nepalese carpet industry, according to UNICEF, resulted in more than 5,000 girls being forced into prostitution."[21] Perhaps we should beware of condemning employment before we know all the realistic alternatives.

Cosmopolitans favor free trade if it really helps the poor. They're skeptical of reliance on national borders in the first place, so they find cross-border trade only natural. Also, if trade moves more people toward prosperity, cosmopolitans support globalization out of equal concern for everyone's welfare regardless of nation.

However, many thinkers believe that globalization harms people in poor countries. Economic historian and political analyst Kevin Phillips thinks the general tendency of globalization is to increase the gap between the world's haves and have-nots.

Economists in the IMF [International Monetary Fund], World Bank, and elsewhere who oppose the notion that globalization and technology are widening the gap between the world's have- and have-not nations invariably acknowledge that India and China, with their huge populations totaling over 2 billion, are central to their case. Without China and India the great bulk of the underdeveloped world that is losing ground would dominate the outcome.[22]

Journalist Tina Rosenberg agrees, writing in the *New York Times Magazine*: "Excluding China, the growth rate of poor countries was 2 percent a year lower in the 1990's than in the 1970's, when closed economies were the norm. . . . Latin American economies in the 1990's grew at an average annual rate of 2.9 percent—about half the rate of the 1960's. By the end of the 1990's, 11 million more Latin Americans lived in poverty than at the beginning of the decade."[23] The benefits of free trade for the world's poor outside India and China remain disputed.

Globalization Takes American Jobs and Drives Down American Wages

Disputes remain also regarding benefits to the United States. In theory, globalization helps everyone, but many people think it harms American workers by making them compete with cheap labor overseas. Consider vehicle manufacturing. Ted Fishman, a contributing editor at *Harper's Magazine*, visited the Wanfeng automotive factory outside Shanghai, which he found to be

a bare-bones machine. Most tellingly—this goes a long way toward accounting for China's current status as an economical juggernaut—there is not a single robot in sight. Instead, there are hundreds of young men, newly arrived from China's expanding technical schools, manning the assembly lines with little more than large electric drills, wrenches and rubber mallets. Engines and body panels that would, in a Western, Korean or Japanese factory, move from station to station on automatic conveyors are hauled by hand and hand truck here. This is why Wanfeng can sell its hand-made luxury versions of the Jeep (to buyers in the Middle East, mostly) for $8,000 to $10,000. The company isn't spending money on multimillion-dollar machines to build cars; it's using highly skilled workers who cost at most a few hundred dollars a month—whose yearly pay . . . is less than the monthly pay of new hires in Detroit. Factory wages in the country's booming east coast cities can be $120 to $160 a month, and half that inland.[24]

China manufactures an astonishing array of items. "China . . . assembles more toys, stitches more shoes and sews more garments than any other nation in the world. But moving up the technology ladder, China has also become the world's largest maker of consumer electronics, like TV's, DVD players and cellphones."[25] Now it's entering the fields of biotech and high-tech computer manufacturing.

Its profitability has attracted investment. "In all," Fishman writes, "foreign companies have been involved in establishing between 200 and 400 of their own research centers in China since 1990." The likely outcome is even greater productivity. "Just as China's abundant unskilled workers feed the world more shoes and more gadgets than it needs—or at least more than it can absorb without forcing prices down—China's abundance of newly skilled industrialists threatens to swamp the world's most highly prized, high-tech markets."

The way American companies compete is typically to lower labor costs by substituting high-tech machinery for labor. Signicast Corporation, which makes metal castings in Hartford, Wisconsin, for example, survives through automation. Fishman writes: "Robots fill its factory, moving everything from thumb-size precision parts to the boxes in the warehouse. Workers are scarce. Walking through the plant is a lesson in how the hardware business has become a software business. The whole plant seems to be run by smart ghosts."[26] This implies that American workers lose either way. American manufacturing survives only by cutting jobs almost as sharply as if the factory had closed and work had moved overseas.

Fishman quotes Sandra Polaski, former State Department special representative for international labor affairs: "If *all* U.S. jobs were moved to

China, there would still be surplus labor in China." Fishman adds: "That fact highlights what is most sobering about China's booming economy: it can force down the value of work in any job that is at all transferable."[27] This covers just about every type of manufacturing.

Globalization accounts for some of the decline in median American incomes during a period of prosperity, Kevin Phillips claims. He writes that one effect of

trade and globalization lay in the weapons they gave to management against employees and unions. A Cornell University study of labor organizing drives determined that in 62 percent of the cases examined, management fought back by threatening to shift production to a lower-wage area. Enough companies had already done so to make the threat itself work in a larger number of instances.[28]

We saw in chapter 13 that immigration, principally from Mexico, also puts pressure on wages in the United States. Some of that pressure comes indirectly from China. Fishman writes, "In Mexico . . . , which has lost nearly half a million manufacturing jobs and 500 *maquiladora* manufacturers, workers earn four times what their Chinese counterparts do. So for Mexican factories to stay competitive, they must get by with fewer hands or smaller profits." When they get by with fewer hands, more Mexicans are attracted to employment possibilities in the United States.

Americans lose high-paying jobs to China and then compete with immigrants for low-paying work. German sociologist Ulrich Beck writes: "For the first time, we are dealing with an upturn in the economy in which 'full employment' is *accompanied* by declining real incomes in the middle levels of society."[29]

The service economy will not come to the rescue, according to Beck, because automation eliminates jobs.

For example, telebanking will lead to the closure of high-street banks; telecommunications will shed . . . jobs through . . . consolidation; and whole occupational categories, such as typists, may simply disappear.

Even if new jobs do emerge, in this computer age they can easily be transferred anywhere in the world . . . , [such as to] southern India.[30]

Kevin Phillips shares this dim assessment of the possibility of high-technology jobs saving the American middle class. In the mid-1990s, for example, Intel, Oracle, Microsoft, Apple, and Sun Microsystems combined offered only 94,800 jobs to Americans, compared to the 709,000 that General Motors used to offer. Phillips adds: "The [t… growth since then has not begun to make up for the U.S. jobs… panies like GM."[31] On this view, contractarians, interested in the… of society's poorer members, would oppose globalization.

Thomas Friedman, by contrast, sees benefits for poor Americans from global trade—low consumer prices. He cites "a study by Morgan Stanley estimating that since the mid-1990s alone, cheap imports from China have saved U.S. consumers roughly $600 billion."[32] Robert Samuelson writes in *Newsweek* of such benefits: "From 1992 to 2002, ownership of microwave ovens by the poorest tenth of Americans went from 39 percent to 77 percent, reports one Census Bureau study. VCRs went from 22 percent to 56 percent, computers from 4 percent to 21 percent."[33] Friedman notes also that imports "have saved U.S. manufacturers untold billions in cheaper parts for their products. This savings, in turn . . . , has helped the Federal Reserve to hold down interest rates longer, giving more Americans a chance to buy homes or refinance the ones they have, and giving business more capital to invest in new innovations."[34]

Friedman claims that when Americans build factories overseas, they often create job opportunities for Americans. For example, "if General Motors builds a factory offshore in Shanghai, it also ends up creating jobs in America by exporting a lot of goods and services to its own factory in China and benefiting from lower parts costs in China for its factories in America."[35] Lower-priced parts can improve the company's market share worldwide, promoting even more employment at home and abroad.

Still, world trade causes disruptive change. A rising tide sinks boats with heavy anchors on short chains, so people must be flexible and the government helpful. With Stanford University economist Paul Romer as his guide, Friedman advocates making

> tertiary education, if not compulsory, then government-subsidized for at least two years, whether it is at a state university, a community college, or a technical school. Tertiary education is more critical the flatter the world gets, because technology will be churning old jobs, and spawning new, more complex ones.
>
> Educating more people at the tertiary level has two effects. One is that it produces more people with the skills to claim higher-value-added work in the new niches. And two, it shrinks the pool of people able to do lower-skilled work, from road maintenance to home repair to Starbucks. By shrinking the pool of lower-skilled workers, we help to stabilize their wages (provided we control

...tion), because there are fewer people available to do those jobs. It is not ...ccident that plumbers can charge $75 an hour in major urban areas.[36]

It seems that Friedman advocates the free flow of money, information, and goods around the world, but not the free flow of people. Limiting immigration plays a key role in protecting the American middle class and poorer workers from the wage-lowering effects of free trade. On these conditions, contractarians might approve of globalization.

Complaints of Hypocrisy that Harms Poor Countries

Tina Rosenberg attributes the failure of most poor countries to benefit from freer trade to the unfair system of trade that has been developed largely by the United States and Europe under the aegis of the WTO.

One problem is subsidies. Rosenberg writes: "European farmers get 35 percent of their income from government subsidies, and American farmers get 20 percent. Farm subsidies in the United States, moreover, are a huge corporate-welfare program, with nearly 70 percent of payments going to the largest 10 percent of producers."[37] As a result, "American corn now makes up almost half of the world's stock, effectively setting the world price so low that local small farmers can no longer survive," a devastating blow to Mexico.[38] Cotton is another example, writes Joseph Stiglitz.

Some 25,000 rich American cotton farmers, reliant on government subsidies for cotton, divide among themselves some $3 billion to $4 billion a year, leading to higher production and lower prices. The damage that these subsidies wreak on some 10 million cotton farmers eking out a subsistence living in sub-Saharan Africa is enormous.[39]

Many African cotton farmers use methods less technologically sophisticated than those used in the United States, but their costs are so low and their land so well-suited to cotton that they can get cotton to market cheaper than Americans, except for American subsidies. Photographer and travel journalist Kate Eshelby reports in *New Africa*:

In 2003, [the West African country] Burkina Faso received $10 million in U.S. aid, but lost $13.7 million in cotton export earnings, as a result of U.S. subsidies. No country ever grew rich on charity, it is trade that holds the key to generating wealth. Fair trade would give the Burkinabe cotton farmers a decent opportunity to make a living by selling their produce, at a decent price, to the richer world; enabling them to work their way out of poverty.[40]

One Burkinabe farmer told Eshelby: "Prices are down so I cannot send my youngest son to school. This makes me sad. I know his only chance of a good future is school."[41]

Subsidies like these have proved a stumbling block in recent rounds of negotiations aimed at lowering tariff barriers. Poor countries promised the elimination of subsidies for agriculture in Europe and the United States have been disappointed by lack of action on this issue. They are therefore reluctant to move forward on other items.

A second concern is intellectual property rights, designed primarily to benefit American pharmaceutical companies. Rosenberg writes:

The most egregious example of a special-interest provision is the W.T.O.'s rules on intellectual property. The ability of poor nations to make or import cheap copies of drugs still under patent in rich countries has been a boon to world public health. But the W.T.O. will require most of its poor members to accept patents on medicine . . . , the very poorest . . . in 2016. . . . Medicine prices will probably double, but poor countries will never offer enough of a market to persuade the pharmaceutical industry to invent cures for their diseases. . . .

The intellectual property rules have won worldwide notoriety for the obstacles they pose to cheap AIDS medicine. . . . The World Bank calculated that the intellectual-property rules will result in a transfer of $40 billion a year from poor countries to corporations in the developed world.[42]

A third problem is belief at the IMF that currently poor countries will develop fastest and best if they open their economies totally to foreign investment and competition. This ignores the fact that today's wealthy countries, such as the United States, Britain, and France, didn't develop their economies through free trade. They protected their infant industries from international competition, thereby creating a national market for their goods. Only when competence at serving the national market was assured did they subject their industries to international competition.

More recently, Japan, China, and India did the same. As matters of national policy, they trained workers and invested in industries that they protected at first from international competition. Indian excellence in engineering, computer science, and software development, for example, results from India's first prime minister, Jawaharlal Nehru, establishing India's seven Indian Institutes of Technology (IIT), beginning in 1951. No one could get in through bribery. Friedman writes: "Given India's 1 billion-plus population . . . , competition [for entrance] produces a phenomenal knowledge meritocracy."[43] But workers alone don't provide jobs. "India . . . closed its market to foreign technology companies, like IBM, [so] Indian companies . . . started their own factories to make PCs and servers."[44] They eventually got good enough to compete internationally. In sum, government provision of infrastructure, including education, can be a first step in successful international competition, and the second step can be plain old protectionism, using trade barriers to allow domestic industries to develop without stiff international competition until they're ready.

Stiglitz summarizes the hypocrisy among rich nations that has made it impossible for many poor countries to benefit as they should from increasing trade:

> While [rich] countries had preached—and forced—the opening of the markets in the developing countries to their industrial products, they had continued to keep their markets closed to the products of the developing countries, such as textiles and agriculture. While they preached that developing countries should not subsidize their industries, they continued to provide billions in subsidies to their own farmers, making it impossible for the developing countries to compete.[45]

Rosenberg adds: "The architects of globalization are right that international economic integration is not only good for the poor; it is essential. . . . But the protesters are also right—no nation has ever developed over the long term under the rules being imposed today on third-world countries by the institutions controlling globalization."[46]

On this showing, cosmopolitans, who generally favor a borderless world and equal rights worldwide, would oppose the current manner of implementing globalization. They would support globalization more in theory than in current practice.

Non-Commercial Values

Globalization could be reformed to protect workers and industries in developing countries from unfairness. The United States could protect American workers from lower wages and job losses incident to globalization by better funding education and more effectively limiting immigration. Still, globalization would remain controversial, because its sole aim is maximizing the production of goods and services for consumers. The problem is that people are more than just shoppers. They have multiple values.

National Security

Although he advocates increased world trade, Friedman also advocates energy independence for the United States, primarily for reasons of national security and international diplomacy. He suggests

a crash program for alternative energy and conservation to make America energy-independent in ten years. . . . [This] would dry up revenue for terrorism, force Iran, Russia, Venezuela, and Saudi Arabia onto the path of reform—which they will never do with $50-a-barrel oil—strengthen the dollar, and improve [our] standing in Europe by doing something huge to reduce global warming.[47]

This seems reasonable, but it's also an unacknowledged departure from globalization, which is geared to increase, not decrease, international (inter)dependence.

Like energy, food might be thought too important to national security for dependence on others. Agricultural subsidies could help maintain food security and independence. Most current subsidies in Europe and the United States don't serve this purpose, but it's easy to imagine subsidies that would. For example, extensive soil erosion jeopardizes the long-term sustainability of American agriculture. When corporations own farm land, they tend to use it to maximize profit on a yearly basis. By contrast, when families own farm land, many people believe, they tend to use it for long-term agricultural productivity, because they look forward to their children and grandchildren farming the same land. Long-term food security in the United States might be advanced by encouraging family farming. We could give tax breaks to help families retain or buy farms. Additional tax breaks might be needed to make these farms price-competitive if it costs more to produce food on smaller farms. But international rules could condemn all such tax breaks as unwarranted subsidies.

Water is in short supply in the United States, as major aquifers in the West are pumped for irrigation faster than they replenish. We could extend the life of those aquifers, thereby extending our food independence, by subsidizing installation of more efficient drip systems of irrigation. Again, such subsidies might run afoul of WTO rules. In these respects, national security is not a value recognized by the WTO.

Animal Welfare and National Sovereignty

WTO rules can also interfere with a country trying to promote animal welfare. Philosopher Peter Singer gives this example:

In 1991 the European Union agreed to prohibit, from 1995, the sale of furs that had come from animals caught in steel-jaw leghold traps. (These traps crush and hold the animal's leg, holding the animal until the trapper returns, which may be several days. Nocturnal animals are terrified at being held out in daylight. Animals may die of thirst or from their injuries. They have been known to bite off their own legs to get free.) Because it is impossible to tell if an individual pelt has come from an animal caught in one of these traps, or by some relatively more humane method, the European Union decided to accept the import of furs only from countries that had banned the steel-jaw trap. The United States, Canada, and Russia threatened to lodge a complaint with the WTO against this ban. The European Union capitulated.[48]

Europe capitulated because they were likely to lose if they forced a decision by the WTO, which distinguishes between products and the processes used to create them. If a product is unsafe, for example, it can be excluded from trade, but the process used to create the product can't be grounds for exclusion. Here, fur is the product; leghold traps the process. Because fur gleaned from leghold traps is the same product as fur gleaned through more humane methods, the European Union had no right to discriminate against fur from countries that allowed leghold traps.

The United States had the same difficulty when the Marine Mammal Protection Act ran afoul of the product/process distinction. Dolphins often swim near tuna, and some types of tuna nets trap these dolphins under water where they drown. Many thousands were killed this way every year. The Marine Mammal Protection Act attempted to protect dolphins by disallowing importation of tuna caught in such nets. The act specified the use of nets from which most dolphins can escape. However, using the same rules as the WTO, its predecessor organization working under the General Agreement on Tariffs and Trade (GATT) sided with Mexico, which complained that the method of catching tuna has no effect on the quality or safety of the tuna caught. The Marine Mammal Protection Act was overridden by the GATT panel. Not only were dolphins harmed, but the United States was denied the sovereign right to protect them.[49]

Child Labor and Unsafe Working Conditions

The product/process distinction makes it difficult to exclude products made with child labor and products made under unsafe working conditions. Jeffrey Sachs commends consumer boycotts for their role in limiting child employment and improving working conditions in some poor countries where textiles are made for the American and European markets. Consumer groups exposed practices that embarrassed the name brand companies that market the products. Threats of boycott influenced the companies to insist that children be excluded from manufacture and that safety conditions be improved for all workers. Such threats were necessary, because in light of the product/process distinction, there's no rule of international commerce that allows countries to exclude importation of products made by children or those produced in unsafe work environments. Officials at the WTO worry that if such exclusions were allowed, they'd be used as pretexts to exclude products whose only sin is successful competition with a politically powerful home industry.

Singer concludes:

Import prohibitions against goods produced in ways that violate human rights— for example, by using forced labor, or pushing indigenous people off their land— would also fail to pass the test of being applied to a product, rather than a process. If any form of protection, no matter how fair it is in the way it treats domestic and foreign enterprises, is ruled out because it targets a process rather than a product, that will drastically curtail the means by which a nation can protect its values.[50]

Socially Responsible Business

American values include limits to exclusive preoccupation with commercial success. We want companies to be socially responsible as well as efficient and consumer-friendly. Yet global competition tends to squeeze social responsibility out of business. The most successful global retail business, Wal-Mart, is notorious for its exclusive emphasis on low prices and high profit without sufficient regard for other aspects of human well-being. Friedman writes:

Some of Wal-Mart's biggest competitors complain that they have had to cut health-care benefits and create a lower wage tier to compete with Wal-Mart, which pays less and covers less than most big companies. . . . One can only hope that all the bad publicity Wal-Mart has received in the last few years will force it to understand that there is a fine line between a hyperefficient global supply chain that is helping people save money and improve their lives and one that has pursued cost cutting and profit margins to such a degree that whatever social benefits it is offering with one hand, it is taking away with the other.[51]

Friedman published this hope in 2005. In 2006, Wal-Mart unveiled a plan to deny medical benefits to a larger percentage of its employees by using more part-timers.[52] Absent consumer boycotts, the tendency of global competition is to reward companies that ignore the welfare of their employees, at home and abroad. Social conservatives see exclusive emphasis on commercial values as inappropriate and dysfunctional for society.

Environmental Limits

Another problem with globalization is that Earth's ecosystems can't sustain the attainment of its goal—worldwide prosperity like that in the United States. Alan Durning of the World Watch Institute noted in 1992:

As income rises . . . , purchases of cars, gasoline, iron, steel, coal, and electricity, all ecologically . . . damaging to produce, multiply rapidly.

The furnishings of our consumer life-style—things like automobiles, throwaway goods and packaging, a high-fat diet, and air conditioning—can only be provided at great environmental cost. . . .

In particular, the fossil fuels that power the consumer society are its most ruinous input. Wresting coal, oil, and natural gas from the earth permanently disrupts countless habitats; burning them causes an overwhelming share of the world's air pollution; and refining them generates huge quantities of toxic waste.[53]

In 1995, development economist David Korten advocated radical improvement for the 20 percent of the world's people in abject poverty, but no great change for "roughly 60 percent of the world's people [who] are presently meeting most of their basic needs in relatively sustainable ways. . . . As members of the world's sustainer class, they travel by bicycle and public surface transport; eat healthy diets of grains, vegetables, and some meat; buy few prepackaged goods; and recycle most of their wastes."[54]

Unfortunately, globalization tends to move people from tolerable, sustainable ways of life to unsustainable overconsumption like that in the United States. Friedman saw this on his trip to Beijing with his wife and daughter, Natalie, in 2004.

Before we left, I said to Natalie, "You're really going to like this city. They have these big bicycle lanes on all the main roads. . . ."

Silly Tom. I hadn't been to Beijing in three years, and just in that brief period of time the explosive growth there had wiped out many of those charming bicycle lanes. . . . I discovered why all the bikes had disappeared. . . . Some thirty thousand new cars were being added to the roads of Beijing *every month*—one thousand new cars a day![55]

Friedman adds: "The Great Chinese Dream, like the Great Indian Dream, the Great Russian Dream, and the Great American Dream, is built around a high-energy, high-electricity, high-bent-metal lifestyle." But this creates pollution. "Already, according to the World Bank, sixteen of the twenty most polluted cities in the world are in China."[56]

China's increasing prosperity is environmentally damaging in other ways as well, Friedman learns from Glenn Pickett, senior vice president of Conservation International.

If you look at what is happening in the Congo Basin, the Amazon, the rain forests of Indonesia—the last great wilderness areas—you find that they are being devoured by China's rising appetite. More and more palm oil is being extracted from Indonesia and Malaysia, soybeans out of Brazil, timber out of central Africa, and natural gas out of all of the above to serve China—and, as a result, threatening all sorts of natural habitats.[57]

Water is a critical limit to economic development. High-yield crop varieties of rice grown in India since the late 1960s use more water than the indigenous varieties they replaced. Water for irrigation is becoming scarce.[58] Water shortage afflicts China as well. As people become wealthier in China, they eat more meat, and much livestock is fed with grain that uses a lot of irrigation water. In both countries, aquifers are being depleted, Lester Brown of the World Watch Institute reported in 1999.

A survey covering 1991 to 1996, for instance, indicates that the water table under the north China plain is dropping an average of 1.5 meters, or roughly 5 feet, a year. . . . This area accounts for nearly 40% of China's grain harvest.

A similar situation exists in India [where] underground withdrawals . . . are at least double the rate of aquifer recharge. . . . Water tables are falling 1–3 meters (3–10 feet) per year almost everywhere in India.[59]

Chinese rivers are also at risk, Brown notes. "The Yellow River [used to irrigate corn and wheat crops] ran dry for the first time in China's 3,000-year history in 1972, failing to reach the sea for some 15 days. Since 1985 [it] has run dry for part of each year. In 1997, it failed to reach the sea for seven months out of the year."[60]

In short, people the world over can't sustainably eat, drive, and waste resources in the American pattern. Recognizing this regarding energy, at least, Friedman writes: "We in the West have a fundamental interest in keeping the American dream alive in Beijing and Boise and Bangalore. But we have to stop fooling ourselves that it can be done in a flat world with 3 billion potential new consumers—if we don't find a radical new approach to energy usage and conservation."[61]

But energy isn't the only problem. People are eating more meat from grain-fed livestock than water supplies can sustain, and while energy won't always require fossil fuels, grains will always require water. There's no technological fix. In addition, rainforests are being decimated, fisheries depleted, and climates changed as a result of increasing world trade. Friedman suggests that Americans set an example of sustainable living for emerging economies so their development can be environmentally friendly. On this view, globalization works environmentally only if Americans change their wasteful ways. How realistic is that?

Conclusion

Libertarians favor globalization because it fosters free trade across national borders, which allows people to exercise their property rights worldwide without unwarranted interference from governments. Globalization thus increases individual freedom.

Free-market conservatives favor globalization because free trade maximizes the efficient production of goods and services, thereby helping all societies to get richer.

Cosmopolitans favor globalization if it tends to improve the life prospects of people around the world, because they don't think national boundaries are morally important in the first place, and they think that people should be given equal moral concern regardless of nationality. However, they oppose any version of globalization that tends to harm people in poor countries, including the WTO's intellectual property regime and current protectionist practices of the United States and Europe.

Contractarians tend to oppose globalization on the same grounds that they tend to oppose immigration—harm to poor people in rich countries.

Social conservatives worry that globalization's emphasis on commercial values tends to undermine a host of other traditional values, such as national security, national sovereignty, and the protection of children from exploitation.

Environmentalists tend to oppose globalization because it fosters more people adopting environmentally unsustainable lifestyles.

The Upshot

Adherents of a political philosophy often adjust their support for government programs according to details or accompanying aspects of proposals. For example, cosmopolitan support for globalization depends on whether it really helps people in poor countries. Cosmopolitans opposed to globalization might change sides if shown that seemingly exploitative labor practices actually help the poor in the long run.

Similarly, contractarian opposition to globalization—based on its tendency to harm poor workers in wealthy countries—might be avoided with a high minimum wage, increased government support of education, and effective policies against immigration.

Again, consider the forced taking of land for economic development discussed in chapter 1. Libertarians oppose such takings regardless of the details, because they support property rights. But environmentalists could go either way. They supported the takings in New London because they liked the energy- and space-saving aspects of the urban village that developers wanted to create. If developers had planned single-family mansions, environmentalists would probably have opposed those takings.

In general, appeals to political philosophies, not just to self- or group interest, can help garner support for political proposals. Viewing politics through the lenses of twelve political philosophies can inspire modification of proposals that help create successful coalitions. This is political philosophy aiding practical politics.

Afterword

We have essentially a two-party political system, so it's difficult to capture from election results the influence on the candidates or the voters of the twelve political philosophies discussed in this book. If, as I've argued, most of us, including the candidates, have sympathy with at least half a dozen of these political philosophies, each candidate probably appeals to at least this number of philosophies when all of his or her positions are considered. So, too, any given voter may vote for a candidate with whom she disagrees on several issues, because she likes the candidate's positions on other issues that she considers more important. Another voter may vote for the same candidate for entirely different reasons. Thus, convergence on a candidate, no less than on a law or public policy, may reflect a coalition of people who come to the same conclusion but have different reasons and underlying justifications. Still, it's worthwhile investigating the major candidates' positions and voter reactions on just a few of the salient issues of the campaign season in 2008 to look for the influence of political philosophies.

The credit-market crisis, and fear of recession or worse, influenced many voters in 2008. John McCain and Barack Obama were roughly even in the polls until economic concerns dominated the news in September, at which point Obama pulled ahead. Of course, we can't know exactly what was in voters' minds as they increasingly leaned toward Obama. This was also the period of the televised debates, which often favor the candidate who is less well known—Obama, in this case. McCain's running mate, Sarah Palin, who energized the Republican base in the first few weeks after her selection, gave some interviews that caused many people to doubt her fitness for office. Still, the economy seems to have been a major factor in Obama's victory.

Part of Obama's advantage may have been his cool demeanor in contrast to McCain's more frenetic reactions to the crisis. Obama was thought to benefit also from his party being out of executive power as economic problems developed. Voters may have associated Republicans in general with economic mismanagement.

Nevertheless, having ample opportunity during the campaign to address issues raised by the crisis, the candidates revealed that different political philosophies underlie their approaches to economic matters. Both championed economic growth, called for more government regulation of financial markets, supported the $700 billion bailout package, and opposed large salaries and golden parachutes for executives of companies being bailed out. Yet they differed in ways that suggest McCain adhered to a more libertarian or free-market conservative philosophy, whereas Obama favored contractarianism.

Contractarians want economic growth that secures equal basic rights and economic opportunities to everyone while protecting the interests of the poorest segments of the population. Improving the economic situation of the poor requires some redistribution from the rich to the poor because the free market has a tendency to concentrate wealth. The United States has been trending toward increasing concentrations of income and wealth for over a generation. By contrast, most free-market conservatives and virtually all libertarians oppose redistribution of wealth. Free-market conservatives worry that redistribution will deprive talented entrepreneurs of monetary incentives to innovate and work hard. They consider such incentives to be the major engine of economic growth. Libertarians oppose redistribution because they think people have a natural right to their property, so redistribution is the moral equivalent of stealing from some people to give to others.

On this understanding, Obama's economic plans were much more contractarian than McCain's. Obama favored raising federal income taxes for families earning $250,000 or more per year. He would do this by reversing tax cuts enacted earlier in the decade. McCain favored continuation of these tax cuts that disproportionately favor wealthy people. For middle-income families, by contrast, both candidates favored tax cuts, but independent researchers calculated that the Obama tax plan would yield three times as much tax relief for these people as McCain's plan. Other things being equal, Obama's plan would produce greater economic equality. Obama's running mate, Joe Biden, referred to this as simple fairness, an echo of John Rawls's contractarian position that is called "justice as fairness." Obama used the phrase "spread the wealth around" in a conversation with "Joe the Plumber" (Joe Wurzelbacher) during a campaign stop in Ohio. When asked by Wurzelbacher about the desirability of a flat tax, Obama said he didn't think it fair for someone as wealthy as himself to pay taxes at the same rate as a waitress. He also said, "My attitude is that if the economy's good for folks from the bottom up, it's going to be good for everybody." This resembles Rawls's view.

McCain also favored some wealth redistribution, but less than Obama, and geared more toward people in higher-income groups. For example, besides retaining Bush-era tax breaks for the wealthiest Americans, McCain would charge only 10 percent federal income tax on money retirees take out of their tax-sheltered 401(k) retirement savings accounts. Middle- and lower-income Americans have relatively little income from such accounts and already pay a low percentage on their federal income taxes. It's primarily wealthy people, those with significant income from retirement savings that puts them in the 25–30 percent tax bracket, who would benefit from McCain's 10 percent plan. Similarly, McCain would buy up troubled mortgages at their face value and then renegotiate affordable terms with homeowners to forestall foreclosure, thus indemnifying lending institutions completely from any loss consequent upon making bad loans. Obama would negotiate with banks to write down the loans, thereby forcing banks to take some loss before the government bought the mortgages to forestall foreclosures.

Perhaps most revealing about the role of political philosophy in these economic issues is not so much the result of the election, but the prospect in electoral advantage of different campaign strategies. For example, evidence suggests that libertarian and free-market conservative appeals attracted some voters in the closing weeks of the campaign when McCain emphasized Obama's willingness to "spread the wealth around." McCain/Palin saw correctly that many voters would object to any of their own wealth being taxed so as to spread some around to other people. Many voters were hostile to the contractarian concept of justice as fairness.

McCain was also more free-market-oriented than Obama regarding education and innovation in technology. His plans to stimulate the economy by improving technological education and innovation featured lowering corporate and capital gains taxes so that the profit motive would provide entrepreneurs with incentives to innovate and students with incentives to become engineers. Obama favored more public money allocated for the direct subsidy of engineering education and basic scientific research that would not likely result in marketable products for many years. In this matter, it seems that the candidates were equally oriented toward growing the economy, as free-market conservatives would want. But McCain thought the free market would allocate enough money for education and basic research, whereas Obama thought the market would fail to produce all the technological education and innovation needed for maximum economic growth. So he advocated targeted government programs.

McCain similarly would rely more on the free market with minimal government guidance to provide more Americans with health care. He proposed giving every family a tax credit of $5,000 to spend as it sees fit on health insurance. He would pay for this, at least in part, by counting employer-provided health benefits as income on which employees must pay federal income taxes. He also favored federal legislation to override any state laws that currently limit the kinds of health insurance policies that can be sold in the free market. Some states disallow policies with very high deductibles or that require mothers to leave the hospital within twenty-four hours of giving birth. McCain would let the market, not the states, decide such matters.

Obama's more contractarian approach was to fund more health coverage for poor Americans by taxing employers (who have more than a certain, unspecified number of employees) if they don't provide their employees with decent health coverage. Republicans claimed the Obama plan was much more expensive than McCain's, whereas Democrats predicted that Obama's plan would drastically reduce the number of uninsured from its current level of 45 million.

Feminist concerns were also prominent in this election cycle. Feminists believe that no person should be disadvantaged for being female. Senator Hillary Rodham Clinton, wife of a former president, was the early leader in the race for the Democratic Party nomination. She eventually lost the nomination to Obama amid cries that the press and electorate were sexist. Independent analyses were conflicting on this issue. Clinton seemed to defeat sexism by doing better than Obama among working-class men in western Pennsylvania, a group often thought to be sexist. (Of course, they may have just found Obama's race more troublesome than Clinton's gender.) Sexism seemed evident, however, in some news coverage of the Clinton campaign, as she was compared on MSNBC to "everyone's first wife standing outside a probate court." Clinton complained about sexism from time to time, but offered no comprehensive perspective on the subject as Obama did on race.

Apparently hoping to capitalize on Democratic women being disaffected by Clinton's loss, McCain chose a woman, Sarah Palin, governor of Alaska, for his running mate. Criticisms of her relative inexperience and poor grasp of issues were sometimes met with charges that the press was sexist. But policy positions probably explain why most women chose Obama/Biden over McCain/Palin. Senator Biden was known for sponsoring legislation to protect women from domestic violence. The Republican platform on which McCain/Palin ran opposed abortion even in cases of pregnancy resulting from rape or incest. McCain had also opposed legislation promoting equal pay for women.

In the end, the campaign reproduced to a large extent the stereotypes of red and blue. The Republican coalition supporting the McCain/Palin ticket combined free-market conservatism with social conservatism and even some theocracy. They called for low income taxes, low corporate taxes, minimal regulation of business (except in the financial sector), little regulation on guns, bans on abortion, abstinence-only sex education, and teaching Intelligent Design along with the theory of evolution in biology classes. The Palin candidacy was meant to highlight the value of traditional families. The campaign tried to ignite the culture war by accusing Obama of consorting with celebrities and seeming elitist, in contrast to Joe Six-Pack and Joe the Plumber.

The Obama/Biden ticket combined contractarian, feminist, and environmentalist themes. They agreed with Republicans that gun ownership is a constitutional right. They conceded also that certain late-term abortions should be illegal, but insisted, as feminists would want, that abortion bans should not apply when the life or health of a woman is at risk. They wanted to help the economy grow by giving more money to poorer (middle-income) people, a contractarian view, and by public works projects of environmentalist inspiration in such areas as energy and transportation. Unlike the Republicans, the Democrats would not let the private sector decide whether or not such investments are a good idea.

The basic cultural divide between red and blue was visible also in many of the referenda that were decided in this election. Red did well on same-sex marriage and affirmative action. California voters approved a constitutional amendment to reverse a California Supreme Court decision that legalized same-sex marriage. There was some reaching across party lines as a majority of African Americans who voted for Obama also voted— on theocratic grounds, it seems—against same-sex marriage, a position generally more popular among Republicans than Democrats. Anti-gay-marriage referenda passed also in Florida and Arizona. Arkansas passed a referendum aimed at denying same-sex couples the right to be foster or adoptive parents. Also trending red was Nebraska passing a ban on affirmative action in government employment. Colorado voters were about equally divided on that question.

Blue did better regarding abortion and physician-assisted suicide. Referenda aimed at limiting abortion were defeated in Colorado, South Dakota, and California. South Dakota was red on the presidential race, but blue on abortion. Washington state passed a "death with dignity" proposition making it the second state, after Oregon, to allow physician-assisted suicide.

In short, to judge by the campaigns for president and vice president in 2008, political philosophies are important in general elections, but they don't tend to catalyze coalitions across party lines. Such coalitions are more common in the contexts of policymaking, legislation, and legal argument, as was evident to some extent regarding ballot initiatives concerning same-sex marriage and abortion.

Notes

Introduction

1. *Barnes v. Glen Theatre, Inc.*, 501 U.S. 560 (1991), at 563.

2. Ibid., at 565.

3. Ibid., at 572.

4. Ibid., at 582.

5. Ibid., at 591.

6. Ibid., at 592.

7. *Church of the Lukumi Babalu Aye v. City of Hialeah*, 508 U.S. 520 (1993), at 525.

8. M. Gonzalez-Wippler, *The Santeria Experience 47*. In Gary L. Francione, "Brief in *Church of the Lukumi Babalu Aye, Inc. v. City of Hialeah*." www.animal-law .org/sacrifice/hialbrf.htm, p. 10 of 11. Accessed 3/4/2004.

9. Ibid., pp. 7–8 of 11.

10. Ibid., p. 3 of 11.

11. Jane Gordon, "Gay Marriage Case Now before the Court," *New York Times*, Connecticut Weekly Desk (April 2, 2006). www.glad.org/marriage/Kerrigan-Mock/ NY%20Times%20Article.pdf, pp. 1–2 of 3. Accessed 4/9/2006.

12. Russell Shorto, "What's Their Real Problem with Gay Marriage?" *New York Times Magazine* (June 19, 2005), p. 39.

13. Ibid., p. 67.

14. Gordon, "Gay Marriage Case," p. 3 of 3.

15. www.marijuana.org/ballot%20arg2Hallin.htm, p. 1 of 1.

16. www.marijuana.org/ballot%20arg4Pro.htm, p. 1 of 2.

17. Sarah Glazer, "Sexual Harassment: An Overview," in *Sexual Harassment*, Louise I. Gerdes, ed. (San Diego: Greenhaven Press, 1999), pp. 16–26, at 16.

18. *Robinson v. Jacksonville Shipyards*, 760 F. Supp. 1486 (1991), in Michael Weiss and Cathy Young, "Feminist Legal Definitions of Sexual Harassment Promote Injustice," in Gerdes, *Sexual Harassment*, pp. 175–187, at 180.

19. Cristina Hoff Sommers, *Who Stole Feminism? How Women Have Betrayed Women* (New York: Touchstone, 1994), p. 271.

1   No Strange Bedfellows

1. Susette Kelo, "Real People Pay Dearly for NLDC Land Grab," *The Day* (February 11, 2001), p. 1.

2. Avi Salzman, "Homeowners Shown the Door," *New York Times*, Connecticut Weekly Desk (July 3, 2005). www.nytimes.com/2005/07/03/nyregion/nyregion special2/03ctdomain.html?pagewanted=print, p. 1 of 3. Accessed 2/13/2006.

3. *Kelo v. New London*, 545 U.S. 469 (2005), at 473.

4. Ibid.

5. Ibid., at 474.

6. Iver Peterson, "As Land Goes to Revitalization, There Go the Old Neighbors," *New York Times*, Metropolitan Desk (January 30, 2005). query.nytimes.com/ search/restricted/article?res=9500EEDE153BF933A05752C0A9639C8B63, p. 1 of 4. Accessed 2/13/2006.

7. Ibid., p. 4 of 4.

8. "High Court Decision Divides New London" (June 23, 2005). 1010wins.com/ topstories/local_story_174110555.html/resources_storyPrintableView. Accessed 2/13/2006.

9. Peterson, "As Land Goes," p. 2 of 4.

10. *Kelo*, at 478–479.

11. Quoted in *Berman v. Parker*, 348 U.S. 26 (1954), at 28.

12. Ibid., at 32–33.

13. Ibid., at 34–35.

14. *Kelo*, at 477.

15. Ibid., at 484.

16. Ibid., at 483.

17. Ibid., at 498.

18. Ibid., at 500.

19. Ibid., at 501.

20. Dahlia Lithwick, "Condemn-Nation," *Slate*, posted February 22, 2005. www .slate.com/toolbar.aspx?action=print&id=2113868, p. 2 of 3. Accessed 2/13/2006.

21. *Kelo*, at 500–501.

22. Ibid., at 505.

23. Ibid., at 522. Internal citations omitted.

24. Quoted in Terry Priston, "Connecticut Homeowners Question Eminent Domain," *New York Times*, Commercial Real Estate (September 8, 2004). www .nytimes.com/2004/09/08/business/08prop.html?pagewanted=all, p. 1 of 4. Accessed 2/13/2006.

25. Peterson, "As Land Goes," p. 3 of 4.

26. Ibid., p. 1 of 4.

27. Pristin, "Connecticut Homeowners," p. 3 of 3.

28. Ibid., p. 2 of 3.

29. Ibid.

30. Among others in 2006, Senators Bill Frist of Tennessee and Orin Hatch of Utah opposed abortion but supported public funding of stem-cell research that involved killing human embryos. See Carl Hulse, "Senate Approves A Stem-Cell Bill; Veto Is Expected," *New York Times* (July 19, 2006), pp. 1 and 18.

31. John M. Broder, "States Curb Right to Seize Private Homes," *New York Times* (February 21, 2006), p. A1.

32. Ibid., p. A17.

33. Avi Salzman, "Eminent Domain; Homeowners Settle, but Their Fighting Spirit Lives On," *New York Times*, Connecticut Weekly Desk (July 9, 2006). query.nytimes.com/gst/fullpage.html?res=9801E0DA1330F93AA35754C0A960 9C8B63, pp. 1 and 2 of 2. Accessed 7/18/2006.

2 Pulling the Plug

1. Jon B. Eisenberg, *Using Terri: The Religious Right's Conspiracy to Take Away Our Rights* (San Francisco: HarperCollins, 2005), p. 48.

2. Arian Campo-Flores, "The Legacy of Terri Schiavo," *Newsweek*, Vol. 145, No. 14 (April 4, 2005), pp. 22–28, at 24.

3. Ibid.

4. Jay Wolfson, "Erring on the Side of Teresa Schiavo: Reflections of the Special Guardian ad Litem," *Hastings Center Report*, Vol. 35, No. 3 (May–June 2005), pp. 16–19, at 16.

5. Ibid.

6. Campo-Flores, "The Legacy," pp. 24–25.

7. Ibid., p. 25.

8. Eisenberg, *Using Terri*, pp. 14–16.

9. Cal Thomas, "The Substance and Symbol of Terri Schiavo's Case." www .beliefnet.com/story/162_16296.html, p. 1 of 2. Accessed 3/8/2006.

10. Frank Pavone, "Terri Schiavo." priestsforlife.org/columns/columns2005/ 05-01-31schiavo.htm. Accessed 3/9/2006.

11. Florida Catholic Conference, "Continued Concerns for Terri Schiavo" (February 28, 2005). www.flacathconf.org/Health/Schaivo%20Statement%202-28-05 .htm, p. 1 of 2. Accessed 3/9/2006.

12. *The Declaration of Independence*, Sam Fink, ed. (New York: Scholastic Inc., 2002), p. 146.

13. David Walker, *David Walker's Appeal* (New York: Hill and Wang, 1995), pp. 41–42.

14. Quoted in Doris Kearns Goodwin, *Team of Rivals: The Political Genius of Abraham Lincoln* (New York: Simon and Schuster, 2005), p. 699.

15. In *A Testament of Hope: The Essential Writings of Martin Luther King, Jr.,* James Melvin Washington, ed. (New York: Harper and Row, 1986), p. 293. Emphasis in original.

16. President George W. Bush, "President Bush Addresses the Nation," speech delivered September 20, 2001. www.washingtonpost.com/wp-srv/nation/specials/attacked/transcripts/bushaddress_092001.html, p. 6 of 6. Accessed 6/27/2002.

17. www.nytimes.com/2004/10/14/politics/campaign/14text.html, p. 17.

18. Jim Wallis, *God's Politics: Why the Right Gets It Wrong and the Left Doesn't Get It* (New York: HarperCollins, 2005), p. 82.

19. Quoted in Frank Pavone, "Terri Schiavo: A Living Sermon for Good Friday." priestsforlife.org/euthanasia/05-03-25priestfax.htm, p. 1 of 2.

20. Ibid.

21. Winthrop D. Jordan, *White over Black: American Attitudes Toward the Negro, 1550–1812* (Chapel Hill: University of North Carolina Press, 1968), p. 17.

22. Ibid., p. 19.

23. *Loving v. Virginia*, 388 U.S. 1 (1967), at 2–3.

24. Ibid., at 3.

25. Thomas B. Edsall, *Washington Post*, June 10, 1998. www.loper.org/~george/trends/1998/Jun/77.html, p. 1 of 1.

26. Cal Thomas, "Substance and Symbol," p. 1 of 2.

27. Florida Catholic Conference, "Continued Concerns for Terri Schiavo," p. 1 of 2.

28. www.vatican.va/holy_father/john_paul_ii/speeches/2004/march/documents/hf_ip_ii_spe_20040320_congress_fiamc_en.html, p. 2 of 4. Accessed 9/16/2008. Emphasis in original.

29. I Corinthians, chapter 14, verses 34–35, in *The Holy Bible*, Revised Standard Version (New York: Thomas Nelson & Sons, 1953), p. 907.

30. Genesis, chapter 1, verse 28, in RSV, p. 1.

31. *Griswold v. Connecticut*, 381 U.S. 479 (1965).

32. John Stuart Mill, "On Liberty," in *On Liberty and Considerations on Representative Government*, R. B. McCallum, ed. (Oxford: Basil Blackwell, 1946), pp. 1–104, at 8.

33. Angela Fagerlin and Carl E. Schneider, "Enough: The Failure of the Living Will," *Hastings Center Report*, Vol. 34, No. 2 (March–April 2004), pp. 30–42, at 32.

34. Ibid., at 33.

35. Ibid., at 34.

36. Ibid.

37. Ibid., at 32.

38. Eisenberg, *Using Terri*, p. 16.

39. Wesley J. Smith, "The Legacy of Terri Schiavo," *Weekly Standard*, Vol. 10, Issue 28 (April 11, 2005). www.weeklystandard.com/utilities/printer_preview .asp?idArticle=5443&R=EB951B, p. 2 of 2. Accessed 3/9/2006.

40. Eisenberg, *Using Terri*, p. 33.

41. Ibid., p. 34.

42. Smith, "Legacy," p. 1 of 2.

43. Frank Pavone, "Atrophy of Compassion." priestsforlife.org/euthanasia/atro phyofcompassion.htm, p. 2 of 2. Accessed 3/9/2006.

44. See studies reported by Eisenberg, *Using Terri*, pp. 88–90.

45. On *Dateline* interview, March 26, 2006. www.msnbc.com/id/12025860/ page/2/, p. 2 of 3.

46. Cal Thomas, "Substance and Symbol," pp. 1 and 2 of 2.

3 Physician-Assisted Suicide

1. Andrew Solomon, "A Death of One's Own," *New Yorker*, Vol. 71, Issue 13 (May 22, 1995), pp. 54–69, 56.

2. Ibid., p. 58.

3. Ibid., p. 63.

4. Ibid., p. 58.

5. Ibid., p. 63.

6. Ibid., p. 65.

7. Ibid., pp. 65–66.

8. Timothy E. Quill, M.D., *A Midwife through the Dying Process: Stories of Hard Choices at the End of Life* (Baltimore, MD: Johns Hopkins University Press, 1996), p. 143.

9. Ibid., p. 144.

10. Lonny Shavelson, *A Chosen Death: The Dying Confront Assisted Suicide* (New York: Simon and Schuster, 1995), pp. 191–192.

11. Barry Rosenfeld, *Assisted Suicide and the Right to Die: The Interface of Social Science, Public Policy, and Medical Ethics* (Washington, DC: American Psychological Association, 2004), p. 155.

12. Mill, "On Liberty," p. 8.

13. Wesley J. Smith, *Forced Exit* (New York: Times Books, 1997), p. 6.

14. Ibid., p. 6.

15. *Quill v. Vacco*, 80 F. 3d 716 (2nd Cir. 1996). caselaw.lp.findlaw.com/scripts/ getcase.pl?navby=search&case=data2/circs/2nd/957028.html&friend=nytimes, p. 13 of 26. Accessed 4/3/2006.

16. Yale Kamisar, "Voluntary Euthanasia Should Not Be Legalized," in *Euthanasia: Opposing Viewpoints*, James D. Torr, ed. (San Diego: Greenhaven Press,

2000), pp. 79–87, at 79, which is edited from "The Reasons So Many People Support Physician-Assisted Suicide—and Why These Reasons Are Not Convincing," *Issues in Law and Medicine*, Vol. 12, No. 2 (Fall 1996). Emphasis in original.

17. Ezekiel Emanuel, "Whose Right to Die?" *Atlantic Monthly* (March 1997), pp. 73–79, at 79.

18. Daniel P. Salmasy, O.F.M., M.D., "Managed Care and Managed Death," *Archives of Internal Medicine* (January 23, 1995), p. 134. In Smith, *Forced Exit*, p. 154.

19. Ada Jacob, R.B., Ph.D., et al., "Special Report: New Clinical-Practice Guidelines for the Management of Pain in Patients with Cancer," *New England Journal of Medicine* Vol. 330, No. 9 (March 3, 1994). In Smith, *Forced Exit*, p. 147.

20. Department of Consumer Affairs, State of California, *Summit on Effective Pain Management: Removing Impediments to Appropriate Prescribing*, report (Sacramento, March 18, 1994), p. 3. In Smith, *Forced Exit*, p. 147.

21. Quill, p. 215.

22. Smith, *Forced Exit*, p. 173.

23. Ibid., p. 174. Emphasis in original.

24. Ibid., p. 164.

25. Rosenfeld, *Assisted Suicide*, p. 55.

26. Shavelson, *A Chosen Death*, p. 39.

27. Ibid., p. 46.

28. Ibid., p. 65.

29. Ibid., p. 53.

30. Ibid., p. 56.

31. Ibid., p. 54.

32. Ibid., p. 59.

33. Rosenfeld, *Assisted Suicide*, pp. 152–153.

34. Ibid., p. 151.

35. Ibid., pp. 151–152.

36. Shavelson, *A Chosen Death*, pp. 136–137.

4 The War on Drugs

1. Dave Bakke, "Meth's Price: One Youth Paid with His Liberty—and Sight," *The State Journal-Register* (Springfield, Illinois, Sunday, July 13, 2003), pp. 1 and 5, at 1.

2. Holly Eitenmiller, "Methamphetamine Abuse: The Dangers of Scoring a Fix," *Illinois Magazine*, Vol. 2, No. 5 (May 2003), pp. 20–24, at 20.

3. David J. Jefferson, "America's Most Dangerous Drug," *Newsweek*, Vol. 146, No. 6 (August 8, 2005), pp. 40–48, at 44.

4. Eitenmiller, "Methamphetamine Abuse," p. 23.

5. Bakke, "Meth's Price," p. 1.

6. Ibid., p. 5.

7. Ibid.

8. Ibid.

9. www.whitehousedrugpolicy.gov/publications/policy/ndcs06/stopping_use .html, p. 1 of 14. Accessed 6/21/2008.

10. www.whitehousedrugpolicy.gov/publications/policy/ndcs06/healing_amer .html, p. 1 of 10. Accessed 6/21/2008.

11. www.whitehousedrugpolicy.gov/publications/policy/ndcs06/disrupt_mkt .html, p. 1 of 40. Accessed 6/21/2008.

12. Thomas Szasz, *Our Right to Drugs* (Syracuse, NY: Syracuse University Press, 1992, 1996), p. 151.

13. James Q. Wilson, "Against the Legalization of Drugs," *Commentary*, Vol. 89, No. 2 (February 1990), pp. 21–28, at 24.

14. Eitenmiller, "Methamphetamine Abuse," p. 23.

15. Wilson, "Against the Legalization," p. 26.

16. Ibid., p. 28.

17. William F. Buckley, Jr. "The War on Drugs Is Lost," Part 1, *National Review* (February 12, 1996), pp. 35–38, at 36.

18. Ibid.

19. Ibid.

20. Steven B. Duke, "The War on Drugs Is Lost," Part 7, *National Review* (February 12, 1996), pp. 47–48, at 47.

21. "Danny Stern," in Jeremy Larner and Ralph Tefferteller, *The Addict in the Street* (New York: Grove Press, 1964), pp. 95–115, at 95.

22. Ibid., p. 98.

23. Buckley, "The War on Drugs Is Lost," Part 1, p. 36.

24. Joseph D. McNamara, "The War on Drugs Is Lost," Part 4, *National Review* (February 12, 1996), pp. 42–44, at 42.

25. George F. Will, "About Cocaine and Bananas," *Newsweek* (September 17, 2001), p. 78. Emphasis in original.

26. Joel Brinkley, "U.S. Lists Its Pluses and Minuses in Fighting Narcotics Worldwide," *New York Times* (March 2, 2006), p. A13.

27. Robert W. Sweet, "The War on Drugs Is Lost," Part 5, *National Review* (February 12, 1996), pp. 44–45, at 44.

28. S. Meddis, "Drug Arrest Rate Is Higher for Blacks," *USA Today* (December 20, 1989). In Szasz, *Our Right to Drugs*, p. 116.

29. "Just the Facts," *FCNL Washington Newsletter* of the Friends Committee on National Legislation (February 1990), p. 2. In Szasz, *Our Right to Drugs*, p. 116.

30. Szasz, *Our Right to Drugs*, p. 118.

31. Ibid., p. 119.

32. McNamara, "The War on Drugs Is Lost," Part 4, p. 43.

33. William J. Bennett, *The Broken Hearth: Reversing the Moral Collapse of the American Family* (New York: Doubleday, 2001), p. 93.

34. Duke, "The War on Drugs Is Lost," Part 7, p. 48.

35. McNamara, "The War on Drugs Is Lost," Part 4, p. 43.

36. Wilson, "Against the Legalization," p. 22.

37. Ibid., p. 23.

38. Will, "About Cocaine," p. 78.

39. Wilson, "Against the Legalization," p. 22.

40. Duke, "The War on Drugs Is Lost," Part 7, p. 48.

41. Ibid., p. 48.

42. Michael Elsner, "The Sociology of Reefer Madness: The Criminalization of Marijuana in the USA," unpublished Ph.D. dissertation (American University, Washington, DC, 1994). In Ethan A. Nadelmann, "U.S. Drug Policy Should Incorporate Principles of Harm Reduction," in *Drug Abuse: Opposing Viewpoints*, James D. Torr, ed. (San Diego: Greenhaven Press, 1999), pp. 116–125, at 120. Nadelmann's article appeared originally as "Common Sense Drug Policy," *Foreign Affairs* (January/February 1998).

43. "Danny Stern," p. 100.

44. Buckley, "The War on Drugs Is Lost," Part 1, p. 37.

45. Quoted in Will, "About Cocaine," p. 78.

46. Sweet, "The War on Drugs Is Lost," Part 5, p. 45.

47. Kurt Schmoke, "The War on Drugs Is Lost," Part 3, *National Review* (February 12, 1996), pp. 40–42, at 40.

48. "Danny Stern," pp. 112–113.

49. Ibid., pp. 105–106.

50. Cited in Robert L. Maginnis, "U.S. Drug Policy Should Not Incorporate Principles of Harm Reduction," Part 1, in Torr, *Drug Abuse*, pp. 126–131, at 128.

51. Quoted in Will, "About Cocaine," p. 78.

52. Quoted in Szasz, *Our Right to Drugs*, p. 113.

53. Herbert Asbury, *The Great Illusion: An Informal History of Prohibition* (Garden City, NY: Doubleday and Company, 1950), p. 86.

54. Szasz, *Our Right to Drugs*, p. 160.

5　The War on Terrorism

1. National Commission on Terrorist Attacks upon the United States, Staff Statement 13, "Emergency Preparedness and Response," May 18, 2004, p. 6 of 26, hereinafter referred to as Staff Statement 13. www.9-11Commission.gov-staff _statements-staff_statements_13.pdf. Accessed June 22, 2006.

2. Ibid., p. 8 of 26.

3. Ibid.

4. Ibid., p. 7 of 26.

5. Ibid., p. 13 of 26.

6. Ibid., p. 14 of 26.

7. Ibid., p. 15 of 26.

8. Ibid., p. 26 of 26.

9. Thomas H. Kean, Lee H. Hamilton, et al., *The 9/11 Commission Report* (New York: W. W. Norton, 2004), pp. 48–49.

10. Ibid., p. 51.

11. Ibid., pp. 50–51.

12. *Hamdi v. Rumsfeld*, 542 U.S. 507 (2004), at 511–512.

13. Ibid., at 512–513.

14. Ibid., at 580.

15. Ibid., at 589, from *Moyer v. Peabody*, 212 U.S. 78 (1909). Emphasis added by Thomas.

16. Ibid., at 591, from *U.S. v. Salerno*, 481 U.S. 739 (1987), at 748.

17. Ibid., at 595.

18. Ibid., at 592.

19. Steven T. Wax and Christopher J. Schatz, "A Multitude of Errors: The Brandon Mayfield Case," *National Association of Defense Lawyers*, September/October 2004. www.nacdl.org/public_test.nsf/PrinterFriendly/A0409p6?openDocument, p. 1 of 11. Accessed 7/21/2006.

20. Ibid., p. 3 of 11.

21. Ibid., p. 6 of 11.

22. *Hamdi*, at 538.

23. Ibid., at 531.

24. Ibid., at 561. Emphasis in original.

25. Ibid., at 555.

26. Quoted from *The Federalist*, Number 8, in *Hamdi*, p. 578.

27. See especially John Rawls, *A Theory of Justice* (Cambridge, MA: Harvard University Press, 1971); *Political Liberalism* (New York: Columbia University Press, 1993); and *Justice as Fairness: A Restatement* (Cambridge, MA: Harvard University Press, 2001).

28. *Boumediene v. Bush*, 553 U.S. (2008).

29. See *Hamdan v. Rumsfeld*, 548 U.S. (2006), Scalia dissenting.

30. Mark Danner, "Torture and Truth," *New York Review of Books*, Vol. 51, No. 10 (June 10, 2004), pp. 46–50, at 47.

31. John Barry, Michael Hirsh, and Michael Isikoff, "The Roots of Torture," *Newsweek*, Vol. 143, No. 21 (May 24, 2004), pp. 26–34, at 28.

32. Ibid., pp. 32–33.

33. Sen. John McCain, "Torture's Terrible Toll," *Newsweek*, Vol. 146, No. 21 (November 21, 2005), pp. 34–36, at 36.

34. Anthony Lewis, "Making Torture Legal," *New York Review of Books*, Vol. 51, No. 12 (July 15, 2004), pp. 4–8, at 6 and 8.

35. Ibid. p. 8.

36. In Byron York, "A Tortured Debate," *National Review* (July 12, 2004), pp. 33–36, at 34.

37. McCain, "Torture's Terrible Toll," p. 36.

38. Lewis, "Making Torture Legal," p. 8.

39. Evan Thomas and Michael Hirsh, "The Debate over Torture," *Newsweek*, Vol. 146, No. 21 (November 21, 2005), pp. 26–33, at 29.

40. Andrew C. McCarthy, "Torture: Thinking About the Unthinkable," *Commentary*, Vol. 118, No. 1 (July–August 2004), pp. 17–24, at 22.

41. Ibid., pp. 23–24. Emphasis in original.

42. Ibid., p. 24.

43. McCain, "Torture's Terrible Toll," p. 34.

44. Evans and Hirsh, "Debate over Torture," p. 30.

45. Harvey A. Silverglate, "The Government Should Not Authorize the Use of Torture to Combat Terrorism," in *Civil Liberties*, James D. Torr, ed. (San Diego: Greenhaven Press, 2003), pp. 184–189, at 187. Emphasis in original.

46. Barry, Hirsh, and Isikoff, "Roots of Torture," p. 29.

47. "Convention against Torture and Other Cruel, Inhuman or Degrading Treatment or Punishment." www.hrweb.org/legal/cat.html, pp. 1–2 of 11. Accessed 7/25/2006.

48. William Safire, "Waterboarding," *New York Times Magazine* (March 9, 2008), p. 16.

49. Silverglate, "Government Should Not Authorize," pp. 187–189.

50. Andrew C. McCarthy, "Unreasonable Searches," *National Review* (August 29, 2005), pp. 17–18, at 18.

51. David A. Harris, "Flying while Arab," in *Taking Sides: Clashing Views on Political Issues*, fourteenth edition, George McKenna and Stanley Feingold, eds. (Dubuque, IA: McGraw-Hill/Dushkin, 2006), pp. 223–227, at 225.

52. Harris, p. 226.

6   Affirmative Action

1. Greg Stohr, *A Black and White Case* (Princeton, NJ: Bloomberg Press, 2004), p. 1.

2. Ibid., pp. 2–3.

3. Ibid., p. 50.

4. Pub. L. 88–352, 78 Stat. 241, July 2, 1964.

5. Roger Clegg, "Affirmative Action Is Counterproductive," in *Opposing Viewpoints: Discrimination*, Mary E. Williams, ed. (Farmington Hills, MI: Greenhaven Press, 2003), pp. 112–117, at 113.

6. Ibid., p. 114.

7. Howard Fineman and Tamara Lipper, "Spinning Race," *Newsweek* (January 27, 2003), pp. 26–29, at 28.

8. Ibid. Emphasis in original.

9. *Brown v. Board of Education*, 347 U.S. 483 (1954).

10. See *Green v. County School Board*, 391 U.S. 430 (1968).

11. Patrick A. Hall, "Against Our Best Interests: An Ambivalent View of Affirmative Action," in *Taking Sides: Clashing Views on Controversial Issues in Race and Ethnicity*, fifth edition, Raymond D'Angelo and Herbert Douglas, eds. (Dubuque, IA: McGraw-Hill/Dushkin, 2005), pp. 310–316, at 311.

12. Stohr, *Black and White*, p. 62.

13. For this general libertarian view, see Robert Nozick, *Anarchy, State, and Utopia* (New York: Basic Books, 1974), pp. 152–153.

14. Carl Cohen, "Affirmative Action in Admissions Harms College Students," in *Opposing Viewpoints: Interracial America*, Mary E. Williams, ed. (Farmington Hills, MI: Greenhaven Press, 2001), pp. 144–152, at 146–147.

15. Fineman and Lipper, "Spinning Race," p. 29.

16. Mary Frances Berry, "Affirmative Action: Why We Need It, Why It Is under Attack," in McKenna and Feingold, *Taking Sides: Political Issues*, fourteenth edition, pp. 182–188, at 186.

17. Robert C. Scott, "Affirmative Action Is Beneficial," in Williams, *Discrimination*, pp. 107–111, at 108.

18. Bryan J. Grapes, ed., "Introduction," in *Affirmative Action* (San Diego: Greenhaven Press, 2000), pp. 6–8, at 7.

19. Robert Jensen, "Affirmative Action Balances White Privilege," in Grapes, *Affirmative Action*, pp. 35–37, at 36–37.

20. Claude Steele and Joshua Aronson, "Stereotype Threat and Intellectual Test Performance of African Americans," *Journal of Personality and Social Psychology*, Vol. 74, No. 4 (1998), pp. 865–877.

21. WorldNetDaily, "Bill Cosby: Poor Blacks Can't Speak English." worldnetdaily.com/news/article.asp?ARTICLE_ID=38565. Accessed 8/13/2006.

22. Hall, "Against Our Best Interests," at 315.

23. *Grutter v. Bollinger*, 539 U.S. 306 (2003).

24. Stohr, *Black and White*, p. 47.

25. Quoted in *Grutter*, at 316.

26. Brief for Julius W. Becton, Jr., et al., *Amici Curiae* 27, pp. 14–15.

27. Ibid., p. 16.

28. Ibid., p. 17.

29. Ibid., p. 7.

30. *Grutter*, at 332.

31. Ibid.

32. Grapes, "Introduction," p. 7.

33. *Grutter*, at 328. Italics in original.

34. Ibid., at 330.

35. Ibid., at 330.

36. Ibid., at 333.

37. Ibid., at 373.

38. Linda Chavez, "Promoting Racial Harmony," in McKenna and Feingold, *Taking Sides: Political Issues*, fourteenth edition, pp. 189–196, at 196.

39. *Grutter*, at 353. Inserted quotation is from *Adarand Construction, Inc. v. Pena*, 515 U.S. 200, 240 (1995) (Thomas concurring in part and concurring in judgment).

40. Ibid., at 352–353.

41. Ibid., at 368.

42. Barbara Grutter, "Making Progress," *National Review Online* (August 19, 2003). www.nationalreview.com/comment/comment-grutter081903.asp, p. 2 of 2. Accessed 7/27/2006.

43. Stohr, *Black and White*, pp. 45 and 107.

44. Michael Martin, "Affirmative Action in Admissions Benefits College Students," in Williams, *Interracial America*, pp. 135–143, at 137. The 1998 report is William G. Bowen and Derek Curtis Bok, *The Shape of the River: Long-Term Consequences of Considering Race in College and University Admissions* (Princeton, NJ: Princeton University Press, 1998).

45. Stohr, p. 108.

46. Charles T. Canady, "Affirmative Action Harms Society," in Grapes, *Affirmative Action*, pp. 38–46, at 43.

47. Derrick Z. Jackson, "Affirmative Action Does Not Create Reverse Discrimination," in Williams, *Discrimination*, pp. 76–78, at 76.

48. Ibid., p. 77.

49. Ibid., p. 78.

7   Pornography, Child Pornography, and the Internet

1. J. G. Ballard, *Crash* (New York: Picador, 1973), pp. 79–81.

2. Ibid., pp. 8–9.

3. Kurt Eichenwald, "With Child Sex Sites on the Run, Nearly Nude Pictures Test Laws," *New York Times* (August 20, 2006), p 1.

4. Ibid., p. 14.

5. Kurt Eichenwald, "Through His Webcam, a Boy Joins a Sordid Online World," *New York Times* (December 19, 2005). www.nytimes.com/2005/12/19/national/19kids.ready.html?emc=etal, p. 1 of 14. Accessed 8/21/2006.

6. Ibid., p. 5 of 14.

7. Ibid.

8. Ibid., p. 6 of 14.

9. Ibid., p. 7 of 14.

10. Ibid., p. 1 of 14.

11. Mill, "On Liberty," p. 8.

12. Ibid., p. 14.

13. Ibid., pp. 14–15.

14. *Board of Education v. Barnette*, 319 U.S. 624 (1943), at 642.

15. Gloria Steinem, "Erotica and Pornography: A Clear and Present Difference," in *Problem of Pornography*, Susan Dwyer, ed. (Belmont, CA: Wadsworth Publishing Company, 1995), pp. 29–33, at 31.

16. Timothy J. Burger, "E-mails Bare Coverup," *New York Daily News* (July 17, 2002). www.nydailynews.com/front/v-pfriendly/story/3695p-3303c.html. Accessed 8/23/2006.

17. Helen E. Longino, "Pornography, Oppression, and Freedom: A Closer Look," in Dwyer, *Problem of Pornography*, pp. 34–47, at 35–36. Emphasis in Longino. Internal quotations are from *Report of the Commission on Obscenity and Pornography* (New York: Bantam Books, 1979), p. 239. Emphasis in original.

18. Ibid., p. 39. Emphasis in original.

19. Ibid., p. 40.

20. Andrea Dworkin, *Letter from a War Zone*, reprint edition (Chicago: Lawrence Hill Books, 1973). www.nostatusquo.com/ACLU/WarZoneChapIVG2.html, p. 2 of 5.

21. Inserted quotation in Diana E. H. Russell, "Pornography Causes Violence," in *Opposing Viewpoints: Pornography*, Helen Cothran, ed. (San Diego: Greenhaven Press, 2002), p. 50.

22. John Hughes, "Pornography: The Social Ill behind Some Dangerous Crimes," *Christian Science Monitor*, Vol. 98, No. 183 (August 16, 2006), p. 9. www.csmonitor.com/2006/0816/p09s02-cojh.html. Accessed 8/17/2006.

23. Michael Weiss and Cathy Young, "Feminist Jurisprudence: Equal Rights or Neo-Paternalism?" Cato Policy Analysis, No. 256 (June 19, 1996). www.cato.org/pubs/pas/pa-256.html, p. 9 of 26.

24. Nadine Strossen, "Defending Pornography: Free Speech, Sex, and the Fight for Women's Rights," in *Taking Sides: Clashing Views on Controversial Moral Issues*, ninth edition, Stephen Satris, ed. (Guilford, CT: McGraw-Hill/Dushkin, 2004), pp. 86–99, at 87.

25. Sheila M. Rothman, *Woman's Proper Place: A History of Changing Ideals and Practices 1870 to the Present* (New York: Basic Books, 1978), p. 82.

26. Strossen, "Defending Pornography," p. 87.

27. In Nicholas Wolfson, *Hate Speech, Sex Speech, Free Speech* (Westport, CT: Praeger, 1997), p. 124.

28. Quoted in Strossen, "Defending Pornography," p. 90.

29. Ibid., pp. 89–90. Emphasis in original.

30. Ibid., p. 88.

31. Ibid., p. 95.

32. Wendy McElroy, "Censoring Pornography Would Harm Women," in Cothran, *Opposing Viewpoints*, pp. 86–90, at 86.

33. Quoted in Strossen, "Defending Pornography," p. 95.

34. McElroy, "Censoring Pornography," p. 88.

35. Mathew Gever, "Pornography Does Not Cause Violence," in Cothran, *Opposing Viewpoints*, pp. 53–56, at 54.

36. Patti O. Britton, Jennifer Maguire, and Beth Nathanson, "Feminism and Free Speech: Pornography," Feminists for Free Expression, 1993. In Gever, *Pornography*, p. 55.

37. *Roth v. United States*, 354 U.S. 476 (1957). In Ronald D. Rotunda, *Modern Constitutional Law: Cases and Notes*, third edition (St. Paul, MN: West Publishing Co., 1989), p. 923.

38. *A Book Named "John Cleland's Memoirs of a Woman of Pleasure" v. Attorney Gen. of Massachusetts* [commonly referred to as *Memoirs v. Massachusetts*], 383 U.S. 413 (1966). In Rotunda, *Modern Constitutional Law*, p. 928.

39. *Miller v. California*, 413 U.S. 15 (1973).

40. *Paris Adult Theatre I v. Slaton*, 413 U.S. 49 (1973). In Rotunda, *Modern Constitutional Law*, p. 934. Kristol quotation is in note 15 and is from "On the Democratic Idea in America 33" (1972).

41. *Paris Adult Theatre*, in Rotunda, *Modern Constitutional Law*, p. 933.

42. Catechism of the Catholic Church, Section 2354. www.vatican.va/archive/ENG0015/_P85.HTM, p. 3 of 5. Accessed 8/30/2006.

43. *American Booksellers Association v. Hudnut*, 771 F.2d 323 (1985), at 324–325.

44. Ibid., at 325.

45. Ibid., at 329–330.

46. *New York v. Ferber*, 458 U.S. 747 (1982). In Rotunda, *Modern Constitutional Law*, p. 938.

47. *Ashcroft v. Free Speech Coalition*, 535 U.S. 234 (2002), at 239–240.

48. Ibid., at 246.

49. Ibid., at 247–248.

50. Ibid., at 249.

51. Ibid., at 241–242.

52. Ibid., at 251.

53. Ibid., at 253.

54. Linda Greenhouse, "Court Upholds Child Pornography Law, Despite Free Speech Concerns," *New York Times* (May 20, 2008), p. A17.

55. See *United States v. Williams*, 553 U.S. (2008).

56. Mark Laaser, "Internet Pornography Is a Serious Problem," in Cothran, *Opposing Viewpoints*, pp. 32–39, at 39.

57. *Reno v. ACLU*, 521 U.S. 844 (1997), at 859.

58. Ibid., at 878.

59. Ibid., at 876.

60. Ibid., at 877. Emphasis in Stevens's quotations.

61. Solveig Bernstein, "Filtering Technology Can Limit Children's Access to Internet Pornography," in Cothran, *Opposing Viewpoints*, pp. 117–119, at 118.

62. *Reno*, at 875. Internal citations omitted.

63. *United States v. American Library Association*, 539 U.S. 194 (2003). In *Taking Sides: Clashing Views on Legal Issues*, twelfth edition, M. Ethan Katsh and William Rose, eds. (Dubuque, IA: McGraw-Hill, 2006), pp. 174–190, at 174.

64. Ibid., p. 180.

65. Ibid., pp. 178–179.

66. Ibid., p. 179.

67. Jay Nordlinger, "Pornography Should Be Restricted," in *At Issue: Should There Be Limits to Free Speech?* Laura K. Egendorf, ed. (Farmington Hills, MI: Greenhaven Press, 2003), pp. 77–82, at 80.

68. Ibid., p. 81.

69. Ibid., p. 82.

70. Eichenwald, "Child Sex Sites," p. 14.

71. See *United States v. Knox*, 977 R.2d 815 (3d Cir. 1992).

72. Kurt Eichenwald, "From Their Own Online World, Pedophiles Extend Their Reach," *New York Times* (August 21, 2006), pp. 1 and 14, at 14.

73. Langdon Winner, "Parents Should Not Use Internet Filtering Software," in Cothran, *Opposing Viewpoints*, pp. 121–123, at 122–123.

8 Abortion

1. "Eliza's Story." www.imnotsorry.net/eliza.htm. Accessed 9/4/2006.

2. John T. Noonan, "An Almost Absolute Value in History," in *Arguing About Abortion*, Lewis M. Schwartz, ed. (Belmont, CA: Wadsworth Publishing Company, 1993), pp. 55–61, at 59.

3. Ibid., p. 56.

4. Robert P. George, "God's Reasons," in McKenna and Feingold, *Taking Sides: Political Issues*, fourteenth edition, pp. 264–269, at 267.

5. Richard Stith, "Abortion Rights Devalue the Fetus," in *At Issue: Should Abortion Rights Be Restricted?* Auriana Ojeda, ed. (Farmington Hills, MI: Greenhaven Press, 2003), pp. 17–25, at 19.

6. Charles A. Gardner, "Is an Embryo a Person?" in Schwartz, *Arguing*, pp. 141–145, at 144.

7. Mary Gordon, "A Moral Choice," in McKenna and Feingold, *Taking Sides: Political Issues*, fourteenth edition, pp. 270–276, at 271–272.

8. Dalia Sussman, "Conditional Support Poll: Thirty Years After *Roe v. Wade*, American Support Is Conditional." abcnews.go.com/sections/us/DailyNews/abortion_poll030122.html, p. 2 of 4.

9. Noonan, "Absolute Value," pp. 57–58.

10. Gordon, "Moral Choice," p. 274.

11. Debra Rosenberg, "The War over Fetal Rights," *Newsweek*, Vol. 141, No. 23 (June 9, 2003), pp. 40–47, at 43.

12. The Catechism of the Catholic Church, second edition, p. 2270. www.scborromeo.org/ccc/p3s2c2a5.htm. Accessed 9/6/2006.

13. Ibid., p. 2273. Emphasis in original.

14. For a fuller account of this argument, see Peter S. Wenz, *Abortion Rights as Religious Freedom* (Philadelphia: Temple University Press, 1992).

15. Mary Ann Glendon, *Abortion and Divorce in Western Law* (Cambridge, MA: Harvard University Press, 1987), pp. 38–39.

16. Ibid., p. 39.

17. Ibid., p. 59.

18. Ibid., p. 57.

19. Ibid., p. 54.

20. Nina Kohl, "Pro-Life Democrats: We're Here, We're Sincere. Get Used to It," *Tikkun*, Vol. 20, No. 3 (May/June 2005), pp. 14 and 16–18, at 17.

21. Ibid., p. 16.

22. Ibid., p. 14.

23. Kristin Luker, *Abortion and the Politics of Motherhood* (Berkeley: University of California Press, 1984), pp. 159–160.

24. Ibid., p. 160.

25. Ibid., p. 161.

26. Ibid., p. 162.

27. Ibid., p. 168.

28. Ibid., p. 162.

29. Ibid., p. 164.

30. Ibid., p. 165.

31. Russell Shorto, "Contra-Contraception," *New York Times Magazine* (May 7, 2006), pp. 48–55, 68, and 83, at 50.

32. Ibid.

33. Ibid., p. 55.

34. Luker, *Politics of Motherhood*, p. 171.

35. See Shorto, "Contra-Contraception," p. 68.

36. 410 U.S. 113 (1973).

37. 505 U.S. 833 (1992).

38. "Religious Tolerance," www.religioustolerance.org/abo_pba1.htm, pp. 1–2 of 6.

39. See Brian Fahling, "Partial-Birth Abortion Is Legal Infanticide," in Ojeda, *At Issue*, pp. 26–30.

40. See *Stenberg v. Carhart*, 530 U.S. 914 (2000).

41. imnotsorry.net/elena.htm.

42. Linda Greenhouse, "Justices Reaffirm Emergency Access to Abortion," *New York Times* (January 19, 2006), pp. 1 and 16.

43. John Leland, "Under Din of Abortion Debate, An Experience Shared Quietly," *New York Times* (September 18, 2005), pp. 1 and 29, at 29.

44. Andrew Lehren and John Leland, "Parental Notice Has Scant Effect in Teen Abortion," *New York Times* (March 6, 2006), pp. 1 and 19, at 1.

45. Ibid., p. 19.

9 Homosexuality, Same-Sex Marriage, and Polygamy

1. *New York Times*, Weddings/Celebrations, May 23, 2004. query.nytimes.com/gst/fullpage.html?res=9907EFDC1E3FF930A15756C0A9629C8B63&sq=Hillary+Smith+Goodridge&st=nyt, p. 1 of 2. Accessed 9/13/2006.

2. Ibid., p. 1 of 2.

3. "We Do," *UU World: The Magazine of the Unitarian Universalist Association*. www.findarticles.com/p/articles/mi_qa4071/is_200405/ai_n9453773, p. 1 of 3. Accessed 9/13/2006.

4. "Gay Marriage: A New Era," *Online NewsHour* (May 17, 2004), p. 2 of 4. www.pbs.org/newshour/bb/law/jan-june04/gaymarriage_5-7.html. Accessed 9/13/2006.

5. "We Do," p. 2 of 3.

6. Margaret Marshall, "Majority Opinion," *Goodridge v. Dept. of Public Health*, 440 Mass. 309 (2003), in Katsh and Rose, *Taking Sides: Legal Issues*, pp. 296–303, at 298.

7. Ibid., p. 300.

8. Ibid., pp. 300–301.

9. Ibid., pp. 301–302. Internal reference omitted in Katsh and Rose.

10. Ibid., p. 302.

11. Ibid., p. 303.

12. Russell Shorto, "What's Their Real Problem with Gay Marriage?" *New York Times Magazine* (June 19, 2005), pp. 36–41 and 64–67, at 37.

13. Ibid., p. 39.

14. Leviticus, chapter 20, verse 13, in RSV, p. 92.

15. Dennis Prager, *Ultimate Issues*, special edition, "Part II: Judaism and Homosexuality" (April–June 1990), p. 2. Also in *Same-Sex Marriage Pro and Con: A Reader*, Andrew Sullivan, ed. (New York: Vintage, 2004), pp. 61–67.

16. Thomas B. Edsall, "Sexual Orientation and Religion," *Washington Post* (June 10, 1998). www.loper.org/~george/trends/1998/Jun/77.html. Accessed 3/7/2003.

17. "Homosexuality and the Natural Law," published by Minnesota St. Thomas More Chapter of Catholics United for the Faith, January 2002. www.mncuf.org/honat.htm. Accessed 3/14/2003.

18. Prager, "Judaism and Homosexuality," p. 11.

19. Ibid., p. 11, quoting Eva Keuls, *The Reign of the Phallus* (New York: Harper and Row, 1985).

20. *Romer v. Evans*, 517 U.S. 620 (1996), at 524.

21. Ibid., at 627.

22. Ibid., at 631.

23. Ibid., at 635.

24. Ibid., at 634. Inserted quotation from *Department of Agriculture v. Moreno*, 413 U.S. 528 (1973), at 534. Emphasis in Kennedy's quotation.

25. Ibid., at 644.

26. *Lawrence v. Texas* (2003), in Sullivan, *Same-Sex Marriage*, p. 107.

27. Ibid., pp. 107–108.

28. Ibid., p. 109.

29. Shorto, "Their Real Problem," pp. 39–40.

30. Ibid., p. 40.

31. Kwame Anthony Appiah, *Cosmopolitanism: Ethics in a World of Strangers* (New York: W. W. Norton, 2006), p. 77. Emphasis in original.

32. Patricia Beattie Jung and Ralph F. Smith, *Heterosexism: An Ethical Challenge* (Albany: State University of New York Press, 1993), p. 19.

33. Shorto, "Their Real Problem," p. 37.

34. Ibid.

35. Maggie Gallagher, "What Marriage Is For," in Sullivan, *Same-Sex Marriage*, pp. 263–272, at 264. From the *Weekly Standard* (August 4–11, 2003).

36. Marshall, "Majority Opinion," p. 300.

37. Gallagher, "What Marriage Is For," p. 265.

38. Ibid., p. 266.

39. Ibid., p. 268.

40. Ibid., p. 263.

41. Ibid., p. 267.

42. Ibid., p. 270.

43. William J. Bennett, *The Broken Hearth: Reversing the Moral Collapse of the American Family* (New York: Doubleday, 2001), pp. 119–120.

44. Gallagher, "What Marriage Is For," p. 269.

45. Bennett, *Broken Hearth*, p. 117. Emphasis in original.

46. Ibid., p. 118.

47. Jonathan Rauch, *Gay Marriage: Why It's Good for Gays, Good for Straights, and Good for America* (New York: Henry Holt and Company, 2004), p. 76.

48. Ibid., p. 107. Emphasis in original.

49. Ibid., p. 74.

50. Ibid., p. 18.

51. Ibid., pp. 19–20, quoting James Q. Wilson, *The Moral Sense* (1993).

52. Ibid., pp. 77–78.

53. Ibid., p. 22.

54. Ibid., p. 26.

55. Ibid., p. 9.

56. Shorto, "Their Real Problem," p. 37.

57. Rauch, *Gay Marriage*, pp. 50–51.

58. Ibid., p. 33. Emphasis in original.

59. Ibid., p. 32. Emphasis in original.

60. Ibid., pp. 90–91.

61. Ibid., p. 53.

62. Ibid., p. 94.

63. Bennett, *Broken Hearth*, p. 113.

64. Ibid., p. 115.

65. Rauch, *Gay Marriage*, p. 15.

66. Ibid., p. 129.

67. Ibid.

68. Ibid.

69. Ibid., p. 130.

70. Ibid., pp. 59–60. Emphasis in original.

71. Ibid., p. 22.

72. Ibid., p. 135.

73. Ibid., pp. 135–136.

74. Ibid., p. 136.

75. Ibid., p. 137. Emphasis in original.

76. In 2007 Warren Jeffs, prophet of the Fundamentalist Church of Jesus Christ of the Latter Day Saints (FLDS), was convicted of performing a marriage between a fifteen-year-old girl and her older cousin. In 2008 a polygamous community in Eldorado, Texas, was raided by police and all children were taken from their parents, at least temporarily. See Ralph Blumenthal, "Court Says Texas Illegally Seized Sect's Children," *New York Times* (May 23, 2008), pp. 1 and 20.

77. Mindelle Jacobs, "Polygamy Comes Out of the Closet," *Edmonton Sun* (September 3, 2006). www.edmontonsun.com/News/columnists/Jacobs_Mindelle/2006/09/03/1798357.html, p. 1 of 2. Accessed 9/13/2006.

78. Ibid., p. 2 of 2.

79. Linda Valdez, "One Arizona Town Puts on Best Face for Polygamy Critics," *Arizona Republic* (July 24, 2005). www.azcentral.com/php-bin/clicktrack/print.php?referer=http://www.axcentral.com. Accessed 9/13/2006.

80. Ibid.

81. Adam Liptak, "California Court Overturns a Ban on Gay Marriage," *New York Times* (May 16, 2008), pp. 1 and 19.

10 Genetic Engineering and Designer Children

1. Geoffrey Cowley and Karen Springen, "Risk-Free Babies," *Newsweek*, Vol. 139, No. 10 (March 11, 2002), p. 58. www.accessmylibrar.com/coms2/summary_0286-25100218_ITM, pp. 1–2 of 3. Accessed 9/27/2006.

2. *The American Medical Association Family Medical Guide*, Jeffrey R. M. Kunz, M.D., and Asher J. Finkel, M.D., eds. (New York: Random House, 1987), pp. 296–297.

3. Amy Harmon, "Seeking Healthy Children, Couples Cull Embryos," *New York Times* (September 3, 2006), pp. 1 and 16, at 16.

4. Ibid.

5. Cowley and Springen, "Risk-Free Babies," p. 2 of 3.

6. Bonnie Steinbock, "Using Preimplantation Genetic Diagnosis to Save a Sibling: The Story of Molly and Adam Nash," in *Ethical Issues in Modern Medicine*, sixth edition, Bonnie Steinbock, John D. Arras, and Alex John London, eds. (New York: McGraw-Hill, 2003), pp. 544–545, at 544.

7. Claudia Kalb and Karen Springen, "Brave New Babies," *Newsweek*, Vol. 143, No. 4 (January 26, 2004), pp. 44–52. findarticles.com/p/articles/mi_kmnew/is_200401, pp. 1–2 of 6. Accessed 9/27/2006.

8. Ibid., p. 2 of 6.

9. Quoted in Dinesh D'Souza, "Staying Human," *National Review*, Vol. 53, No. 1, pp. 36–39. findarticles.com/p/articles/mi_m1282/is_1_53/ai_69240190, p. 2 of 8. Accessed 9/28/2006.

10. "Frontline Interview with Lee Silver," www.pbs.org/wgbh/pages/frontline/shows/fertility/interviews/silver.html, p. 4 of 19. Accessed 9/28/2006.

11. D'Souza, "Staying Human," p. 2 of 8.

12. "Frontline Interview," p. 13 of 19.

13. Allen Buchanan, Dan W. Brock, Norman Daniels, and Daniel Wikler, *From Chance to Choice: Genetics and Justice* (Cambridge: Cambridge University Press, 2000), pp. 156–158.

14. Ibid., p. 158.

15. Ibid., p. 159.

16. Ibid., p. 160.

17. Ibid., p. 34.

18. Ibid., p. 44.

19. Ibid., pp. 44–45.

20. Bonnie Steinbock, "Sex Selection: Not Obviously Wrong," *Hastings Center Report*, Vol. 32, No. 1 (January–February 2002), pp. 23–28 at 26.

21. Dan W. Brock, "Shaping Future Children: Parental Rights and Societal Interests," *Journal of Political Philosophy*, Vol. 13, No. 4 (2005), pp. 377–393, at 393.

22. Steinbock, "Sex Selection," p. 27. Inserted quotation is from L. Belkin, "Getting the Girl," *New York Times Magazine* (July 25, 1999), p. 38.

23. Brock, "Shaping Future Children," p. 386.

24. Robert Sparrow, "Defending Deaf Culture: The Case of Cochlear Implants," *Journal of Political Philosophy*, Vol. 13, No. 2 (2005), pp. 135–152, at 136–137.

25. Ibid., p. 138.

26. See *Wisconsin v. Yoder*, 406 U.S. 205 (1972).

27. Sparrow, "Defending Deaf Culture," p. 140.

28. Brock, "Shaping Future Children," p. 386.

29. Michael J. Sandel, "The Case against Perfection," *Atlantic*, Vol. 293, No. 3 (April 2004), pp. 50–62. web.ebscohost.com.ezproxy.uis.edu:2048/ehost/detail ?vid=3&hid=108&sid=449d85a6-ea4a-4e23-8620-c09d5aa0c791%40session mgr107, p. 9 of 11. Accessed 9/28/2006.

30. Ibid.

31. Ibid.

32. Ibid., p. 5 of 11.

33. Ibid.

34. Ibid.

35. Ibid., p. 6 of 11.

36. Bill McKibben, "Why Environmentalists Should Be Concerned," *World Watch*, Vol. 15, No. 4 (July/August 2002), pp. 40–41, at 40–41.

37. "Frontline Interview," p. 17 of 19.

38. Ibid., p. 6 of 19.

39. Ibid., p. 17 of 19.

40. Ibid. p. 13 of 19.

41. Francis Fukuyama, *Our Posthuman Future: Consequences of the Biotechnology Revolution* (New York: Farrar, Straus, and Giroux, 2002), p. 117. Emphasis in original.

42. Ibid., p. 125.

43. Ibid., p. 78. Quotation is from Edward O. Wilson, "Reply to Fukuyama," *The National Interest*, No. 56 (Spring 1999), pp. 35–37.

44. Ibid., p. 92.

45. Ibid., p. 98.

46. Ibid., p. 171.

47. Ibid. p. 172.

48. Ibid.

49. Ibid., p. 173.

50. Lee M. Silver, *Challenging Nature* (New York: HarperCollins, 2006), p. 168.

51. Leon R. Kass and James Q. Wilson, *The Ethics of Human Cloning* (Washington, DC: American Enterprise Institute Press, 1998). In Silver, *Challenging Nature*, p. 169.

52. In Silver, *Challenging Nature*, p. 327.

53. Appiah, *Cosmopolitanism*, pp. 53–54. Emphasis in original.

54. *Lawrence v. Texas*, 539 U.S. 558 (2003).

55. Harmon, "Seeking Healthy Children," p. 16.

56. Buchanan et al., *From Chance to Choice*, p. 259.

57. Ibid., p. 155.

58. Dean Clancy, "Against the Gene Genies," *National Review*, Vol. 55, No. 13, pp. 47–48, at 48.

59. Buchanan et al., *From Chance to Choice*, pp. 296–297.

60. "Frontline Interview," p. 18 of 19.

61. Glenn McGee, "Parenting in an Era of Genetics," *Hastings Center Report*, Vol. 27, No. 2 (1997), pp. 16–22, at 18.

62. "Frontline Interview," pp. 18–19 of 19.

63. Ibid., p. 12 of 19.

64. BBC News, "Back to the Future: Lee Silver, Geneticist," news.bbc.co.uk.hi/ english/static/special_report/1999/12/99back_to_future/lee_silver.stm, p. 1 of 4. Accessed 9/28/2006.

65. Buchanan et al., *From Chance to Choice*, p. 95.

11 Wages and Taxes

1. Eric Dash, "Off to the Races Again, Leaving Many Behind," *New York Times*, Section 3 (April 9, 2006), pp. 1 and 5, at 1.

2. Ibid.

3. Dean Olsen, "Central Illinois Incomes Slip," *State Journal-Register* (September 5, 2006), pp. 1–2, at 1–2.

4. David Cay Johnston, "Richest Are Leaving Even the Rich Far Behind," *New York Times* (June 5, 2005), pp. 1 and 17, at 1 and 17.

5. Gary Strauss and Barbara Hansen, "CEO Pay Soars in 2005 as a Select Group Break the $100 Million Mark," *USA Today* (April 1, 2006). www.usatoday.com/ money/companies/management/2006-04-09-ceo-compensation-report_x.htm. Accessed 10/13/2006.

6. Steven Greenhouse, "Borrowers We Be," *New York Times*, Week in Review (September 3, 2006), p. 12.

7. Robert Nozick, *Anarchy, State, and Utopia* (New York: Basic Books, 1974), p. 169. Emphasis in original.

8. Ibid., p. 172. Emphasis in original.

9. Milton Friedman and Rose D. Friedman, *Free to Choose* (New York: Harcourt Brace Jovanovich, 1979), p. 30.

10. Christopher C. DeMuth, "The New Wealth of Nations," in *Taking Sides: Clashing Views on Controversial Political Issues*, fifteenth edition, George McKenna and Stanley Feingold, eds. (Dubuque, IA: McGraw-Hill, 2007), pp. 241–248, at 242. Originally in *Commentary* (October 1997).

11. Ibid., p. 243.

12. Ibid., p. 244.

13. Ibid., p. 246.

14. Barbara Ehrenreich, *Nickel and Dimed* (New York: Henry Holt and Company, 2001), p. 25.

15. Ibid., p. 27.

16. Ibid., p. 80.

17. Ibid., p. 82.

18. Kevin Phillips, *Wealth and Democracy* (New York: Broadway Books, 2002), p. 162.

19. Ibid., p. 163. Emphasis in original.

20. Ehrenreich, *Nickel and Dimed*, p. 106.

21. Ibid., p. 89.

22. Ibid.

23. Ibid., p. 220.

24. Thomas Rustici, "A Public Choice View of the Minimum Wage," in *Taking Sides: Clashing Views on Controversial Economic Issues*, eleventh edition, Thomas R. Swartz and Frank J. Bonello, eds. (Guilford, CT: McGraw-Hill/Dushkin, 2004), pp. 242–253, at 242. Originally in *Cato Journal*, Vol. 5, No. 1 (Spring/Summer 1985).

25. Ibid., p. 248. Emphasis in original.

26. Steven Greenhouse and David Leonhardt, "Real Wages Fail to Match a Rise in Productivity," *New York Times* (August 28, 2006), pp. 1 and 13, at 1.

27. Dash, "Off to the Races," pp. 1 and 5.

28. Charles Craypo, "In Defense of Minimum Wages," in Swartz and Bonello, *Taking Sides: Economic Issues*, pp. 254–263, at 256.

29. Ibid., pp. 259–260.

30. Ibid., p. 258.

31. Nina Manzi and Joel Michael, "Federal Earned Income Tax Credit and the Minnesota Working Family Credit" (February 2006). www.house.leg.state.mn.us/hrd/pubs/feicwfc.pdf, p. 4 of 26.

32. Citizens for Tax Justice, "Are Americans Overtaxed?" in *Taking Sides: Clashing Views on Controversial Political Issues*, twelfth edition, George McKenna and Stanley Feingold, eds. (Dubuque, IA: McGraw-Hill, 2001), pp. 323–331, at 324. Emphasis in original.

33. Ibid., p. 327.

34. Joseph E. Stiglitz, *The Roaring Nineties: A New History of the World's Most Prosperous Decade* (New York: W. W. Norton, 2003), p. 302.

35. Johnston, "Richest Are Leaving," p. 17.

36. "Gilding the Elite," *Economist*, Vol. 379, No. 8481 (June 10, 2006), pp. 25–26. web.ebscohost.com.ezproxy.uis:2048/ehost/delivery?vid=53&hid=2&sid=769f, p. 2 of 3. Accessed 10/11/2006.

37. Liam Murphy and Thomas Nagel, *The Myth of Ownership: Taxes and Justice* (New York: Oxford University Press, 2002), pp. 36–37. Emphasis in original.

38. Stiglitz, *Roaring Nineties*, p. 302.

39. Johnston, "Richest Are Leaving," p. 17.

40. "Wake Up America: A National Sleep Alert," *Wikipedia*. www.answers.com/topic/wake-up-america-a-national-sleep-alert. Accessed 10/18/2006.

41. Dorothy Wickenden, "The Talk of the Town Comment: Top of the Class," *New Yorker* (October 2, 2006), pp. 35–36, at 35.

42. Ibid., p. 36.

43. Johnston, "Richest Are Leaving," p. 17.

44. Phillips, *Wealth and Democracy*, p. 419.

45. Ibid., p. 323.

46. Ibid., p. 326. Emphasis in original.

12   Health Care in America

1. Ronald Munson, "Robert Ingram: Dilemma of the Working Poor," in *Intervention and Reflection: Basic Issues in Medical Ethics*, seventh edition, Ronald Munson, ed. (Belmont, CA: Wadsworth/Thomson, 2004), p. 508.

2. Ibid., pp. 508–509. Emphasis in original.

3. Paul Krugman and Robin Wells, "The Health Care Crisis and What to Do About It," *New York Review of Books* (March 23, 2006), pp. 38–43, at 39.

4. Jennifer Lee, "For Insurance, Adult Children Ride Piggyback," *New York Times* (September 17, 2006), pp. 1 and 18, at 18.

5. Paul Krugman, "Death by Insurance," *New York Times* (May 1, 2006), p. A25.

6. Krugman and Wells, "Health Care Crisis," p. 39.

7. Ibid., p. 38.

8. Thomas A. Mappes and David DeGrazia, "Social Justice and Health-Care Policy: Introduction," in *Biomedical Ethics*, sixth edition, Thomas A. Mappes and David DeGrazia, eds. (New York: McGraw-Hill, 2006), pp. 615–628, at 615.

9. Krugman and Wells, "Health Care Crisis," p. 41.

10. Ibid., p. 41.

11. Carol Levine, "Should There Be Payment for Body Parts? Issue Summary," in *Taking Sides: Clashing Views on Controversial Bioethical Issues*, tenth edition, Carol Levine, ed. (Guilford, CT: McGraw-Hill/Dushkin, 2004), pp. 306–307, at 306.

12. Ibid., p. 307.

13. Krugman and Wells, "Health Care Crisis," p. 40.

14. See *Medicare News*, "Medicare Campaign to Emphasize Preventive Care," (June 19, 2006). www.seniorjournal.com/NEWS/Medicare/6-06-19-medicare Campaign.htm. Accessed 10/25/2006.

15. Krugman and Wells, "Health Care Crisis," p. 38.

16. Ibid., p. 41.

17. Ibid., p. 39.

18. Krugman, "Death by Insurance," p. A25.

19. Ibid., p. A25.

20. Fareed Zakaria, "How We Drive Our Jobs Away," *Newsweek*, Vol. 145, Iss. 16 (April 18, 2005), p. 43. www.newsweek.com/id/49659/page/1, p. 1 of 2. Accessed 9/22/2008.

21. Allen Buchanan, "Managed Care: Rationing Without Justice, But Not Unjustly," in Mappes and DeGrazia, *Biomedical Ethics*, pp. 652–660, at 653. Originally in *Journal of Health Politics, Policy and Law*, Vol. 23, No. 4 (August 1998), pp. 617–634.

22. Norman G. Levinsky, "Truth or Consequences," in Carol Levine, *Taking Sides: Bioethical Issues*, pp. 292–296, at 293. Originally in *New England Journal of Medicine*, Vol. 338, No. 13 (March 26, 1998), pp. 913–915.

23. Ibid., p. 292.

24. Ibid., p. 294.

25. See Erik Eckholm, "To Lower Costs, Hospitals Try Donating Care to Uninsured," *New York Times* (October 25, 2006), pp. 1 and 13.

26. Marcia Angell, "The Truth about the Drug Companies," *New York Review of Books*, Vol. 51, No. 12 (July 15, 2004), pp. 52–58, at 52.

27. Ibid., p. 52.

28. Ibid., p. 53.

29. Alex Berenson, "A Cancer Drug's Big Price Rise Disturbs Doctors and Patients," *New York Times* (March 12, 2006), pp. 1 and 19, at 1.

30. Ibid., p. 19.

31. Angell, "The Truth," p. 52, quoting Sharon Levine on ABC Special with Peter Jennings, "Bitter Medicine: Pills, Profit, and the Public Health," May 29, 2002.

32. Ibid., p. 56.

33. Ibid., p. 55.

34. Ibid.

35. Ibid., p. 54.

36. Ibid., p. 58.

37. Ibid., p. 52.

38. Adam Smith, *The Wealth of Nations*, Edwin Cannan, ed. (New York: Random House, 1994), p. 109.

39. Ibid., p. 527.

40. Ibid., p. 715.

41. Ibid., p. 287.

42. Kevin Phillips, *Wealth and Democracy* (New York: Broadway Books, 2002), and *American Theocracy* (New York: Viking, 2006).

43. Smith, *Wealth*, p. 288.

44. Alex John London, "Bone Marrow Transplants for Advanced Breast Cancer: The Story of Christine deMeurers," in Steinbock, Arras, and London, *Ethical Issues*, pp. 187–194, at 188.

45. Ibid.

46. Ibid., p. 189.

47. Ibid., p. 191.

48. Ibid., p. 190.

49. Levinsky, "Truth or Consequences," p. 295.

50. Leonard M. Fleck, "Rationing: Don't Give Up," in Mappes and DeGrazia, *Biomedical Ethics*, pp. 660–662, at 661. Originally in *Hastings Center Report*, Vol. 32 (March–April 2002), pp. 35–36.

51. Ibid.

52. Daniel Callahan, "Limiting Health Care for the Old?" in Carol Levine, *Taking Sides*, pp. 278–282, at 280. Originally in *The Nation* (August 15, 1987).

53. Ibid. p. 280.

54. Ibid., p. 281.

55. Ibid.

56. Amitai Etzioni, "Spare the Old, Save the Young," in Carol Levine, *Taking Sides: Bioethical Issues*, pp. 283–287, at 284. Originally in *The Nation* (June 11, 1988).

57. Ibid., p. 285.

58. Ibid., p. 286.

59. Ibid., p. 284.

60. Steven H. Miles, "Informed Demand for 'Non-Beneficial' Medical Treatment," in Levine, *Taking Sides: Bioethical Issues*, pp. 120–124, at 120. Originally in *New England Journal of Medicine*, Vol. 325, No. 7 (August 15, 1991), pp. 512–515.

61. Ibid., p. 122.

62. Ibid., pp. 122–123.

63. Felicia Ackerman, "The Significance of a Wish," in Levine, *Taking Sides*, pp. 125–128, at 126. Originally in *Hastings Center Report*, Vol. 21, No. 4 (July–August 1991). Emphasis in original.

64. Sarah Lyall, "Court Backs Broton's Right to a Costly Drug," *New York Times* (April 13, 2006), p. A3.

65. Clifford Krauss, *New York Times* (February 28, 2006), p. A3.

13   Immigration

1. Mae M. Ngai, "The Lost Immigration Debate," *Boston Review* (September/ October 2006). bostonreview.net/BR31.5/ngai.html, p. 3 of 10.

2. Ibid., p. 4 of 10.

3. Ibid., p. 6 of 10.

4. Ibid., p. 7 of 10.

5. Arian Campo-Flores, "America's Divide," *Newsweek* (April 10, 2006), pp. 28–38, at 34.

6. Corey Kilgannon, "Dreaming of U.S. Citizenship," *New York Times* (April 16, 2006), p. 23.

7. Nigel Dower, *World Ethics: The New Agenda* (Edinburgh: Edinburgh University Press, 1998), p. 20.

8. Michael Walzer, *Spheres of Justice: A Defense of Pluralism and Equality* (New York: Basic Books, 1983), p. 37.

9. John Isbister, *The Immigration Debate: Remaking America* (West Hartford, CT: Kumarian Press, 1996), pp. 126–127.

10. Walzer, *Spheres*, p. 39.

11. Ibid., p. 38.

12. Arthur M. Schlesinger, Jr., *The Disuniting of America: Reflections on a Multicultural Society*, revised and enlarged edition (New York: W. W. Norton, 1998), pp. 51–52.

13. Ibid., p. 146. Emphasis in original.

14. Christopher Jencks, "Who Should Get In? Part II," *New York Review of Books*, Vol. 48, No. 20 (December 20, 2001), pp. 94–102, at 102.

15. Christopher Jencks, "Who Should Get In?" *New York Review of Books*, Vol. 48, No. 19 (November 29, 2001), pp. 57–63, at 59.

16. Jencks, "Part II," p. 95.

17. Schlesinger, *Disuniting*, p. 138.

18. Richard Alba, "'Who Should Get In?' An Exchange," *New York Review of Books*, Vol. 49, No. 9 (May 23, 2002). www.nybooks.com/articles/15423, p. 1 of 6.

19. Michael Walzer, *On Toleration* (New Haven, CT: Yale University Press, 1997), p. 104.

20. Ibid., p. 110.

21. Ibid., p. 111.

22. Schlesinger, *Disuniting*, pp. 144–145.

23. Frank Sharry, "Comprehensive Immigration Reform II," in McKenna and Feingold, *Taking Sides: Controversial Political Issues*, fifteenth edition, pp. 286–292, at 287. Originally testimony before the Senate Committee on the Judiciary, October 18, 2005.

24. Ibid., p. 288.

25. Elisabeth Bumiller, "Bush Is Facing a Difficult Path on Immigration," *New York Times* (March 24, 2006), pp. 1 and 16.

26. Mark Krikorian, "Comprehensive Immigration Reform II," in McKenna and Feingold, *Taking Sides: Controversial Political Issues*, fifteenth edition, pp. 276–285, at 280. Originally testimony before the Senate Committee on the Judiciary, October 18, 2005.

27. Ibid., p. 277.

28. Roger Lowenstein, "The Immigration Equation," *New York Times Magazine* (July 9, 2006), pp. 36–43 and 69–71, at 70.

29. Krikorian, "Comprehensive Immigration Reform," p. 280.

30. Lowenstein, "Immigration Equation," p. 43.

31. Ibid., p. 69.

32. Eduardo Porter, "Here Illegally, Working Hard and Paying Taxes," *New York Times* (June 19, 2006), pp. 1 and 14, at 14.

33. Nicholas D. Kristof, "Compassion That Hurts," *New York Times* (April 9, 2006), p. 13.

34. John M. Broder, "Immigrants and the Economics of Hard Work," *New York Times* (April 2, 2006), p. 3.

35. Ibid., p. 3.

36. James K. Galbraith, "'Who Should Get In?' An Exchange," *New York Review of Books*, Vol. 49, No. 9 (May 23, 2002). www.nybooks.com/articles/15423, p. 2 of 6. Emphasis in original.

37. Ibid., p. 3 of 6.

38. Porter, "Here Illegally," p. 14.

39. Krikorian, "Comprehensive Immigration Reform," pp. 278–279.

40. Ibid., p. 284.

41. Jencks, "Part II," p. 101.

42. Abby Goodnough and Jennifer Steinhauer, "Senate's Failure to Agree on Immigration Plan Angers Workers and Employers Alike," in *Annual Editions: Public Policy and Administration*, ninth edition, Howard R. Balanoff, ed. (Dubuque, IA: McGraw-Hill, 2007), pp. 161–162, at 162. Originally in *New York Times* (April 9, 2006).

43. Jencks, "Part II," p. 97.

44. Robert L. Chapman, "Immigration and Environment: Setting the Moral Boundaries," *Environmental Values*, Vol. 9, No. 2 (May 2000), pp. 189–209, at 192.

45. Patrick J. Buchanan, "La Reconquista," in *Taking Sides: Clashing Views on Controversial Political Issues*, thirteenth edition, George McKenna and Stanley Feingold, eds., pp. 294–299, at 296. Excerpted from *The Death of the West: How Dying Populations and Immigrant Invasions Imperil Our Country and Civilization* (New York: Thomas Nunne Books, St. Martin's Press, 2002).

46. "Sierra Club Population Report, Spring 1989." www.susps.org/history/popreport1989.html, p. 1 of 2. Accessed 11/4/2006.

47. Buchanan, "La Reconquista," p. 296.

48. Ibid., p. 297.

49. Lowenstein, "Immigration Equation," p. 39. Emphasis in original.

50. Peter Brimelow, "Immigration: Dissolving the People," in D'Angelo and Douglas, *Taking Sides: Race and Ethnicity*, pp. 38–41, at 41. Excerpted from *Alien Nation* (New York: Random House, 1995).

51. Campo-Flores, "America's Divide," p. 32.

52. Walzer, *Spheres*, p. 57.

53. Ibid., p. 61.

54. Fareed Zakaria, "To Become an American," *Newsweek*, Vol. 147, No. 15, (April 10, 2006), p. 39.

55. Quoted in Sharry, "Comprehensive Immigration Reform," p. 290.

56. Ibid., p. 291.

57. Peter D. Salins, "Assimilation Nation," *New York Times* (May 11, 2006), p. A31.

58. See Isbister, *Immigration Debate*, pp. 138–163 and 176–177.

14   Globalization

1. Thomas L. Friedman, *The World Is Flat: A Brief History of the Twenty-First Century* (New York: Farrar, Straus, and Giroux, 2005), p. 5.

2. Ibid., pp. 6–7.

3. Ibid., p. 8.

4. Johan Norberg, *In Defense of Global Capitalism* (Washington, DC: Cato Institute, 2003), p. 22.

5. Anita Roddick, "There Is a Human Being behind That Label," *The Ecologist*, Vol. 34, No. 6 (July/August 2004), pp. 23–27, at 24.

6. Ibid., p. 25.

7. Ibid., p. 26.

8. Ibid., p. 27.

9. Dean Olsen, "Central Illinois Incomes Slip," *State Journal-Register* (Springfield, Illinois, September 5, 2006), pp. 1–2, at 2.

10. Douglas A. Irwin, "The Case for Free Trade: Old Theories, New Evidence," in McKenna and Feingold, *Taking Sides: Controversial Political Issues*, fifteenth edition, pp. 300–307, at 300–301. Excerpted from *Free Trade under Fire* (Princeton, NJ: Princeton University Press, 2002).

11. Norberg, *In Defense*, p. 117.

12. Irwin, "Case for Free Trade," p. 305. The quotation from Mill is from *Principles of Political Economy* (1848).

13. Ibid., p. 306.

14. Surit S. Bhalla, "Today's Golden Age of Poverty Reduction," in *Annual Editions: Developing World (07/08)*, seventh edition, Robert J. Griffiths, ed., (Dubuque, IA: McGraw-Hill, 2007), pp. 15–18, at 15. Originally in *The International Economy* (Spring 2006), pp. 22–25.

15. Ibid., pp. 16–17.

16. Ibid., p. 16.

17. Jeffrey D. Sachs, *The End of Poverty: Economic Possibilities for Our Time* (New York: Penguin Press, 2005), p. 11.

18. Ibid., p. 12.

19. Norberg, *In Defense*, p. 217.

20. Ibid., p. 218.

21. Ibid., p. 199.

22. Kevin Phillips, *Wealth and Democracy: A Political History of the American Rich* (New York: Broadway Books, 2002), p. 269.

23. Tina Rosenberg, "The Free-Trade Fix," *New York Times Magazine* (August 18, 2002), pp. 28–33, 50, and 74–75, at 31.

24. Ted C. Fishman, "The Chinese Century," *New York Times Magazine* (July 4, 2004), pp. 24–31, 46, and 50–51, at 28.

25. Ibid.

26. Ibid., p. 46.

27. Ibid. Emphasis in original.

28. Phillips, *Wealth and Democracy*, p. 264.

29. Ulrich Beck, *What Is Globalization?* Patrick Camiller, trans. (Cambridge, UK: Polity Press, 2000), p. 61. Emphasis in original.

30. Ibid., p. 60.

31. Phillips, *Wealth and Democracy*, p. 160.

32. Friedman, *World Is Flat*, p. 120.

33. Robert J. Samuelson, "Trickle-Up Economics?" *Newsweek*, Vol. 148, No. 14 (October 2, 2006), p. 40.

34. Friedman, *World Is Flat*, p. 120.

35. Ibid., p. 123.

36. Ibid., p. 289.

37. Rosenberg, "Free-Trade Fix," pp. 33 and 50.

38. Ibid., p. 33.

39. Joseph Stiglitz, "Social Justice and Global Trade," in Griffiths, *Developing World*, pp. 33–35, at 34. Originally in *Far Eastern Economic Review* (March 2006), pp. 18–21.

40. Kate Eshelby, "Cotton: The Huge Moral Issue," in Griffiths, *Developing World*, pp. 40–41, at 41.

41. Ibid.

42. Rosenberg, "Free-Trade Fix," p. 33.

43. Friedman, *World Is Flat*, p. 104.

44. Ibid., p. 106.

45. Joseph E. Stiglitz, *Globalization and Its Discontents* (New York: W. W. Norton, 2002), p. 244.

46. Rosenberg, "Free-Trade Fix," p. 30.

47. Friedman, *World Is Flat*, p. 283.

48. Peter Singer, *One World: The Ethics of Globalization* (New Haven, CT: Yale University Press, 2002), p. 60.

49. Ibid., p. 59.

50. Ibid., pp. 62–63.

51. Friedman, *World Is Flat*, p. 137.

52. Paul Krugman, "The War against Wages," *New York Times* (October 6, 2006), p. A27.

53. Alan Thein Durning, *How Much Is Enough? The Consumer Society and the Future of the Earth* (New York: W. W. Norton, 1992), p. 52.

54. David C. Korten, *When Corporations Rule the World* (West Hartford, CT: Kumarian Press, 1995), pp. 279–280.

55. Friedman, *World Is Flat*, p. 407. Emphasis in original.

56. Ibid., p. 408.

57. Ibid., p. 412.

58. See Vandana Shiva, *The Violence of the Green Revolution* (London: Zed Books, 1993), p. 125.

59. Lester R. Brown, "Feeding Nine Billion," *State of the World 1999* (New York: W. W. Norton, 1999), pp. 115–132, at 124.

60. Ibid. For an update on the river, see Jim Yardley, "China's Path to Modernity, Mirrored in a Troubled River," *New York Times* (November 19, 2006), pp. 1 and 14–15.

61. Friedman, *World Is Flat*, pp. 412–413.

Index